CUe0021534

Postmodernism and the Other

DATE DUE

PRINTED IN U.S.A.

Postmodernism and the Other

THE NEW IMPERIALISM OF WESTERN CULTURE

Ziauddin Sardar

Pluto Press
LONDON • CHICAGO, ILLINOIS

First published 1998 by Pluto Press
345 Archway Road, London N6 5AA
and 1436 West Randolph, Chicago, Illinois 60607, USA

Copyright © Ziauddin Sardar 1998

The right of Ziauddin Sardar to be identified as the author of this work
has been asserted by him in accordance with the Copyright, Designs and
Patents Act 1988.

British Library Cataloguing in Publication Data
A catalogue record for this book is available from the British Library

ISBN   0 7453 0748 5 hbk

Library of Congress Cataloging in Publication Data
Sardar, Ziauddin.
  Postmodernism and the other : the new imperialism of Western
culture / Ziauddin Sardar.
    p.   cm.
  ISBN 0–7453–0748–5
  1. Civilization, Modern—1950– 2. Civilization, Western—20th
century. 3. Postmodernism. 4. Difference (Philosophy) I. Title.
CB430.S28 1997
909.82—dc21   97–32972
                                                         CIP

Designed, typeset and produced for Pluto Press by
Chase Production Services, Chadlington, OX7 3LN
Printed in the EC by T J International, Padstow

Contents

For Anwar and Aziza

Introduction: 'Be Seeing You'

Before the beginning there are signs and portents. Make of them what you will. They are indicators of choices that need to be made. 'Be seeing you' was the standard greeting in Patrick McGoohan's cult television series, *The Prisoner*, first broadcast in October 1967. Then postmodernism was hardly a twinkle in the eye of its principal champions. The term had been used by the Spanish writer Federico De Onis in 1934 to describe a reaction to and within modernism. Subsequently, it was used by the historian Arnold Toynbee in his *A Study of History* published in 1947, and by literary critics Irving Howe and Harold Levine and writer Leslie Fiedler in the 1960s. But as a full-blown theory and practice, postmodernism was still at least a decade away. It is hardly surprising then that *The Prisoner* is not seen as a postmodern product. Yet it prefigures and plays a number of features we have come to associate with the postmodern genre. The opening sequence of each episode included the following dialogue:

Prisoner: 'Where am I?'
Voice: 'In The Village.'
Prisoner: 'What do you want?'
Voice: 'Information.'
Prisoner: 'Whose side are you on?'
Voice: 'That would be telling. We want information ... information ... information ...'
Prisoner: 'You won't get it.'
Voice: 'By hook or by crook we will.'

Prisoner: 'Who are you?'
Voice: 'The new Number Two.'
Prisoner: 'Who is Number One?'
Voice: 'You are Number Six.'
Prisoner: 'I am not a number, I am a free man.'

With its Orwellian and Huxleyan tones, the opening sequence appears to establish *The Prisoner* as an action-cum-suspense drama in which the eponymous hero, a secret agent, angrily resigns, only to be kidnapped and transported to an exact replica of his own home recreated in a bizarre new location, the Village. The premise, then, is a conscientious individual fighting for his freedom from an unseen Big Brother. But nothing in *The Prisoner* is as it appears; everything is laced with multiple layers of meaning. The profusion of meanings is aptly reflected in the confusion of architectural styles. The Village is Portmeirion, situated on the Mawddach estuary in North Wales, which is nothing more than a latter-day grand folly. Built by the eccentric architect Sir Clough Williams-Ellis, Portmeirion is an eclectic mix of real buildings, fake façades and imported structures, ranging from the Oriental to Italianate. Many of its edifices and ornate flourishes are no more than props: the onion dome on the tower is a copper cut-out concealing a chimney stack; the Gloriette, modelled on the Schonbraunn Palace in Vienna, is all front and no back as in a film-set; and the miniature Chatsworth on the hill is no more than a cottage aggrandised by plaster porticoes. Portmeirion also prefigures postmodern architecture in its most amusing and ironic stance: combining, in the words of Charles Jencks, 'modern techniques with something else (usually traditional building) in order for architecture to communicate with the public and a concerned minority'.[1] The real artificiality of Portmeirion is transformed into the imagined reality of the cosmopolitan village of *The Prisoner*.

Bryan Turner explains postmodernism as a response to modernity:

> with the spread of modern mass technology of communications, it is not only that there is a great expansion of services and the leisure industry (and a concomitant new middle class), but there is a growing

simulation of reality. The implosion of signs eventually undermines our sense of reality. The result is that, in our media dominated world, the concept of meaning itself (which depends on stable boundaries, fixed structures, shared consensus) dissolves.[2]

The Prisoner excels both in dissolving meaning and simulating reality. The culmination of the series, its final episode, 'Fall Out', purports to reveal the identity of Number One and thus decode all that has gone before. Yet here the generally linear narrative of earlier episodes dissolves into chaotic meaninglessness. There is no structure, no logic, only word-games and the promise of a return to the beginning: the whole cycle repeating itself. The episode 'Living in Harmony' is presented as a conventional Western. Lacking the usual opening sequence, our eponymous hero appears as a nameless stranger who arrives in a menacing Western town. The action revolves around the stranger's efforts to evade being made sheriff and his refusal to carry a gun. Its climax seems to be a gunfight with the trigger-happy, mute Kid in which the stranger is finally forced to resort to the gun, kills Kid, but is himself shot by the town judge. Yet on regaining consciousness, the stranger is again Number Six, back in the Village in his usual attire; he rushes out to find that the town was nothing but a façade complete with wooden cut-out figures of the characters he has just encountered. The whole exercise was a manipulation of images to produce a simulated reality.

In 'The Chimes of Big Ben', the second episode, Number Six enters an abstract carving in the Village's Arts and Crafts Exhibition. The judges are intrigued:

Judge: 'We are not quite sure what it means.'
Number Six: 'It means what it is.'
Number Two: 'It means what it is. Brilliant. Oh no, you mustn't let me influence you. You are the awards committee.'
Judge: 'What puzzles me, Number Six, is the fact you've given the group a title: Escape.'
Number Six: 'This piece – what does it represent to you?'
Judge: 'A church door?'
Number Six: 'Right first time!'
Judge: 'I think I see what he is getting at.'

Meaning is totally relative, *The Prisoner* seems to argue. One sees what one wants to see: there is no universal truth. In Number Six's mind, truth is dependent on which side you are on. But the guardians of the Village are more sceptical of any grand notion of the truth: they show, in Lyotard's words, an 'incredulity towards metanarratives' which for Lyotard is both the defining characteristic and the definition of 'postmodern';[3] or, as this dialogue from 'The Chimes of Big Ben' puts it:

> *Number Two*: 'There are some people who talk and some people who don't. Which means there are some people who leave this place and some people who do not. You are obviously staying.'
> *Number Six*: 'Has it ever occurred to you that you are just as much a prisoner as I am?'
> *Number Two*: 'Oh my dear chap, of course! I know too much. We're both lifers. I am definitely an optimist. That's why it doesn't really matter who Number One is. It doesn't matter which side runs the village.'
> *Number Six*: 'It's run by one side or the other.'
> *Number Two*: 'But both sides are becoming identical – what in fact has been created is an international community. A perfect blueprint for world order. When the sides facing each other suddenly realise they're looking into a mirror they will see that this is the pattern for the future.'

Thus ideologies, truth and even reason are all relative: everything is a mirror-image of the other, and in the final analysis, there is no real escape from the all-encompassing relativism and oppression. All that remains are language-games; and *The Prisoner* is saturated with elaborate language-games, word-plays and plays with words:

> *Number Two*: 'I'll kill you.'
> *Number Six*: 'I will die.'
> *Number Two*: 'You're dead.'

But even the throwaway lines in *The Prisoner* have an indisputable tone of irony and self-mockery: 'I am reporting a breakdown in control. Number Two will need to be replaced ... Yes, this is Number Two reporting' (from 'Hammer into Anvil').

In conventional television dramas, the protagonists search for and pursue rather mundane subjects – the one-armed killer of *The Fugitive* being a notable example. In today's postmodern counterparts, the primordial quest becomes much more illusive: *Nowhere Man* is looking for his identity which has been totally erased by powerful global interests; the young hero of *Dead Before 21*, who has a microchip implanted in his head as part of a government experiment, is looking for his cyber-past; and the survivors that manage to land on a new planet in *Earth 2* are looking for an earth of the future. *The Prisoner*, however, prefigured the postmodern paradigm thirty years ago, before its features had become paradigmatic. Number Six's quest for the identity of Number One is in fact a quest for the discovery of his own identity as well as an attempt to define his own future – Number One turns out to be the *alter ego* of Number Six.

The Prisoner deliberately mixes facts and fantasy and collapses the past (that is, the fictional past of the actor, Patrick McGoohan) into the present, and the present into the future. The symbol of the modern-cum-postmodern tale of *The Prisoner* is the traditional penny-farthing bicycle: the old and the new are combined to suggest both continuity and rupture. *The Prisoner* itself is really a continuation of *Danger Man* (aka *Secret Agent*), McGoohan's earlier television series, in which he plays secret agent John Drake. Number Six certainly behaves like Drake: he prefers to use his head rather than his fists or a gun, he is astutely ethical, and he shows no Bond-like interest in women. A real John Drake appears in the episode 'The Girl Who Was Death': a real actor playing the part of a bowler in a cricket match. The fictional village of *The Prisoner* draws heavily on the real village in Scotland where, during the second world war, ex-secret agents were sent for an 'enforced holiday' by the (now extinct) Inter Services Research Bureau (ISRB). In other words, the Village of *The Prisoner* actually existed. In one episode, Number Six gives his address as '20 Portmeirion Road, Filey Clyde, Scotland'.

In one respect *The Prisoner* is decidedly *not* postmodern: in its uncompromisingly moral stance. *The Prisoner* does not argue for some illusive notion of freedom, including individual freedom (which it actually posits as a myth), but against all forms of manipulation, including manipulation by images. It does not argue that we are all prisoners in a world dominated by manufactured images and futile word-plays, but rather rejects such a world. As Steven Best and Douglas Kellner argue, postmodernism 'delight[s] in the world as it is and happily coexist[s] in a pluralism of aesthetic styles and games.'[4] In contrast, *The Prisoner* uses the aesthetic style of postmodernism to undermine its message: ultimately, a moral stance is necessary to escape the perpetual cycle of oppression.

The Welfare Committee

Almost three decades after *The Prisoner*, postmodernism has become a key term of our times. It conditions our thoughts and politics, forms our art and architecture, frames much of the entertainment industry, and is actively shaping our future. We can watch it, hear it, read it, shop within its precincts, be awe-struck by it – in short, we live and breathe it. Slowly but surely, postmodernism is taking over the world we inhabit, the thoughts we think, the things we do, what we know and what we don't know, what we have known and what we cannot know, what frames our nature and our being. It is the new, or perhaps not so new, all-embracing theory of salvation.

Postmodernism emerged from western critical movements in art and architecture. It was, is, largely a reaction against the suffocating embrace of modernity, its instrumental rationality, the alienating idea of perpetual, linear progress and elitist notions of culture. Postmodernism grew as a rebellion against the Enlightenment, the eighteenth-century European movement that grounded all human thought and behaviour in a specific notion of Reason and sought to represent European civilisation, culture and society as the universal yardstick against which all other civilisations, societies, cultures and modes of thought and behaviour were to be measured. Postmodernism stands against totalising Reason, against the racist European notion of culture and civilisation, and seeks to represent all classes and races. It champions variety, pluralism and eclectic mixing of different traditions and modernism. But the nature of postmodernism has been totally transformed. A number of key intellectual and social developments over the last two decades have not only undermined modernity, but have also changed the character of postmodernism itself. These developments include:

- the demystification of scientific objectivity by Kuhn, Feyerabend and a host of Marxist critics of science;

- the collapse of Western philosophy as a worthwhile enterprise thanks largely to Wittgenstein, Derrida and Rorty;

- the emphasis on indeterminacy in quantum physics and mathematics;

- the emphasis on discontinuity and difference in history, primarily by Foucault but also by other historians;

- the rise of the 'magical realism' school of fiction pioneered by Borges, Marquez and other Latin American novelists;

- the concern over representations of the 'Other' in history, anthropology and politics;

- the secularisation of Christianity and its removal from society as a moral force;

- the triumph of the market economy and the emergence of the pathological concern with consumer 'choice'.

These developments have given postmodernism its new foundation. Thus, contemporary postmodernism is not concerned simply to dethrone Enlightenment Reason, or to give voice to the voiceless. Neither is it limited to art and architecture. Postmodern theory is derived from philosophy, science, history, literature and cultural criticism, as well as numerous other disciplines, and the theory has in turn given rise to postmodern philosophy, history, anthropology, fiction and even religion. Postmodernism has thus penetrated all spheres of disciplinary thought, established deep roots in daily life, while becoming a global cultural force underpinned by free market, bourgeois liberalism. The postmodern world is being built by the mass media. The glue that binds it all together: the postmodern economy.

Given its multifaceted and pluralistic character, postmodernism is not an easy beast to pin down. The nature of postmodernism is further complicated by the fact that it seems to be for everything and against (apparently) nothing. The eclectic nature of postmodernism has been used by its champions and apologists to mystify it; to present it as a pragmatic, intellectual force that cannot be fathomed, let alone resisted. Many writers on postmodernism insist that it cannot be defined. Yet, there is nothing mysterious about postmodernism.

So, what defines postmodernism? *The Prisoner* was indeed prescient. Let me elaborate further. Postmodernism, as the label suggests, is *post*-modernity: it transcends modernity, which in turn surpasses tradition. Thus the first principle of postmodernism is that all that is valid in modernity is totally invalid and obsolete in postmodern times. Modernity was framed by what are called, in the jargon of cultural studies, Grand Narratives: that is, Big Ideas which give sense and direction to life. Such notions as Truth, Reason, Morality, God, Tradition and History, argue postmodernists, do not live up to analytical scrutiny: they are totally meaningless. And all worldviews that claim absolute notions of Truth – for example, Science, Religion, Marxism – are artificial constructions that are totalitarian by their very nature. Truth is relative, contingency is everything: or as Richard Rorty, the American guru of postmodernism, puts it, nothing has an intrinsic nature which may be expressed or represented, and everything is a product of time and chance. Thus postmodernism rejects all forms of truth-claims; it accepts nothing as absolute; and rejoices in total relativism.

When Truth and Reason are dead, what becomes of knowledge? Postmodernism considers all types, as well as all sources, of knowledge with equal scepticism. There is hardly any difference between science and magic, as Feyerabend took such pains to demonstrate. For postmodernists, knowledge is acquired not through inquiry but by imagination. As such, fiction rather than philosophy, and narrative rather than theory, provide a better perspective on human behaviour. Wittgenstein argued that all we have is language, even though its representation of reality is, at best, approximate and faulty. Rorty asserts that we should drop even the idea of language as representation, and the postmodern project should consist only of attempts 'to de-divinize the world'.[5] Irony, ridicule and parody are the basic tools with which this postmodernist goal is to be achieved.

The second postmodern principle is the denial of Reality. Postmodernism suggests that there is no ultimate Reality behind things: we see largely what we want to see, what our position in time and place allows us to see, what our cultural and historic perceptions focus on. Thus even in science the easiest thing to find is what we are looking for. As science gets closer and closer to its ultimate goal, the formulation of a Theory of Everything, it assumes postmodern proportions. Relativism was introduced into science by quantum mechanics. Light can be simultaneously wave and particle, and a particle can simultaneously pass through a double slit producing wave-like patterns (Newton's rings). Heisenberg introduced a measure of permanent uncertainty in science with his principle: the impossibility of predicting both the mass and velocity of a particle at any given moment. The 'elementary' particle has turned out to be more and more elusive as we discover that the atom consists not only of protons, neutrons and electrons, but all varieties of gluons, charms, quarks ... there is, it seems, a plethora of elementary particles which turn out to be 'strings' rather than points. New developments in mathematics suggest that there are fundamental limits to our scientific knowledge. The emerging theories of chaos and complexity demolish the notion of control and certainty in science. Chaos can be defined as a kind of order without periodicity. Complexity is concerned with complex systems in which a host of independent agents interact to produce spontaneous self-organisation. Both theories promise a postmodern revolution in science based on the notions of holism, interconnection and order out of chaos and the idea of an autonomous, self-governing nature. These new developments in science point not towards the existence of an ultimate reality 'out there', but to the all-pervasive influence of contingency.

Rather than reality, what we have, contends postmodernism, is a simulacrum: a world in which all distinction between image and material reality has been lost. This is the third principle of postmodernism. Postmodernism posits the world as a video game: seduced by the allure of the spectacle, we have all become characters in the global video game, zapping our way from here to there, fighting wars in cyberspace, making love to digitised bits of information. All social life is now being regulated not by reality but by simulations, models, pure images and representations. These in turn create new simulations, and the whole process continues in a relentless stream in which the behaviour of individuals and societies bears no relationship to any reality: everything and everyone is drowned in pure simulacrum.

The fourth principle of postmodernism is that of meaninglessness. In a world without Truth and Reason, where no knowledge is possible and where language is the only tenuous link with existence, where Reality has been drowned in an ocean of images, there is no possibility of meaning. As Umberto Eco seeks to show in *Foucault's Pendulum*[6] the world is nothing more than an onion: once we have 'deconstructed' it layer by layer, we are finally left with – nothing. Deconstruction – the methodology of discursive analysis – is the norm of postmodernism. Everything has to be deconstructed. But once deconstruction has reached its conclusion, we are left with a grand void: there is nothing, but nothing, that can remotely provide us with meaning, with a sense of direction, with a scale to distinguish good and evil. This fourth principle of postmodernism thus takes us back to the first, reconfirming the arbitrary nature of truth and morality, science and religion, physics and metaphysics, while generating a fifth principle: doubt. Doubt, the perpetual and perennial condition of postmodernism, is best described by the motto of the cult television series *The X Files*: 'Trust No One'. In postmodern theory, this is extended to include no theory, no absolute, no experience: doubt everything.

In addition to these five principles, there is one other, perhaps more positive, defining characteristic of postmodernism. Postmodernism is concerned with variety, with multiplicities: it emphasises plurality of ethnicities, cultures, genders, truths, realities, sexualities, even reasons, and argues that no one type should be privileged over others. In its concern to demolish all privilege, postmodernism seeks a more equal representation of class, gender, sexual orientation, race, ethnicity and culture.

Once we appreciate these defining principles of postmodernism, it becomes easy to identify ideas, personalities, products and artefacts – buildings, movies, pop songs and videos, advertisements, television shows, politicians and individuals – of the global culture currently known as postmodernism. A typical postmodern product may incorporate any number of these defining features, embracing or parodying them, playing with them or taking them all too seriously.

Questions are a Burden to Others

Postmodernism is said to herald the beginning of a new age on earth, an age that transcends the modern, and which, in the words of John Gibbons,

> both explains contemporary behaviour and attitudes and offers a radically new set of experiences, practices and life worlds for its inhabitors. The move from the modern to the postmodern worlds, like that from the classical to the medieval to the modern, was at first imperceptible. But unlike these transitions, and more in line with the development of the Renaissance and Enlightenment movements, postmodernists are conscious of the change.[7]

In modernity, 'Other worlds' are excluded, overlooked and marginalised. Over four decades of 'modernisation' programmes in the Third World have compelled pre-colonial dependencies into post-colonial underdevelopment, destroying traditional societies, cultures and environments in the process. But, argue the exponents of postmodernism, all that was in the bad old days:

> Postmodernism signals the death of such 'metanarratives' whose secretly terroristic function was to ground and legitimate the illusion of 'universal' human history. We are now in the process of awaking

from the nightmare of modernity, with its manipulative reason and fetish of the totality, into the laid-back pluralism of the post-modern, that heterogeneous range of life-styles and language games which has renounced the nostalgic urge to totalize and legitimate itself ...[8]

In postmodernism, marginality takes centre-stage as western culture discovers Otherness and its own ethnocentric perspectives. 'Today', notes George Yudice, 'it is declared, the "marginal" is no longer peripheral but central to all thought.' As such, marginality has become a liberating force:

by demonstrating that the 'marginal' constitute *the* condition of possibility of all social, scientific, and cultural entities, a new 'ethics of marginality' has emerged that is necessarily decentered and plural, and that constitutes the basis of a new, neo-Nietzschean 'freedom' from moral injunctions.[9]

So, of what does this 'ethics of marginality' consist? Is 'freedom from moral injunction' necessarily a good thing? Indeed, is postmodernism really a liberating force? Does the rejection of suffocating and totalising metanarratives – the arch-concern of postmodernists from the Left and the Right – and close attention to 'Other worlds' and 'Other voices' the emphasis on understanding differences and Otherness, as well as the representation postmodernism gives to a whole host of social movements (women, gays, blacks, ecologists, regional autono-mists, colonised peoples with their own histories, etc.) spell a liberatory potential? Or is it a new twist to an old narrative? A new form of cultural exploitation? A new theory of imperialism? These are important questions especially for those in 'Other' non-western 'worlds' whose 'voices' have been silenced and whom postmodernism seeks to represent; particularly when, as Andrew Ross points out, postmodernism 'holds the promise of a cultural politics that would have no institutional boundaries, high or low, and that would fight over, if not infiltrate, every last inch of new historical terrain'. The issue of 'Other worlds' is central to postmodernism; an issue that raises a number of natural questions:

What world? Whose world? and What possible world? Suddenly postmodernism has become an epic production almost in spite of itself, or at least in spite of what many saw initially as one of its possibly vital impulses – a dissenting response to the epic, or universal, claims of modernism.[10]

The main thesis of this book is that far from being a new theory of liberation, postmodernism, particularly from the perspective of the Other, the non-western cultures, is simply a new wave of domination riding on the crest of colonialism and modernity. Alterity (along with other euphemisms signifying the Other or the non-west) is a key postmodern term. Postmodern relativism embraces the Other, making alterity far more than just the representation of all non-western cultures and societies. Alterity is the condition of difference in any binary pair of differences; there is even alterity within the self. Thus postmodernism avoids, by glossing over, the politics of non-western marginalisation in history by suddenly discovering Otherness everywhere, and arguing that everything has its own kind of Otherness by which it defines itself. While this proves the triumph of the postmodern thesis that everything is relative, it is incapable of suggesting that anything is in some distinctive way itself, with its own history. The postmodern prominence of the Other becomes a classic irony. Instead of finally doing justice to the marginalised and demeaned, it vaunts the category to prove how unimportant, and ultimately meaningless, is any real identity it could contain. We are all Others now, can appropriate the Other, consume artefacts of the Other, so what does it matter if Others want something different in their future – such as the chance to make it for themselves! Postmodernism is thus several quantum leaps above colonialism and modernity. Colonialism was about the physical occupation of non-western cultures. Modernity was about displacing the present and occupying the minds of non-western cultures. Postmodernism is about appropriating the history and identity of non-western cultures as an integral facet of itself, colonising their future and occupying their being.

While postmodernism is a legitimate protest against the excesses of suffocating modernity, instrumental rationality and authoritarian traditionalism, it has itself become a universal ideology that kills everything that gives meaning and depth to the life of non-western individuals and societies. It represents a partial displacement from repression to seduction, from the police to the market, from the army to the bank, from the depth reading of epistemology to a surface reading of hermeneutics. If postmodernism had a slogan it would be 'anything goes'; but when 'anything goes', everything stays and expediency guides thought and action. Postmodernism preserves – indeed enhances – all the classical and modern structures of oppression and domination. Hence, Other cultures are becoming prisoners in the world that postmodernism is creating. Indeed, the real postmodern world is coming more and more to resemble the Village of *The Prisoner*. In that televisual precursor, information is the desired commodity; and information has become the prime commodity of our global village. The indigenous knowledge of the Others, along with their history, is now being appropriated on an unprecedented scale to become consumer fodder for the west, to be recycled and exported back to non-western cultures. Instead of money, the Village uses a fictional credit unit system: much of the global economy is now based on either the production of imaginary money which is lent to non-western countries or the purchase of manufactured images by nations of the 'Third World'. The daily newspaper of the Village, *Tally Ho*, prints mostly lies, much as the global media nowadays largely recycle the images of Orientalism and 'demon Others' or 'poverty-stricken Others' or 'blood-thirsty warring Others' or simply publish lies, half-baked truth and manufactured versions of what is really happening in 'Other worlds'. Despite its cosmopolitan nature, English is the language of the Village and its dominance is symbolised by a standard and standardised form of greeting and farewell: 'Be seeing you.' The diversity of the modern world is similarly being replaced by the uniformity of the linguistic and visual domination of Hollywood and American television; indeed, it often seems as though the world is being run by the American entertainment industry. As in the Village, everyone is being manipulated, most of the time, into a craving for consumption and desire for manufactured love and happiness. The Village is guarded by Rover, the killer ball permanently on duty, ensuring that no one leaves, no one moves without permission. The global village is policed by the IMF, the World Bank and the United Nations, the mouthpiece of the western powers – the forces that ensure no one escapes the straitjacket of 'structural adjustment'.

Seen from this perspective, postmodernism emerges as a worldview conjured from the pathological necessity of the west to define reality and truth as *its* reality and truth. Now that the west itself doubts the validity of its own reality and truth it seeks to maintain the status quo and continue unchecked on its trajectory of expansion and domination by undermining all criteria of reality and truth. Western oppression of Other cultures seems to move in endless spirals, each ushered in with the promise of infinite freedom and expansion of civilisation. Postmodernism is the latest of these spirals, taking over from modernity, which itself is a product of colonialism. In the last reel of the last episode of *The Prisoner*, Number Six finally returns to his London home, having escaped the Village in an embryo 'cage' driven by the dwarf butler. The front door (now with a large number 1) opens automatically to admit the butler – exactly as all the doors in the Village opened. The prisoner enters, but we do not see him from the other side, coming into the room. There is a nagging feeling that somebody is waiting inside to start the cycle all over again. He emerges once more to climb into his parked Lotus car, to speed along a deserted motorway – just as he did at the very beginning of the first episode. The prisoner has not gained his freedom; this is no mythic quest complete with an apotheosis, it is merely another stage of an continuous cyclical restatement. The alleged promise of postmodernism is a similar myth. We are simply being taken from one domain of oppression into another. As the door closes on modernity, the modes and mechanisms of oppression of the Other continue, albeit in a new and more allusive form.

Thus postmodernism takes the civilising mission of the west to render the Other in its own image, into new arenas of oppression and subjugation. As the judge in the mock-trial in the last episode of *The Prisoner* declares: 'We desire that these proceedings be conducted in a civilised manner, but remind ourselves that humanity is not humanised without force.' *Postmodernism and the*

Other explores how the west continues the proceedings of colonialism and modernity, pushing the project to 'humanise' the Other towards its postmodern endgame: to absorb and consume the Other; it examines the nature of the force that is being used to accomplish this task.

When it looks out from the dark enclosure of its soul, western civilisation now perceives nothing but the echo of its inner emptiness. Unless it is consciously resisted, this dismal emptiness will envelop all that is distinctive about Other cultures and makes them genuinely Other: alternatives to the west. As they say in the Village: 'Be seeing you.' Or perhaps not, if we can help it!

1. Take Me, I'm Yours

Humanity is always on the edge of transformations. World history and the history of ideas have been written as a series of breathless leaps over impediments to the fuller realisation of the human spirit. Each transformation is perceived as a sharp break with the past, a discontinuity from what has gone before. Each transition is heralded as a harbinger of new promises, new opportunities, new freedoms. The transition from modernity to postmodernism is no exception. Our epoch will see 'our' total liberation from the shackles of the past, from the dogmas of the present, from the very anchors of our being that bind us to ourselves: it will be the culmination of 'the ascent of man', the zenith of our evolution and the final triumph of the human will.

According to Walter Anderson, there are three major forces shaping the transition from modernity to the postmodern age: (1) the breakdown of old ways of belief – this has been going on for the last century; (2) 'the birth of global culture', with a worldview that is truly a 'world view'; and (3) the emergence of a conflict about the nature of reality, social truth and epistemology which, like class, race and nationality, are now contested by all groups in society. These forces are so powerful that nothing can stand before them: 'it is impossible to return to a previous culture and industrial form,' says Charles Jencks – the transition, the onward march to postmodern times, is 'irreversible'.[1]

The postmodern age forces us to be free: it is, in Anderson's words, 'a time of incessant choosing'. It is a period, Jencks says, when it is 'not only the rich who become collectors, eclectic travelers in time with a superabundance of choice, but almost every urban dweller'; in this age 'Everyman becomes a Cosmopolite and

Everywoman a Liberated individual'.[2] But postmodernism does more than give us choices about lifestyles and cultures, consumer goods and technologies; it offers us a whole array of realities. As Anderson puts it:

> In the postmodern world we are all required to make choices about our realities. You may select a life of experimentation, eternal shopping in the bazaar of culture and subculture. Or you may forgo the giddy diversity of contemporary life-style swapping and fall into step with some ancient heritage: be an Orthodox Jew or fundamentalist Muslim or a Bible-toting Christian or a traditional native American.[3]

The freedom to choose to do and be anything and everything makes us all into 'consumers of reality'. In postmodern times, the emphasis is squarely on cultural and traditional diversity. The byword for postmodernism, Jencks tells us, is 'pluralism, the "ism" of our time'. Pluralism is both the great problem and the great opportunity of our age:

> The challenge for a Post-Modern Hamlet, confronted by an *embarras de richesses*, is to choose and combine traditions selectively, to 'select' (as the verb of eclecticism would have it) those aspects from the past and present which appear most relevant for the job at hand. The resultant creation, if successful, will be a striking synthesis of tradition; if unsuccessful, a smorgasbord. Between inventive combination and confused parody the Post-Modernist sails, often getting lost and coming to grief, but occasionally realising the great promise of a plural culture with its many freedoms. Post-Modernism is fundamentally the eclectic mixture of any tradition with that of the immediate past: it is both a continuation of Modernism and its transcendence. Its best works are characteristically doubly-coded and ironic, making a feature of the wide choice, conflict and discontinuity of traditions, because this heterogeneity most clearly captures our pluralism.[4]

Is postmodernism really a pluralistic enterprise? Is it really going to produce a synthesis of all our traditions and cultures? And, who is this 'we' who must 'choose' to be what 'we' want to become? Who is this individual, 'born out of the collapse of the medieval monolith',

who Anderson insists, 'must "choose" and keep choosing, whether
or not he or she knows it or wants such freedom: must determine
who to be, what to believe in, how to live'?[5]

Pay As You Enter

Let us begin with a banal but necessary point. This 'we' and these
'individuals' do not include those dying of famine in Africa: they
cannot choose to live, let alone how to live. We need a proper
perspective on who is in and who is out of the inescapable
postmodern world of free choices. We know that at least one
billion global citizens – that's one in five – live in abject poverty,
with insufficient shelter, food and other basic amenities. These are
the smallholder farmers, landless peasants, artisans, fishermen,
nomads, indigenous peoples, the bulk of whom live in rural areas.
These individuals do not suffer from richness of choice: they
cannot choose not to live below the poverty line. As Idriss Jazairy
and his colleagues show in the International Fund for Agricultural
Development (IFAD) report, *The State of World Rural Poverty*,[6]
rural people not only sustained themselves for thousands of years,
they also kept their societies fed and functioning. Now they have
become abjectly poor because choices related to agricultural and
pastoral practices have been systematically removed from them.
They exist in a twilight zone between life and death simply
because they have no other choice.

But the 'we' must also exclude an estimated three billion traditional people, living in the larger civilisations of India, China and
Islam, and numerous smaller civilisations in Asia, Africa and South
America, both urban and rural dwellers. These people cannot choose
to be what they want to be, what they have always been, because the
environment that sustained and nourished them, that allowed them
to be what they want to be, has been and is systematically being
destroyed. They cannot live as they choose to live, because the sciences, the technologies, the medical systems, the architecture, the
natural habitat that sustained their lifestyles have been suppressed
and destroyed. They cannot buy what they choose to buy, because
their mode of production has been replaced by imported western

consumer goods and services. They cannot even choose not be the victims of the dominant culture: their victimisation is embedded in the global economic and political system.[7]

There are other groups of people who cannot be part of the postmodern 'we'. The refugees who cannot return home and have no choice but to exist in squalid camps and survive on handouts; the asylum seekers who – thanks to European immigration policies – have no choice but to face despotic regimes or 'ethnic cleansing'; the increasing number of inner city poor in the west who have no choice but their grinding poverty; the rapidly multiplying homeless in Europe and North America who do not have the choice of a roof over their heads, let alone how to live ...

All these people – the vast majority of the earth's population – without much hope, let alone a bundle of choices, are not – cannot be – part of the postmodern 'we'. The postmodern 'we' is thus not a pluralistic, global we: it applies to those in North America and Europe who are, consciously or unconsciously, genuinely confronted by choices about lifestyles, belief systems and 'realities'. Those enslaved by poverty and those trapped in an oppressive modernity do not have the luxury of postmodern freedom of choice: circumstances dictate their lifestyles and reality. Thus, postmodernism is not only an occidental challenge and a western opportunity, it is the privilege of a particular group within western society.

However, the non-western world – four-fifth of the planet's population – does not even have the choice not to be *victims* of postmodernism. For despite its claims to be pluralistic, postmodernism is ravenously monolithic. Its surface pluralism masks a monolithic matrix at its core. Its language, logic, analytical grammar, are intrinsically Eurocentric and shamelessly cannibalistic of Others. Postmodernism does not mark a break, a discontinuity from oppressive modernity; rather, it represents an underlying continuity of thought and actions about Other cultures, which formed the bedrock of colonialism, was the foundation of modernity and is now housed in postmodernism. Colonialism signified the physical occupation of the territory of Others, the non-western cultures. Modernity signalled their mental occupation. Postmodernism now moves in to take possession of their total reality.

As an example of the Eurocentric logic inherent in arguments for postmodernism, consider the three 'global' forces Anderson identifies, which are making the transition from modernity to postmodernism 'inevitable'. The alleged 'total breakdown of old ways of belief', if at all true, is purely a western phenomenon. For example, in the Muslim world, the last century has seen a remarkable resurgence in belief.[8] Christianity played a large part in dethroning communism in Eastern Europe. The rise of belief is a recurrent theme among the liberation movements in Latin America.[9] The 'loss of hope' and disillusionment engendered by modernity have not led to a loss of faith but to a robust revival of belief as well as increased popularity of indigenous social, cultural and political movements throughout the non-western world. Postmodernists regularly generalise a purely western trend (and even here there are doubts) and present it in global terms.

The emergence of a 'global culture' is often presented as yet another indication of the imminence of postmodernism. We all wear T-shirts, jeans and trainers, eat McDonalds and Kentucky Fried Chicken. Memes – the cultural equivalent of genes – which replicate mental patterns, are now so firmly embedded in the cultural body of the globe that everyone is singing the same tune, discussing the same ideas, talking in the same catchphrases and expressing themselves in the same fashions. But, argues Anderson, we must not be too concerned about the monolithic nature of emerging culture:

> This looks to some people like nothing more than the Westernisation of the world. They're not entirely wrong, and the spread of Western influence is something you can view with dismay or perhaps a bit of hope. It includes not only junk food and junk bonds, but also concepts of democracy and human rights ... [But] it is a fragment of the whole picture ... Every Westerner knows about tea and Zen and the thoughts of Chairman Mao, and every Western businessman has heard about Japanese management.[10]

There are several layers of ethnocentricity in this argument. It is claimed that the westernisation of the globe may be a good thing; that non-western cultures do not have their own ideas of governance and notions of human dignity; that 'tea', 'Zen' and 'thoughts of Mao' are ahistorical, and that knowledge of these products in the West has nothing to do with colonial or recent history; that the flow of ideas between west and non-west is equal and at par.

The westernisation of the globe is suffocating non-western cultures: this point is so well established that it is hardly necessary to labour it here.[11] Suffice it to say that a world dominated by a single culture will not only be a much diminished world, it will also be an endangered place. In social life, as in nature, monocultures are doomed to extinction.

The assumption that the flow of ideas between the west and non-west is equal and will lead to a richness of cultures at worst and a 'synthesis' of cultures and traditions at best is widespread in postmodern writings and thought. However, the flow of cultural ideas and products, as those of commodities and goods, is strictly one-way: from the west to the Third World. One doesn't see an Indian Michael Jackson, a Chinese Madonna, a Malaysian Arnold Schwarzenegger, a Moroccan Julia Roberts, Filipino 'New Kids on the Block', a Brazilian Shakespeare, an Egyptian Barbara Cartland, a Tanzanian *Cheers*, a Nigerian *Dallas*, a Chilean *Wheel of Fortune*, or Chinese opera, Urdu poetry, Egyptian drama, etc. on the global stage. The global theatre is strictly a western theatre, a personification of western power, prestige and control. Those non-western individuals who occasionally get walk-on parts are chosen for their exotica or because they specifically subscribe to western ideas and ideals, or promote a western cause. When non-western cultural artefacts appear in the west, they do so strictly as ethnic chic or empty symbols.

The quest for synthesis of cultures in postmodernism should be seen as a logical step in the process of the westernisation of the globe, and universalisation of western civilisation itself. Having subsumed its own diversity into modernity, including its religious heritage of Judeo-Christianity, into seemingly superior principles of secular meliorism, the west now feels confident that a truly universal civilisation, stripped of all confessional content is feasible. Synthesis can only occur between two equally powerful cultures which are equally represented on the global stage. A powerful and dominant culture does not combine with a weak and dependent one to produce synthesis: it simply absorbs it. The weaker partner is not synthesised it is overwritten, reforged according to the principles and agenda of the dominant order. Postmodern synthesis is a euphemism for absorption of Other cultures into western civilisation.

Both the assertions about breakdown of belief systems and the birth of global culture are based on a third, and perhaps the most important, force of transition in the postmodern armoury: the social construction of reality. All we do as humans, it seems, is to construct realities to fit our own mental picture of the world. Everything 'out there' is a figment of our imagination. And since we are all equal in this best of all possible postmodern worlds, all realities are on a par with each other, all truth is relative, and all objectivity is but a charade. Anderson puts the postmodern case aptly:

> Reality construction is a process, and although some constructs may be tenacious they are still only temporary manifestations of a dynamic flow of thought that no philosophy or science has yet been able to map or describe in its entirety. Cognition ... is a process of computing a reality – not the reality. And it appears that we construct not just one reality, but realities and realities and realities and that they overlap and enclose one another and sometimes conflict.[12]

This means that the world has been transformed into a theatre where everything is artificially constructed. Politics is stage-managed for mass consumption. Television documentaries are transformed and presented as entertainment. Journalism blurs the distinction between fact and fiction. Living individuals become characters in soap operas and fictional characters assume 'real' lives. Everything happens instantaneously and everybody gets a live feed on everything that is happening in the global theatre. 'This theatricality', writes Anderson, 'is a natural – and inevitable – feature of our time. It is what happens when a lot of people begin to understand that reality is a social construction.' In other words, we are being constantly manipulated – and, perhaps, we in turn are manipulating others; that is, those of us who have the choice to manipulate.

Baudrillard has the courage to take the argument about social construction of all reality to its logical conclusion. The entire global theatre is in fact 'fluctuating in indeterminacy', he argues, so much so that reality is being absorbed into the fictionally created 'hyperreality'. All social life is now being regulated not by reality but by simulations, models, pure images, representations. The postmodern age has unleashed a process in which reality is systematically manufactured as representation. But the process does not stop there: the representations themselves produce new simulations totally divorced from the original reality, and the simulations themselves go on to produce pure images, the progeny of other images. This is how Baudrillard describes the process:

> Representation starts from the principle that the sign and the real are equivalent (even if this equivalent is Utopian, it is a fundamental axiom). Conversely, simulation starts from the Utopia of this principle of equivalence, *from the radical negation of the sign as value, from the sign as reversion and death sentence of every reference.* Whereas representation tries to absorb simulation by interpreting it as false representation, simulation envelops the whole edifice of representation as itself a simulacrum. These would be the successive phases of the image:
>
> 1. It is the reflection of a basic reality.
> 2. It masks and perverts a basic reality.
> 3. It masks the absence of a basic reality.
> 4. It bears no relation to any reality whatever: it is its own pure simulacrum.
>
> In the first case, the image is a good appearance: the representation is the order of sacrament. In the second, it is an evil appearance: of the order of maleficence. In the third, it plays at being an appearance: it is the order of sorcery. In the fourth, it is no longer in the order of appearance at all, but of simulation.[13]

It is futile to look for 'reality' in a world of pure simulation. It is not that we lack a way of telling the 'real' from the artificial; we can never discover the distinction. As such, we would do well to accept the postmodern condition for what it is and learn to enjoy it, instead of chasing the chimeras of antiquated belief systems and outmoded paradigms, whose truths possess not an iota of credibility.

What, then, should a postmodern consumer, with a modicum of conscience, think about all that pain, suffering, injustice and oppression? Is it all just a simulation, or are there real people enduring real hardship and cruelty? Baudrillard's answer came in the form of his analysis of the Gulf War. A few days before war broke out, he argued in the *Guardian*, that the war would never take place.[14] The whole exercise was an artificial construction: the real thing was not going to be any more real than an arcade video game played out on the world's television screens. After the war, Baudrillard declared: 'The Gulf War Has Not Taken Place'.[15] Notwithstanding the deaths and devastation, it was a 'virtual' engagement and so it was 'idiotic' to be for or against it.

In many respects, the Gulf War *was* a postmodern phenomenon. The blanket media coverage did convey the feeling that everything was being examined in minute detail and transmitted live to every household of the planet. The extensive coverage, served up with simulations, computerised footage of bombings, meaningless statistics, instant press conferences and expert opinion, the ridiculous claims of 'precision bombing' and 'pinpoint accuracy' with no civilian casualties, the eagerness of the media, European politicians and religious divines alike to accept the blatant propaganda of the US military machine – all this did blur the distinction between fact and fiction, the actual and the staged, the real and the hyperreal. But does it mean, as Baudrillard claims, that we cannot know whether the war actually took place, that there is no way of knowing what really happened and, most important, that we are in no position to take a moral stand on the issue?

For a world that claims that all reality is socially constructed, that promotes simulation as the norm, the pain, suffering and the death of the Other is particularly unreal. Postmodern simulacra serve as an insulating space, which isolates those who live in a world of countless choices from those whose only choice is to be their unwilling victims – the Others. The true postmodern character of the Gulf War is summed up, as Christopher Norris shows so powerfully, in the depth of complacency 'that exists between such forms of extreme anti-realist or irrational doctrine and the crisis of moral and political nerve among those whose voices should have been raised against the actions committed in their name.[16] Unable morally to justify its ceaseless oppression, the western world now postulates that no moral stance is possible. Since all moral positions are equally valid or equally absurd, none is possible, and one might as well learn to enjoy the status quo. From the patently sensible assertion that culture cannot be grasped as a true or false representation of reality – as Marxists have argued for decades – postmodernism manufactures the absurd theses that the real is no longer real, that reality is but an illusion, that there is nothing but a perpetual and endless reconstruction of realities as Anderson would have us believe, or truth and arguments are little more than free-floating language-games, as Baudrillard would argue. From here the next step, that of taking oppressive political and economic actions as representation of social reality and proving them to be totally unreal, is a short one. Postmodernism is the ultimate justification, the master alibi, for the continued exploitation and oppression of non-western cultures.

Yet there are factual and moral truths which are as real as the 'smart bombs' that (mistakenly?) landed on people's homes in Baghdad. There are real truths which stand above bare disagreements between competing viewpoints, that can be argued, that are amenable to historical evidence, and that, as Norris notes, 'involve determinate standards of veridical warrant and accountability'. Using Noam Chomsky's work, Norris catalogues a few factual truths concerning the Gulf War:

> Popular support for the Gulf War was secured through a large scale campaign of media disinformation that suppressed many truths – historical, geo-political, and factual-documentary – and which traded on widespread ignorance of what was *actually occurring* from day to day, in the bombing of civilian populations, the extent of so-called 'collateral damage', and the pursuit of war-aims that greatly exceeded the official UN provisions with regard to the Iraqi occupation of Kuwait.
>
> Thus for instance it is a claim borne out by knowledge of the relevant background history that the 'Allied' campaign was fought with the object of securing Western hegemony in the region through the survival of client regime (Kuwait) which could then be relied upon

to keep the oil-supplies flowing and to exert a 'stabilizing' influence on adjacent territories. It is also a matter of documentary record 1) that Saddam Hussein was bought to power and maintained over a long period by US intelligence and 'long-arm' strategic agencies; 2) that his regime was backed up *until the very last moment* by constant supplies of weapons and resources (not to mention diplomatic support) provided by the US and other Western powers; 3) that his invasion of Kuwait was prompted – or at least given what appeared to be the green light – by indications that the US would not intervene since it also wished to push up the oil-prices by exerting pressure on Kuwait; 4) that the Gulf War was fought *first and foremost* as a war of retribution against the erstwhile ally who had proved too difficult to handle; 5) that its conduct involved not only enormous military and civilian casualties but also – contrary to professed 'Allied' war-aims – a full-scale campaign of aerial bombardment launched against electricity generating stations, water-supply systems, sewage disposal plants, and other components of the urban infrastructure whose collapse could be predicted to cause yet further death and suffering through the breakdown of emergency services and the spread of infectious diseases; 6) that the attack on the retreating Iraqi forces (along with civilian hangers-on and hostages) continued to the point where any justifying talk became merely a cover for mechanized mass-murder; and 7) – still within the realm of documentary evidence – that the war might well have been averted had the 'Allies' held out against US pressure and listened to those well informed sources who argued that sanctions were already (in early January) taking their toll of Iraqi war-fighting capability. Of course all these claims are properly subject to reasoned argument and counter-argument, some of them (like item 3, 4 and 7) involving a considerable measure of interpretative hindsight. But to treat such disputes – in the Foucault–Lyotard manner – as so many rival, incommensurable 'discourses' beyond any hope of just and truthful arbitration is to adopt the kind of doctrinaire relativist outlook that leaves no room for genuine debate.[17]

But the Gulf War was also very real in another term: it was paid for in hard cash by Kuwait and Saudi Arabia and it involved the transfer of real wealth from the Middle East to the west.

'We Are Controlling the Horizontal, the Vertical ...'

Despite its claims to be a revolutionary departure from the past, postmodernism is in fact a continuation and further expansion of the essential dynamic of western culture. It is 'revolutionary' in that, in the Baudrillardian terminology, it has created a world of pure 'simulacra'. As Baudrillard writes,

> the transition from signs which dissimulated something to signs which dissimulate that there is nothing, marks the decisive turning point. The first implies a theology of truth and secrecy (to which the notion of ideology still belongs). The second inaugurates an age of simulacra and simulation, in which there is no longer any God to recognise his own, nor any last judgement to separate truth from false, the real from its artificial resurrection, since everything is already dead and risen in advance.[18]

But this 'turning point' does not mark postmodernism as a discontinuity from the past of the Other. Far from being a 'radical break' which effects all theoretical and cultural practices, as Fredric Jameson suggests in *Postmodernism or the Cultural Logic of Late Capitalism*,[19] postmodernism takes the subjugation of the Other to a new level of all-consuming transcendence. Western culture has continuously used five of its basic internal traits to oppress the Other: representation, duality, control, instrumentalism and the gaze. These facets of western culture remain intact and provide a continuous link between colonialism, modernity and postmodernity. When stripped of their outer camouflage, the three are one and the same theory of domination.

Representations of reality are not a new concern unique to postmodernism. Western culture has always been obsessed with representation. During the colonial period, European visitors to the Middle East were particularly perplexed by the lack of perspective of Muslim cities. A labyrinth of narrow streets without names, a complex maze without plan, the city looked nowhere except to itself. It was there: the real thing. Visiting Cairo in 1856–57, Herman Melville complained that it had no point of view; to appreciate the city he wanted a plan. In Constantinople, he complained, there was 'no plan to the streets. Perfect labyrinth. Narrow. Close, shut in. If one could but get up aloft ... But no. No names to the streets ... No numbers. No anything.'[20] Since it was not built according to a 'plan', a 'picture', the city did not represent anything:

> nothing stood apart and addressed itself ... to the outsider, to the observing subject. There was no name to the streets and no street signs, no open spaces with imposing facades, and no maps. The city refused to offer itself ... as a representation of something, because it had not been built as one.[21]

But to colonise these cities it was necessary 'to determine the plan'. Colonialism required the creation of a plan or a framework that would transform non-western cities and cultures into representations, make them legible, and hence amenable to political and economic calculations. But representation was not simply a 'plan' that colonialism brought to the non-western world; it was a process, a process of enframing non-western cultures, constructing an image of their reality, and directing their gaze in a particular way.

At the 1889 World Exhibition in Paris, Muslim visitors were intrigued by western obsession with representation. As Timothy Mitchell relates in *Colonising Egypt*, the Egyptian visitors noticed that 'on the buildings representing a Cairo street even the paint was made dirty', the donkeys were from Cairo and the Egyptian pastries on sale tasted like the real thing. The exhibition's perspective was that of Paris and the exhibits were arranged and illuminated so that an observer felt that he was standing at the centre of Paris. The city itself was represented as the imperial capital of the world, and exhibits from the empire were laid out according to a strict hierarchy. But it was not just the exhibition that simulated reality; the real world outside appeared as though it was an extension of the exhibition. As Mitchell notes, no one realised this except the Egyptian visitors. Egyptian authors who visited the exhibition and toured Europe regularly described what they called *intizam al-manzar*, the organisation of the view:

The Europe one reads about in Arabic accounts was a place of discipline and visual arrangement, of silent gazes and strange simulations, of the organisation of everything and everything organised to represent, to recall like the exhibition some larger meaning. Outside the world exhibition, it follows paradoxically, one encountered not the real world but only further models of the representation of the real. Beyond the exhibition and the department store, everywhere the non-European visitors went – the museums and the Orientalist congress, the theatre and the zoo, the countryside, encountered typically in the form of a model farm exhibiting new machinery and cultivation methods, the very streets of the modern city with their deliberate facades, even the Alps once the funicular was built – they found the technique and the sensation to be the same. Everything seemed to be set up before one as though it were the model or the picture of something. Everything was arranged before an observing subject into a system of signification (to use the European jargon), declaring itself to the signifier of a signified.[22]

Colonialism used representation to construct a particular image of the Other. This was a distinctive construct, an image based on knowledgeable ignorance – that is, it was constructed with the full knowledge of the reality of the Other yet designed to project an ignorant image of non-western cultures. It represented negative projections of the west's own fears as well as a rationale for domination, offering only a choice of enduring subservience to non-western people, or exclusion beyond the pale in a zone reserved for implacable hostility to the true cannibal savage or barbarian who existed before civilisation began. The construction of a distorted image of the Other – what, in the case of Islam is known as Orientalism[23] – reflected the internal insecurity of the west which forced it to see everything in terms of duality. Unable to face the real Other, it had to create an artificial image, painted in terms of its own categories and concepts, to which it could relate.

Colonialism perceived Other cultures in terms of a conceptual schema, first introduced by the anthropologist Adam Ferguson, a leading figure of the Scottish Enlightenment.[24] Anthropology equated specific social and cultural features as indicative of a three-fold ranking of living cultures: savagery, barbarism and civilisation. From the outset, however, civilisation was a unitary term: savagery and barbarism were seen as transitional phases in the progressive emergence of civilisation, the highest achievement of which was represented by European society. Colonialism directed the gaze of non-western cultures towards Europe and insisted that they become like the west. Both colonialism and Christianity were seen as the instruments of this 'civilising mission'. The salvation of the Other lay in accepting Christianity, in accepting the superiority of Europe and in coming as close to the ideal model as possible.

Taking over where colonialism and Christianity had left the Other, modernity became, in the words of Ashis Nandy, a 'secular theory of salvation'.[25] In the post-colonial world, non-western cultures came to be described as traditional, as opposed to modern, and naturally superior, western culture. It was their traditionalism that made them 'underdeveloped'; to become like the west they had to 'develop'. The literature of modernisation is replete with examples of how inferior traditional lifestyles impede the growth of economy and thwart the development of non-western societies: 'multi-stranded instead of single-stranded relationships, kinship ties, labour immobility, restrictions on the sale of land, subsistence rather than open-market production, mystical or religious instead of scientific ways of approaching production, and gift or reciprocity instead of commodity exchange'[26] are just a few of the ways in which the march of modernity is blocked by traditional societies.

But modernity did not limit itself to forcing non-western cultures to become like the west – that was an antiquated colonial goal. Modernity presented itself as a universal aspiration and sought the absorption of the Other into the west as a natural process of accretion, the inevitable outcome of the Other seeking their own betterment. Here hierarchical control came in terms of history: the present of the Other was described as the past of the west; the west had already lived through the present of the Other which was merely a representation of the real history of the west. Histories of all non-western cultures were so many tributaries and insignificant rivers which all flowed into the mighty ocean of Universal History, the history of the west.

To absorb non-western cultures into itself, modernity required a new schema of representation. Modernity not only forced an internalisation of the image of the Other constructed under colonialism, it also led the west to see its own construction as the real thing. The theory of modernisation was based on this construction of non-western cultures as innately inferior; the practical programme to absorb the non-west into the west came as 'Development Plans'. It was what Tariq Benuri describes as 'hegemonic panopticism'[27] – meaning centralised surveillance and control – inherent in western liberalism's method of binary opposition, which became the cornerstone of all theories of modernisation. The inferior dialectical relationships so evident in non-western cultures had to be replaced by superior hierarchical ones: the personal emotions of the populace had to make way for the impersonal 'animal spirit' of a certain class. This shift from 'personal' to 'impersonal' forms of understanding and acting could be justified on the basis of a host of western social theories which, in the words of Benuri, 'helped to legitimate this asymmetry as intrinsically desirable' and made 'it an important and valued aspect of Western culture'. Benuri shows how these theories have shaped and directed the discussion of valued goals in society:

1. Exchange theory: impersonal relations between buyer and seller ensure freedom of exchange. In many writings this is seen as a primary form of freedom.

2. Production theory: impersonal relations between employers and employees ensure that resources will flow to their most efficient use.

3. Jurisprudence: 'blindness' of justice, and the principle of natural law, 'that no man shall be a judge in his own cause', suggests that impersonal relations between the judge and the litigants are necessary to ensure justice.

4. Education theory: the separation of the content of education from the personality of the participant may be necessary not only for the pursuit of efficiency, but also to maintain the myth of the equality of opportunity.

5. Political science: a bureaucratised, efficient state is seen as one which will be able to implement most effectively the will of the citizens, leading not only to effective decision-making, but also to the protection of freedom.

6. Technology: the notion of experts, and the partitioning of knowledge that it entails, is legitimized on grounds of efficiency, as well as of innovation and growth.

7. Moral philosophy: based on abstract rather than relational principles, it is legitimized on the grounds of its being universal and objective – and thus fair.

8. Communication: that a free, impersonal, and impartial press will provide true information, in contrast to the tainted news supplied by politically motivated sources.[28]

The theories of modernisation produced during the 1950s and 1960s were based on these, and similar, theories generated by western social sciences. Blueprints for modernisation, like Daniel Lerner's *Passing of the Traditional Society: Modernizing the Middle East*,[29] contain a step-by-step guide to the eradication of 'personal' traditional, non-western cultures and their replacement with a pale representation of 'impersonal' western culture and lifestyle. Since the cities of non-western people have no perspectives, they must be structured hierarchically; since most of the population of 'developing countries' live in rural areas, urbanisation must be introduced, and they must be motivated to move to cities where they can have a modern lifestyle; since their subsistence agriculture is not efficient, it must be replaced with modern methods of agriculture ... and most important: they must be persuaded, by any means necessary, to think with modern categories, so that they see basic human values such as freedom, justice, equality, creativity and even power solely as they have been experienced and defined by the west: only then would non-western cultures become truly western, truly modern. Modernity sought nothing less then to replace the ways of knowing, being and doing of non-western cultures.

The goals of modernity could best be achieved by separating traditional cultures from their reality. Traditional cultures approach reality not just in epistemological terms, but also experientially. As Benuri notes, such things as land, the village, the home, trees, forests, animals, stars, goods, even people are not seen simply in terms of personal gratification, as in the western culture, but in a 'relational context: a home is not just a place where you are living at the moment, but also an integral part of your history as well as of your future'.[30] It is this experiential and relational perception of reality that guides individual behaviour, in non-western cultures, towards what the society holds as essential, valuable and desirable.

Modernity applied two basic instruments to break this experiential and relational bond: instrumental reason and an instrumental notion of the person, or 'individualism'. Instrumental reason was the weapon that sought to transform the experiential reality of non-western cultures into an experimental one. New forms of institutionalised violence were justified in the name of such values as competition, control, production, achievement, efficiency, growth, progress, development. Everything was made subservient to a rationality that could be reduced to a set of variables, a collection of figures, which gave primacy to statistical and laboratory reality over the personal, social, communal, spiritual and cultural realities of non-western cultures. Instrumental reason fostered the notion that the means by which social and political development is sought are separate from its ends; and it is only the ends that need to be given moral consideration. Thus freed from any moral constraints, the means of systematically separating Other cultures from their reality unleashed ruthless violence, in the shape of instrumental science, capitalist technologies, agribusiness and instrumental nation-states, against traditional societies. The emphasis on individualism was designed to generate a sense of personal identity independent of relationships, autonomous from cultural, social and communal concerns, and based on such impersonal elements as preferences, desires, fashions and professional occupations. Goals and preferences of (westernised) individuals were presented as metaphysical entities – the only realities that mattered – while the desires and aspirations of communities were dismissed as irrelevant to modernisation. In this way, modernity has succeeded, to a considerable degree, in shaping traditional societies in the image of the west.

We see, then, that the internal traits of western culture – its obsession with representation, insistence on duality and control, ruthless instrumentalism and persistent gaze – are in fact a metalanguage of oppression and domination. Postmodernism exhibits the same traits; but in as much as it is a transcendence of modernity, it gives the western metalanguage of oppression a few new twists. The enframing of non-western cultures continues, but the process itself of enframing is now presented as an illusion, a mirage, a simulation; simultaneously simulations and mirages are constructed to make it appear as though all hierarchy and control, and hence domination and oppression, have disappeared. The object of postmodernism is not simply to absorb the non-west – that is the goal of hackneyed modernity – no: postmodernism aims at nothing less than to exhaust and consume the non-west.

Jencks sees postmodernism in terms of 'paradoxical dualism' or 'double coding'.[31] What that means is the duality principle of western culture remains intact. Listen to the terms of debate that postmodernism has imposed: either reality represents something 'real' or it represents nothing; either religions, Marxism and other 'metanarratives' will be transcendental or they will not be; 'works of art either represent something more real than themselves which is therefore the depth beneath their surface (making them susceptible to a hermeneutic reading) or they are absolutely autonomous, indeterminate and therefore "unanalyzable"; either the subject is master of itself, its own thought and actions or it has simply vanished into the pure systematicity of the historical present.'[32] Moreover, as Warren Montag argues,

the first set of alternatives (transcendentality, art as representation, the subject as origin-center), is often placed in historical opposition to the second set (the absence of transcendentality, the indeterminacy of art, the death of the subject) as a once existing past that has given way to the present as one historical totality to another. So, for example, the classically conceived subject once existed but no longer does, just as art once represented reality but has somehow ceased to do so.[33]

Of course, the binary oppositions presented by postmodernism are just as much an artificial construction as the duality championed by colonialism and modernity. Anderson, for example, argues that there are 'two faces of God': religion thus comes in binary oppositions of 'exoteric' and 'esoteric' varieties. 'Exoteric religions, such as institutionalized Christianity and Islam', he tells us, 'are reified and deified belief systems that explain all reality and are capable of serving as a complete system of values and beliefs for a society.'[34] Esoteric religions, such as Sufism and Zen Buddhism, 'are primarily traditions of individual instructions'. It does not occur to him that there may be non-institutionalised forms of Christianity and Islam, which do not explain 'all reality', but leave the exploration of reality to their followers. Nor does it occur to him that there may be 'esoteric religions' which are not systems of 'individual instructions', but ways of experiencing 'reality' in a communal form. However, this neat binary categorisation excludes the vast majority of Christians and Muslims altogether: 99.9 per cent of Muslims are not fundamentalists or Sufi mystics; 99.9 per cent of Christians, of all denominations, are not Bible-thumping fundamentalists; 99.9 per cent of Hindus are not fundamentalists nor do they subscribe to the mystical beliefs and practices so readily available in India. Fundamentalism recurs in postmodern writings as a straw man to burn. Modernist cultural phenomena in non-western countries are taken as representations of the social reality of religion and then represented as the norm of Other cultures. Postmodernism is thus championed not just by projecting a fear of fundamentalism, but also by showing Other cultures to consist of so much irrational and obscurantist theology.

But there is another point that needs consideration. Modernity limits all theoretical criticism to the intra-paradigmatic sphere (where the assumptions and proposition of theories are questioned within a given paradigm) and inter-paradigmatic sphere (where writers in different disciplines who may share the worldview of the impugned paradigm though not all of its maintained assumptions are examined). Postmodernity, on the other hand, first focuses criticism on 'texts' – which could be anything from written words to cultural practices and artefacts – and then renders all criticism meaningless: once the text is 'deconstructed' one is left with nothing but inescapable textual predicaments.

However, there are other forms of criticism that are not amenable to modernist or postmodernist analysis – resistance, for example. Fundamentalism, especially Islamic fundamentalism, is not just a religious phenomenon: it is a critique of both modernity and postmodernity. Certainly, fundamentalism emerged in Islam as a critique of imposed modernity.[35] Similarly, some 1,300 years ago, Sufism emerged in Muslim societies as a critique of the arid legalism of the dominant system.[36] To understand fundamentalism and Sufism, one has to read them as critiques.

However, in postmodernism, critiques, debates, intellectual and critical positions have little meaning for its fundamental postulate is that nothing can count as an argument when all criteria for assessing reality and truth, as well as reality and truth themselves, have been deconstructed and shown to be chimeras. This is the control principle of postmodernism. At one level, it demolishes the hierarchy of truth established under colonialism and expanded by modernity. But on another, it creates a new monopoly through which control of the Other is exercised. To understand how it works we need go no further then Baudrillard himself – the guru of postmodernism. To maintain control, Baudrillard tells us, monopoly tactically creates a double:

> In all domains, duopoly is the highest stage of monopoly. It is not political will that breaks the monopoly of the market (state intervention, anti-trust law etc.); it is the fact that every unitary system, if it wants to survive, has to evolve a binary system of regulation. This changes nothing in the essence of monopoly; on the contrary, power is only absolute if it knows how to diffract itself in equivalent variations; this is, if it knows how to redouble itself through doubling. This goes for brands of detergent as much as for 'peaceful coexistence'. You need two superpowers to maintain a universe under control; a single empire collapses under its own weight. The equilibrium of terror is what permits a strategy of regulated oppositions to be established, since the strategy is really structural rather than atomic.[37]

A structured strategy of control and regulation can, of course, produce an infinite number of homologous and competing differences: a universe of competing 'realities', 'truths', 'worldviews', 'texts', 'cultures', 'positions' generating a perception of thriving pluralism and diversity. But a monopoly, *the* monopoly of western culture, controls and directs this apparent pluralism. Pluralism has meaning only when the participants in plurality have equivalence of representation, equivalence of access to resources and opportunities, and a modicum of equality in terms of power. Postmodernism perpetuates the monopoly of western culture not just by producing a binary system of regulation (post-cold war, the new super-demon is Islam),[38] but also by generating a simulated plurality which veils the continuity in oppression and inequality.

Postmodernism also legitimises western representations of the Other by a sleight of hand. Since there is nothing but representation, all interpretation is misinterpretation, there is no hope of rescuing the truth of non-western cultures from the constructed images of the west. The status quo is preserved: both the historic, current and the future enframing of the Other in images of ignorance continues una-bated. Of course, the representations of the Other are constructions; but the ignorance and oppression they perpetuate are very real! There is a corollary: the past of the Others is also erased by this metaphysical incantation. As all texts are embedded with narrative or story-telling interests, it is not possible to distinguish the factual and documented writing of history from fiction, imaginative and simulated events. There is thus no possibility of unearthing the truth about the histories of all Others, the myriad of non-western cultures that exist and have existed in history. With one con-trick, postmodernism absolves western culture of its historic guilt while propelling its historic themes.

While colonialism and modernity sought moral justification (however facile) for its ends, if not the means, postmodernism does away with the need even for a moral justification of its ends – indeed, all ends. Pure instrumentalism becomes the norm. This is what is meant by postmodern pragmatism. As William James put it, what we need are 'instruments, not answers to enigmas, in which we can rest'.[39] Rorty concurs. And Anderson adds: 'to be a postmodern pragmatist is to recognize all constructs as theories – and hence as instruments to be used where appropriate and periodically replaced.'[40] In its instrumentalism, postmodernism takes a quantum leap from modernity and colonialism: here everything is an instrument towards the cultural ends of western civilisation, including human beings, and particularly non-western individuals, communities, societies and cultures which are just so many consumables. In postmodernism, the Other becomes an instrument for the realisation of the full potential of the west.

The postmodern desire to consume the Other is not just a collective cultural phenomenon: it is also an individual quest. Postmodernism takes individualism to a new level. As Anderson notes, 'the rush of postmodern reaction from the old certainties has swept some people headlong into a (radical) worldview ... Many voices can now be heard declaring that what is out there is not only what we put out there. More precisely, what *I* put there – just little me, euphorically creating my own universe.'[41] Postmodern individuals – being so many points of greed within the western civilisation – are forever acquiring new identities, creating new universes of realities, consuming whatever they think would satisfy their insatiable quest for meaning, identity and belonging: largely at the expense of non-western cultures.

In this eternally empty and meaningless universe what is there to guide us? Baudrillard has already given up: for him, it's *Apocalypse Now!* Rorty and others have opted for 'literature' and 'irony'. Anderson suggests that individual conscience will become our guiding star. 'We do not', he asserts boldly, 'cease to be moral animals and slide into hedonistic or savage normlessness.'[42] No: we will use psychology as well as our own conscience to help us evolve into new 'moral beings'. As an example, Anderson suggests that something like Lawrence Kohlberg's moral development scale will become a standard instrument. This postulates six different levels of growth. In stage one people understand little more than their own needs and notions of reward and punishment. Stage two arrives when they begin to recognise that other people have needs and a few trade-offs may be necessary. In stage three they move into a 'good boy' orientation based on gaining approval for pleasing and helping others. At stage four they begin to see society as a system of rules. In stage five people begin to recognise that all systems of rules are arbitrary and negotiate a 'social contract'. The postmodern individual reaches his moral apex in stage six when he/she begins to rely on personal conscience.[43] Here then is the zenith of postmodernism: after all has been said and done, we have nothing but shoddy pop-psychology to take us to the next stage of our evolution – and the schemata are nothing but a scale whose conception and early stages would have been instantly recognisable to Adam Ferguson!

Reliance on individual conscience has meaning only when individuals have a conscience. All of postmodernism's traits work towards depriving individuals of their conscience. If neither the ends nor the means need justification then anything goes. Both thought and action are motivated by expediency: witness the Gulf War, the first trial of Rodney King, the denial of assistance to Bosnian Muslims subjected to 'ethnic cleansing'; it's all so very pragmatic. Postmodernism engenders double standards. And the individual is not just trapped into a system of ambiguous morality and double standards, perpetual and insatiable quest for consumption, inescapable bombardment of images and representations, and constant manipulation of and by all: there is also the very real fear created by the postmodern need to choose an identity wrapped in a manufactured reality: 'when we choose to adopt one, we know – even if we are terrified by the knowledge and do all we can to repress it in ourselves and others – that we could choose an entirely different one.' What role can conscience play in a world of such fear, angst and darkness?

In its most oppressive and totalitarian phase as postmodernism, western civilisation wants to drown the globe in the absolute blankness of its vision. Postmodernism continues the exponential expansion of colonialism and modernity. It is a worldview based on that pathological condition of the west, which has always defined reality and truth as its reality and truth, but now that this position cannot be sustained it seeks to maintain the status quo and continue unchecked in its trajectory of consumption of the Other by undermining all criteria of reality and truth. Postmodernism takes the ideological mystification of colonialism and modernity to a new, all-pervasive level of control and oppression of the Other while parading itself as an intellectual alibi for the west's perpetual quest for meaning through consumption, including the consumption of all Others.

'They Identified Their Realities Accurately'[44]

Non-western cultures have been aware of both diversities of
reality as well as its social construction (although they do not
state their realisations in the jargon of modern sociology). For
example, in Islamic culture reality is designated by a number of
technical terms. *Haqiqah* is reality per se; *haqiqah ahadiyah* is
unitary reality; *haqiqah al-haqaiq* is the reality of realities;
haqiqah muqayyadah is determined reality (as for example in
science and other rational inquiry); *haqiqah mutlaqah* is absolute
reality; *haqiqah al-insan* is the reality of man (that is, socially
constructed reality); *haqiqah al-shay* is the reality of things;
haqiqah wahidah is single reality; and so on. Each reality reveals
its essence through a particular methodology, and while they are
different realities, they could be aspects of the same; multiplicity can be seen as unity and unity as multiplicity. Absolute
reality is the reality of God and it cannot be known: 'God in
His essence is only known to Himself.' Determined reality, the
reality of the world, is acquired through sustained use of reason
and physical human faculties. The reality of man is the self he
shapes through his cultural, social and communal identity.
Some realities can be acquired by sustained effort, some are
lived, some are experienced. Various realities can sometimes
combine to produce new realities: for example, a unitary reality
occurs when the determined reality glimpses the Absolute.[45]
This is not the place to examine the universe of realities in
Islam; the point is that postmodernism is not what 'inevitably
happens' when people discover that there are many realities and
many ways of knowing, as Anderson asserts: Muslims, and other
non-western people, have always known this.

Not only does postmodernism recycle notions well established
in non-western cultures, it makes two further assertions. The
argument that since there are many realities there can be no
criteria for determining their validity becomes quite meaningless
when viewed, for example, from the perspective of Hindu logic.
Western logic is based on the principle of 'valid inference' and
formulated in a content-independent 'formal' language which

aims to translate everything into mathematical symbols. In contrast to western logic which uses sequential techniques of quantification and negation, Indian logic uses a geometric system to demonstrate configurational relationships of similarity and convergence: it is both mathematical and symbolic. Instead of a universe seen through an either/or duality, the Indian system sees the world through a fourfold logic (X is neither A, nor non-A, nor both A and non-A, nor neither A nor non-A) and Jain logic expands these categories into a sevenfold logic. Being a logic of cognition, the Indian system achieves a precise and unambiguous formulation of universal statements in terms of its technical language without recourse to quantification over unspecified universal domain.[46] Again, I do not want to give an exposition of Indian logic here: the point is that non-western cultures are not only aware of the diversity of realities but they have also developed criteria for the validation of different realities. The universe is not as meaningless as postmodernism would have us believe.

Postmodernism also posits that realities are something that we can all acquire, or buy at a cut-price sale in the 'bazaar of realities' like ready-to-wear designer clothes. The only reality that is amenable to purchase is the one that postmodernism already sells: consumer goods. Other realities have to be lived and experienced. Watch a craftsman in a traditional society and see how his reality shapes his craft. The craft may be for sale, but the reality isn't. Experiential realities have to be lived and experienced. They are not amenable to a culture totally submerged in the instant, spontaneity, hyperreality, self-delusions, anxiety and angst. The dupes of somnolent wishfulness who buy Karma Kola mysticism, quick-fix Hindu meditation schemes and perverted Sufism are getting just what they pay for: consumer products. The realities of Other cultures are not for sale in the supermarkets of postmodern nihilism.

The totalising and transcendental pretensions of postmodernism can be undermined by the realities – lived, experienced, thought, constructed, discovered – of non-western cultures. In their ability to demonstrate that a universe of diverse realities does not abolish metanarratives – on the contrary, it makes certain metanarratives essential to our survival – non-western cultures could actually offer true resistance to the consuming and globalising tendencies of postmodernism. A meaningful world with meaningful relationships can only be based on meaningful content and meaningful worldviews.

Ashis Nandy has described progress as 'an expansion in the awareness of oppression'.[47] Western radicals and radical movements need to realise that postmodernism perpetuates oppression by foreclosing the possibility of discovering alternative visions of society. It is designed to instil a state of total helplessness in those who buy its credo. Genuine progress demands that we direct our intellectual and physical energies to vanquishing the metalanguage of oppression, so deeply ingrained in western culture, that postmodernism is now using to re-conquer the world.

2. The Joys of Cynical Power

'Barbarism in our backyard' declared an advertisement that appeared in most daily newspapers in Britain after a 'safe haven' in Bosnia was ransacked by Serbs and its inhabitants murdered, tortured, raped and 'ethnically cleansed'. Beneath the banner headline, and next to a photograph of a terrified woman and crying children, the story read:

> Bosnia today is the stuff of nightmares. As you read this newspaper, please spare a thought for a woman and child you have never met ... [she was] sitting on a coach full of Muslims leaving Srebrenica. As the coach slowed to a halt at a military checkpoint, the women and children on board cowered behind the seat rests in the vain hope that they would escape the soldiers' attention. This woman and child were unlucky. According to observers, the soldiers took their pick of women and dragged them off as they cried for help. And it certainly wasn't to give them desperately needed food or water. Refugees who were interviewed spoke of systematic rape. Others talked of unspeakable torture – young boys mutilated, young girls defiled, women and men murdered.[1]

Barbarism has not been the exception in the twentieth century; it has been the norm. Between 1914 and 1990, an estimated 187 million people perished in warfare: the twentieth century has been the epoch of 'mega-deaths'. In modernity, barbarism, and the ideologies which promote its gory associates – genocide, torture and rape, ethnic cleansing, white supremacy – evoked moral repulsion. Barbarism was and remains the unthought of modernity – it is integral to it, as Stjepan Mestrovic, amongst others, has shown.[2] Just as there is honour amongst thieves, there is some moral discernment in barbarism. Modernity with its technology and management and organisational techniques, as Zygmunt Bauman has argued, facilitated the Holocaust;[3] but it also produced a will to stop the barbarism of the Third Reich. In modernity, the will to act against perceived barbarism (often in Other, non-western cultures) is intrinsic and automatic. But postmodern times are about acceptance of barbarism as one amongst many modes of behaviour; postmodernism, in Eric Hobsbawm's words, makes 'barbarity seem unimportant, compared to more important matters like making money'.[4] In other words, postmodernism, unlike modernity, embraces evil.

But modernity laid the foundations on which the postmodern embrace of evil rests. By positing a devilish Other whose barbarity had to be checked, by instituting the ideas of total war and Cold War, and by giving common currency to barbaric practices – which include not only the deployment of weapons of mass destruction and the development and sale of technologies of torture, but also such practices as the displacement of people in the name of progress and development and the eradication and marginalisation of indigenous cultures – modernity domesticated barbarity. In its struggle against the devilish Other, modernity also legitimised the idea that ends justify all means. As Hobsbawm notes:

> nothing could conceivably be worse than the Devil's triumph. As the Cold War phrase went, 'Better dead then red', which, in any literal sense, is an absurd statement. In such a struggle the end necessarily justified any means. If the only way to beat the Devil was by devilish means, that is what we had to do. Why, otherwise, would the mildest and most civilised of Western scientists have urged their governments to build the atom bomb? If the other side is devilish, then we must assume that they would use devilish means, if they are not doing so now.[5]

Modernity, then, made barbarity a routine, everyday business. Postmodernism has taken the business of barbarism a step further: it has turned it into an irrelevance. The ambivalence of postmodern morality does not allow a value judgement to be made against barbarity; neither does the moral ambiguity of postmodernism allow action to be taken against those who engage in barbaric behaviour. The authority of postmodernism is based on this moral – and hence political ambivalence – 'this ability to see all sides, to defer judgement and to refuse agency'. It suggests, writes Diana Brydon, 'that action is futile; that individual value judgements are likely to cancel each other out; that one opinion is as good as another; that it would be futile and dishonest to choose one path above any other; that disinterested contemplation is superior to any attempt at action'.[6] Thus postmodern ambivalence not only preserves the status quo, it also generates a culture that readily accepts all modes of behaviour as long as its own privileges and advantages are not threatened – what Galbraith has called the 'culture of contentment'. In the post-Cold War era, when communism has failed and capitalism has seemingly triumphed, the power of contentment to override moral imperatives and codes of moral behaviour has become universal: 'What is new in the so-called capitalist countries', suggests Galbraith, 'is that the controlling contentment and resulting belief is now that of the many, not just of the few. It operates under the compelling cover of democracy, albeit a democracy not of all citizens but of those who, in defence of their social and economic advantage, actually go to the polls.'[7]

So what do we get when we combine 'controlling contentment', moral ambivalence and the doctrine of intrinsic futility of action? Cynicism. In postmodern times, power is not about financial and military muscle over and above anything else, it is about cynicism. Those with and in power are motivated purely by self-aggrandisement, which is itself enhanced by demonstrations of the total helplessness of their victims. This is true not just of political power but also of corporate power: postmodern politics and corporate behaviour are all about cynical power. Nothing illustrates this better than how the west approached the war in Bosnia.

Die you scum!

The death of the small nation that is Bosnia-Herzegovina marks the true birth of postmodern cynical power. The west buried every one of its self-proclaimed values, every norm of civilised, modern behaviour in the countless mass graves of civilians who were taken to the 'butcher's shop' where 'their throats were cut';[8] the women who were raped repeatedly and who were left with 'nowhere to go'[9] reflect the abandonment of all civilised values; the agony of hundreds of thousands of people who were ethnically cleansed, displaced and left to freeze in the Bosnian winter as voyeuristic television cameras relayed their plight to an apathetic western audience in an effort to increase their ratings; the suffering of those who were tortured and mutilated; the bewildered appearance of concentration camp victims – all bear witness to the domestication of barbarity and the cynical use of power. The Bosnians, as their history shows so vividly, are model liberals and true multiculturalists. The war in Bosnia was all about racism and fascism, about morality and ethics. This is precisely why the west did nothing for three years, and then acted only when Bosnia could serve its cynical ends.

The issues in the Bosnian conflict could not be more straightforward. The Serbs desired to absorb Bosnia-Herzegovina as a realisation of their dream of 'Greater Serbia'. At the beginning of the conflict, the Serb military was well equipped, consisting largely of the battalions of the army of the former Yugoslavia, while the Muslim Bosnians were largely unarmed. The United Nations imposed an arms embargo on both countries, thus effectively ensuring that the Bosnians could never defend themselves. Given a free hand, the Serbs began to butcher the Bosnians, launched a massive ethnic cleansing drive, and transported those they could not kill to concentration camps. The west and the UN declared its outrage but did nothing. Indeed, as we are repeatedly told, the west was unable to do anything. Security Council resolutions do not allow the UN to take sides: they allow them only to observe the enactment of barbarism and feed the victims. As Europe's third largest military force, the Serbs are invincible; it would require 250,000 NATO troops on the ground to halt them; military action, we are told by UN and NATO experts, would endanger UN peacekeepers (who were not keeping the peace anyway) and pulling them out would require at least 125,000 troops. Moreover, the arms embargo against the Muslims could not be lifted, for it would only escalate the war. Absolutely 'nothing we can do will stop the Serbs', Lord Owen, the go-between of the 'Contact Group' of countries overseeing the UN operation, repeatedly declared. But why such poor – and blatantly false – excuses for inaction? To add insult to injury, the UN repeatedly announced that the Bosnians were bombing their own people to get the attention of the media and gain support for their cause. Any kind of proactive approach would simply have threatened the status quo. The western strategy was simple: create a simulacrum of doing something while allowing the Serbs all the freedom in the world to exercise their barbarity.

The sharp contrast with the Gulf War is telling. There, the aggressor had to face the full might of the west within months. But, whereas the Gulf War was a war about a vital commodity – oil – Bosnia cannot be commodified: it has nothing that the west needs. And unlike Saudi Arabia and Kuwait, which paid for the Gulf War and will continue to pay for another two decades, Bosnia cannot pay. The Gulf War was about demonisation. But while Saddam Hussein could easily be associated with the Devil as he was clearly non-European; the European Serbs cannot be so demonised: 'Serbs 'R' Us' – they are western culture and civilisation and former victims of Nazi atrocities. 'As inflated as the term "fascism" is', notes Paul Hockenos, the 'Serb Republic has all the characteristics of the real thing: concentration camps, extensive paramilitary and police force, and an extreme clerical-nationalist ideology.'[10] But even though they may be fascists. Serbs are Serbs: they are not 'terrorists', 'fundamentalists', 'savages', 'blood-thirsty' or 'debased' – the kinds of label that are so easily appended to non-western groups in general, and Muslims in particular. Indeed, the media generally shy away from describing them as fascists. The common element between the Gulf and the Bosnian wars is that both were about cynicism. Cynical power is motivated purely by self-aggrandisement. The Gulf War was a demonstration of the military muscle of the west and about humiliating the aggressor: showing him to be powerless in the face of western might – that is why 400,000 young Iraqi conscripts had to die. But the war in Bosnia, unlike the Gulf War, did not provide an opportunity to increase the conceit or the power of the west. The west did not use its power to stop the Serbs because that could not lead to its self-aggrandisement. It could conceivably have led to loss of British, French or American lives, but it would not have brought any tangible benefit to the 'Contact Group' of countries. What enhances self-aggrandisement is demonstrations of the helplessness of the victims of power. Hence the 'safe havens' where the defenceless victims are trapped in enclaves, fed by aid agencies and survive courtesy of the western military: dependency is added to despondency, and dignity is sacrificed at the altar of 'humanitarian aid' – giving western self-importance a boost.

But, as we now know, even the 'safe havens' were a cynical ploy. No sooner than 'safe havens' were established, the west abandoned them: as the *Independent* reported: 'Six weeks before the Bosnian Serbs forces overran Srebrenica and murdered thousands of its inhabitants, the United Nations top military man in the former Yugoslavia told UN diplomats to abandon the Muslim enclave and the other so-called "safe areas" in Bosnia to their fate.'[11] Then, when the Serb army ransacked the allegedly protected town and slaughtered thousands and gang-raped women and children,[12] the UN troops turned a blind eye. Indeed, in Srebenica, where 'the UN troops hated the Muslims they protected', the Dutch troops had a drink or two with the Serbian army as they went about compiling a list of 2,700 men, who were systematically killed in the presence of their protectors.[13] Finally, just to drive home the message, the UN and western nations covered up the massacre. As reported in the *Observer*:

> United Nations spin-doctors have destroyed film showing shaming scenes of UN troops standing by while Bosnian Serbs organised the massacre of Muslim men in Srebrenica ... The destruction of the film is part of the pattern of events that was designed to ensure that the full story of the massacre of Srebrenica would never be told ... three western governments ... played down, sat on and destroyed evidence of the massacre.[14]

And just to give a twist of postmodern irony to the whole affair, the very people who enabled the massacre to take place and tried to hide the evidence, declared: 'it is hard to see the presence of the UN forces as anything other than some sort of accomplice to this barbarism'![15]

However, a year before the US presidential elections, and after an unexpected vote in the US Congress in favour of lifting the arms embargo against the Bosnian government, the narrative changed. Self-aggrandisement now dictated that something had to be done about Serbian barbarity. The same mandates that tied the UN's hands and allowed the Serbs to continue unimpeded suddenly permitted NATO to bomb the Serbs. The Serbian dictator, Slobodan Milosevic, who started the war, who initiated ethnic cleansing, who was branded a war criminal by Washington, suddenly becomes a multiculturalist peacemaker. The invincible Serb army collapsed when confronted with a better equipped Bosnian army and Croat artillery and tanks. Instead of '250,000 NATO troops and years of bloody war', the Serbs were expelled from Krajina in three days. Within a month, the UN almost disappeared from Bosnia. And when the Bosnian army started taking the land that had been ethnically cleansed by Serbs, Washington introduced a new term to the Balkan lexicon: 'show restraint'. Within weeks the Serbs had been bombed into submission; and the Bosnians had been forced to accept a worse deal than the one rejected earlier by the Americans, the so-called 'Owen–Vance' plan – as a betrayal of the ideal of a multi-ethnic Bosnia. The Bosnians were forced to hand over the land they had liberated to allow 33 per cent of the Bosnian population, the Serbs, to control 49 per cent of the country. The once multicultural state of Bosnia-Herzegovina is now carved up into different ethnic enclaves. And those US troops who could not be sent to Bosnia to preserve peace arrive, three years on, to preserve the new peace.

Western behaviour in the face of Serb aggression demonstrates the amorality of postmodern politics. To a large extent, what motivated the Serbs also motivated the west. Bosnia, a multicultural Muslim republic at the heart of Europe, is an affront to all that the west stands for; it personifies all that it has always projected on the Other. The Bosnians are the wrong people in the wrong place. The UNHCR soldiers supposedly protecting the Bosnians did not try to hide their hatred of Muslims. One UNHCR official described Sebrenica to an *Observer* reporter as a 'zoo where people are fed by the UN and kept in by the Serbs'.[16] But Bosnians have even less value than animals. With the exception of France, where one demonstration was held, western capitals have seen no public protest on behalf of Bosnia. In contrast to the animal rights movements, movements for multiethnic, multicultural emancipation are conspicuous by their absence. When Europe was celebrating VE and VJ Days, occupied Bosnia was witnessing ethnic rape and massacres perpetuated on the basis of racial hatred, while slave labourers dug trenches and their own graves. The long appeasement of the Serbs has been nothing but an invitation for ethnic cleansers from Bulgaria to Birmingham. The 'peace' in Bosnia has confirmed the axiomatic western assumption that everyone belongs in an ethnic niche: peace means never having to live alongside anyone different. 'Bosnia's enemy is cynicism,' declared Martin Bell, who covered the conflict for the BBC.[17] But cynicism is the bosom pal of postmodernism. Evil may be transparent, as Baudrillard tells us,[18] but in these best of all possible postmodern times, the west finds excuses for it, rejoices in the absolute powerlessness it produces in its victims, even celebrates it.

Postmodern political cynicism expresses itself in a number of ways. It can, for example, simply amount to turning a blind eye in the face of barbarity. Thus, the atrocities committed by 'democrat' Russian leaders in Georgia, Azerbijan and Chechnya have hardly elicited a comment from western leaders. An estimated 25,000 civilians – including 3,700 children – perished in the Russian army's clumsy onslaught on Grozny alone; after it fell, the Russian army went on a rampage of terror and random executions.[19] Numerous mass graves of people executed in this way have been discovered:

> With his mouth opened wide in a silent scream and his muddied bare feet he is just one of a crowd. More than 100 men, women and children lie jumbled in two open graves on a stretch of ground between Grozny's central cemetery and a main road; dozens of mouths screaming silently, bare feet, baby soft stomachs and contorted limbs. There are some skeletons, some decomposing and some fresh corpses – all turning the colour of mud. Nothing shields these Chechen bodies from the rain, the appetites of hungry dogs, or the terror-stricken gazes of passers-by.[20]

Western leaders reacted to these atrocities, first, by describing the entire Chechen people as a nation of thugs; and then by conveniently airbrushing the Chechnian state from their atlases.

Apart from overlooking the barbarities of one's own allies and collaborators, cynical power manifests itself in showing two fingers to the world. The collaboration of the oil multinational Shell with the military junta in Nigeria is an example of power taking postmodern expression. Under modernity, clandestine arrangements would have been enough. The postmodern dimension is added by the presentational factor, the creation of appropriate images and the cynical display of the helplessness of the victims: while Shell does not attempt to hide its collaboration with the military junta, it declares its innocence in the shooting and burning of those who demonstrated against it; while Shell promotes the image of an environment-friendly company in global television advertisements it blatantly pollutes and destroys the environment of the Ogoni people while accusing them of poisoning their own environment (resonance here of the UN claims in Bosnia that the Bosnians themselves shelled Sarajavo and killed their own people to get attention); while the multinational colludes in 'framing' those who object to the destruction of their environment and silently promotes their executions,[21] it takes out full-page advertisements in the European press to protest its innocence.

French nuclear tests in the South Pacific, carried out during the 50th anniversary of Hiroshima and Nagasaki, are an example of how postmodern cynical power is expressed politically. For France, it was a matter of letting the world know of its continuing nuclear strength. For the non-western world, it is terror tactics. Imagine the reaction from the US or Britain if Pakistan, Brazil or North Korea were to announce plans to carry out a nuclear test in the mid-Atlantic. Nuclear capability is, of course, a declaration of brute power; and when it comes to brute power some nations are more equal than others. This inequality is enshrined in the Nuclear Non-Proliferation Treaty (NTP), which guarantees the right of the five nuclear powers – USA, Britain, France, Russia and China – to hold the rest of the world to ransom while denying nuclear power to every other nation. Under the Treaty, the nuclear powers retain a legal monopoly over the most destructive weapons known to humanity. But there is more: the NTP not only allows the nuclear powers to have whatever weapons they want, to continue their own programmes of nuclear rearmament, it also gives them the power legally to keep the rest of the world under surveillance and intervene in the affairs of other nations they suspect of developing nuclear weapons. The nuclear powers can impose sanctions, or take military action, including threat of nuclear force, against those who think they should have the same rights as the privileged to develop nuclear capability. Thus the NTP ratifies double standards of cynical power in international law.

Postmodern cynical power comes in two forms. First, there is the simulacrum of power we are presented with in the persona of western leaders at such public events as the annual G7 summits. But the political leaders are decoys for the cynical power that is being exercised behind the scenes in corporate boardrooms and the corridors of multinational corporations, drawing attention away from the corporate colonisation of the poor and working classes in the west and markets and cultures of the non-west. The 1990s have witnessed the climax of a systematic evolution within global capitalism towards oligopolistic and conglomerate forms of economic concentration. Power is now concentrated in the hands of some 200 global corporations which, in the aftermath of the deregulatory movement initiated by the Thatcher, Mitterrand, Kohl and Reagan administrations, effectively rule the postmodern world:

By acquiring earth-spanning technologies, by developing products that can be produced anywhere and sold everywhere, by spreading credit around the world, and by connecting global channels of communication that can penetrate any village or neighbourhood, these institutions we normally think of as economic rather than political, private rather than public, are becoming the world empires of the 21st century. The architects and managers of these space-age business enterprises understand that the balance of power in world politics has shifted in recent years from territorially bound governments to companies that can roam the world. As the hopes and pretensions of government shrink almost everywhere, these imperial corporations are occupying public space and exerting a more profound influence over the lives of ever larger numbers of people.[22]

The function of the political leaders in the west has been reduced to ensuring that the new empires continue to flourish and expand. This function is performed by enhancing the powers of international regulatory agencies such as the International Monetary Fund (IMF), the World Bank and World Trade Organisation (WTO). The policies and procedures of the recently negotiated WTO, which replaced the GATT agreement and is now the main international tool for the defence and expansion of free trade, clearly reflect the interests of the multinationals and international banks, as the agreement regarding Trade Related Investment Measures (TRIM) and Trade Related Intellectual Property (TRIP) measures show. Under WTO, foreign investment and technology-transfer procedures are decided not by national laws but by an international capitalist procedural framework designed and monitored by WTO itself – an organisation, like the IMF and World Bank, that is staffed almost exclusively by western nationals and provides moonlighting opportunities on its dispute arbitration network for experts who work for multi-national corporations and international commercial banks. The self-declared *raison d'être* of WTO is to promote free trade and provide a stronger framework for accelerating the liberalisation of non-western economies. Free trade is increasingly seen by non-western countries as a euphemism for multinational colonialism; and WTO is there to promote liberal imperialism. Countries such as the US, Germany and France find it easy to circumvent WTO authority – as is the case with the authority of the IMF. But WTO, like IMF and the World Bank, will be able to put unbearable pressure on small, poor countries to reduce their national sover-eignty and restructure their economies in a way which facilitates profit-maximisation for the multinationals and the international banks. Effectively, WTO is there to exercise surveillance over the third world, while the IMF has de facto statutory powers to intervene in the internal affairs of sovereign states. Thus, while international regulatory agencies facilitate the expansion of multi-national empires in the background, our attention is constantly directed towards pronouncements by political leaders about inflation, unemployment, economic recoveries, proliferating choices and good times ahead.

In the Cold War era of modern development, multinational companies were content to dump shoddy goods, products they were prevented from selling in the west – such as certain kinds of contraceptives and medicines – and redundant technologies on the third world. While this practice continues, there has been a cynical shift in multinational practice in non-western countries. 'Economic liberalisation' has led to a scramble for territories and markets reminiscent of colonial engagement. Just as European imperial powers waged war against the peoples of Asia and Africa for control of land and resources in the nineteenth century, so today multinational companies are engaged in a territorial war for markets: the victims, as before, are the peoples of the non-west. The postmodern equivalent of the colonial weapons of war is the counterfeit product. There is, of course, a thriving pirate market of counterfeit products in the developing countries, most notably in southeast Asia. But the reference here is to another kind of counterfeit product, one that is cynically promoted by multinational corporations themselves. When a multinational company carves out a new market in a non-western state, it does not manufacture its product lines itself. Instead, it subcontracts a local company to manufacture its goods and then markets them under its brand names. The advantages to the parent company are obvious: it can avoid all responsibility for exploitative practices such as poor working conditions, wages well below the legal minimum and the use of child labour; it can keep the costs to a bare minimum and ensure maximum profit; and it can boast about helping local businesses. But what of the product itself? While it carries the brand name of the multinational corporation, it is in fact a totally different product, not least because its formulation has been changed and original ingredients have been replaced by cheaper ones:

Western logos and names frequently mask an article that consumers in the west would not recognise: a debased, altered or down-market imitation. The real culprits in the counterfeiting games are not the pirates of their products, but the transnational companies. Take almost any such product. Savlon, for instance, from Johnson and Johnson, is in India a lurid, deep orange colour that stains everything it touches.

The item sold in the west looks and smells quite different. The Indian version contains both Quinoline Yellow WS and Sunset Yellow FCF. The same thing is true of Dettol; Colgate Red toothpaste seems to consist largely of cloves, which can be bought far more cheaply in their natural form.[23]

Thus, most of the western products sold in non-western countries are simulacra: while they look like the real things, and have been marketed by real western companies, they are in fact shoddy replicas.

This cynical treatment of non-western consumers is based on the assumption that people from Other cultures are not only ignorant and foolish, but their life is not worth much either. In modernity, this supposition went unstated. But in politically ambivalent postmodern times, one does not have to hide such assumptions: they can be publicly declared. Thus in evaluating the impact of climatic change on the world, which itself is largely a product of western technologies and patterns of consumption, western advisers to the UN treated non-western people as expendable fodder. The UN's Intergovernmental Panel on Climate Change (IPCC) has recommended that lives of non-western people are worth 15 times less than those of people in the west; the death of a white person costs $1.5 million; but a person living in Asia, Africa or Latin America is only worth $100,000.[24] This, then, is the end of postmodern cynicism: a quantum leap forward in the axioms of colonialism.

He Who Would Govern Others

While postmodernism insists on a plurality of cultures and discourses, postmodern political theory and practice are based exclusively on the modernist notions of, in the words of Richard Rorty, 'bourgeois liberal democracy'. Postmodern discourses, Agnes Heller and Ferenc Feher tell us, contain 'certain moral principles of democratic politics'[25] which may appear to be parasitic on modernity but nevertheless lead to pluralism. But a pluralism based on liberal democracy is the Orwellian notion that all positions in culture and politics are open and equal, although European ideas are more equal than others. By championing democracy, and its associated notions of 'liberalism' and 'human rights', postmodernism seeks an expression of the privileged status of the west. Moreover, given that liberalism is a creed of those who have accepted capitalism, and the division of wealth that goes with it, postmodern liberal democracy serves only as a poor excuse for the global expansion of the western economy and the transformation of non-western societies into havens of western consumerism. This is why we have heard so much about the export of 'western democracy', seen how international regulatory agencies tied Third World 'aid' to 'liberalisation' and 'democratisation' policies, and have witnessed the shameful triumphalism of the 'end of history' in the final victory – solution? – of 'liberal democracy' discourse. All of which are euphemisms for the euphoric vindication of free market capitalism.

But who are the western states to tell the non-western countries to embrace liberal democracy? Especially when the greatest non-participatory democracy in the world, the USA, finds that only billionaires can now afford to make unfettered appeals to the populace, while the entire operation of government can be hijacked by the cynicism of a single congressional leader; the government of Britain can be reshaped through the authoritarian insistence of a single 'leaderene' whose determination to roll back the frontiers of the state was a cynical smokescreen for more centralisation and aggregation of power than had ever been experienced in British history and where the politics of cynicism, double standards and sleaze has been institutionalised;[26] France, the birthplace of liberty, equality and fraternity is embodied in the electoral popularity of an avowedly fascist party and run by a president with 'dictatorial' powers;[27] the Italians have recognised that they have been ruled by democratically institutionalised corruption for the last forty years ... If this is liberal democracy then Russia has clearly made a highly successful transition: it is now run by its own Mafia!

But democracy itself is a movable feast. It is desirable only when the pro-western side wins an election in a non-western country. It can be 'cancelled', to the applause of the west, as it was in Algeria, when the undesirable 'Islamic fundamentalists' won the general election. Just as it was when Salvador Allende won electoral office in Chile only to be ousted by a bloody coup organised and operated by the unholy alliance of the Chilean generals and the CIA; and not withstanding the fact that despite all the propaganda and explicit, unconstitutional interference in the internal affairs of another nation, the Sandanista government accepted the verdict of the Nicaraguan people and peacefully handed over power when its political opponents won the election. Still 'our' democracy is always superior: so democracy in Pakistan is always 'fragile'; Malaysia, one of the most democratic states in Asia by any standard, is always an 'authoritarian' enclave; and an absolutist, undemocratic monarchy is fine as long as it is 'our' ally and buys weapons from 'us'. Democracy has become a cynical postmodern ploy based on changing principles that are used to beat the non-west when it suits the west.

In the postmodern world, where the distinction between illusion and reality has been lost and issues are determined by 15-second soundbites and manipulated images, democracy has become meaningless. The power it gives the citizen is the fictive power of voting every four or five years without markedly affecting the accountability or responsiveness of elected representatives. The end of the Cold War supposedly makes western democracy the only viable system. But nothing can hide the fact that western democracies are dominated by an elite who offer simplistic, one-dimensional solutions to problems that concern the voters. British MPs are chosen by a handful of party activists. An electorate of 43 million is represented by 652 full-time politicians who are the only ones with a direct say over government and play a direct role in framing legislation. In a typical general election, only a few MPs stand down and only a handful of seats usually change hands. Thus, at best estimate, fewer than 100,000 people each decade play a direct part in deciding which of the 7,000 would-be MPs, selected by the party activists, occupy the seats in the House of Commons.[28] Other countries of Europe and North America follow a similar sort of representative logic. Liberal democracy thus legitimises elite rule – which is exactly why it is being forced on the non-west. When western-educated elites are in power, they not only pursue pro-western policies but also suppress and marginalise more popular traditional leadership, which tends to be anti-western. Thus, the west supports authoritarian rulers and military dictators as long as they are pro-west; and insists on democracy when traditionalists are in power or when it opens up opportunities for western-educated elites to rule. The stance taken towards democracy is determined by western interests and not what is appropriate for the non-west or what the people of Other cultures desire themselves.

But democracy also serves as a tool for the westernisation and postmodernisation of Other cultures. The development of liberal democracy is an historic process inconceivable and inexplicable except for secularisation. The nation state began in Europe as a religious state, the only citizens being those created by the compulsory rite of baptism; the only good citizen was the believer as defined by the Roman Catholic Church. The secularisation of the nation state and the concept of citizen alone permitted the expansion of the franchise: the right to representation on the basis of freedom of conscience. Secularisation did nothing to alter the other basis for citizenship: property. It was the firm contention of Oliver Cromwell, the ultimate advocate of freedom of conscience, that only the property owner had a 'natural interest' in the affairs of government. This dictum effectively delayed mass enfranchisement of the populace of Britain for more than three hundred years, and the principle did not pass into extinction until 1929, when the first general election operated on universal adult suffrage was held. Cromwell would have been at ease with Margaret Thatcher's ideas about a property-owning democracy. Secularisation was the only concept which could place the self-subsisting individual citizen prior to the concept of the state, replacing compulsory obligation defined by religious rite, with the notion of consensual delegation of powers to elected representatives. Morality and conscience were privatised to enable the franchise to be extended to a religiously heterogeneous citizen. The enfranchised citizen, however, long remained the property qualified citizen. So the rise of secularism as a force to temper the restricted, ascriptive origins of citizenship in modernity has a corollary in the rise to dominance of consumerism, the

quintessential characteristic of the postmodern era. Mass production, mass markets, the spread of ownership, the commodification
of lifestyles all seem to spread access to and privatise the ability of
the individual to accumulate property, and thus temper the
perception that ultimately it is the concentrated power of wealth
and property, rather than the dispersal of its signs and symbols,
that dominates the decision-making of governments. Secularism
and consumerism are essential handmaidens not merely of the
genesis, but of the ongoing operation of western liberal democracy. These fundamental assumptions ensured that the wealthy,
educated elites could maintain control of political institutions.
Only the wealthy and highly educated had the qualifications, time
and resources to master the skills necessary to pass laws and
debate conflicting points endlessly, and during the rise of
modernity only they had the franchise. As in Athens, the first
citizens of the new democracies of the late seventeenth and early
eighteenth centuries were men of property. So democracy comes
with its own ideological baggage which, in the case of Other
cultures, requires acceptance of western liberalism, secularism and
the notions of the nation state – all of which are eagerly endorsed
by postmodernism.

Just because the term 'democracy' was coined in the west, it
does not mean that Other cultures did not have, or do not have,
representative or participatory political structures. The non-west
is replete with multiple mechanisms by which governance has
operated and citizens participated in the free discussion of issues
which affect their life, liberty and pursuit of happiness, not
forgetting their standard and quality of life. The vaunted
principle of the separation of powers enshrined in the American
constitution is analogous to the structural arrangements of
traditional Yoruba society. Chiefless societies in Africa and
elsewhere that practised moot politics could be said to be the
ultimate in direct participatory decision-making where citizens
represented themselves in public meetings which did not end
until an acknowledged and binding consensus had been
negotiated. In fact, as Jeremy Corbyn acknowledges, 'European
democracy has been ... heavily influenced by its contact with
Islam.' It 'is not the result of a superior enlightenment

rationality, but of a backward and mystical feudalism'.[29] Both humanism and democratic ideals were adopted in Europe from Islam, as George Makdisi demonstrates in his study, *The Rise of Humanism in Classical Islam and the Christian West*.[30] However, the transmission of humanism from Islam to Europe also involved a radical transformation: Europe accepted the ideal but changed the axioms – as was also the case with science and philosophy. The notions of community and social responsibilities and duties which were so central to Islamic forms of participatory governance were abandoned in favour of individualism.

Individualism is *the* absolute of both liberal democracy and postmodernism: the notion that society is nothing more than the sum of individuals and that the individual is a self-contained, autonomous and sovereign being who is defined independently of society. The assumption that the individual is prior to society is unique to western culture: it is the defining principle of liberal democracy and shapes its metaphysical, epistemological, methodological, moral, legal, economic and political aspects. In non-western cultures, the individual does not define him/herself by separating from others, but in relation to a holistic and integrated group: the family or clan, the community or culture, religion or worldview. The Chinese, for example, see the family as an organism linking the past, the ancestors, with the present and the future, the descendants.[31] Muslims see the individual as an integrated part of society, which in a local area is defined by the Friday mosque and on an international level by the collectivity of all Muslims: the *ummah*. Society is ontologically prior to the individual and social obligations come before individual dictates.[32] In most indigenous cultures, the individual is defined by the tribe or the clan: the individual cannot be distinguished from the tribe and seeks his/her fulfilment as an integrated part of the whole tribe.[33]

In the western liberal framework, the individual is constantly at war with the community. The individual's main concern is to keep his/her identity intact, separate from all others, to preserve the boundaries at all cost, to enclose herself/himself within a protective wall. Whereas in non-western cultures, morality is defined by the community or society, in postmodern liberal thought individuals make their own morality, or make choices as the euphemism has it, as they pass through life. Thus there can never be substantive agreement between the individual and the community as a whole. Morality becomes a matter of individual behaviour: the emphasis is not on what is of ultimate value and what ends should be sought, but how whatever ends are chosen ought to be pursued.[34] The goals of postmodern democracy therefore focus on providing the individual with all possible avenues to pursue whatever is desired, even if it is at the expense of the community, as it so often is. Everyone makes his or her own rules, creates his or her own universe, and pursues his or her own happiness in his or her own way. How can one create a community from so many individual points of greed?

The postmodern contention is that individualism has to be enhanced further for democracy to be humanised. In the age of cyberspace, this means providing citizens with computer terminals giving them direct access to their representatives, by-passing pressure groups, party politics, the media, special interest groups and other undemocratic ways of opinion formation. Technology will improve both the individual as well as the political system. Miklos N. Szilagyi explains:

> The information revolution will change the political system automatically. The commercialization of computer networks will create a situation when everyone will be connected to everyone else with the ease of using a telephone today. In this environment ideas will be exchanged free of charge and with the speed of light. No government or special interest group can stop this process. It will lead to the collapse of representative democracy as it is known today. Money will be eliminated from politics and replaced with this independent information system to present a broad range of political choices for every caring citizen. Participation will be open to all qualified persons. The electronic information system will provide forums to express ideas. Competing opinions will be freely publicized, criticized, and discussed. Paid political advertising, financial campaign contributions and political action committees will become obsolete. Politicians will be selected in a free competition of ideas. Their power will be limited

and decentralized. They will be accountable to the citizens. Success and status in society will not depend on political power. Representative democracy will be dead and the sooner it is replaced by the democracy of the information age the better it is for all of us.[35]

Thus, in the cybervision of democracy, the 'representatives of the people' would perform that function only on the people's daily sufferance. Much of the technology needed for this kind of vision to be realised already exists: satellite networks, cheap fibreoptic connections, the Internet, videoconferencing, two-way cable systems, and the desktop computer in almost every (western) home.

But cyberspace democracy does little to fix the bugs in the system and a great deal for individualism and fragmentation.[36] The very idea of the citizen sitting in front of his or her computer terminal interrogating the political representatives divorces that individual from the community. While leaving the nation state and all its oppressive apparatus intact, cyber-democracy introduces a new element of lynch law. It fosters the delusion of the frontier mentality while implying that you can get the laws you want simply by pressing a button. But laws are not products of individual clamour but of collective and consultative acts that have to reflect the balance of the community. To be humane, just and protective of all segments of society, laws need the context of discussion, information and testing against the needs of all – the very things you cannot get from an instant reflex in cyberspace. Instant decisions by cyber-polls obviate the need to understand and consider, thereby taking us further and further on the march from knowledge and wisdom.

Where individualism sets the pace, the government can never seek communal, social, cultural, economic or political goals, such as ensuring equal distribution of wealth, creating a classless society or providing equal economic and educational opportunities for all. Thus inequality and an inability to promote community are intrinsic to the liberal, postmodern notion of democracy. Bhikhu Parekh outlines five reasons why this tends to be so:

Firstly, the government owes its existence and authority to the fact that its subjects are self-determining agents wishing to pursue their self-chosen goals under conditions of minimal constraints. Its task therefore is to maximise their liberties and to facilitate their goals, which by definition it cannot do if it pursued large-scale goals of its own.

Secondly, citizens of a liberal society do not all share a substantive conception of the good life. There is therefore no moral source from which the government can derive, and in terms of which it can legitimise, its substantive goals. Whatever goals it chooses to pursue are bound to be disowned by, and thus to violate the moral autonomy of, at least a section of them. An attempt to create a 'better' or 'more humane' society flounders on the fact that its citizens deeply disagree about the under-lying criteria. A government that goes beyond laying down the necessary framework of formal and general rules therefore compromises its subjects' humanity and risks committing a moral outrage.

Thirdly, a government engaging in a programme of large-scale economic redistribution or radical transformation of the social order uses some of its citizens as instruments of its will and treats their interests as less important than others, violating the principles of human dignity and equality. Since it is unlikely to enjoy their consent, it is also bound to be oppressive and risks forfeiting its legitimacy.

Fourthly, a programme of economic redistribution implies that the government has something to distribute, that it is the owner of what it seeks to redistribute. For the liberal the assumption is wholly false, for property belongs to its owners and not to the government, and is a product of their labour and not its. It is entitled to claim from them, with their consent, only that portion of their property which is necessary to help it undertake its legitimate and collectively agreed activities.

Finally, for the liberal almost all social institutions are grounded in and propelled by specific natural desires. This is as true of the economy as of the others. People work hard, exert themselves, accept privations, and save up for the future because they are driven by self-interest and the desire to better their condition. The dynamic interplay of these impulses creates the complex economic world with its own autonomous logic. Government interference with the economy, as with other social institutions, runs up against the inescapable limits of human nature and the inexorable logic of the economy, and is ultimately counter-productive.[37]

Thus the postmodern democratic ideal, and the liberal notion of a human being that goes with it, is always suspicious of communal concerns and values. Hardly surprising then that community has all but disappeared from the western world, leaving isolated, autonomous individuals in its wake.

Non-western cultures, however, have managed to retain most of their 'basics': community, a sense of belonging, a source of morality, a worldview that gives meaning and direction to their existence. When western countries insist on imposing liberal democracy on non-western countries, they deny them their histories, break up their communities, destroy the coherence and integrity of their ways of life, and reduce them to mimics, unable and unwilling to be true either to their traditions or to the imported alien norms.

What happens when democracy is imposed on non-western cultures is well illustrated by Africa. African political thought evolved on an organic conception of social and political order premissed on the natural formation of kinship.[38] The major elements of this thought, Godwin Sogolo notes, continue to dominate the political formations of contemporary African societies. This conception is further strengthened by various myths of creation which shape the communal identities of Africa. Thus the exercise of political power in Africa was grounded in the consensus of the people who in turn gave their blessings to both the authority and actions of the rulers. The rulers derived their power from the people and held it in trust on their behalf. The whole complex was organically knitted by the belief systems and religion of the community. The ruler was thus not just a person who could impose his will on the people, but the axis of the political relations of the community, the symbol of its unity and identity, and an embodiment of its basic values. The claims by some western scholars[39] that traditional African systems were not 'democratic' and did not allow for participation in political issues has no historical support. Sogolo writes:

> powerful though African monarchs were, their powers were circumscribed by the customs and usages of their kingdoms. The kings were expected to work within a structure characterized by inhibitions and social control. In fact, the social system prescribed elaborate and explicit rules of behaviour and a king had to forfeit the right to rule if his conduct fell below expectation.[40]

Indeed, the citizens exercised an automatic right to remove the ruler once his misconduct or abuse of power was proved. In many African cultures, power was collectively shared through a council of elders. Again, the plurality inherent in the membership of the council checked any tendency towards tyranny. Thus traditional African systems of governance involved both participation and accountability – much more so than the modern forms of representative democracy. It is 'bad history', declares N. Sithole, that has led many western scholars to declare that 'Africans never had democracy until the coming of the white man to Africa.'[41] And there is a considerable body of evidence to support the assertion that it was colonialist interpretation of African kingship, seeing its content and meaning in purely western terms and subverting its operation to facilitate colonial control – by paying kings and chiefs a stipend to maintain a 'dignity' of their position that had no indigenous warrant and which inevitably led to the overthrow of traditional methods of selecting office holders by the creation of unnatural non-indigenous self interests – that deformed these institutions. The much derided reactionary nature of traditional governance then becomes a consciously created product of colonial ignorance. Similar arguments have been made in respect of the fate of traditional rulers in other parts of the world, for example, India.

What the white men did bring was the idea of the modern nation state – a key component of democracy. The notion of the state with its impersonal institutions and emphasis on geographical boundaries was not only alien to African thought, it led to a total dislocation and disruption of African societies. The imposition of the nation state on Africa effected profound changes by destroying the indigenous social fabric of villages and communities, chieftaincies and kinship. It replaced these organic structures with alienating state institutions such as bureaucracy, law courts, political parties and, of course, the military. The nation-state structure made Africa an appendage of western civilisation and plunged Africa into the world capitalist system dominated by the colonial powers where Africans, with their communal and sharing values, were ill-equipped to compete with the dictates of aggressive individualism. Fragile state structure, the crisis of legitimacy and economic underdevelopment have reduced Africa to ruins.[42] According to Meddi Muguenyi, it took post-colonial Africa less then a decade to lose confidence in democracy.[43] Given the distrust of democracy, it was natural for the vacuum left by the displaced traditional political structures to be filled by military and authoritarian regimes. And the consequent violations of human rights were just as natural.

Let Us Show You How To Be Human

There is, though, nothing 'natural' about human rights. Along with liberal democracy, postmodernism has embraced the notion of human rights: a truly democratic state is seen as a state that shows total respect for human rights. But just as democracy is a cynical ploy for postmodernising the non-west, human rights too have become an instrument for promoting the western agenda. The western liberal notion of human rights, which is the basis for the UN Declaration of Human Rights, reduces the issues of the rights of human beings simply to preserving the civil liberties of individuals and provides a moral high ground for these rights to be imposed, by coercion if necessary, on all non-western, and by definition illiberal, people. But non-western countries, and post-colonial writers, have started to raise questions about this supposedly altruistic endeavour.

Postmodernism, eschewing all grand narratives, would endorse the suggestion that no culture, tradition, ideology or religion has a right to speak on behalf of humankind or impose its notion of what it means to be human on others. But when it comes to human rights, this arch-principle is overlooked. Rich Falk, for example, argues that 'individual conscience' has a high priority in postmodernism and 'this postmodernist priority is emphasised by adherence to international human rights standards' and its unconditional acceptance by all postmodernists.[44] But not all postmodernists are so forthright: they recognise that the idea of 'universal' and 'absolute' human rights is problematic from the postmodern perspective, but fall back on 'liberal humanism' to provide a loose basis for some notion of human rights. But this reluctance is more apparent than real. Even when the notion of human rights is accepted as a western social construction, as for example by Anderson,[45] its imposition on, and acceptance by, non-western nations is actively sought. When it comes to human rights, postmodernists happily suppress what Donald Kuspit has described as their 'own intellectually honest, unhappy admission of the problematic character of postmodernism' lest it 'should make us aware that it has ideological import and is protected by a mystique'.[46]

The very idea that other cultures are not paying attention to human rights, that non-western cultures had no notion of human rights before the west appeared on the scene (as, for example, is argued by Anderson) presupposes an indisputable superiority of western culture. Logically, of course, such a proposition also means there is no such thing as universal human rights; there is merely a practice that has been abstracted from the ideas of one culture and termed universal. The universalising principle of western civilisation has always been to see its way as the only way and therefore the universal way. The west's use of the term universal is an intentional statement of the becoming of the Other. Wherever it occurs it is always intended to be an act of will and force. Even if human rights were desirable, even universal, their introduction in other cultures, by force or tying it to foreign aid if necessary, amounts to the continuation of the colonial belief that the perceptions of a particular culture (about God, Church, Empire, Civilisation, Reason, Science, Progress, Modernity) inherently contain superior values giving them a moral right to spread them all over the planet.

The Universal Declaration of Human Rights assumes a universal human nature common to all peoples. It further assumes that this human nature is knowable and that it is known by a universal organ of knowledge: human reason. Moreover, it posits that this human nature is essentially different from the rest of creation: other forms of life are inferior to humans and have no rights, and living beings superior to humans are not likely to exist. Thus, humankind is the master of all creation, of itself and the universe: it is not only the supreme legislator on Earth but also the source of all moral principles. The whole question of an external Creator, a

Supreme Being, can be debated endlessly but it is largely irrelevant and ineffective. The Declaration presupposes a social order based on liberal democracy where the society is simply a collection of 'free' individuals. Again, the individual is seen as absolute, irreducible, separate and ontologically prior to society. But more than that: it assumes, like postmodernism itself, that the individual is the whole person. Self-interest and desire for absolute autonomy are all there is to a person: the links between history and community, environment and nature, cosmos and the universe, do not exist. But the person and the individual are not the same thing. The individual is simply an abstraction, a truncated and selected version of the person for the sake of practical convenience. Postmodern ahistoricalism notwithstanding, a person incorporates his/her parents, children, extended family, ancestors, community, friends, enemies, ideas, emotions, self-image, perceptions, visions and self-identity. Violence inflicted on a person equally damages the whole community, not to mention the perpetrator of the violence. Thus in the perspective of the whole person, rights cannot be individualised. The insistence of many non-western cultures and religious traditions on consensus rather than majority opinion is based on the corporate and collective nature of human rights.[47] These traditions see God as the source of all morality and originator and guarantor of all rights and duties. Theological worldviews regard the idea of humankind as the source of morality as misplaced arrogance and the notion of an autonomous individual as naive. They see the notion of the human being presented in the Declaration as a defective reading of what constitutes a human being: are humans simply packages of material and psychological needs, wrapped in an atomised microcosm? Is this all there is to being human? Non-western cultures beg to differ.

The liberal humanistic notion of human rights, argue many post-colonial writers, has become a political device in the hands of the west, used largely to defend the status quo and maintain western dominance. Vinay Lal considers 'the discourse of human rights' to be an example of 'the most evolved form of Western imperialism'. It is 'the latest masquerade of the West – particularly America, the torchbearer since the end of World War II of

"Western" values – to appear to the world as the epitome of civilization and as the only legitimate arbiter of human values'.[48] What, from an Islamic perspective, writes Parvez Manzoor, 'is, at best, a fluid theory, a wishful moral sentiment, or a misguided foundationalism', presents itself 'as a sacred canon, a legal fait accompli, and a binding charter, to which the only permissible Muslim response is compliance and submission'.[49]

In this atmosphere of liberal inquisition, being against human rights seems akin to being in favour of sin. Questioning human rights is seen by western and westernised individuals as being against humanity itself. But to have misgivings about the theory of human rights does not amount to the renunciation of the ideal of a common humanity; indeed, there are strong arguments to suggest that human rights themselves have religious origins.[50] Neither does it mean abandoning the quest for a humane politics – it is simply a way of resisting western hegemony and rejecting the prevailing world order.

Since an autonomous, isolated individual does not exist in non-western cultures and traditions, it does not make sense to talk of his or her rights; and where there are no rights, it is quite absurd to speak of their denial or annulment. However, this does not mean that the individual is totally unprotected. Indeed, notions of the individual's dignity and the respect that is due to it exist in all non-western cultures even though they may not be formulated as political theories.[51] Since the starting point is the complex web of relationships between an individual and his or her personhood, a balance is sought between rights and duties. In Hinduism, for example, the notion of *dharma*, one of the fundamental concepts of Indian tradition, leads us to a symbolic correspondence with the western idea of human rights. *Dharma* is a multilayered concept and incorporates the terms, elements, data, quality and origination as well as law, norm of conduct, character of things, rights, truth, ritual, morality, justice, righteousness, religion and destiny. In Sikhism, the prime duty of a human being is *sewa*: there is no salvation without *sewa*, the disinterested service of the community. The rights of the individual are thus earned by participating in the community's endeavour and thereby seeking *sakti*. Cultures based on such notions as *dharma* and *sewa* are not concerned with the reductive exercise of defining the 'rights' of one individual against another, or of the individual against the society: the individual is but a single knot in the web of material, social, cultural and spiritual relationships and his/her duty is to find a harmonious place in relation to the society, the cosmos and the transcendent world.[52] Indian thought on human rights, therefore, contrasts sharply with the western model. According to Raimundo Panikkar, the Hindu, Jain and Buddhist vision of human rights insists that:

1. Human rights are not individual human rights only. The *humanum* is not incarnated in the individual *only*. The individual is an abstraction, which cannot be an ultimate subject of rights. The individual is only the knot in and of the net of relationships which form the fabric of the Real. The knots may individually be the same, but it is mainly their position in the net which determines the set of 'rights' an individual may have.

2. Human rights are not human only. They concern equally the entire cosmic display of the universe, from which even the Gods are not absent. All sentient beings and supposedly inanimate creatures are also involved in the interaction concerning 'human' rights. The human is a peculiar being, to be sure, but neither alone nor so essentially distinct.

3. Human rights are not rights only. They are also duties and both are interdependent. Humankind has the 'right' to survive only insofar as it performs the duty of maintaining the world (*lokasamgraha*).

4. Human rights are not mutually isolatable. They are related not only to the whole cosmos and all their corresponding duties; they form, among themselves as well, a harmonious whole. It is for this reason that a material list of definitive human rights is not theoretically feasible. It is the universal harmony that ultimately counts.

5. Human rights are not absolute. They are intrinsically relative. They are relationships among entities – entities determined by the relationships themselves. The classical Indian vision would start from a holistic conception and then define a portion of reality by function of its situation in the totality. In a certain sense, the knot is nothing – because it is the whole net.[53]

This vision has many similarities with Islamic ideas. In contrast to the 'western liberal tradition of personal freedom which signifies the *ability to act*', Abdul Aziz Said tells us, 'in Islam it is the *ability to be, to exist*.'[54] The emphasis in Islam, therefore, is on creating a material, social and spiritual environment in which the individual can realise his or her full potential to *be*. This is done by protecting the life, liberty and property of the individual by law while making the government accountable to the citizens. In Islam, justice and equality go hand in hand and the judiciary is kept at a respectable distance from the state to ensure its independence. Caliph Ali, the fourth Caliph of Islam, for example, insisted that the judiciary should be above all kinds of executive pressure and advised judges that when the truth is presented they must pass judgment without fear, favour or prejudice. The whole notion of accountability, ingrained in such fundamental Islamic concepts as *akhira* (accountability before God in the hereafter), *khilafa* (our trusteeship of our environment), *shura* (consultation with the public on important matters) and *istislah* (public interest), has become an integral part of Islamic philosophy.

The notion of an individual person's rights is not unknown to Islam. Mohammad Kamali shows that even though Muslim jurists never articulated a precise definition of 'human rights', Islamic law was not only cognisant of these rights (*haquuq*) but even developed other more comprehensive and precise concepts such as *hukum* (judgments or legal decisions of God concerning an individual's rights), which subsumed the former.[55] Thus, individual rights in Islam do not stop at personal freedoms but include economic, social, cultural, civil and political rights as well. The poor in Muslim societies, for example, have a right to the wealth of the community: *zakat*, the 'poor tax', is one of the five pillars of Islam and is on par not just with prayer and fasting but with the declaration of belief in the unity of God. Moreover, Islam makes numerous other provisions: for example, all persons in a Muslim society have a right to meet their basic necessities of food, shelter, clothing, education and health care irrespective of age, sex, colour or religion.[56] But Islam always combines rights with responsibilities. Indeed, there can be no rights without responsibilities. For example, freedom of expression is a fundamental right but it is also a responsibility that has to be met with a sense of justice and commitment to truth.[57] In the Qur'an the freedom of expression to propagate virtue and righteousness is not only a right but an obligation. Thus, rights become responsibilities and responsibilities become rights. Similarly, the individual has a number of obligations towards the community: to resist oppression of all kind, to promote peace and harmony, to promote communal values, to safeguard the lives and property of others and to seek socially relevant knowledge.

The main difference between western and non-western perspectives is that while the former focuses exclusively on individual rights, the later emphasises the rights of *humanity* – including the humanity of the individual – and combines these rights with responsibilities. 'The Universal Declaration of Islamic Human Rights', a document formulated by a group of Islamic scholars in 1981 based on the values and principles of the Qur'an and the examples of the Prophet Muhammad, for instance, connects the standard rights to life, freedom, equality, justice, fair trial, protection from abuse of power, free speech, et cetera, with the rights of the individual to fulfil his/her basic needs, the rightful claim of the individual on the wealth of the community, the right to protection of honour and reputation, and combines these with the individual's responsibilities towards the community.[58] So why do such holistic notions of rights and responsibilities cause such problems for the west?

Responsibilities only make sense in a moral universe. When postmodernism undermines all absolute bases for morality, it also takes away any reasons for fulfilling responsibilities. The postmodern world is a world free of all responsibilities; it is about total liberation of the individual; not about tying the individual down with obligations and communal duties. Indeed, responsibilities and obligations have come to be seen as intrinsically oppressive to the individual: the extended family is oppressive to its young generation; marriage is oppressive to women; wearing *hijab* (Islamic dress) is oppressive to women – while being chic is not. Moreover, the liberal model of human rights thought and action, as Upendra Baxi notes, finds the problems of needs rather irritating.[59] It is frequently transformed into a contest between 'bread' and 'freedom', and freedom always wins in the western perspective, despite the fact that without 'bread', 'freedom' of speech and assembly, of association, of conscience and religion, of political participation, is existentially meaningless for its 'victims'. Indeed, it is characteristic of classical and contemporary western liberal thought to ignore the entire problematic of basic human needs. The whole tradition of discourse from John Stuart Mill to John Rawls illustrates the tendency. In his *Essay on Liberty*, Mill excluded the backward nations, along with women and children, from the rights to liberty.[60] John Rawls, in *Theory of Justice*, acknowledges that societies where the basic needs of the individuals are not fulfilled do not fit in his framework of liberty.[61]

Liberalism also has a serious problem with the notion of community. The liberal perspective sees the egalitarian approach of non-western cultures as denying the basic characteristics of freedom: belonging to a community consciously demands discipline and sacrifice. No community can exist if every individual goes his or her own way and defines his or her own morality. But the cultural anarchy of individualism, a hallmark of postmodernism, is not only a direct route to alienation and the fragmentation of society, but also inconsistent with ecological balance. Its creative potential is oversold and it overlooks the capacity for creativity in non-coercive communities: look at the artistic, cultural, architectural and scientific achievements of India, China and Islam. The Islamic heritage of communal concern and social consciousness allowed independent non-Muslim cultures to flourish and pluralism to bloom in Islamic Spain, and in more recent times, in Bosnia and today in Malaysia. In contrast, western individualism has led to the destruction of numerous native cultures – Tasmanian Aboriginal and Native American nations to give just two examples – as well as anti-Semitism and other forms of racism in recent years. Indeed, liberal secularism is unable to deal easily with any kind of collective identity except those defined by geography. It is not surprising then that postmodern liberalism is only happy when non-western cultures ditch their traditions and sacred notions and subscribe fully to the liberal creed.

This then is the crux of the matter. The discourse of human rights serves as an instrument for the pathological expansion of modern and postmodern liberalism and what accompanies it: free market capitalism. At best, it focuses attention on local dictators, on the despotic tendencies and practices at the level of individual nations, distracting us from the real culprits: the multinational corporations, international banks, the global regulatory agencies, the arms merchants and cynical postmodern politics. When western nations accuse non-western nations of human rights violations and declare them, in the jargon of *The Prisoner*, 'unmutual', they are cynically exposing alleged suppression at the national level to hide the authoritarianism of the international system. As Noam Chomsky has repeatedly suggested, it is time that we understood the deep totalitarian strain in western society and the savagery and cynicism of which it is capable. Focusing on the civil liberties of individuals, in the guise of 'universal human rights' is an attempt to deny non-western countries the right to point out the excesses of state formation in the west and the inherent injustice and authoritarianism in the global economic system.[62]

For the vast majority of the people, writes Malaysian human rights activist, Chandra Muzaffar, the right to food, housing, basic sanitation and the preservation of one's own identity and culture are far more important than the preservation of an individual's civil liberties. 'Of what use is the human rights struggle', asks Chandra,

> to the poverty-stricken billions of the South if it does not liberate them from hunger, from homelessness, from ignorance, from disease? Human rights interpreted mainly in terms of political and civil rights will not satisfy the quest of the poor for human dignity and social justice. Life and liberty, food and freedom, should go hand in hand if we want to develop a more holistic, integrated vision of human rights.[63]

For the non-west, emphasising the rights of the collectivity as a whole is not just a matter of developing a more complete and holistic perspective on human rights: it is also a matter of survival. When most of the world's political, cultural, intellectual, economic, scientific and technological resources are controlled and dominated by a few industrialised states of the North, it is inconceivable that the people of the South would not insist on their right to justice and equity. 'By equating human rights to civil and political rights', argues Muzaffar,

> the rich and powerful in the North hope to avoid coming to grips with those economic, social and cultural challenges which could well threaten their privileged position in the existing world order. What the rich and powerful do not want is a struggle for economic transformation presented as a human rights struggle, a struggle for human dignity. If, on the other hand, the discourse on human rights is confined to civil and political rights, it will be much easier to put governments in the South on trial for alleged violations of freedom of expression or freedom of assembly. Consequently, governments in the South will be on the defensive. If economic rights become the central issue, it is not inconceivable that the North which dominated the global economy will be in the dock.[64]

The control and domination by the industrialised countries of the structures and institutions of global economy, information systems and media networks, and the relentless and ruthless imposition of western culture on the South, have a direct bearing on a whole range of rights in the South. For example, IMF-imposed economic structural adjustment programmes in developing countries, which reflect the interests of the North, force developing countries to neglect the basic needs of the poor.[65] This is why in many countries of Africa and Latin America, food production, housing, healthcare, education and other basic needs are set aside in favour of export crops, tourism and debt-inducing prestigious 'development projects'.[66] In sub-Saharan Africa, IMF and World Bank structural adjustment programmes imposed harsh reductions on government spending on basic needs. The result was massive de-industrialisation and a steep rise in poverty as social and economic infrastructures were gradually destroyed. In the South, over 1 billion people – that is, one in five of the world's total population – live in absolute poverty; over 1.5 billion are deprived of primary health care; and 1 billion are illiterate.[67] What about the rights of these individuals simply to live?

This is why the human rights discourse in many non-western countries has shifted away from individual civic rights toward humanity and communal rights, basic needs and social empower-ment. In India, for example, human rights action has taken the form of organisation and empowerment of tribal people, the *dalits*, the rural poor, and women. Through such organisation, writes D. L. Sheth, it is hoped, these marginalised groups would be able to 'articulate their needs and press for their rights, not as passive subjects, but as self-confident citizens advancing their legitimate rights to survival and well being'.[68] The state, argue the more open-minded activist groups, is not the sole adversary: there are the local power structures, the structures of global dominance and the multinationals – all of whom are collaborating with the state to deny basic rights to the marginalised. This collaboration, argues Sheth, has led to inhuman models of development which reduce vast segments of the rural population to abject poverty, rendering them helpless and incapable of survival. These models have an inbuilt bias against the citizens in unorganised and informal sectors who have to be kept in their place as a perpetual source of cheap and trouble-free labour.[69] Their survival problems are attributed by the established economic and political institutions to overpopulation and deteriorating law and order. It is these populations, written off by development and organised politics, that are now increasingly becoming a focus of human rights activism in India. A similar shift is evident in Bangladesh, where meeting the basic needs of the rural population is now seen as the priority for human rights movements. In Malaysia, the human rights struggle is increasingly seen as a struggle against western domination.

Saving Other Souls, Again!

The 1990s have also witnessed the emergence of a new instrument of western domination of Other cultures: relief and aid work. In the last decade, relief and aid agencies have grown from relatively small, and often insignificant organisations, doing 'development' work on the sidelines, to global giants allegedly tackling the bulk of the world's development effort. Non-governmental organisa-tions, or NGOs, are now an unregulated, global industry worth

£2,500 million a year. The bulk of the development funding of western governments, as well as organisations like the European Union and the United Nations, is now channelled through the NGOs. But NGOs are undertaking much more than just old-fashioned development projects. Quite a few are simply fronts for the colonial mission of converting and civilising non-western people. After the end of the Cold War, 'when embassies and intelligence services have been scaled down, NGOs have become the eyes and ears of western governments'.[70] After the spectacular failure of five decades of direct government-to-government development aid, NGOs keep up the pretence that western nations are doing something to alleviate poverty in the South while propping up the development enterprise: they provide a cynical ploy for easing the conscience of the west.

The NGOs are exercising their newly acquired power and prestige in a classically postmodern way: cynically. 'Humanitarian work', 'charitable work', 'development assistance' and 'disaster relief' are all smokescreens for the real motives behind the NGO presence in the South: self-aggrandisement, promotion of western values and culture, including conversion to Christianity, inducing dependency, demonstrating the helplessness of those they are supposedly helping and promoting what has been aptly described as a 'disaster pornography'.

Bangladesh provides a good example of the cynical use of power by the NGOs. Since the turn of the decade, there has been open war, with the government and the people of Bangladesh fighting the NGOs. There are 16,000 foreign aid and charity organisations working in Bangladesh, a country the size of England and Wales. Of the 66,000 villages in Bangladesh, 33,000 have one or more NGOs working in them, giving a density of 3.5 foreign NGOs per square mile. What the NGOs were really doing became apparent in the aftermath of the tragic cyclone of 1991 when thousands of people stormed the office of an NGO in Kutubdia area of Chittagong to protest at being asked to change their faith if they wanted to receive relief material. The protest set off a chain-reaction of demonstrations throughout Bangladesh against the NGOs, which were accused of buying Bangladeshi souls with bribes of money, jobs and schooling. The Bangladeshi press accused NGOs of using their aid and charitable funds to buy influence, funding political parties, setting up candidates in the local government elections and campaigning in favour of certain candidates in the National Assembly elections. Under pressure, both from the public and the press, the government instituted an inquiry into the activities of the NGOs. The NGO Bureau Inquiry Report, published in 1992, showed that these allegations were only the tip of the iceberg.[71] The Bureau auditors examined the accounts of 100 NGOs and found that 80 per cent were involved in monetary corruption and financial irregularities, including maintaining secret bank accounts. The NGOs do not necessarily spend all that has been apportioned for a project; part of the funds, the report claimed, was regularly being siphoned off. The report also claimed that some 70 per cent of the NGO funds and resources are spent on the salary and perks of the foreign workers, experts and consultants, and on travel and transport; 15 per cent goes towards the salary of the Bangladeshi staff; 10 per cent on office and administration; and only 5 per cent goes to the much talked about target groups. In a country where the minimum monthly wage is $25, heads of NGOs award themselves monthly salaries of $3,000 to $7,000. The Bureau Report identified 52 NGOs as engaged directly in converting people to one or other Christian sect and also provides an interesting insight into the colonial mission to civilise the natives. The main target for proselytisation are the vulnerable: women, children, the poor and uneducated rural peasants. Some NGOs make Bible-reading compulsory for their staff, including Muslims. Most try to buy or browbeat the poor and vulnerable into changing their faith. One big missionary NGO employed only Christian teachers in its schools and a student has to be a Christian before he is given board and lodging in its hostels. In most NGO schools Christianity is compulsory, and all students are converts. Government education inspectors who came to assess the syllabus and standards were told, 'we are not funded by your government and are not accountable to you' and were regularly refused entry to these schools. Many NGOs were lending money to illiterate peasants at exorbitant rates of interest: with interest calculated on a daily, weekly or fortnightly basis, the peasants were paying 25–30 per cent. One NGO,

Prashika Manabid Unnayan Kendra, is alleged to have been receiving 226 per cent interest! As a result, whole villages, like Feni and Manikganj, have become virtual serfs of NGOs.

The NGOs now function as alternative, western power structures in developing societies. They have created a new class amongst the indigenous people: those who work for the NGOs and receive salaries, cars (normally), foreign travel and various perks that other members of society, those working in the civil service, education or business, can only dream of. The western press makes a bee-line for NGO officials who are supposed to 'know' what is 'really' going on in a developing country and who now speak on (western) television, meet visiting dignitaries, have open access to local ministers and lobby the United Nations and its subsidiaries. NGO officials pronounce on human rights, the condition of the rural and urban poor, what needs to be done, what policies should be followed and whether the IMF or the World Bank should or should not deal with a certain country. At the extreme, notes Alex de Waal,

> this means that NGOs can call for international military intervention. CARE International headed the campaign for US troops to Somalia; Oxfam called for a UN force for Rwanda. CARE and its US NGO supporters succeeded. When the US Marines landed in Mogadishu, their job was to protect international aid operations – not to protect the Somali people. In effect, a handful of private American charities had taken on the job of representing – or rather, misrepresenting – the interest of the Somali nation before the international community.[72]

The NGOs are not accountable to the victims of war and poverty they supposedly help, or to the public in western nations to whom they regularly appeal for donations, not even to governments who finance their work. The relief débâcles of the 1990s, in Ethiopia, Somalia, Rwanda, Bangladesh and Chechnya, passed without comment or criticism. The western press seems to have declared criticisms of aid and relief organisations a forbidden territory. Indeed, the media collude in keeping the self-made image of NGOs spotlessly clean. The London *Observer* journalist, Lindsey Hilsum, admits:

I, like other journalists, often travel to trouble-spots in aid agency-planes or jeeps. It is nearly always the cheapest, and sometimes the only, way to get there. Perhaps that is one reason reporters rarely give aid workers tough interviews or write critical reports. Wars are frequently reported through humanitarian eyes – the dying child and the aid agency nurse is an easier story to tell than the complex cause of war.[73]

The NGO monopoly on communication, transport, jobs, and primary and secondary educational facilities, as well as the moral high ground is such that all local opposition is silenced. NGO development projects and programmes, just like the aid projects of the western governments that were in vogue during the 1950s, 1960s and 1970s, are of little consequence in removing poverty and empowering the poor. International food aid in recent African famines has amounted to less than 10 per cent of the overall diet of famine-stricken people; those who survive, do so not because of international aid, but because of the resources of the community itself. NGOs have become a prime vehicle for direct western intervention in the South and a new instrument for inducing dependency in the developing countries. They have become businesses, big businesses in some cases. Those who are victims of NGO cynicism and imperialism are increasingly bitter and resentful: 'they see organisations suffused with arrogance born of power without responsibility, and a new hegemony of humanitarianism that allows no criticism'.[74]

The non-western critique of NGOs, liberal democracy, human rights and postmodern cynicism and ambivalence is evocative: and what it evokes is exactly the same corpus of arguments and, as we have seen, even the same problems that preceded and prompted the drive for independence in the non-west, the search for release from the modernist political hegemony of colonialism. The location of colonial paternal authority may have changed, as in the case of development aid, yet the enterprise remains the same. Victorian imperial mission is postmodern privatised paternalism in another guise, so it is hardly surprising that ideas that for a time did not dare to speak their name have returned to the arena of supposed intellectual discourse. The fear of Other civilisations, the expression of the neurotic insecurity and angst that defines western self-perception, always required externalisation, which was answered by the demonisation of the Other. The Other was not merely different, but inherently opposed to, indeed inimical to, the west. The only defence was aggressive, first-strike capacity: the destruction of the Other or their reformation and cooption within the body of all that was/is the west. Or, as Samuel P. Huntington describes it, the future belongs to 'the clash of civilizations'.[75] Such an old chestnut can only sound like an apposite timely analysis, a 1990s idea, when temporality itself has been collapsed by the notion that the project, even the existence, of history is at an end. Ahistorical, atemporal discourse re-establishes all the old discourses with their attendant baggage of ideas and reflexes.

Francis Fukayama's 'The End of History' argument is not so much a re-examination of history as an attempt to shape a particular future. Its consequence comes in the form of the 'clash of civilization' thesis which internalises all of the past within postmodern times as well as the future. In this perspective, all regain their history only to re-establish the imperatives whereby Other civilisations confront and threaten the west much as their existence did before Columbus. The end of the Cold War may have created a new world, but old history will come to haunt our new existence. Thus, according to Huntington,

> the fundamental source of conflict in this new world will not be primarily ideological or primarily economic. The great divisions among humankind and the dominating source of conflict will be cultural. Nation states will remain the most powerful actors in world affairs, but the principal conflicts of global politics will occur between nations and groups of different civilizations. The clash of civilizations will dominate global politics. The fault lines between civilizations will be the battle lines of the future.[76]

But where exactly are these 'fault lines'?

> The most significant dividing line in Europe ... may well be the eastern boundary of Western Christianity in the year 1500. This line runs along what are now the boundaries between Finland and Russia and

between the Baltic states and Russia, cuts through Belarus and Ukraine separating the more Catholic western Ukraine from Orthodox eastern Ukraine, swings westward separating Transylvania from the rest of Romania, and then goes through Yugoslavia almost exactly along the line now separating Croatia and Slovenia from the rest of Yugoslavia. In the Balkans this line, of course, coincides with the historic boundary between the Hapsburg and Ottoman empires. The people to the north and the west of this line are Protestant or Catholic; they share the common experiences of European history – feudalism, the Renaissance, the Reformation, the Enlightenment, the French Revolution, the Industrial Revolution; they are generally economically better off than the peoples to the east; and they may now look forward to increasing involvement in a common European economy and to the consolidation of democratic political systems. The peoples to the east and south of this line are Orthodox or Muslim; they historically belonged to the Ottoman or Tsarist empires and were only lightly touched by the shaping events in the rest of Europe; they are generally less advanced economically; they seem much less likely to develop stable democratic political systems.[77]

This is, of course, as Fouad Ajami notes, the classical divide where civilisation ends and the wilderness of the Other begins.[78] We now return to the beginning: Islam, with its 'bloody borders' is poised to pounce on the West. Worse, the entire host of non-western civilisations, who have no share in 'European history', are ganging up on the righteous, defenceless west: 'Confucian, Japanese, Islamic, Hindu, Slavic-Orthodox, Latin American and possibly African civilizations', argues Huntington, are rediscovering their identities and 'have the desire, the will and the resources to shape the world in non-western ways' (God forbid!). A west, at the peak of its power, is now seriously threatened by the non-west. One of the most pernicious post-Cold War developments, states Huntington, has been the 'Confucian–Islamic connection that has emerged to challenge Western interests, values and power'. The countries of the Confucian and Islamic civilisations are 'weapons states' (as if the western nations are non-weapon states) hell-bent on acquiring 'weapons technologies needed to counter the military power of the West'. Faced with such a heinous onslaught from the Other, what should/can the west do? Huntington's prescription for keeping history on its true course is simple: the west should do what the west has always done. It should 'limit the expansion of the military strength of Confucian and Islamic states' (that is, continue with imperialism); 'exploit the differences and conflicts among Confucian and Islamic states' (that is, divide and rule); 'support in other civilizations groups sympathetic to Western values and interests' (that is, promote insurrection); and 'strengthen international institutions that reflect and legitimate Western interests and values' (that is, retrench western global domination).

The cynicism of postmodern politics is contained in its history, and its history is the beginning of its future.

3. A Grand Memory for Forgetting

Postmodernism achieves its effects through deconstruction, ridicule and parody. None of these features comes rootless into the contemporary imagination; postmodernism arrives as a stance, a convention in history, which is also a point of attack on history. For modernity, history is a record of the self-aggrandisement of the victors, a self-interested portrayal of how they saw themselves and those ranged against them. The history of modernity, as much as the writing of history in the conventions of modernity, is a linear progress. Even when the Marxist notion of rupture between eras is introduced it implies a new linear trajectory, whether it be through time or conceptual improvement. Linear progress is the triumph of an implicit rightness, the record of the vindication of ideas and people by their coming to dominance through time. Postmodernism leaves behind precious few heroes and no noble causes. It also collapses the sense of linear connection. What happened in history is on a par with today's news; by corollary today's news can attain no greater significance or transparency from a knowledge of history, which consists of a collection of divergent, opposing interpretations, all of equivalent dubiety. History becomes so many competing attempts to author non-authoritative explanations of reality through the disposition of representations, manipulation of images and obfuscation of unfortunate facts.

Postmodernism has a particular take on the end of history: it is truly the end of history as we have known it because it envelops all historical events in meaninglessness. Significance can only be an act of interpretation – postmodernism recognises only multiple competing interpretations. How can one subject them all to truth or reality tests? The grand school of history sought objective verification, but postmodernism suggests a new possibility – that all interpretations are in their way cogent and valid. The end of history is not just Fukayama's simplistic, totalitarian terminus, the consummation of modernist historical understanding. The postmodern end of history is the conversion of all temporal sequence into simultaneity, the coexistence of all possibilities as some grand kaleidoscope with no pattern being more persuasive, dominant or significant than any other. Today, one can choose one's designer history, link one's contemporary choices with a refashioning of the past that suits one's mood. Felipe Fernandez-Armesto's *Millennium*,[1] for example, offers an eclectic selection from a thousand-year history – with Muslim civilisation's intellectual and global dominance of the first half of the millennium dismissed as 'the tower of darkness' and China written off in 24 pages – designed to show that the supremacy of the white man is a product only of natural development. In designer history any choice can be fitted with a tradition by associating it with a chosen historical pattern of ideas or events or characters that are selectively assembled. History returns not to its fictional, putative father – Herodotus – as he was constructed by nineteenth-century historians, but to the spirit that moved the civilisation that produced him: history becomes myth-making. But the magical realistic myths of postmodernism are quite different from the tales of wonder and reverence infused with moral purpose any ancient Greek would recognise. It is not the mythic qualities of historical understanding that mark out postmodernism, but the way they affect the use of history. The overriding purpose of today's mythic reality is that it magically renders history irrelevant as a charter for any action, the complete antithesis of the uses of myth in history, archaic or modern. The consequence of postmodern historical mythicism is that everything stays just as it is, since everything that has happened is valid, while nothing that has happened leads to a moral conclusion, a sense of purpose or direction that could warrant redress of the legacy of history. The old myths were about heroes and heroines. Postmodern historical mythicism is the realm of the anti-hero, the jaded viewer who sees it all, who sees lamentable events but accepts that 'shit happens'. Postmodern historical myth becomes obfuscation, selective indulgence and a transport of forgetting. The ultimate response to history is a magical talent for total neutrality, which makes no challenge whatever to the status quo.

The uses of history become a fairytale, a fiction. Imagination, the fairytale or other fictional literary forms become as cogent a means to appropriate and disseminate historical understanding as historiography. As it was at the beginning so, once again, the storyteller becomes the historian. But when history dissolves into atemporality, the images, words and actions of the past do not cease to have consequences. We merely become less capable of discerning how the past is imprinting itself once again, or of detecting that we are hearing only what the annals recorded of the past; the deficiencies of received and recorded history are as chimerical as the authorised versions rendered in the scholarly tomes. Postmodernism traps historical understanding in the limitations of what the annals record, by making all annals, folk tales or mythic history the same: works of self-interested human expression. What the overwhelming impulse to neutrality in the face of history anaesthetises is our recognition that whether as storytelling, myth-making or truth and reality testing the sources of history contain a voicelessness, a silent lacuna that makes the dethroning of history a continuation of the grand historic narrative with even less let or hindrance to the dominating, overwriting and distorting powers it possesses. The use of history in postmodern convention becomes the empowerment of imagination, but what postmodern imagination cannot envisage is any alternative.

It may seem bizarre to consider history through a Hollywood cartoon, but it is precisely the place where the postmodern dispensation is at its most insidious and potent. It is the place where the use and abuse of history in a distinctly postmodern fashion intersects with the reality of the postmodern order: its fashion of style, its commodification of everything, its eclectic relativism and its genuine talent for forgetting that becomes simultaneously the forging of new icons that will be remembered. Postmodernism empowers images, when images are all we have.

How it makes and manipulates its images is where the cunning of the postmodern project can and must be recognised. When the process of making new iconography is examined we have to acknowledge that we have not entered a new era of liberation from the flaws of history, but are tied more firmly to the very old and familiar ideas of dominant history that postmodernism must deploy to give itself a language and work its effects. What emerges is a new surface, a superficial expression that is consolidated by the continued dominance of the old language, that gives precedence to the dominating ideas of modernism even when it appears to parody and ridicule them.

Consider the ghost invoked for the quintessential act of postmodern historicism in Walt Disney's *Pocahontas*. In this cinematic endeavour the fairytale teller becomes the teller of a fairytale that refashions history for future use.

The film begins with a jolly song as a motley crew prepare to sail from old London. 'In 1607 we sailed the open sea, for glory, God and gold in the Virginia Company.' The company would be incomplete without our lithe, blond hero: 'You can't fight Indians without John Smith.' And so they set sail, only to meet a violent storm, providing our hero an opportunity to show his metal by diving into the boiling ocean to save a young lad. Adventurous, lusty manhood is ready to make landfall on its greatest glory.

Meanwhile, in the virgin forests of America, for the unsuspecting natives life goes on. They tend their village and gather the fruits of Mother Earth. The noble chief, Powhatan, returns with his warriors to his happy village after a successful campaign and looks for his daughter, Matoaka, whom he calls by her pet name, Pocahontas. But Pocahontas is in the forest trying to resolve the mystery of the dreams that have been troubling her sleep. She has seen strange clouds (which turn out to be the sails of the ship bringing John Smith) – do they portend some new path she must follow? Her father presents her with just such a new proposition, that she should marry Kocoum, a young warrior who has newly proved his worth. Pocahontas finds him too stern and serious – the standard wooden Indian? For counsel she visits Grandmother Willow, the ancient talking tree, cast much after the fashion of Tolkien's Ents in *The Lords of the Rings*.

And so the scene is set for the new ideological meeting in the New World, according to the postmodern handbook. The film works a host of timely effects. The historic Pocahontas is represented as contemporary tastes and sensibilities need her to have been: female, feisty, full of acuity, an independent actor in the midst of momentous events. The symbolic love-story that is her legend is a timeless idyll of a better, more peaceful way; the rapprochement that can be made at the end of history. The object of Pocahontas' desire and affection becomes even more empowered by being sought by this new historic icon. Without John Smith to save, what would be the use of Pocahontas? There are two sides of a power equation being re-fabulated in this cartoon.

In the animated cartoon version of the future history fairytale Walt Disney has conspicuously consumed history to provide a subtle reading of the old story, re-propagandising a tale that gained currency precisely as polemic masquerading as history. Today, films are not merely made, they are accompanied by documentaries of their making, a self-conscious examination of the existence of cultural power that acts as far more than a device of advertising and self-promotion. The merchandising spin-offs that fill shops around the world, television transmission time taken up by programmes about films, all stress the centrality of image-making, and the locale from which the image-making emanates – Hollywood, the place where arbitration and the exercise of fashion, taste and understanding are made for everyone. In the television documentary of the making of *Pocahontas*, all the participants – the animators, the musicians, the voice-overs, the producers, the director – stress how they sought to be true to history, in a streamlined, digestible way, which allowed them to concentrate on the love-story at the heart of history.[2] Portentously, we are told this is the first time Disney has ventured into history, as opposed to fiction and fairytales. To emphasise this departure, stylistic reminders are included in the film: the playful animal familiars of the heroine have no voice and sing no songs – they are real animals, because this is real mythicism, not pure imagination. Walt Disney, assured of its stranglehold on the young consumers of the world, is consciously engaged in authoring a message about history, based, according to their publicity department, on real history.

What the animated cartoon finds significant about the discovery of the New World is a highly significant, postmodern
ideological centrepiece. It is not some nonsense put out by a
mindless leisure industry, but a conceptual refinement to be found
at the cutting edge of intellectual fashions in history, anthropology, philosophy – or any 'ology' you care to mention. The
argument concerns the Other, the awareness of difference and the
recognition of ethnic and cultural diversity through stereotypes.
The chic is to assert, definitively, that both sides operate on
stereotypes, one as bad as the other.

We've heard them all before: 'Savages, savages, barely even
human' sing the settlers, adding, 'not like you and me, which
means they must be evil.' The native Americans reply in similar
vein as they prepare to defend their land: 'The Paleface is a
demon. Beneath that milky hide there's emptiness inside', and
ending with the neatly matched refrain: 'Savages, savages different
from us, which means they can't be trusted.' So here we have the
essential postmodern twist on history – we are all Others now and
all concepts of others are pretty much the same. The differential
power granted to some stereotypes by the historic record of
dominance is at a stroke dematerialised, abolished, leaving behind
only equivalence that unifies all peoples in the need to be
politically correct. The effect is to vindicate the current resurgence
in usage of the term 'savage' since it now has a validity that is
universal, as opposed to a sole historic implication, which is the
prejudicial imposition of a dominating and discriminating order.
While it brings the Other into the category of the dominant order,
it throws a cloak of invisibility over the effect the differential
power of description and stereotyping has had on non-western
peoples, now and in history. In effect, dominance is made to look
like chance, one that would not have been different if the history
of the peoples of the non-west had been other.

This new sense of equivalence is brought to bear on the central
mythic act that animates the film: the laying down of the shapely
head of Pocahontas to save the life of John Smith. The dénouement of the film seems to imply a new resolution to the old
conflict that preoccupies history books. Or as the promotional
material put it: 'Two different worlds, one true love.' For

Pocahontas, as she peeps through the undergrowth to get her first sight of the strange newcomer, it is love at first sight, or at least the fulfilment of all those strange dreams, the new direction, the something more than her world has to offer, which Disney has established as part of her character. John Smith, we are told, is an old campaigner: 'I've seen hundreds of new worlds, Thomas, what could possibly be different about this one?' But this new land is something different. He sets out in a small boat to explore the misty river – looking for all the world like an earlier version of George Washington on his way to Valley Forge. And the young maiden he meets is like no Indian he has encountered. Fascinated, he allows her to open his eyes to new possibilities and experience. Not only does Pocahontas show John Smith corn, the only gold she can think of in her land, but she also introduces him to the spiritual path of her insight, for at least in this version she takes him to talk to the tree, old Grandmother Willow.

Pocahontas is a clever foil for the assured assumptions John Smith has about the fate of this new world. His cinematic paraphrase of the American colonists' vision of a city on a hill prompts Pocahontas to burst into Oscar-winning song:

If the savage one is me,
How come there's so much you don't know?

Pocahontas lays down her head to save the life of John Smith, challenging the desire for revenge for unjust wrongs on the part of her own people. Peace and reconciliation appear possible, impelled by the love of two free spirits. But this does not provide a proper dénouement for future history. So the cartoon has Ratcliffe, the representative of the perfidy of the Virginia Company, take aim at Powhatan, to fulfil his own instruction that 'anyone who so much as looks at an Indian without killing him is guilty of treason' (the only good Indian is a dead Indian). John Smith leaps forward and takes the bullet himself. Disney places a neat balance, reciprocal acts of heroism, at the heart of history.

The mutual acts of loving self-sacrifice are what unite the 'two different worlds' and seem to validate the new availability of the native Other for inclusion on a par in the multicultural relativism of postmodernism. It seems as if a new pole of tradition has been entered into the annals. As John Smith lies wounded, in danger of his life unless he is taken to England, he asks Pocahontas to accompany him. 'I am needed here', she says. Pocahontas belongs to the new world of history Disney has fashioned out of America. The Native American 'babe' and the spirit of the 'all-American' he-man, are bound together and will be with each other forever, the bond between them, 'one true love', makes something new in this new world. The balanced role given to the Other, which makes Pocahontas the iconic heroine standing on a high cliff watching the sailing ship depart, diverts attention and obfuscates the exact dimensions of the remaking authored by Disney's mythic history. It is the balanced attention to the Other that makes Pocahontas an even more dependent utility of the dominant order than did her legend in modern history. While a new myth has been made, all the old ideas, the content of the annals of history have been deployed, reaffirmed and consolidated to strengthen and serve the power of dominance. Disney has made a pastiche, one that is curiously full of attention to historic detail. The film makes much use of a compass, and indeed it is recorded in various sources that John Smith presented a compass to a Powhatan Indian. Their magical confabulation makes it possible to revisit history in a new, improved fashion, simultaneously it makes it more difficult to disentangle the mythical refashioning from recorded history and both confidence tricks operate to distract attention form the main import of the exercise: the making of a confirming myth of absolute dominance, just as the legend of Pocahontas did for modernity.

Me Poca, You John – We PC

Walt Disney is the fast food of modern cinema entertainment. It is not surprising that to 'celebrate' the release of *Pocahontas*, McDonald's launched a 'McChief Burger' – making the connection between the two, McDonald's and Walt Disney, that much clearer. Packaged, promoted and always ready off the shelf. More importantly, as the participants in the making of the film assert, they know they are remaking history, that a Walt Disney feature will last forever as a new iconography, a new history. Pocahontas will be an icon for future generations of children, who receive most of their information from television and cinema, video games and CD-ROMs. With the information revolution, new characters populate history, there are new ways to revisit the past and see it in new ways.

Alas, the reality is otherwise. The postmodern information revolution – whether in the hands of Disney or the makers of 'edutainment' computer products – is more ruthlessly selective, with a more ruthless ideological purpose than the extant annals of modern history. What is selected, what is omitted and how the details are joined into compelling, entertaining mythic history validate the old and familiar ideas of modernity to produce a sophisticated realignment that confers more power on the dominant order and more potently eradicates the Other than even the early settlers of America could have contemplated. It is the mechanics of selection and silence which must be examined to perceive what postmodern mythic history means.

The famous incident of the laying down of Pocahontas' head would have occurred in 1608, if it ever did, when the 27-year-old John Smith was indeed captured by the Powhatan Indians. The legend of his life being saved by the intervention of Pocahontas was not written until 1624 in the *General History*, John Smith's third book about Virginia, and the only one to mention the story. The *General History* was published after the death of Powhatan and John Rolfe, and when Pocahontas herself was safely dead and buried in Gravesend, England – a site that Disney has now turned into a tourist attraction. In the history books, John Smith is Captain John Smith, the rank acquired fighting in the armies of Emperor Rudolph II, but Smith also fought in Hungary, Transylvania, Russia and Morocco before setting off for the New World. It has been noted that John Smith 'took the same eyes to the Holy War against the Turks and the invasion of America'.[3] In contrast to Disney's 'good guy with a bit of cultural rethinking to do',[4] Smith's own writings demonstrate that he was a man with a fund of fully fashioned opinions on the subject of the 'innocent savage'. Far from having his mind opened to new possibilities by talking to Grandmother Willow, Smith was resolutely convinced, as were all his contemporaries, that the religion of the indigenous peoples was devil worship. As he wrote in his second book, *A Map of Virginia*, published in 1612, 'their chief god they worship is the devil'.[5] In the same volume, Smith also records the Powhatan practice of child sacrifice.[6] His general summation of the character of these people: 'they were inconstant in everything but what fear constraineth them to keep'. They are further:

> crafty, timorous, quick of apprehension and very ingenious. Some are of disposition fearful, some bold, most cautious, all savage. Generally covetous of copper, beads and such like trash. They are soon moved to anger and so malicious that they seldom forget an injury.[7]

John Smith was one of those who established the very terms of the dominant convention of understanding the Other. The object of the 'one true love' that makes a new mythic history is not fortuitous; he is an essential selection for reasons more significant than his afterthought anecdote about an Indian girl.

In 1608 Matoaka, or Pocahontas, would have been a girl of 11 or 12, which adds a salacious, paedophilic overtone to the explicitly amorous relationship, 'one true love', depicted in the Disney cartoon. According to William Strachey, until they were 12 years of age, Indian girls went naked. Strachey had seen Pocahontas, 'the playful one', 'a well favoured but wanton young girl'.[8] In Jamestown, Pocahontas would

> get the boys forth with her into the market place and make then wheel, falling on their hands, turning their heels upwards; whom she would follow, and wheel herself, naked as she was, all the Fort over.[9]

The Disney film is scrupulous in including Pocahontas cartwheeling, though in this case it is not through the streets but by the maize fields.

In 1609, the Virginia Company underwent a major restructuring to increase its powers and refashion the problems of the administration of its colony. A new Governor with absolute powers was appointed, Lord De La Warr, to replace the 'elected

president', who happened to be John Smith. Lord De La Warr
spent virtually no time in America; the implementation of the
new policies of colonial administration was undertaken by a
number of Deputy Governors, among whom were Sir Thomas
Gates, Sir Thomas Dale and Samuel Argall. The objective of the
new policy was immediate, large-scale settlement and expansion of
the Jamestown colony. In facilitating the policy, Gates carried
with him to Virginia instructions for the conversion of the
Indians 'which the better to effect you must procure from them
some convenient number of their children to be brought up in
your language and manners'.[10] Procuring would be done by force.

In 1610, it seems, Matoaka married Kocoum, the Indian Disney
alleges she refused as 'too serious'. In 1611, Sir Thomas Dale set
off up the James River to found a new settlement, Henrico, 70
miles away. The new settlement speedily set about implementing
the policy of procuring. In 1613, Dale and Argall had a showdown
with the Indians, demanding that they lay down their weapons: 'if
they would do this we would be friends; if not, burn all'. The
Indians fired arrows at the English, so Dale 'killed some, hurt
others, marched into the land, burnt houses, took their corn' and
proposed 'to burn all if they would not do as we demanded'.[11]
There followed a truce which included provision for Pocahontas
to be taken into the custody of Sir Thomas Dale to be instructed
in the Christian religion. In a letter written in 1614, Dale wrote:

> Powahatan's daughter I caused to be carefully instructed in Christian
> religion; who after she had made some good progress therein,
> renounced publicly her country idolatry, openly confessed her Chris-
> tian faith; was, as she desired, baptised.[12]

It is this event that ensured Pocahontas' place at the centre of
American history, a fact confirmed by a painting of her baptism
done in 1840 by John Gadsby Chapman to adorn the Rotunda of
the Capitol building in Washington DC. In the history of the early
settlement of America, Pocahontas was the first and, for a very
long time the only, documented convert – the living proof, in the
battery of European claims, for the right of dominance over the
newfound lands.

Pocahontas is wedded forever to the colonial endeavour in the new world Europe made of America, appropriated into the dominant culture's history of appropriation. Disney omits the real wedding of Pocahontas. In 1614 Rebecca, the baptismal name of Pocahontas, married John Rolfe, one of the passengers of the *Sea Venture*, the ship under the command of Sir Thomas Gates, which was cast adrift on its way to Jamestown.

Rolfe's marriage to Rebbeca/Pocahontas, the sometime Matoaka, united the two strands of significance and fascination she held for her contemporaries: the wanton, sexually suggestive woman and the symbolically tractable, converted Indian. Consummation of a marriage was not an impulsive, romantic decision as his correspondence makes clear. It was a matter which 'toucheth me so nearly as the tenderness of my salvation',[13] Rolfe wrote in a letter to Sir Thomas Dale.

The settlers of the Virginia colony were as conscious as any later Pilgrim Father of the Biblical warrants of the Old Testament, by which they continually justified their actions and rights to dominance in America. And in the Old Testament there were the words of Ezra, which gave instructions against miscegenation: 'you have transgressed, and have taken strange wives, to increase the trespass of Israel' (10: 10). As Rolfe stated in his letter: 'nor am I ignorant of the heavy displeasure which Almighty God conceived against the sons of Levi and Israel for marriage of strange wives; nor of the inconveniences which may arise thereby'.[14] His trouble was 'a mighty war in my meditations' prompted by passion for Pocahontas. But even while Rolfe declared himself 'in love', he could not ignore the fact that Pocahontas was 'descrepant in all nutriture from muself', that 'her education hath been rude, her manners barbarous' and that her 'generations' have been 'cursed'. This last is a reference to Genesis 9: 25: 'Cursed be Canaan: a servant of servants shall he be unto his brethren' – a biblical text which was conventionally used to place the new peoples of the New World within the existing framework of European anthropological understanding, their place being that of natural slaves.

To bring himself to the matrimonial altar Rolfe had to find alternative biblical warrant if he was to overcome his feeling that his affections were 'wicked instigations hatched by him who seeketh and delighteth in man's destruction'. To Calvinist Puritans such as Rolfe, the words of St Paul – 'Wherefore come out from among them, and be ye separate, said the Lord' (I Corinthians 6: 17) – had a distinct resonance. Yet it was in Pauline pronouncements that he also found his justification for marriage, as well as in the *Institutions* of Calvin, which he also quotes. So he was able to deduce that Pocahontas had 'capableness of understanding', 'aptness and willingness to receive any good impression', 'desire to be taught and instructed in the knowledge of God' and 'great appearance of love for me'. Therefore he could fulfil the 'duty of a good Christian', by 'converting to the true knowledge of God and Jesus Christ an unbelieving creature'. As Porter so rightly emphasises, in all of Rolfe's tortuous 'mighty war in my meditations' his problem is never one of 'colour', but the true origins of all European racial consciousness: 'the unclean seed of idolatry'.[15] What tipped the balance for Rolfe was the alternative construction of the barbarian character: the native as a natural child who could be instructed and brought to the benefits of civilisation. The actual words of Rolfe, the real husband, mirror the pastiche mouthed and parodied in the character of John Smith in the movie.

In 1616, Mr and Mrs Rolfe set sail for England with their baby son, Thomas. On her arrival in London Mrs Rolfe was given an allowance of four pounds a week by the Virginia Company and seems to have been the event of the season: she met Samuel Purchas, arch-scribbler in the cause of Empire, friend and collaborator of John Smith, was grandly entertained by the Bishop of London; her portrait was drawn by a Dutch engraver; she was presented to James I and well seated at the Masque given on 6 January 1617, Ben Johnson's *The Vision of Delight*. The last detail comes from a letter of John Chamberlain, who noted that her return to Virginia had been planned 'sore against her will'.[16] The Rolfes set sail from London in 1617. The ship put in at Gravesend where, as Samuel Purchas put it, Rebecca/Pocahontas, 'the Virginia born Lady' came 'to her end and grave, having given demonstration of her Christian sincerity, as the first fruits of Virginia conversion'.[17] She was indeed proof of the rightness of the election of the colonisers of America. As John Rolfe wrote

shortly before taking her to England: 'what need we than fear' in
our 'zealous work' in the land of Virginia 'but to go up at once as a
peculiar people, marked and chosen by the finger of God to
possess it'.[18] This is the vision from the city on the hill of the
departing Pocahontas, heroine of the earliest annals of America:
symbolic confirmation of the right of European expropriation,
appropriation and overwriting of all that they had come to claim
as their own. In effect it is hardly different from the readjusted
iconography offered by Disney.

All the contemporary sources of the early settling of North
America – the travellers' tales, company propaganda and learned
works – had a polemic purpose not just in the pursuit of profit but
in staking and legitimising the claim to Empire. In all these
sources Matoaka and her people have no independent voice. They
are the reported objects only of the European gaze and its fervid
imagination; their actuality, history and experience are voiceless,
except as reported by the appropriators and remakers.

Pocahontas the movie is a representation in a gallery of representations. Most eloquently it tells us that the dominant order still dominates the terms, content and means of description. Now, however, in
its incarnation as postmodern relativism it seeks to assert that it
includes and gives voice to the Other, that it represents a refashioned
statement sensitive to the history and experience of the Other. The
fault of the original sources, the absence of independent presence of
the Other, it would seem, has been made good in new history. What
these claims amount to is little more substantive than the whispered
advice of Grandmother Willow when Pocahontas and John Smith
discover they have no mutual language: 'Listen with your heart and
you will understand.'

Digging Deep into the Other

Disney's new history is a subtle selection, highly significant in
how it chooses to paraphrase, collapse and conflate the details
from the contemporary sources and the legend that constitute
western civilisation's colonial/colonising history. To compound
their new stereotypes Disney is deeply indebted to old familiar

stereotypes which root their postmodern refurbishment in a
continuing tradition.

The earliest iconography of the new continent depicted
America as a nubile, available maiden with long, loose tresses.
Certainly the languor of the sexually charged figure of America in
the earliest European representations was intended to suggest she
was ready to be husbanded by Europe.[19] The drawing of Pocahontas in the cartoon version makes Pocahontas the most sexually
endowed of all the female forms that appear. Or as Mel Gibson
puts it in the TV documentary of the making of the film: 'I mean
Pocahontas is a babe, isn't she? You've got to say it.'[20] Her
costume, a figure-hugging number, hardly suggests a deerskin
robe and is obviously informed by the famous drawings John
White made at Roanoke. Characteristically, all the females in
White's paintings wore short shifts, baring one shoulder, and so
does Pocahontas.[21] Within the family viewing conventions of
Disney, there is no doubt that the lusty manhood of John Smith is
roused and taken by his first glimpse of this icon of America. How
easily supposed political correctness betrays its origins and ends
up redeploying the oldest stereotypes of all.

In the early representations, America, while sexually charged
and available, is always a passive figure, reposing in a hammock,
lying in a languid pose (not unlike those famous harem postcards
of Arab maidens, it was a conception of colonial womanhood that
was widely deployed, a long-standing tradition, a conventional,
stereotypical notion).[22] But Disney's Pocahontas is something new
– she is entranced by John Smith even before he is aware of her
presence. It is Pocahontas who gets the love light burning in eyes
first – the multicoloured, windblown feathers and leaves which are
the representation of the chemistry of physical attraction in the
cartoon version. It is a little like Anne Frank falling in love with
an SS officer. By this twist of the palette Disney confirms its own
statement in the television documentary: Pocahontas is looking
for heightened experience, something more than her world offers.
She is explicitly made to say that Kocoum is too serious, not
exciting enough for a red-blooded, all-American girl. So it is that
native America stalks the animus it desires – all that is embodied
and represented by John Smith. In today's postmodern refashion-

ing, instead of passivity, the tractable native awaiting the coloniser, the native is yearning to make herself sexually available to
her destiny: the coloniser. On one level, the character of Pocahontas is a proof of the new dispensation of multiculturalism – she is
an independent, intelligent, opinionated woman, who challenges
the notion that she is savage and uncivilised. At a more important
level we get proof positive of the limits of postmodern multiculturalism: all Pocahontas' liberation is for is to be included,
beloved perhaps, but subsumed in the dominant society of her
own volition. Postmodernism can conceive of no alternative
desire; it can know the Other no better than did modernity.

Before the arrival of the Virginia Company's sailing ship, strange
portents trouble Pocahontas' dreams. She asks Grandmother
Willow whether these omens indicate a new path her life should
follow. This seemingly innocuous piece of hokum demonstrates
once again the sophistication of Disney's selection from the tropes of
modern history. It evokes the legend that the Aztec permitted a
bedraggled band of Spaniards to penetrate to the heart of their
empire because they believed them to be the white god mythology
foretold would come from the West. Peter Schaffer's play, and the
movie based on it, *Royal Hunt of the Sun*, use this conventional European legend, this time concerning the arrival of the Spaniards in the
Inca empire. Schaffer has a more complex reading of first encounters
and emphasises the infinite attractiveness to European colonisers of
being taken for gods by simple savages. In its instructions to the
settlers the Virginia Company was careful to insist that no Indian
should become aware of any white man who was killed or fell sick:
the godlike role was to be consciously played to aid the process of
colonisation. It became a convention in European writing, and conventionally the arrival of a new 'god' would require omens and portents, modelled on the basic source of so many colonising thoughts,
the Bible. The white man mistaken for a god has become the oldest
cliché in books, cartoons and movies – think of the Rudyard Kipling
story made into the John Houston film, *The Man Who Would Be
King*; or the adventures of Indiana Jones in the *Temple of Doom*, or
almost any adventure that sets off for Darkest Africa. These are not
disinterested reports or literary deceits, but a consciously deployed
ideology to explain the innate superiority of Europe. At first, the

white man-as-god is the missionary bringing the Christian message; then he becomes the god of scientific wonder and superior technology. The bearers of such advancement must be a thing of wonder for the unsophisticated Other, who could not conceive of such refined and civilised marvels for themselves. For Disney, it is a super handsome hunk; love at first sight is the equivalent of the god-from-afar syndrome, yet another restatement of the innate superiority of all that is the west.

Indigenous women have always been libidinous in the western convention from Amerigo Vespucci's accounts through to Margaret Mead's now discredited reports of sexual licence granted to Samoan girls, by way of the *Arabian Nights* and image of the harem. The Disney animators who made Pocahontas this vision of sexually explicit girlhood – and their characterisation is definitely adolescent – also explain that they wanted to express an animality in her movements. There is something decidedly feline in the way she slinks through the undergrowth as she follows John Smith. Once more Disney evokes a much older and redolent tradition linked to some very powerful colonising ideas. The conventions of early modern Europe, which describe the natives as scantily clad with long flowing hair, who use bows and clubs and inhabit the forests, had a specific meaning that became central to the conception of 'savagery'. This highly stereotyped representation of barbarians, people who lived in nature, who operated within natural law, separates the Other from the existence of redeemed European Christian humanity.[23] The sexual availability and abandon of native women was in contrast to the chastity and probity of the Christian way. The feline movements connect Pocahontas to the old associations. The wild woman was conceived to have a store of learning about the natural world, was skilled in herbs and potions, and conventionally conceived to have a familiar, a cat, for company, much in the fashion that Disney gives Pocahontas playful animal friends – the ones that have no voice to remind us all this is real history. In short, the wild woman of the Middle Ages was the origin of the concept of the witch, precisely the concept the Disney studio deployed in its first full-length cartoon, *Snow White*: 'Mirror, mirror on the wall, who is the fairest of them all?' The beautiful woman/old crone who tempts Snow White is the conventional representation of libidinous woman on the outside, who in reality is the gnarled old crone, the actuality of her unnatural evil within.

The bows and clubs of the natives were the implements of the Cyclops, the original Other in Greek mythology. Living in nature, as feral creatures who modelled themselves on animals in whose skins they clothed themselves, the natives were not possessors of 'dominium', real property rights in the land they inhabited, or as the early settlers of Virginia explicitly stated, they had no 'meum and teum' (mine and yours). They ranged through the natural world living on the fruits it offered, said the Virginia settlers. Such is the litany repeated in the words of Columbus and Vespucci, the famous 'they have no': private property, hierarchy, hereditary principles, religion, 'but all is common'. These negative descriptions had very precise meaning within the terms of European law and the self-interested rationalisation it gave to the colonising enterprise: those who had no property except in common could commonly have everything taken from them, justly according to the law. Disney has put the animality back into the native, the meaning of this necessary decision is just what it always was. The more Pocahontas is the child of nature, the better what she is and has can be taken from her and appropriated for its own uses by the dominant order.

Disney is not merely trying to be historically accurate by the prolific use of the term savage put into the mouths of the European characters portrayed in the film. The supposedly politically correct, improved, postmodern vision of the Native American invokes and relies on potent ideas that are so widespread within western culture that they can only be refashioned and refurbished, not overturned or dispensed with. Thus postmodernism is a continuation of the colonising mission, another totalising, absolutist frame of reference: when postmodernism speaks, even in its multicultural mode, what it says relies on all the old conventions. Thus, in its own terms and for its own purpose, it fills in the silence that remains, the Other.

Pocahontas ends with the Indians bringing offerings of corn to the settlers who will remain when John Smith leaves, the symbolic evocation of the traditions and understanding of Thanksgiving

Day (25 November). The Other remains, depicted as apologetic suppliants bidding for the good opinion of the dominant order: as Janet Siskind has convincingly argued, it is clear in the repository of the American mind that on Thanksgiving the Indian is the dead, trussed, cooked turkey offered up to ensure the survival of American family values.[24] Disney's new history does not need to continue, the rest is history as it has always been written, history whose very familiarity and ubiquity postmodernism depends upon to author its effects of seeming revision while effecting no change.

What Pocahontas is permitted to say of the Native American worldview is a postmodern convention, the shorthand for New Age ideas. She speaks of an animate universe, spiritually alive and interconnected. In the Powhatans' village there is an old wise man, not called a medicine man but embodying all the conventions of every representation of the Indian medicine man from every Western movie ever made. Sure enough he is the one given the line 'my old medicine does not work on these new injuries' as he shakes his rattle over a gunshot wound. This repository of spiritual learning and wisdom conjures information about the newly arrived Europeans in portents from the fire: the Europeans take visible shape in the smoke and then transmute into ravening wolves as the natives look on, mesmerised. This is the classic representation of the Werowance from the annals of the first settlers, a basic modern trope. To this Disney adds the fascination of native peoples for New Ageism. The spiritual power of native peoples, indigenous Others, is psychic power, an acuity to the irrational rationality that modernity drove out of the Western mind through its total dedication to scientific rationality. Of course, in modernist terms, the irrationality of routine recourse to psychic power was not deemed rational, it was the negative antithesis of scientific rationality: magic (cf: Evans Pritchard and Azande witchcraft which has become a seminal work in the postmodern debate) or in Levy Bruhl's term 'pre-logical'. In the postmodern vision, it is the psychic acuity that is the attraction of the Others, the property common to all that is to be and can be appropriated. It is the psychic spirituality, the being in touch with their inner premodern natural world that adds nobility to the Other and gives them the last laugh on the modern dispensation.

Innumerable films in recent years depict the whole panoply evoked in *Pocahontas*: everything from Chief Dan George in *Little Big Man*, who sees through dreams and visions and therefore knows what happens to Little Big Man when he is living in white society, to Russell Means in *Windwalker* as the reincarnated spirit of Olympic champion Jim Thorpe, who becomes the wise old Indian who mysteriously attaches himself to a young white boy to counsel and teach him through his difficult adolescence and then mystically departs from the world. A good example is Lou Diamond Phillips' unreconstructed character in *Avenging Lance*, in which the lance is a sacred object stolen from a museum, which must be tracked and retrieved by Phillips and his white sidekick played by Keifer Sutherland. The tracking takes in much visionary seeing and knowing, plus the 'magical' revenge of the lance itself, which eventually engulfs its thief in flames. As the sceptical character played by Sutherland incredulously asks: 'You don't believe all that Indian shit, do you?' To which Phillips responds, 'I am that shit.' Whereas the postmodern eclectic can make judicious selection of the useful and potent aspect of the Other insights and psychic spirituality, the Other has no alternative definition even of Self. Native American psychic spirituality can have beauty and inform, fill in some of the increasingly obvious gaps in postmodern perfection, but it could never have produced a washing machine. Native peoples are the last repository of the psychic/spirituality that has been forsaken in the progress of Western civilisation. New Age lifestyles need a model, they need to appropriate ecological learning that has been lost in the rise of modern science. Pocahontas is in the mainstream of the postmodern project of domination of the Other through appropriation of the eco-dream, and like all postmodern expressions of this process, it is the dominant society that interprets, reports, analyses, selects and determines what is the Other psychic/spirituality it is appropriating.

Even the appropriation of Other psychic/spirituality is not a departure from norms and convention of western civilisation. In large part, the selection from the religious perspectives of the

Other that dwell upon an animate universe and the interconnect-edness of man and nature answer the agenda of western romanti-cism. It is the pathetic fallacy of Wordsworth in a rather more exotic setting. At the beginning of the nineteenth century, in rejection of the totalitarian rationalism and violence of the Terror that began as the French Revolution, Romanticism was born. It spawned a whole convention of sympathy for nature to be found in the poetry of Wordsworth and Coleridge. It included the idealisation of the simple life of 'savages' and peasants, whose insight was comparable to that of innocent children. It is the positive pole of that old idea of the barbarian as natural child. Even children to the Victorians, who invented the concept of childhood, were unrefined, uncivilised, and hence more in touch with the intimations of the fallacy than adults could be. So conventional was this Romanticism that it is gently and subtly satirised in the novels of Jane Austen: every fashionable young lady should be painting a view of rocks and trees; while she accurately incorporates the fashion for visits to natural settings in the trip to Box Hill in *Emma*, Elizabeth Bennet's tour of the Pennines in *Pride and Prejudice* and the trip to Lyme Regis in *Persuasion.* Postmodern appropriations of the eco-dream of the Other is nothing more than the utilisation of Other systems of ideas to enable internal reform of the dominant, colonising convention. This is a function the Other has been performing since Thomas More wrote *Utopia* in 1516, in the form of a dialogue between More and Ralph Hythlodyus, a traveller who sailed to the New World on one of Vespucci's voyages. The travellers' tales he brings back of the idyllic life of the natives he encountered represent More's virulent denunciation of European corruption. The literary device of employing an invented report of native habits was to protect More from the charge of heresy, which his views would otherwise have attracted. By utilising the Other the west has been able to say the unsayable, think the unthinkable, and remodel its own internal conventions to taste. The only one who has no alternative is the Other.

But what voice did Disney's new history give to white America? The explicit purpose of Disney's new postmodern history is to wrest superpower America, the dominant culture of western civilisation, from the calumny of European origin. The artefact it uses for the ideological purpose is John Smith, and the elements it deploys, appropriately enough, were originated by none other than the historic John Smith himself.

There is an explicit dichotomy between the representation of John Smith and the representation of John Ratcliffe. Ratcliffe is the villain; he is also the man who wields the Union Flag and plants it on the soil of America where, of course, honest, God-fearing and liberty-loving republican Americans will not, in the not too distant future, permit it to remain. Ratcliffe's character is given all the unremitting expression of naked colonialism as greed and exploitation. He is the personification of the Virginia Company, which is implied to be a vehicle for his personal enrichment rather than a commonly shared objective. He diverts the colonists from building homes and planting crops, sending them on a mad, eco-destructive and futile search for gold. He is implacably hostile to the native people. He is the evil genius sending others forth to despoil this new land, hardly moving from the fort he has constructed on the seashore alongside his ship, his lifeline back to England. And the only reason Ratcliffe wants to be in the New World is to make his fortune and thus establish his position at the Court of St James, outshining even King James himself. He is the kind of rapacious, overbearing imperialist any colony that hopes to have a future could well do without. On cue, at the end of the film, he is wrestled to the ground by the salt-of-the-earth colonists to be sent off in disgrace, evoking another prefiguring of the American Revolution.

By way of complete contrast stands the representation of John Smith, the light to all of Ratcliffe's darkness, trim and fit in contrast to Ratcliffe's effete obesity (rather a falling off from political correctness these overtones of sizeism, but no doubt justifiable for the greater ideological good!). Smith is clearly weary of the Old World, though he can wax lyrical about its achievements, and has a jaded edge to his character. It is through the eyes and experience of John Smith that the wonder of this new world of America is revealed to the audience. It is John Smith who appreciates the true and enduring significance of the kind of life and society that can be built in America. It is John Smith who fearlessly sets off alone to explore the new land and falls in love with it before he ever meets its embodiment, Pocahontas. John Smith is not bound by ties to England and therefore can appreciate the new learning that must be undertaken to master this new land of America, and sufficiently open-minded to embrace, not merely the physical form of Pocahontas, but her challenge of relative pluralism – a dispensation of the dominant order.

So why does Disney work so hard to manufacture such a stark contrast between Ratcliffe and John Smith? The characterisations evoke and depend upon a specifically American hagiography of its own history, and in particular certain notions introduced into American thinking by John Smith himself. Smith, as we have noted, was a prolific writer about the project of colonialism and one of his most consistent themes was the need for artisans fitted for the task of building and servicing a new society to be sent out to the colonies. When he was the President of the Council of Jamestown, a post he held for a year before injury forced him to return to England, he was vitriolic about the unsuitability of gentlemen settlers for the job. These references have spawned a great tradition in America. On the one hand, there is the notion that Virginia, a southern state, derives from English gentlemen who were unwilling to roll up their sleeves: hence the ease with which the 'peculiar institution' – slavery – came to be adopted there. Information on the first slaves – or servants as they were euphemistically called at the time – comes, incidentally, in a letter written by John Rolfe. He says some 20 or so were bought 'at the best and easiest rate' from a Dutch ship that put into Jamestown in August 1619.[25] It was not just artisans who would be serviceable to the ends of colonialism, even in the mind of John Smith. In a book published in 1616, he drew a telling distinction between the 'poor savages' of Virginia and the 'black, brutish Negers of Africa'.[26] But what has passed most trenchantly into the self-image of Americans is John Smith's clarion call for honest artisans. What he argued for is summed up in the hagiography of the northern settlements, also under Letter Patent to the Virginia Company, which became the home of the Pilgrim Fathers of the 1620 Mayflower expedition. Here were ordinary people yearning to be free of the yoke of English intrusion, who set off to build a new society, a city on the hill, in a new land, by the sweat of their own brow, with courage, determination and beholden to none. The imagery of American history is that of pioneering and the frontier – the very images evoked in Disney's characterisation of John Smith. Everything about the historic John Smith that detracts from received ideas is jettisoned to support that imagery.

Disney's portrayal of Smith and Ratcliffe, their new history, must conform to American self-description and sensibility. America's self-consciousness is to see itself not as a repository of European heritage, but as a new distillation, a new civilisation arising out of the wreckage of the old decaying Europe. From the founding of the Republic, with its Declaration of Independence, the United States of America self-consciously sees its standards as universal, and its social and constitutional practice as the acme of the best universal principles. In his approach to the work of domination, through his relations with Pocahontas, as the object of her love and desire, as much as through the fearless courage by which he makes the Indians tractable and serviceable to the new colony, this is what John Smith symbolises and must be understood to symbolise in Disney's new history, the most important point of political correctness they must endorse. The subtext of the characterisation of Smith and Ratcliffe is the confirmation of the rightness of *Pax Americana*, because America is the desire of all peoples, not just the huddled masses yearning to be free.

Go West, Young Person

America is a consciously created artefact, as is its self-image. The manufacture of this self-image must be sustained through its cultural products to imprint itself on a heterogeneous population, to forge them into a coherent body by passing them through not just a social melting pot but an ideological forge. It is the ideology of American colonialism, the colonialism of the Pilgrim Fathers, the colonialism of the pioneer of the frontier that moves ever westward, as evoked by the characterisation of John Smith, that underpins the rationalisations and justification for the right of global dominance of *Pax Americana* today. It is worth noting that in representing John Smith as a loner, critical and rebellious towards old established authority, who easily forms relations with and acquires an understanding of the indigenous culture, who intervenes to protect the interests of 'loh the poor Indians'27 and the struggling settlers, Disney is invoking the essential lineaments of the hero of every classic western movie. John Smith's character is a compound of John Wayne, James Stewart and *Shane* and, as in many classic Westerns, at the finale he sails into the sunset, having made the settled land a better place: the place that will become America. The historical two-year span of the narrative need never concern itself with the details, for they are implied and evoked through representations, located in a familiar and inflexible context, which must be carried forward in new postmodern American history to confirm the continuity of what is America, the dominant culture of the globe.

So insistent is this dominance of the ideology of American history that not even historic American cultural products are immune from its overwriting. Thus, Michael Mann's *The Last of the Mohicans* is violently adjusted to conform to contemporary ideological needs. There are many ways in which Fenimore Cooper's seminal drama could have been adapted to contemporary sensibilities, for every strand of his story, first published in 1826, has become the stuff of stereotypes. The selection of those half-remembered but potent threads in the collective memory is therefore highly telling. The latest *Last of the Mohicans* (1992) is based on the 1936 screenplay rather than the book itself. The capable, responsible, individualist, liberty-loving frontier settlers who are betrayed, used and abused by the English, clearly form a better society marked by their inherent virtues for future greatness and world domination. This is the American frontier as self-aggrandisement. Holding the centre, as he must, is Natty Bumpo, as Cooper christened his protagonist. But it's a preposterous name, so Hawkeye and Nathaniel must suffice. Natty Bumpo/Hawkeye is the original literary instance of an idea whose time has now come. This character is the first of the appropriators, the white child raised with all the knowledge and skills of the Native American, who synthesises these strands into the unquestionable hero who is the spirit of America. Today he is the laconic, intense Daniel Day Lewis, whose stock in trade is the classic Western movie device of being short on words. Natty Bumpo in the pages of Cooper's five Leatherstocking tales is never to be found without at least three pages of dialogue at the height of any action sequence. Now brooding looks have to speak his volumes. Chingachgook, his adoptive father, and Unca, his adoptive brother, are, as they ever were, attendant players who substantiate the appropriation of the native world of the Other into the integrated persona of Hawkeye. Fitted with such appropriation, Hawkeye can become the moving spirit necessary to lead the settlers and enable them to fulfil their manifest destiny to subdue a new continent, forge a new society and supplant a failed European civilisation.

Michael Mann's retelling of the tale has all the clean lines of a dominant ideology of the dominant society, providing the historical background to the beneficence of *Pax Americana* of postmodern popular culture. The opening sequence, when Hawkeye, Chingachgook and Uncas hunt deer, suggests respect for their quarry, the eco-dream vision of existing in harmony with the natural world seamlessly sewn into the ideology of dominance. It would come as a considerable shock to Fenimore Copper who ceaselessly used Natty Bumpo as a critic of the depredations of settler society. Natty, in the novels, always comes to the aid of white society, is never sure that he approves of the new society and the life it is making in America. Old, alone and deeply saddened by what is happening around him, Natty goes to his grave in *The Prairie* (published in 1827) more redolent of the last of a vanishing breed.

In the film, when Hawkeye and his adoptive family visit their settler friends, Chingachgook and Uncas are welcomed participants in the simple meal, at ease as members of an inclusive society. So the dream of the melting pot society is prefigured in a scene which is such an historical improbability that its only purpose can be to eradicate the experience of the Other. If this was how things were at the dawn of the Great Society, then the contemporary concerns of Native Americans can have no legitimacy. The genocide visited on Native Americans must have been some unfortunate incident, not a deliberate working out of the policy and ideology of American society. The inclusion of the

Other in so many recent politically correct products of American dominance delivers the same message. In television series such as *The Young Riders*, with its token Indian and token free black, and the banal *Dr Quinn, Medicine Woman*, Others, all the minorities, are used as regular characters who move with the dominant society as on a par and beloved of all the lead characters. How can an unfailing and unending history of marginalisation, exclusion and oppression be comprehensible from such routine falsification? *Young Riders* is set in the years preceeding the American Civil War. Though the leading characters are divided in their loyalty between North and South, the only substantive issue they recognise is how to operate and realise the life, liberty and pursuit of happiness scenario. Wherever they originate, whichever side they support, the regular characters are uniformly and aggressively united on the anti-slavery issue. Slavery, racism and the extermination of the Indians are all dealt with, but their characterisation is a guest spot – a reality off centre. *The Young Riders* does not deny the existence of racism or slavery, but it draws all the sting from their historic meaning and the meaning of colonialism as an ongoing structure of dominance by its use of 'ethnics' as leading characters and the attitudes of its real heroes – who nevertheless are all WASPs, true scions of the dominant society.

Fenimore Cooper was a much more honest man. In the pages and pages of Hawkeye's musings are to be found his ample reflections on his 'red brothers' and their nature. Cooper's Natty was always true to the duality of the western perspective. His Indians came in two types: noble savages and savage barbarians, summed up in the characters of Chingachgook and Magua (*Le Renard Subtil* – the sly fox – as the character is more frequently termed, to underline a point that is never understated). The portrait Cooper adduces is the reflection of western ideology, the separate and distinctively different being of the native. The noble savage is and ever will be a 'savage' for the noble savage is the barbarian as natural child with childlike innocence, and therefore capable of a better rapport with the natural world, but without the innately superior understanding and creative ability of the dominant Christian civilisation. And, like all children, when they are bad they are not very, very bad, they are horrid, indeed horrific, as is the deceitful, innately untrustworthy, blood-seeking, barbarically cruel Magua, an embodiment of incarnate, demonic evil. Even good Cooper Indians always stand at a remove from white society: they are never invited into the parlour to take tea or break bread, and it would be against their nature to allow themselves so to transgress the rules. As they stand over the grave of Uncas at the end of the novel *The Last of the Mohicans*, Hawkeye vows that Chingachgook will never be alone. But Cooper was honest enough to incorporate into *The Pioneers* the vignette of Chingachgook as a whisky-swilling Christianised Indian abandoned to his fate by Natty Bumpo, who in his later career encounters virtually only bad Indians, who by their nature justify their destruction.

The explicit superstructure of the concept of the Other in Cooper's writing enabled him to include a plot device that is far too rich for Mann's film. Cooper amply suggests a love affair between Uncas and Cora Munroe, prompting Uncas' brave and doomed attempt to save her from the clutches of the dastardly Mingoes. This is not quite the 'liberal' conception it would appear. A true son of his times, Cooper makes it clear that Cora, though the daughter of Colonel Munroe, the army commandant of Fort William Henry and an English gentleman, is the product of a shameful early alliance contracted in the West Indies with a lady of dubious and definitely tainted racial ancestry. Cora is not just the brunette, the woman with character flaws and a past as opposed to the blond innocent who is the true heroine, she has a distinct touch of the tarbrush running through her veins as well. So Cooper frees himself to suggest a love affair across the lines between the English lady of resolute, sturdy strength and the noble, brave, young 'savage' while not risking frightening and outraging his readers. Of course, both characters are marked from the outset of this plot device as 'incipient stiffs' – those who must die before the story is over in a convention that has unerringly survived the entire history of the Western. Yet, Cooper goes a lot further than his postmodern successors dare to imagine – and this is the most telling script selection of all. In the film version of *Last of the Mohicans*, Cora Munroe loses her tainted blood and becomes the love-interest of Hawkeye. Cora survives to the end of the picture, she is one Hawkeye will never leave, while blonde Alice plunges to her death with Uncas, who is permitted only one lingering glance at Alice which bears no moment of interpretation unless one has read the book and is looking for some indistinct hint of verisimilitude in the movie. Not only is politically correct postmodernism shy about dealing with love across the ethnic and racial divide – in *Dances with Wolves*, Lieutenant Dunbar pairs off with a *white* captive of the Lakota – but to leave Hawkeye as Cooper wrote him would go far too far towards implying a 'gay' hero. Natty Bumpo/Hawkeye for all his benign comments on the 'fair sex' never so much as thinks about them as women, let alone approaches one in a heterosexually companionable way. 'Anything goes' may be the dictum of postmodernism, but in the cinema the guy's still gotta have a girl, and if you are going to cast an ethnic as hero then you definitely have to write the love-interest variant out of the script, as befell Denzel Washington in *Pelican Brief* and Wesley Snipes in *Murder at 1600*. Just as in *Pocahontas*: the appropriation and consumption of the Other must be made serviceable to the dominant tradition of the feel good factor.

All is America, America is all!

It is, however, impossible to 'feel good' about the dominant power in the global popular culture from the perspective of the Other: it is a totalitarian imposition that can only be resisted. Through its stranglehold on the production of popular culture and information sources, the American postmodern revolution has acquired the most truncated lens with which to gaze upon the whole of human history. Much of history and literature are now palatable only when they conform to the interests and sensibilities of the American marketplace. Thus every telling of any tale must incorporate the journey of the manifest destiny of *Pax Americana* to dominate the globe with all that that implies about vindicating the marginalisation of all Others. Similarly, all tales must be reset within the confines of America, as the only tenable space where stories can be told. To set a story or locate events or characters outside America is to risk losing market share by overtaxing the historical interest, knowledge or awareness of the prime audience, ticket-buying Americans. Since postmodern ideology through its representation of the Other in the land of the melting pot enables America to claim itself as the literal embodiment of everywhere, the universal standard of applicability, it becomes the only place that is represented. So a classic English children's story, *The Little Princess*, becomes the most bizarre of cinematic representations. Francis Hodgson Burnett's novel concerns a daughter of the Raj, Sarah, who is sent to boarding school by her single parent, soldier father. This is far too complicated for the film, so new plot justifications must be interpolated: Sarah is sent to school because her father is summoned to serve in the First World War. A curious choice because the novel was written and published before that conflagration took place. For reasons that strain the logic of the narrative beyond the endurance of anyone except a total illiterate, the school is relocated in New York. Sarah was supposedly raised in India, which one still resolutely maintains was a work of British imperialism, but in the film nevertheless speaks with a pronounced American accent and the kind of idiom that Hodgson Burnett could never have written on pain of all the tortures of hell. To keep from crying the Little Princess tells stories with magical properties, entrancing her schoolmates with the narrative of Rama and Sita and their conflict with the evil Ravana. The movie gives these interludes the correct visualisation – courtesy of the *Little Buddha* handbook of how it should look. So colonialism of India, here appropriated to America, appropriates Indian culture to itself: bigger fleas having littler fleas to bite them. But does the American setting allow the novel to be understood? Essential to the fairytale narrative is the presence of a gentleman next door with an Indian servant. In the novel, the Indian servant befriends Sarah and makes it possible for the sad, lonely old man with a guilty secret to become the Fairy Godfather who transforms the misery of the Little Princess's life to provide a happy ending. In the movie the old man retains his Indian servant but loses his guilty secret: he is sad and lonely because his son goes off to war. We open with the film dating itself precisely: 1914. Yet no sooner has the Little Princess arrived in New York than the old gentleman next door is sobbing, bidding his son farewell. The son is dressed in a British uniform, yet the old gentleman is clearly an American. But all this is played as normal, a plot device that serves to generalise the sense of the isolation that has befallen Sarah, the little Princess. In 1914, America was at the height of its isolationist policy, and had no intention of becoming implicated in a European fiasco, the indisputable proof of the decay of the Old World. Such a scene on a New York street would have dumbfounded everyone in the crowd that hustles past. Without the need for explication, the British Raj and its colonisation of India and the entire history of the First World War are appropriated to American history because all stories and histories now belong to the dominant culture and can only be told through the perspective of American experience. America rules, and its rapacious will to consume determines what will be told and how it will be told.

The explicit moral of Frances Hodgson Burnett's fairytale is a denunciation of capitalist hierarchy and the materialist values it breeds, most especially its insensitivity to poverty. Burnett herself had gone from comfortable circumstances to ungenteel poverty, the transition she gives to Sarah. What Sarah learns is how to be nobly poor, sharing the little she has with others worse off than herself. But most of all she learns to recognise how offensive affluence is in the eyes of the poor, how thoughtless and uncaring are the nice affluent people who have no awareness of the poor they make serviceable to their needs, how interconnected and interdependent is the system of dominance that keeps the poor poor. In effect, though written and first published in America, Burnett's fairytale is a typical Victorian socialist tract, a powerful morality tale from a working-class point of view. Sarah is sent into the child labouring working class to become humane, refined, a newly civilised person who retains these essential lessons to apply to the good fortune that befalls her at the end of the book. No wonder the film has to give the fairytale such a radical revisionist setting. Far better to consume history than permit such un-postmodern conventions any room at all.

The history that is being told in a plethora of computer games and 'edutainment' products continues both to cleanse colonialism of blood and further postmodern absorption of the Other. CD-ROMs and video games are not just the locus of consumer culture at play, they are also the repository of information about the past, present and future of the Other. Quite apart from the fact that cyberspace itself is being 'colonised' on the lines of the American 'frontier' as though it were new 'virgin territory' in a newly discovered 'New World',[28] computer games like *Big Red Adventure, Merchant Colony* and *Death Gate* are poorly disguised re-runs of the great European 'voyages of discovery'. Nintendo's *Super Mario Brothers*, as Mary Fuller and Henry Jenkins note, is essentially the 'cognate version' of the mythical narrative of Pocahontas and John Smith (with Princess Toadstool representing Pocahontas and Mario and Luigi standing for John Smith).[29] 'The tradition of civilization continues' with *Colonisation*, which presents the postmodern players with 'colonies' complete with friendly natives and challenges them to recolonise them all over again and 'create a new nation'.[30] Thus the imagery of computer games is ruled by the implicit stereotypes of colonial domination.

Edutainment CD-ROMs that combine information with entertainment, and serve as potent educational tools, also serve as the perfect counterpart to the ideology of *Pocahontas*: everything now belongs to a world dominated by America and America is the apogee of all human civilisations and experience, the only perspective through which history is meaningful, which all of history explains. CD-ROM encyclopedias and multimedia packages like *Microsoft Bookshelf, Microsoft Encarta*, the *Compton Interactive Encyclopedia* and *The Story of Civilization* by Will and Ariel Durant not only repackage the old paradigm of history as linear progress from the bush to the white man, but also add a new twist. *Microsoft Bookshelf*, for example, presents the rest of the world – including much of Europe – as an unnecessary and awkward appendage to American civilisation.[31] *Bookshelf* is one of the most popular and readily available information CD-ROMs now being sold, and is used throughout the world. The Encyclopaedia and Almanac that come as part of the package are dominated by reference to American history, society, literary and cultural products; the rest of human history, culture and civilisation is presented as secondary and subsidiary, and reduced to thumbnail sketches. The torch of civilisation starts in Europe and is passed westwards to America. As we move through time in the year lists of the Almanac towards the present, the significant events are more and more those that led inevitably to the establishment of the United States. Potent and blatant ideology is thus presented as history and information.

History is the explicit subject of Dorling Kindersley's CD-ROM *History of the World*, which offers 'in depth coverage of world history'.[32] Its contents are replete with all the requisite post-modern sensibilities: political correctness, feminism, concern for and representation of the Other. But this distillation of the whole of human existence offers exactly the same ideological voyage as *Pocahontas*. While Other cultures are represented we see them exclusively from western perspective: comments, reconstructions and images are derived from western travellers' tales. For example, the selection in the years 1700–1825 for Asia and Australia has two topics: the South Seas and the settling of Australia. Both selections deal with the region only as caught in the gaze of the west. The South Seas includes a subsidiary section on Fijian dancers, which turns out to be a selection of illustrations and a quote from the work of an unnamed 'British adventurer' of the 1870s. The selected description of a ceremonial Fijian dance concerns how the glowing bodies of 'fantastically feathered' warriors carrying clubs performed their dance in perfect time, making a 'picturesque' scene. There is, however, the inevitable inclusion of the reflex of guilty conscience: 'Sadly they [the Europeans] brought deadly diseases and interfered with the customs of the native Polynesians.' Thus the contemporary reality of Polynesian society is eradicated for the future: it is truncated by the two prongs of the vanishing syndrome that is ingrained in the western imagination. First, there is the familiar trope of disease, whose corollary is the clearing of the country. In America the white settlers, the scions of John Smith, regarded this genuine holocaust as a providential blessing, a proof of God's favour. It was the fate of the native to dwindle, to vanish either absolutely through dying, or to become dependent, supplanted by the stronger and innately superior Europeans. A second and related point is that native society lacks authenticity today, even as Other, because disease and the crucial, 'adulterated' customs of the native make today's representatives of Polynesians bastardised in a

cultural sense, less real than their ancestors, who were genuine
Other. The representatives of the Other in contemporary times are
synthetic products of a past that has been tampered with. What
has been done is done. If such people are not wholly vanished by
the great dying, then they are vanishing, have become shadows of
their authentic identity, because their customs have been altered
in a process that is assumed implicitly to be irreversible and total.
Caught only in their connection to the overwriting of dominance,
no true, discrete authenticity can be claimed by the descendants of
the process of contact with Western dominance. They no longer
have access to the customs, traditions, history and experience that
are real Polynesia, which exists only in the description given by
the travellers of early contact. Or, in other words, only the west
knows truthfully what the Other once was and is the source from
which everyone, including contemporary Others, must learn of
that past.

History of the World does mention that the Aborigines arrived in
Australia some 40,000 years ago, but then moves on swiftly to deal
exclusively with white arrival and settlement. Naturally, there is a
subsection on the voyages of Captain Cook. However, here
compression of detail allows the claiming of the continent, with a
highlighted picture of Cook with Union Jack in hand, to be
included but neglects the most salient detail of the event. Despite
explicit instructions to the contrary, Cook claimed the continent
for Britain without making any treaty with the native inhabitants
– the only instance in colonial history where even fictive
recognition was not given to the existence of the original people of
the land. Australian Aborigines acquired redress of this most
notorious violation of their rightful existence as people only in
1996, and it does little to alter the status of today's Aborigines
within Australia. Genuine inclusion of Other perspectives would
require reference to the assumption of an innate right to rule,
expropriate and appropriate and to be the only author of history.
Captain Cook described the Aborigines as feral inhabitants of the
land, a civilisation too poor to be deemed competent to negotiate a
treaty for the expropriation of their land. Cook's action, despite
being contrary to instruction, was accepted and became the basis
of British possession. Thus Australia is the clearest case of the

application of the framework of colonialism. The selective ideol-ogy of postmodern representation of the Other has a different agenda: one that does not author change through salient informa-tion, but continues the conventions of received history while simulating caring, fair and plural representations. First, European contact with the Other, with all its inherent distortions, is perpetuated into the future as the authentic and only voice on any topic under the sun. The Other has a history which is summed up in the old convention of 'tradition' as unaltering, inflexible imposition and retold as history through the ideological strictures of western perceptions. In short, the Other is here caught in all the patronising condescension the west on its best behaviour can summon up.

As one moves through the historical timeframes, geographic regions and categories of *History of the World*, the dominance of the United States becomes evident as the message and meaning of history. Of the gallery of historical biographies that can be selected through the programme's Who's Who, one gets a most bizarre balance of names to conjure with. These are names, not history, since each character gets the same amount of space and therefore precious little context in which to measure their relevance in terms of their impact on human history. As postmod-ernism dictates, representation is given to all; but it is ideology that dominates the selection, not objective historical conscious-ness. Thus, women fare extremely well, though one wonders why Lucrezia Borgia or even Boudicca and Zenobia are chosen in a list that includes just 78 people to represent the whole of human history and placed in the company of Jesus Christ, Buddha and Prophet Muhammad. The reason is ideological: they represent fighting, ruling, strong and determined women from the ranks of the west and the Other, as does the Dowager Empress of China, Tz'u-shi. Therefore it is obvious that Susan B. Anthony, the American feminist, and Harriet B. Tubman, the African-Ameri-can activist, will also be included. The proportion of the women is neatly matched by the proportion given to the Other: 24 and 25 out of 78, respectively. The selection from among the Others mirrors that of women. Those selected are strong, resilient characters, though this can cut both ways: there is Timur and

Attila the Hun; and there are Akhenaton, Atahuallpa and Montezuma along with the Native American Tecumseh and Shaka Zulu. Akhenaton is the most aberrant figure in all the millennia of Ancient Egyptian History, notable for his failure to convert Pharaonic society to the monotheistic worship of Ra, the sungod, as opposed to the pantheistic worship of a whole panoply of gods. The only other name from Ancient Egypt is Hastphshut, included because she is a woman, but of whose life we know virtually nothing except for the resplendent temple built at the entrance to the Valley of Kings near Luxor. This is historical significance dictated by tourist guides. Boudicca, Zenobia, Tecumseh, Shaka, along with Haile Salasse, Atahuallpa and Montezuma are all notable for the fact that their opposition to colonialism failed, nobly but inevitably. While their inclusion represents the Other, it also underwrites the inflexible ideological moral of the history that is being presented: dominance of the west is the innate pattern of all history as a conveyor belt which inexorably passes the mantle ever westward until it comes to rest in the United States. The ideology of defeated resistance can call forth strange bedfellows. In Africa, South Africa is represented through the Boer experience which dwells on the Great Trek, the exact parallel of the American frontier motif of the prairie schooners that moved the frontier ever westward. This parallel experience on another continent includes the defeat of the overwhelmed natives, who had no answer to western weaponry, at Blood River. South Africa occurs only fleetingly afterwards so that the role of the Boer society in the construction and maintaining of Apartheid is consciously erased from this history.

The 'modern history' presented in the *History of the World* is the proof of the ideological design on the selective history of all the world presented on the CD-ROM as a contemporary educational resource. Since the conclusion of the second world war, the whole world is viewed through the Cold War perspective of the ideological battle between American democracy and its benighted Communist opponent, whose failure is amply detailed. To follow Asia through the divisions of nineteenth- and twentieth-century history is to see the vision of the world required by the American perspective. Japan, for example, features through the arrival of the

American Captain Perry, who forced its opening to the world and provided the impetus for the Meiji reform, the overthrowing of the unpopular Shogunate and the adaptation of western standards and technology by Japan. The only other mention of Japan in modern times is as the opponent in the Pacific in the Second World War. The war itself is described as the cause of the eventual independence of all the countries of southeast Asia from European rule (the natives, of course, played no part in gaining their own independence!). There is a fleeting mention that the Philippines had been ruled by the United States and acquired independence in 1947. So Asia in the modern world is described through the Vietnam War and Maoist China. In China we learn that once popular Maoism became communist oppression under the Great Leap Forward and Cultural Revolution. But after the death of Mao, Communist leaders in China 'looked for ideas and money from the United States, Japan and others', having decided it was permissible 'for people to buy goods and improve the quality of their life through private enterprise'. The Vietnam War is relevant because 58,000 Americans died there between 1961 and 1973 and it spawned an anti-war protest movement in the United States; the representations of the war focus on the American experience, whose presence is explained solely by the need to oppose Communism.

The 'eyewitness' account of world history amply provides silence, the silence of the Other, through its perpetuation of the ideology of dominance as the postmodern, simulated pluralistic representation of everything. The ideological selection and concise statements of the whole of the world's history re-establishes all the stereotypes of the Other as the only ongoing concern on the face of the globe. Thus oil and Islam brings all the previous racist references to Muslim society into the most pernicious of stereotypical statements. Even the basic entry on Islam contains the most blatant errors: Caliph Ali, for example, is said *not* to have been elected a Caliph – which will come as a great shock to over a billion Muslims. According to the over-simplified *History of the World*, it is the failure of Ali to be elected Caliph that explains the origin of Shi'ism, Shi'a being the party of Ali, from which arises the militant Shi'ite Islam in fundamentalist Iran. In fact, Shi'ism

originates in the acceptance of Ali as the proper successor of the
Prophet Muhammad, and the belief that he therefore is the most
authoritative of the Rightly Guided Caliphs and who should have
been the first, not the fourth Caliph. Shi'a as much as Sunni
Muslims accept all four Caliphs. Contemporary Islam has nothing
to offer, if the *History of the World* is to be believed, except oil,
fundamentalism and terrorism.

Postmodern 'infotainment' and 'edutainment', as well as postmodern cinema, reaffirm the context of dominance and its
ideology, both explicitly and implicitly, when it claims to give
voice to the Other as much as when it speaks of the Other.
Children reared on this standard fare, which places today's
unrealised idealism as the true mainstream of their history, can
have no empathy for the struggle, history and contemporary
concerns of the Other. John Smith said of Virginia that it was a
'tabernacle of miracles, a wonder of the world'.[33] Now this
tabernacle of miracles is demonstrating that the project of
colonialism has finally succeeded in its first and only aim. It rules
not only the globe, but the future by its control and selective
manipulation of all that is human history. The rest had best be
forgotten, there is no alternative and there is no other future.

4. Recycling Shampoo

A helicopter flies over the Amazon jungle. It hovers over a sparse patch of land, which turns out to be a village. A ladder is thrown out, and someone descends, swinging like Tarzan, from the helicopter. A close-up reveals the person to be Anita Roddick, founder of *The Body Shop*, bearing gifts for the women of the village. She embraces and hugs them as though they were long-lost friends.

This is a scene from a comic that I was given when I bought a copy of *The Body Shop Book* and *Mamatoto: A Celebration of Birth* which is written by 'The Body Shop Team'. In her Foreword to *The Body Shop Book*, Roddick writes:

> the idea of *The Body Shop* is not new. In India and the Arab world for centuries perfume has been decanted and sold in the amounts the customers wanted ... the ideas for the products were based on my experiences travelling around the world. I saw raw ingredients being used, as they have been for centuries, to polish the skin, to cleanse the hair and to protect both. They worked, without hype, without claims and without millions spent on advertising.[1]

Later, we read:

> It is essential for us to pursue new discoveries and unearth the knowledge of the past which has been lost by our modern technological society. Constant travel enables us to learn from the cultural traditions handed down from generation to generation among different peoples of the world. When she was travelling in Mexico, for example, Anita Roddick observed that aloe plants were kept in the home; if

there was an accident in which someone was burnt, an aloe leaf was broken off and its gel applied directly to the wound. In less sophisticated societies than our own, raw ingredients are still used automatically in the treatment of skin and hair problems.[2]

Imagine the opposite scenario. An indigenous businesswoman, say from Brazil, comes to Britain to learn about new discoveries in skin and hair care preparations. Comes? Well, let us assume that she can get a visa and enters Britain without harassment by the immigration authorities. She goes to a famous manufacturer of skin care products and inquires about the secrets of their preparation. She wants to set up her own business using their methods and raw materials, she says. What would she be told? How would she be treated? She would soon discover that western knowledge is not freely available. She will have to pay patent and licensing fees and even then she won't get the 'secrets'; she will only get the finished product or a few ready-made chemicals to mix on site back home. But her own knowledge, the product of centuries of experimentation and experience, is there for anyone to grab and sell.

The Body Shop is an archetypal postmodern institution. It does not have to hype itself, for its image thrives on the longing for the exotic and ethnic Other that is ever-present in western society; it deliberately conflates business expediency with moral endeavour; it appropriates the knowledge and the products of non-western cultures (it is estimated that the ingredients acquired by the company under fair trade conditions account for less then 1 per cent of its sales);[3] it commodifies and repackages them; and in a genuine twist of postmodern irony, it sells what was always theirs to the non-west in smart green bottles with shiny labels. Non-western cultures may constitute 'less sophisticated societies than our own', but their knowledge, ideas, history, experiences and products have acquired much greater currency in postmodern times than ever before. During the colonial period and under modernity, everything non-western and indigenous to traditional cultures was reviled and shunned; in postmodernism, concern for Other cultures has revived, and they are now appropriated, repackaged and marketed in the name of plurality and multiculturalism. *The Body Shop* has simply transformed the products and experiences of Other cultures into a marketing ideology: Roddick's claim that her business is inspired by Mahatama Gandhi, Martin Luther King and African tribal chiefs completes the process of appropriation.

When the appropriated ideas, experiences or products are exported back to the Third World, they lose their innocence, context, significance and meaning. When *Body Shop* products arrive in a non-western country, they are no more 'natural' than any other processed commodity. They have the cachet of a western product and are consumed by the natives as such: the inferiority of the indigenous cultures is therefore reinforced and the myth that a traditional product becomes worthy of consumption by the locals only when it is refined by the west is further entrenched. Often the re-exported item comes back in a totally perverted form. Consider, for example, massage therapy, which has been used in the non-west for thousands of years. Mothers regularly massage their babies, little children climb on the backs of their grandparents every evening to give them a walk-on massage, it is a commonly used remedy for muscular pain, arthritis, backache and other ailments. The Chinese therapy of reflexology, an ancient body of theory and practice, involves vigorous massage of the feet to cure a host of physical illnesses and promote general well-being. During pregnancy and childbirth, as *Mamatoto* explains,

> Malaysian mothers like to have their navels massaged with coconut oil – they say it helps the baby to descend. Japanese women like to have their muscles massaged during a difficult labour, for they believe that leg muscles are linked to muscles in the vagina and pelvic floor. If your leg muscles are relaxed, then your vaginal muscles will relax too and birth will be easier. Another Japanese remedy for labour pains is to press on the side of the woman's little toe on each foot, at a shiatsu pressure point on the inside of her ankles, and on her sacrum. The traditional Jamaican midwife has a whole repertoire of massages for different stages of birth. At the beginning, she massages the labouring woman's abdomen with the slimy part of toona leaves to make sure the baby gets into the right position; to help the contraction along she wraps the abdomen in hot towels and then rubs the woman's whole body lightly with olive oil; and

to ease the intense pains that come before pushing starts, she pats her belly with a warm, damp rag. Mayan women have their abdomens massaged by the midwife, who puts two fingers under the uterus and pulls it up towards her ...[4]

However, once the notion of massage was appropriated by the west, it lost all its innocence and therapeutic connotations. In Europe and North America, massage came to signify something totally different: it became something you did with a 'model' in a massage parlour. Thus a medical practice of the non-west is seized, infused with the orientalised images of non-western sexuality, and re-exported as a euphemism for prostitution. Today, it is almost impossible to have a therapeutic massage in southeast Asia: 'traditional' massage in 'modern' massage parlours is now regularly administered to postmodern voyeurs and tourists. Even in prim Singapore the ceaseless throughput of tourists at moderately priced hotels will be bombarded by business cards slipped under their door offering massage in much the same terms as 'French lessons' are advertised in a London newsagent's window, and meaning exactly the same thing. The sensuality of non-western cultures, such as Thailand's, is thus commodified and whole cities are transformed into markets for sex.

Postmodernism thus turns established practices in non-western societies into commodities – often causing frictions and fissures where none existed before. Consider homosexuality which, for some non-western cultures, has never been a 'problem'. Indeed, many Other cultures, like the Pathans on the north-western frontier in Pakistan, the Malays, the Thais, and many tribal cultures in Iraq and Iran, are renowned for their open acceptance of homosexuality. In certain cultures homosexuals play an important social role: in India and Pakistan, for example, homosexuals and transsexuals (*hijras*) have a virtual monopoly in providing entertainment at weddings and other social celebrations – they have the privilege of freely moving amongst the women. It was this tolerance and acceptance of homosexuality that made the 'Orient' such a haven for colonial European travellers and adventurers who were motivated to visit the 'east', amongst other reasons, by their desire for sexual gratification. Sir Richard Burton, T. E. Lawrence, André Gide and Isabelle Eberhardt provide us with accounts of the sexual 'liberation' they discovered in the east. Even in modern times, the Maghreb has attracted angst-ridden western males: Paul Bowles, William Borroughs and a host of 1960s pop stars found a sexual liberation in Morocco they were denied back home. All that seemed to change in the 1970s and 1980s: homosexuality became a 'lifestyle' which, like any other western 'style' could be exported to the third world. Culturally reconstructed postmodern homosexuality and lesbianism owe little to the Greeks or Romans – as Foucault has pointed out neither of these civilisations had a word for it. Most men in classical Greece loved young men, but they also loved their wives. And they certainly had no notion of homosexuality as a lifestyle, let alone as a fashionable accessory. When postmodern notions of homosexuality are exported to non-western cultures as a commodity, a lifestyle or a chic fashion, often by pop groups such as 'Fem to Fem', or in advertising, as in the campaign for Calvin Klein perfume 'CK One' (which shows nine carefully designed street kids without any primary or secondary sexual characteristics: flats chests, no bodily hair, no genital bumps, faces that could happily sit on a male or female), it is seen for what it is: an arrogant imposition, a cynical exercise in marketing, an extension of western cultural imposition. In the backlash, bonds of toleration and acceptance that can be traced back over centuries are broken and a minority that was never seen as a problem suddenly acquires the gloss of imperialism. History evaporates; bigotry becomes operational.

Eaten Any Human Flesh, Lately?

Postmodernism is not content to appropriate the ideas, experiences and products of the non-west. It also wants to take the history of non-western cultures away from them; or more appropriately, it desires to cleanse it of blood, repackage it in multicoloured wrappers and sell it back to the third world. The last decade has seen the emergence of a number of global clothing

128 POSTMODERNISM AND THE OTHER

stores whose main selling point is the glorification of colonialism. *The East India Company* and *British India* chain stores, for example, represent British and Dutch imperial history as a glorious phase in world history. The English and Dutch East India Companies went to India and Indonesia, respectively, to discover new markets, to bring these countries under the sovereignty of their respective crowns, enslave their cultures with the aid of advanced military technology and turn these countries into goldmines for the homeland. But *British India* stores present colonialism as a joyful experience. The interior of the shops is tastefully decorated with colonial artefacts – nineteenth-century luggage, bowler hats, old rifles – while the walls are adorned with colonial photographs showing white men, and sometimes white women, being waited on by the Indians and Malays, going hunting and engaging in other chores of imperialism. *The East India Company* thoughtfully supplies a tag with every garment which describes the company's history:

> The East India Company was founded in 1600 by a group of English merchants. Their ships voyaged to and fro the new trade route around the Cape of Good Hope and across the Indian Ocean, forming a life-line between the small, isolated British outposts and the mother country. The merchants traded spices, gems and precious stones. Their lifestyles, marked by adventure, inspired the creation of utilitarian garments especially suited to the sweltering tropics. They are made of one hundred percent finely woven cotton and are tailored for comfort and durability.[5]

What the 'adventures' of these 'merchants' amounted to we are not told. Nor are we told anything about the natives these merchants encountered – the very natives that both companies are selling to.

While *The East India Company* and *British India* operate predominantly in Asia, *Banana Republic Travel and Safari Clothing Company*, owned by the clothing retail corporation 'The Gap', sells exclusively in the United States. *Banana Republic* was established in 1983, has some 50 branches, and in addition to department stores, it also functions as a mail order business. Here too colonial history is pumped with a heavy dose of anaesthesia and recycled as a cause for celebration. In the company's catalogue, postmodern irony and historic nostalgia are combined to produce an image of the third world, in the words of Paul Smith as 'a kind of benign theme park for adults, as well as a place redolent of a certain kind of purity'.[6] All economically disadvantaged third world countries are comically described as 'banana republics' in which the Company executives 'visit vanishing cultures ... to celebrate their uniqueness and discourage them from slipping into global homogeneity'. One of the catalogues proclaims that 'in Africa the dawn of the twenty-first century casts its shadow on the dawn of man. On this continent there's no mistaking it: You know where you come from.' Such announcements are accompanied, writes Smith,

> by quotations from the travel writings of men such as Sir Richard Burton, Henry Stanley, and Theodore Roosevelt. These in turn are juxtaposed with the writings (very often 'reports' on a particular item of clothing) of contemporaries like the photographer Carol Beckwith, Wildlife biologist Mark Owen, a self-described glacier and bush pilot, and contemporary writers as various as Gerry Trudeau, Lawrence Ferlinghetti, Cyra McFadden, and Roy Blount Jr. In most of the season catalogs this peculiar admixture of the historical and the contemporary, along with fairly unabashed reference to current affairs or historical event (such as Watergate, Lord Kitchener's subjection of the Sudan, or – in a piece of copy designed to sell 'paratrooper briefcases' – the Israeli raid on Entebbe), is accompanied by some thematic motif ... [such as] a discourse on Africa ('we've opened the pages of this issue to many voices from Africa', few of which turn out to be 'native') ...[7]

Whatever its impact on the Other, in the case of the *Banana Republic* on the blacks in America, the descendants of the African slaves, the object of the exercise is to make the (white) postmodernist consumer feel at home all over the world: wherever you are, you will always be cool, chic, confident and never short of pockets. This discourse also gives the white postmodern consumer in the North, which has lost all sense of history, a sense of tradition. But the narrative does not end here: it also aims to make the consumer feel at home with the injustices of history and legitimise the injustices of the present. As Smith notes:

> By adopting its own 'brand' of postmodernist discourse, *Banana Republic* has re-placed or reconstructed a whole history and its discourses – the history of colonialism – and re-represented the current phase of domination in such a way that those discourses cannot properly be called mystification. Rather, they are de facto the active, effective, and the real truths of contemporary American culture and need to be treated as such.[8]

Such representation of history is much more than simply insulting to non-western cultures. It has deep and profound consequences.

In Other cultures, history and tradition are the prime source of meaning and identity. History and tradition provide non-western worlds with their modes of knowing, being and doing. History, to use the words of Ashis Nandy, is a 'means of reaffirming or altering the present'.[9] The fractures in the present are amended with reference to the past and the present is constantly remade to yield a new past. Such a view of the past gives an authority to history, but the 'nature of authority is seen as shifting, amorphous and amenable to intervention'. History therefore has a constant presence in traditional cultures not least by its periodic re-enactment. The ever-present historical memory provides a source of cultural identity, social cohesion, a sense of permanence amid change and a means of rejuvenating the present and shaping the future.

In contrast, postmodernism is concerned solely with the present, the immediate and, in rejecting Enlightenment metanarratives, abandons all sense of historical continuity and memory. Just as Rorty makes the philosopher redundant, Foucault reduces the role of the historian to an archaeologist of the past. But postmodernism does more than simply abandon a sense of historical continuity in values and beliefs; it conceives itself as a struggle against history, as a site where the final battles against history will be settled. Postmodernism thus seeks to represent the very form and substance of historical reality. The tendency of postmodernism to rewrite history, to drain it of invested (non-secular) meaning, to appropriate it for secular and consumer culture, has two specific purposes. On the one hand, it neutralises the identity of the Other by subsuming all non-western identities and histories in the grand western narrative of secularism; and, on the other hand, by inflating the history of secularism as *the* history, the yardstick of reality, leads to the collapse of all histories into the postmodern spectacle. Thus, postmodernism is ushering in an era of inflated, manufactured truth which reasserts the claims to power of the Author, the Producer. In as much as any history has any role in postmodernism, it is as the history of victors who are now rightly claiming the spoils. *Banana Republic*, *The East India Company*, *British India* and *The Body Shop* – what are they saying to non-western cultures: 'This is as good as it gets for you, boyo!' Consume and be consumed.

Postmodernism, then, reconstructs history, represents it as the real truth of contemporary reality, to absorb the identity of the Other in its own discourse. A feature of *Banana Republic* catalogues is its multivocalism; it gives representation to 'Other voices', but only, as in postmodern fiction, on its own terms. The Other is not allowed the use of its own categories and concepts, partly because they have been suppressed (in colonialism and modernity), partly because they been rendered meaningless (in postmodernism) and partly because they would be quite incomprehensible to its audience. The new genre of postmodern advertising, pioneered by *Benetton*, illustrates how ahistorical representation of the Other can combine colonialist notions with contemporary oppression to yield images of the Other that take us back to the days of the cannibal savages. The notorious *Benetton* campaign, which at any given moment covers billboards in over 100,000 streets around the world, takes Marshall McLuhan's famous adage 'the medium is the message' to a new dimension: 'image is all'. The object of advertising now is not merely to create dreams and desires, but to engender a new commodified reality shaped by a company's logo or slogan. Gone are the days when advertisements actually named, and showed, the products being promoted: 'Murray mints, Murray mints, too good to hurry mints.' Nowadays, it is sometimes even difficult to discern what is being advertised and by whom. The *Benson and Hedges* ads which use gold to convey a subliminal message or the *Silk Cut* ads that play on torn purple fabrics, are pure postmodern concept designs. The *Benetton* campaign consists of bold photographs: a white woman and a black woman holding an oriental baby wrapped in a towel; the breasts of a black woman being sucked by a white baby; a white infant made up to look like an angel and a black infant with devilish looks; a child's black hand resting on a white male hand – accompanied with the company logo: 'United Colors of Benetton'. The photographs themselves do not convey any message about buying brightly coloured knitwear. But the message about the Other is quite clear: in colonial history blacks were projected as infantile, in modernity blacks were projected as irrational – a black infant hand in an adult male hand cashes in on these subconscious stereotypes to suggest that blacks need to be guided by whites, they cannot look after themselves; the breasts of the black woman play on all the archetypes of black female sexuality as well as recycling the image of black women's place in western society – as a nurse, sexual object, the 'big black Mama' of 1940s and 1950s Hollywood; the black devil simply confirms what most white folks think of the Other.

In popular consciousness, advertising is the antithesis of 'truth'. Advertising images are recognised by most people as unreal. *Benetton* appropriates and transforms photo-journalism both to undermine the cultural codes by which advertising images are seen as unreal as well as to commodify the hyperreality of the news photo and cash in on the news value of the images.[10] *Benetton* advertisements have carried news photographs of a dying AIDS patient with his distraught family, a picture of a graveyard with rows of white crosses after the Gulf War and of an African mercenary holding a human thigh bone in the wake of the civil war in Rwanda. The African mercenary is an iconic image: deprived of history and context, it none the less excavates all that represents Africans as barbaric flesh-eaters incapable of embracing civilisation. The image refers to a moment of barbarism, having no reference to the chain of events which lead to it, while depriving the African of a voice. The *Benetton* campaign encapsulates the past, present and future in a single timeframe offering images which conjure historic, futuristic and apocalyptic elements within a grammar of race. In most of these images the diversity of national culture is reduced to a stylised, hackneyed individual. Difference is commodified and a portrait of plurality is produced which designates the colourful individuals within the image to be a race apart. This is advertising as the consumption of difference: difference is glorified for its own sake, wrapped in colonial and modernist subconscience, to create an artificially constructed reality that is then used to sell an oppressive brand name.

Of course, the Others need not be used to confirm difference; they can also be used simply to make a comparison. The amusing Phileas Fogg advertisements for various Indian condiments use Indian artefacts to bounce off messages about their own products. The 'Pakora' campaign, for example, featured four stylised cartoonish drawings of an Indian couple making love and eating pakoras, underneath the caption: 'Pakora. The *only* spicy Indian pickle to offer strangers at parties.' The copy in smaller print explains: 'Our new Pakora and The Kama Sutra both share a reputation for satisfying the most insatiable appetites. One is a crisp potato snack with sesame seeds, battered and lightly fried before being coated in a sweet and spicy Brinjal pickle. The other is not.' The Phileas Fogg ads employ self-mocking humour and ironically deconstruct colonial archetypes (one running theme in its television advertisements is that everyone knows where its non-western food products come from, but no one knows where on earth 'Medomsley Road, Consett' is, where they are made) to make the point that what they are selling is clearly appropriated.

In contrast, the act of representation in *Benetton* ads, as in the (ab)use of colonial history by the *Banana Republic* and *The East India Company*, involves both perpetuation of stereotypes and constitutes a new form of imperialism. In fact, these companies are engaged in acts of brutality. Their concern for the Other is nothing more than murderous love for the non-west. The presentation of history as a hamburger – the 'Whopper' – not only humiliates and deprives Other cultures of their historic identity, it also undermines their future: without historic identity Other cultures do not have a future as *Other* cultures, their future becomes an extension of the future of postmodernism. Without a sense of continuity and a confidence in their history, Other cultures become archaeological sites fit only to be represented in museums or as a source of entertainment or exploitation for the postmodernist tourist.

This is exactly what is increasingly happening to Other cultures. The tourists look at Other societies as a new location for culture, as a source of fulfilment of their wildest desires, as a fountainhead for difference. Conscientious backpackers seek culture in non-western destinations because culture has disappeared in the west: it has been replaced by talk shows. What is increasingly seen in art galleries, watched in theatres, read in novels is trivial, banal, ephemeral. The serious, the complicated, the strenuous, the enduring, the profound are not just conspicuous by their absence but are also feared and shunned. Rather, culture in the west has come to mean an awareness of prize-winners and prize-givers, of festivals, magazine and newspapers profiles, the prejudices and paranoia of reviewers, biographies, best-seller lists, stock questionnaires, publicised feuds, chat show hosts interviewing chat show hosts, abused individuals baring their soul on national television, home videos, lawsuits for plagiarism, scandals, celebrity interviews, obituaries and signing sessions. In postmodern times, culture is something that happens to us, increasingly at home, or something we pick up at an airport, or read or listen to. It is not experiential; it does not transform our perceptions; it does not reach out and stir our soul: it entertains, focuses our attention on the spectacle for a fleeting moment and then moves on. Under such circumstances, Other cultures are seen as articulate objects.

Thus, an essential item in the itinerary of the western tourist is an encounter with gracious eastern tradition. On the southeast Asian package tours and backpacker trails. a rendezvous with exotic natives is essential. So in rapidly developing nations that are economically outperforming the west, an appearance of the authentic is sustained. Hence, for example, the floating market of Bangkok where the modern and the postmodern western tourists can touch an older and immensely more primitive world. It pays very well for the women plying their sampans who can sell vegetables and fruits at rates well above the local market price. And the whole floating market has been moved to an area removed from the tourist hotels, generating business for coach operators, and the guides who shepherd the tourist along the wooden walkway on the banks of the *klong*, beginning and ending in large sheds where enormous arrays of 'authentic' handicrafts are ready to be purchased as momentoes of the tourists' brush with the ancient and unchanged Orient. For the tourist what is important is taking back the snapshot that looks just like the image in the holiday brochure and the knick-knack to be placed on the shelf to impress the neighbours. What it means for the locale, the site of all this wish fulfilment, is the end of culture as a system of meaning and communication, and of skill and enterprise that has any relevance in Asia for Asians. The dance-drama and song traditions, the culinary delights and the entire repertoire of crafts are debased, bastardised and brutalised to support the escapist delusions of tourists, while culture as lived and understood by Asians is atrophying and dying. The younger generation do not want to learn the old crafts, only how to make shoddy goods that will sell to tourists so that they can earn enough to buy western-style goods. Dance troupes and cultural shows are ripped violently from their contexts to be parodied, poorly executed and shoddily mounted for an audience that has not the faintest idea of what they are, merely requiring they exist to while away one evening out of a fortnight. Postmodernism is not merely ingested, it is willingly connived with and its products manufactured in Asia by Asians for tourists. The results are the daily sights and sounds, the order of normality for those who are Asian in Asia, even when there is no tourist in sight.

Not all tourists seek cultural encounters. Many seek the fulfilment of their sexual desires. There is an Other side to the *Club 18–30* advertisement that asks, on a picture of a conspicuously full Y-front, 'Girls, can we interest you in a package holiday?' or another that simply states: 'It's not all sex, sex, sex ... there is a bit of sun and sea as well' (with the word 'sex' multiplied across the bottom of the poster). These ads betray the true origins of tourism in war and colonialism. Rape and pillage were the original forms of tourism. The lone European tourist of the eighteenth and nineteenth centuries followed in the footsteps of the East India Company and the conquest of the third world to taste the sexual fruits of the vanquished. The notions of Other cultures as passive and willing participants in their sexual exploitation is intrinsic in tourism. Hence the massive market for sexual tourism. The heterosexuals go to Thailand, Indonesia,

Kenya, Cuba or Mexico; homosexuals go to the Maghreb; the paedo-philes go to Sri Lanka or the Philippines; and ageing white women go to the Gambia to entrap young black men. In their turn, non-western countries engage in a truly postmodern exercise of image-making, creating an image of the image of the Other that lies deep in western consciousness. For what must be created is an industry based on selling to the west that which conforms to the west's dis-torted image of what the 'Orient' never was. The 'Singapore Girl', the slogan of Singapore's state's airline, panders to western notions of the compliant eastern female. The 'Singapore Girl' is merely a sanitised version of the syndrome that supports the sex tourism of Thailand and the Philippines. The existence of the one underpins the allure of the other. The difference is that now it is Asians who are imposing the illusion upon themselves.

But tourists do have other interests: hunting out a good bargain, or a game of golf, for example. Tourism is consumerism writ large, naked and unashamed, and to feed the insatiable need of tourists whole nations are converting themselves into vast emporia, havens of everything under the sun that can be bought. Thus Dubai, Singa-pore, Hong Kong: the emerging postmodern phenomenon of na-tion-state as shopping complex. Shopping complexes vie with golf courses in claiming land and resources that should go to those who need them most: in other words, the vast majority of the poor in the Third World. 'Golf tourists' vie with sex tourists to play their favour-ite game in exotic paradises. Both shopping complexes and golf courses make the poor landless, homeless and economically margin-alised. Consider, for example, the fate of Thailand's Pee Pee Island whose virtues were extolled in print in the 1950s by Jacques Coust-eau. Fifteen years later an Austrian set up Moskito Diving there. The following year four more tourist businesses were established. Then corporate developers moved in with a $30 million scheme to develop a hotel resort complex and golf course. Then, the Thai authorities realised the ecological problems of too many tourists. So the natives were isolated further and the resort limited to the very rich: the well-off can continue to degrade Pee Pee's environment. The golfer goes back after his rest and recreation, the global bargain-hunter returns with a suitcase full of Thai silk and imitation antiques – but the oppressive patterns they leave behind are there for everyone who lives among and around the resorts, hotels and shopping outlets 365 days a year rather than for dreamy excursions that come in 14-day packages.

Not surprisingly, natives across the Third World are becoming increasingly restless about tourism. Campaigns against tourist hotels and golf courses are increasingly common. A few communities are taking up arms: for example, in the summer of 1995, the peasants in Topoztlan, an unspoilt town 50 miles south of Mexico City, took over the town hall and held a few officials hostage in protest against plans to build a huge golf course, hotel and tourist projects.[11] Others are resorting to terrorism: the campaign of Muslim fundamentalists in Egypt led to the killing of tourists during 1993 and 1994. But tourism and terrorism are not as far apart as they seem. As the radical Sufi writer, Hakim Bey, points out, terrorists and tourists have much in common:

> Both are displaced people cut loose from all moorings, drifting in a sea of images. The terrorist act exists only in the image of the act – without CNN, there survives only a spasm of meaningless cruelty. And the tourist's act exists only in the images of that act, the snapshots and souvenirs; otherwise nothing remains but the dunning letters of the credit-card companies and a residue of 'free mileage' from some foundering airline. The terrorist and the tourist are perhaps the most alienated of all the products of post-imperial capitalism. An abyss of images separates them from the objects of their desire. In a strange way they are twins ... [they] suffer an identical hunger for the authentic. But the authentic recedes whenever they approach it. Cameras and guns stand in the way of that moment of love which is the hidden dream of every terrorist and tourist. To their secret misery, all they can do is destroy. The tourist destroys meaning, and the terrorist destroys the tourist.[12]

The idea of tourism with all its terrorist underpinnings, contrasts sharply with non-western notions of travel. Travel is intrinsic to the metaphysical ideals of many non-western cultures. In Islam, for example, everyone, whatever their sex, class or status in society, is urged to travel at least once in their lifetime: to go on a pilgrimage to Makkah. Indeed, this pilgrimage, the *hajj*, is an essential article of faith. The Hindus travel to the holy city of

Benares. The Chinese undertake pilgrimages to monasteries and shrines of great saints and Masters. But while the tourist seeks cultural difference, the non-western pilgrim seeks *baraka* or *mana* (blessings), spiritual upliftment, presence in the midst of the sacred. While one journey involves a flight away from the profane towards the sacred, the other involves escape from the homogeneity of 'home' to the (often imagined) heterogeneity of the destination. One journey is undertaken for the sake of a transcendental ideal, while the other is taken for the sake of consumption. One involves dissolution in experiential ecstasy and a shift in consciousness, the other involves a swim in materialism, the gaze of insatiable desire and submersion in fleeting images. The pilgrim brings back blessings; the tourist takes home souvenirs and trinkets. The two ideas of travel could not be further apart.

Sacred journeys are an integral part of the identities of non-western cultures. The pilgrimage connects distant history with living history and breathes life into culture and tradition. For non-western cultures, historical identity provides tradition with its motivational power: without history, tradition loses its impulse and the difference of Other cultures is subsumed into an amorphous, global postmodernism. Postmodern global stores, advertising and tourism appropriate non-western history, tradition and cultures to consume difference and transform them into marketable commodities. The process separates the present lives of non-western people from their living history and thus deprives non-western cultures of the very oxygen that sustains and nourishes them. Beyond dislocated and commodified history and tradition, beyond exotic cultures that exist only to be consumed, lies a whole universe of fractured identities.

Save Yourself, Change Your Colour

In traditional societies, identity is shaped by history, tradition, community, ancestors and extended families. Postmodernism seeks to replace all this with a new resource: consumer products. Shopping is now a cultural enterprise and a cultural experience. We buy things to acquire identity; we shop to complete the Self.

Consumer objects are systematically invested with meaning in the way they are marketed, in their advertising, in carefully chosen contexts. Banking is thus no longer simply a question of finding a convenient and safe place to put your money; it is a matter of lifestyle. As a long-running advertisement for 'First Direct' Bank put is: 'Change your life. Change your bank.' Consumerism defines who you are, what your are, where you are coming from and where you are going to.

Postmodernism consumerism – that is, consumerism which transfers meaning inherent in age-old sources of meaning such as history, tradition and community to consumer products – undermines non-western cultures in two ways. To begin with, it creates an illusion of plurality which shrouds the west's real perception of Others. The marketplace brings Other worlds collapsing upon each other in the local shopping arcade: all manner of the world's commodities, with all manner of ethnic cultures juxtaposed, are assembled under a single roof for the western consumer to experience 'different worlds'. Most western cities have an array of ethnic restaurants where one can dip into an 'Other culture' for the evening: Indian curry, sweet and sour Chinese, Thai chilli paddi, Mexican burritos have now become regular fare in the west. Supermarkets sell exotic fruits, department stores stock baskets from the Philippines, cane furniture from Thailand and Malaysia, recycled paper from India, fabrics from Pakistan, carpets from Iran, erotic sculptures from Peru, ethnic dresses and African cultural artefacts. But this cultural plurality of the contemporary marketplace has all the familiar features of postmodernism. The plurality it presents is apparent rather than real: racism and bigotry remain dominant in Europe and North America; ethnic minorities in the west are marginalised from the sources of power; and oppressive global institutional arrangements continue. The encounter with the products of Others does not lead to a meaningful appreciation of Other cultures – even if they are your neighbours. Thus the illusion of plurality created by the market serves only to hide the reality that the west continues to despise non-western cultures while it continues to consume them.

Postmodern consumerism also acts as a torrential force for assimilation of Other cultures. In modernity, the Third World was seen simply as a market for western goods: fast foods, electronic gadgets, obsolete high technology, 'professional' aid and services. Third World people were required only to buy; and to buy more they were encouraged to change their lifestyle. In postmodernism, the emphasis has shifted: now the requirement is to abandon all that gives meaning to their lives, to throw away not just values but also their identity, stable relationships, attachment to history, buildings, places, families, people, and received ways of doing and being. The focus of attention is the youth.

Youth is a diminishing resource everywhere except in the non-west. While the civilisations of China, India and Islam support young populations with average ages between 20 and 25, the population of Europe and North America is ageing. The baby boom of the postwar years reshaped marketing and advertising to create the phenomenon of a youth-oriented consumer culture afraid of ageing. Now postmodern consumerism must take on a global focus to meet the demographics of the 1990s. So it is the increasing spending power of east and southeast Asian youth that is the lodestar of postmodern marketing techniques and multinational merchandising concerns. An advertisement for the Hongkong Bank says it all: 'There are 3 billion people in Asia. Half of them are under 25. Consider it a growing market'.[13]

This 'growing market' is being targeted in a specific way. In a truly postmodern, pluralistic strategy, multinational companies promote their goods using western pop music, local television channels and specially produced style products. Cigarette companies, for example, do not only sell cigarettes: they sell cigarettes as a total style and identity package. The cigarette-hawking cowboy, 'The Marlboro Man', may be under siege back home, but in Asia it is almost impossible to escape his craggy all-American face: it is plastered on billboards, peers out from magazines and newspapers, flickers across television screens. He is 'sponsoring' American movies and television series, gazing at everybody in crowded shopping malls, selling 'Marlboro Classic' clothes in shops fitted out in the style of the Wild West, and enticing the young to smoke in shopping malls and pubs where teenage girls, dressed as cowboys, offer free cigarettes to passing youngsters. The multitude of style products are used for the construction of images and sign systems emphasising 'freedom', individualism and a postmodern international identity.

Multinational corporations in general, and cigarette companies in particular, have a powerful hold on television channels in the non-western world. According to Arthur Kroker and David Cook, television has

> entertainment as its ideology, the spectacle – as the emblematic sign of commodity form, lifestyle advertising – as its popular psychology, pure, empty seriality – as the bond which unites the simulacrum of the audience, electronic images – as its most dynamic, and only form, of social cohesion, elite media politics – as its ideological formula, the buying and selling of abstracted attention – as the locus of its marketplace rationale, cynicism – as its dominant cultural sign, and the diffusion of a network of relational power – as its real product.[14]

Young people in the non-west are subjected to exactly the same television programmes as their counterparts in the west. Local programming is at best marginal and at worst almost non-existent in many non-western countries. This is not because these countries cannot make their own programmes, or that they do not wish to do so; it is largely because the economics of programme-making, combined with the agenda of multinational advertisers, makes it almost impossible to produce local programmes. The system works like this. A hit show like *The X Files* or *The A-Team* is made for approximately a million dollars per episode. This money is recouped by selling the show to a single network in the United States and Canada. The European sales are pure profit. Once the American and European markets are sewn up, the programmes are dumped on Third World television stations according to a long-established formula for payment. The higher up a country is on the ladder of 'development' the more it pays. Thus, while a British channel will pay something in the region of £100,000–150,000 for an episode of a prestige, high-rating show, Malaysia may acquire the same show for less then US$70,000 and Bangladesh for only US$25,000. Thus a programme which cost $1 million to produce is bought for peanuts; local production can never hope to compete with the production values of the bought-in programme. Hence local programming always looks inferior to imported shows. But programmes are not bought individually; they are bought in package deals. Thus a major proportion of the seasonal output of a local channel in a non-western country may be dominated by the imported package.

Moreover, each programme of the package will be subsidised or 'sponsored' by a multinational company: the programme will be associated with its name or one of its products. As a general rule, multinational companies do not sponsor local programmes, even if they attract high ratings. They sponsor only those programmes – *Model Inc.*, *Melrose Place*, *Baywatch* – which promote a particular image: the images of high consumption, of unrestrained freedom, of the young individual as consumer. When what is being shown on terrestrial television is combined with what comes from satellite – 24-hour MTV, QVC (Quality, Value, Convenience) shopping channel, Star TV's mixture of Kung Fu, the worst of American and British 'cops and robbers', situation comedies and consumer quiz shows – we get a more accurate picture of the almost total displacement and disfigurement of the mind of the young in the Third World by the image production industry that is western television.

Not surprisingly, Asian youth are becoming eager and willing purchasers not just of western pop music and designer outfits, but the entire personality profile of postmodernity – much to the consternation of the societies in which they live. Street rappers wearing reversed baseball caps, baggy sweaters and cut-off jeans atop Doc Martens, heavy metal fans in global heavy metal black jeans and T-shirts and waist-length hair, don't merely want to look and sound like disaffected American black urban youth, they imbibe the psychological profile as well. So crime, truancy, drug addiction and promiscuity, along with breakdown of parental authority, are all on the rise in small but significant levels in societies where 'youth' was never a separate lauded concept, and the extended family and disciplined personal behaviour were the norm. The most notable feature of this culture of disaffection in Asia is that it is confined to those with the greatest purchasing power – the children of the privileged elite. Western pop music, MTV and television programmes, notes *Asiaweek*, 'have created a money minded youth culture that demands instant gratification and thrives on audio-visual bombardment ... as pre-schoolers they start out with Christian Dior sneakers. Then they want Beverly Hills 90210 spectacles. They even use designer pencil boxes.'[15] But these goods only generate disaffection, for the accent in imported culture is on constant and continuous disaffection. Disaffection is the youth culture of the haves who would like to find meaning in the outrage of the have-nots. Thus the interests of affluent youth everywhere in Asia seem to mirror that of the *lepak*, as Malaysia has dubbed its most recently identified social problem – loitering around malls and having all the goods that go with the lifestyle, where style is essential to signify meaninglessness, where a designer fashionplate is the essence of disaffection. And beyond that lies the flirtation with self-destructive addictive behaviour.

But what of those who cannot afford the designer labels? Southeast Asia has produced its own answer to this question: here the postmodern premise that reality and its image are indistinguishable has espoused a thriving culture and economy based on fakes. If the real and its representation cannot be distinguished, what is the difference between a real Gucci watch and a fake? 'Genuine imitations' are freely available. Counterfeit CDs not only look the same as the real ones but have exactly the same sound quality, making it practically impossible, even for industry experts, to tell the difference. But it's not just fake watches, cassettes and CDs that are being marketed in Thailand, Taiwan, Hong Kong, South Korea, Malaysia, Indonesia and Singapore. Counterfeit culture produces everything from designer clothes to shoes, leather goods, antiques, even spare parts for cars and industrial processes. A common sight in the cities of southeast Asia is people dressed in fake designer labels looking every bit as chic as their rich neighbours with the real thing or their western counterparts on the streets of New York, Paris and Geneva. 'Made in Thailand, a thousand years ago' mocks a famous Thai pop song, 'made in USA two hundred years ago'. An astonishing 20 per cent of the region's economy is based on fakes: an ambiguous burgeoning of enterprise, it is both a postmodern product and a potential weapon for the subversion of western capitalism. It does, however, enable all members of society to purchase the all-

powerful image that makes or breaks individuals as they participate in the quest for postmodern individual identity, self-
realisation and meaning.

Pop music, television and style products come together in postmodern times to entrap the young of the Third World, to transform
their identity into a commodity: from television shows to Hollywood, MTV to designer catwalks, pop music to style products, the
youth are being bombarded with glamorised white trash, the whole
'stuff you' attitude that is presented as a fashion trend, the entire
culture of drugs, suicide, criminality and nihilism which is projected
as an essential prerequisite for being 'cool'. Inherent in this package
is loathing, which transforms into self-loathing in the non-west, of
anything that is not western. The package is sold with the allure of
'freedom'. But this 'freedom' – or more appropriately, libertarian
individualism, every individual's potential for fulfilment, the pursuit of endless consumption, withdrawal of all collective, communal
and social responsibility – is a synonym for licence. In western parlance, this is a message that goes back to Rousseau, that great apostle
of freedom and child-centredness (who, of course, dumped all five
children his mistress bore him in the nearest orphanage). But in
non-western societies, this notion of 'freedom' undermines everything that their tradition and history stands for. It does not include
the freedom of the non-western young to have access to their own
cultural products. Traditional non-western music, for example, has
become fair game for postmodern appropriation. Music from Zaire,
the Solomon Islands, Burundi, the Sahel, Iran, Turkey and elsewhere is freely blended with New Age electronics and rock beats to
make them palatable to western tastes and sell them back to the third
world. African Pygmies go postmodern on 'Deep Forest'. Tradition
is deprived of its context and history, commodified and combined
with glamorised self-destruction to produce a mass market culture.
Words like commitment, duty, obligations, family and community
are all relegated to the margins; dissatisfaction, self-realisation, consumption including self-consumption come to the fore. The young
are encouraged to make their own individual way to self-destruction.

Apart from generating an acute identity crisis in non-western
youth, the trinity of style, pop music and imported television
programmes has a devastating effect on local culture. Local

cultural production becomes at best marginalised, or worse, totally suppressed. Since there is no place for local programming on local television, one of the main institutional frameworks for the support of indigenous culture is not available to local writers and artists. Indigenous music is either totally marginalised or has to be torn away from its context and westernised to be acceptable to those who are supposed to be its inheritors. Consider, for example, the case of Quawwali, the devotional music of India, Pakistan and Bangladesh. Of Sufi origin, it is sung to the simple rhythm of traditional drums and hand-clapping in praise of God, Prophet Muhammad, Ali the fourth Caliph of Islam and classical Sufi masters. In its re-emerged form, in the form that has become acceptable to the hip youth of the subcontinent, it has gone funky and is sung to a syncopated rock beat generated by synthesisers. What was originally designed to induce mystical ecstasy is now used to generate hysteria for rock music and disco dancing. Given the dominance of a 'master' language in postmodern products, local languages acquire the stigma of inferiority. In other words, the production of indigenous culture ceases, leaving nothing to which the growing generation can relate. No wonder the politics of identity has become so important in most of the Third World.

Spaced-out Hoodlums Run Riot

Identity and a sense of direction have become major issues in non-western societies, not simply because postmodernist culture places a strong accent on disorientation and self-loathing, but also because the feeling of a total lack of perspective is enhanced by postmodern architecture and space. Modern architecture and planning were about imposing a single set of western standards and aesthetics on non-western cultures – the goal was often achieved simply by denigrating and bulldozing traditional buildings, neighbourhoods and communities in non-western societies and replacing them with arrogant, perpendicular brickworks that served as monuments of the western will to power. The fabric of traditional life was torn apart and replaced with centralised, mass-produced monotony. In contrast, postmodern architecture appropriates tradition and juxtaposes it with modern classicism, high-tech gloss and playful elements to produce an eclectic mix: for example, the combination of white classicism and black modernism of the Sainsbury Wing of the National Gallery in London, designed by Robert Venturi and Denise Scott Brown. In general, postmodern architecture 'observes other laws in addition to functional aptness and maximum simplicity of basic forms', moves away from 'abstraction and tends towards representational objectivisation'.[16] The laws that postmodern architecture observes, or should observe, according to Charles Jencks, are the laws of the new science of complexity. Buildings should be designed according to the theory of chaos and Fuzzy logic, in the manner of fractals and quarks, echoing black holes and other esoteric concerns of modern cosmology. Postmodern architecture thus reflects the 'moral order' of the heavens.[17] Charles Correa's science campus for the Inter-University Center for Astronomy and Astrophysics in Pune, India, melting ancient cosmology with modern astrophysics, using black on black, fractal patterns and the symbol for infinity, combining traditional and modern material, is what postmodern architecture is all about. With or without complexity, however, postmodern building compresses space and time, while retaining all the ostentation and will to power of modern architecture – witness the proliferating number of postmodern corporate headquarters such as Richard Rogers' Lloyds building in London with its unashamed embrace of glitzy yuppie euphoria or the entertainment architecture of Disneyland and Las Vegas. Postmodern architecture, like postmodern culture, tends to glorify the camp and the kitsch, the fake and the phoney, the chaotic and the disoriented.

The link between postmodern architecture and global capitalism is provided by its concern with fiction. Postmodern buildings are designed to create a world of appearances – allusions and associations are created that go beyond the building itself. Postmodern architecture contains abundant allusions to tradition, antiquity and other images and signs; just as global capitalism is now predominantly concerned with the productions of signs and images. The world stock markets trade not in commodities but social and political signs and electronic images. The western economy is now largely based on the production of fictitious capital which is lent to real estate agents who inflate prices on behalf of the stock brokers and bankers who manufacture fictitious capital. During the 1988 Writer's Guild strike, when the image production machine of Los Angeles came to a sudden halt, people realised 'how much of its economic structure is based on a writer telling a producer a story, and that finally it's the weaving of the tale [into images] that pays the wages of the man who drives the van that delivers the food that's eaten in the restaurant that feeds the family who make the decisions to keep the economy running'.[18] Postmodern concrete monuments of capitalism too are based on a similar fiction: the pink granite Philip Johnson's AT&T building, for example, is 'debt-financed, built on the basis of fictitious capital, and architecturally conceived of, at least on the outside, more in the spirit of fiction than of function'.[19]

But the 'narrative content' of this fiction, from the perspective of non-western cultures, is as old as western domination. Postmodern architecture and planning in the non-west is singularly as out of place, as destructive of community, tradition and history as was (is) modern building practices. While modern architecture was turning Third World cities into replicas of Dallas and Houston, postmodern architecture is turning them into theme parks and extensions of Los Angeles. Singapore is undoubtedly the most postmodern city in the non-west, as the cyberpunk author, William Gibson, discovered on a visit:

> The sensation of trying to connect psychically with the old Singapore is rather painful, as though Disneyland's New Orleans Square had been erected on the site of the actual French Quarter, obliterating it in the process but leaving in its place a glossy simulacrum. The facades of the remaining Victorian shop-houses recall Covent Garden on some impossibly bright London day. There was very little to be seen of previous realities: a joss stick smouldering in an old brass holder on the white painted column of a shop-house; a mirror positioned above the door of a supplier of electrical goods, set to snare and deflect the evil that travels in a straight line; a rusty trishaw, chained to a freshly painted iron railing. The physical past, here, has almost entirely vanished.[20]

Singapore represents the future of many southeast Asian cities – if they do not first become victims of pollution and traffic jams. While virtually all of Singapore is a replica of a theme park (the double-coded irony is that the whole island of the city state has actually been turned into a theme park), the malling of many southeast Asian cities is moving them in the same direction. Numerous segments of these cities are turned into huge complexes, with shopping centres, hotels, cinemas and condominiums – rather like 'The Mall of America' in the Minneapolis suburb of Bloomington. 'The Mall' complex in Kuala Lumpur is a good example. The whole complex consists of three elements: The Mall Shopping Centre, The Legend Hotel and the attached network of condominiums. The condominiums are modern perpendicular tower blocks crossed with rationalised Mediterranean flavour. The Legend Hotel has no particular point of view: its dark, circular lobby looks onto nowhere. Nor do its rooms, which not only look exactly the same (gaudy and claustrophobic) but appear to be specifically designed to deprive the visitor of all sense of space and location. The cornerstone of the Mall is the Japanese superstore, Yohan. The first floor contains a multiplex cinema showing both Hollywood and Chinese (mainly Hong Kong) movies. The top floor is split into two halves: one houses a mini theme park containing video games, rides and miscellaneous electronic attractions; the other is a replica of the historical Portuguese city of Malaka with streets, houses, hawker stalls and typical street furniture, where artists, craftsmen and other traditional businessmen sell their products. In the lobby of the Mall, 'Delifrance', a globalised, French boulevard café, and McDonalds are locked in a constant struggle for attention and customers. The lobby itself undergoes seasonal changes – in a country which has no seasons. During Christmas, it is decked with cottonwool snow as Tamil Indians (who have dark complexions) and Chinese men dressed as Father Christmas dispense sweets and try to convince sceptical little children that they are actually white. During the Chinese new year, the lobby houses the longest dragon in the world. During Eid, which marks the end of the fasting month of Ramadan, the lobby is turned into a huge stage where ethnic dancers from all over Malaysia entertain the crowds. During the Hindu Deepavali celebrations, the stage plays host to *baratnatyam* and *khatak* dancers. Out of season, the stage is often used by public relations companies for product promotions. Any number of different worlds, histories, traditions, artforms are collapsed in the Mall, homogenised, commodified and sold. Kuala Lumpur has dozens of such postmodern malls.

The disorientation and lack of perspective are increasingly reflected outside. Not just streets, but all profiles are disappearing. In Makkah, the holiest city of Islam, for example, there are hardly any streets left. Makkah, of course, is the prime focus for the one billion Muslims who face towards the city during their five daily prayers. But the city itself has no sense of direction, no perspective: its looks everywhere and nowhere. Underground tunnels, overhead flyovers, spaghetti junctions and multi-lane motorways compete for attention with hotels that look like colossal Bedouin tents and *Arabian Nights* mansions. Intricate, winding shopping complexes vie for attention with postmodern palaces, which combine fictional traditional architecture with high-tech modernity and virtually sit on top of the kabbah, the cubical black structure that is the prime focus of all Muslim prayer and the symbol of immutable Islamic values, in the Sacred Mosque. Inside the mosque itself, giant escalators and lifts take worshippers to second and third floors so they are floating on top of what they are suppose to be circumambulating. Nothing, absolutely nothing, is left of the history of the city or its invaluable cultural property. What then is left of its sacred nature, its holy status? A city that is supposed to give a sense of direction to the Muslim world becomes a postmodern image of Los(t) Angeles.

Los Angeles, of course, is the archetypal postmodern city and houses the archetypal postmodern building: the Bonaventure Hotel. The Bonaventure Hotel, with its baroque interior and phoney natural and public spaces, dislocated from its neighbourhood, is a total world to itself, a placeless world without perspective. The same lack of perspective can be found in the city's urban sprawl, endless freeways, glitzy downtown area, decaying inner city areas, labour-intensive low-wage industries expanding into manufacturing and services *à la* East Asia, high immigrant population (Asian, Mexican, Central American) and the fortress-like character of the buildings that shape its skyline.

Both Los Angeles and the Bonaventure Hotel are considered in the literature to be the acme of postmodern experience. But

Bombay can offer an experience to match. There's hardly any difference between Bombay and Los Angeles: apart from the fact that both cities house prolific film industries, Bombay is as diffused, as decentralised, as much a melting pot of cultures and ethnicities and as connected to the global economy as Los Angeles. Most people in Bombay may live in slums, but they receive satellite television (Zee TV, CNN, Star Channel) and are hooked up to cable. As Jim Masselos suggests, 'the archetypal postmodern architectural experience may not at all be the plunge into the Escher-like structures of the Westin Bonaventure in Los Angeles but an excursion into the shanty slums'.[21] The architecture of Bombay slums is a product of human ingenuity, the necessities of survival and the demands of physical space. Thus, dwellings are made of old wood and brick, tins and plastics, bits of cloth and aluminium sheets, pipes and tyres. Tightly packed together they sprawl endlessly in all directions generating

> unplanned pathways that wend their way through the massed huts, the pathways out into the space that leads nowhere (though sometimes to space that serves as a latrine), the dead ends, the hidden and clear exits, the makeshift entries through holes and in fences and walls, and the juxtapositions of satellite saucers, make-do machines, trailing electric wires, bits and pieces of past and present crafts and technologies. All of these are, if anything, more consistently decentralised and diffuse in their experiential quality, more drawing on the pasts as needed, than anything the Westin can produce with its ordered pathways and hidden exits. All are the subjects of an overall if confused planning process designed to appeal to a limited and selective stratum of society.[22]

Of course, such a postmodern space cannot retain the ties of tradition or the sensibility of historic identity. In a space that provides no direction, everyone hankers after a modicum of direction. In a space that fractures all identities, the politics of identity becomes the norm. In a space that is the product of an imaginary capital, stagflation takes its deadly toll. Thus, it is not surprising that postmodern Bombay is the locus of Hindu fundamentalism in India. The historic ties between Hindu and Muslim communities as well as age-old relationships between

Bombay's ethnic minorities have withered away. The price of land in Bombay is now probably higher than that in Los Angeles, making it difficult for even the well-off middle classes to buy a small apartment. In January 1993, Bombay experienced a riot unlike any other in its history: it lasted 18 days and resulted in some 550 deaths. What is happening to geographical space in Bombay, suggests Jim Masselos, is essential in understanding both the intensity and the duration of the riot:

> Perhaps they might be classed as the first postmodern riots in the city's history, whereas past riots occurred in and between different localities, and were expressions of matters of particular emotional import of the day: Hindu–Muslim antagonism, anti-plague emotionalism, regional cultural tensions (such as that between Marathis and Gujaratis), and the like. All such outbreaks took the form of a fight for territory and control of the peripheries of the locality. The January riots were different; they were diffused through the city and not limited to one or two areas. People in the slums burnt each others' shanties and killed one another. Slum dwellers went out and attacked middle-class dwellings, middle-class people defended themselves and attacked others, slum dwellers attacked high-rise apartments and demanded that Muslims be produced for killing, middle-class Hindus went on a pogrom against Muslims, burning shops and houses, killing and injuring ... The lack of central control was demonstrated by the inability of the police or their unwillingness to control what was going on, and an equal inability or unwillingness on the part of the government to quell the situation.

> A sense of interconnectedness between differing sections of the city's population as a whole was replaced by a sense of interconnectedness with certain parts only of the population, not all of it. The sense of separateness as represented in the communal antagonisms was what emerged as uppermost in the riots. Similarly, diffuseness and lack of central and government control was equally demonstrated during the riots and to telling effect in terms of the cost to lives and property. The consequences of disorder are such as to lead to a questioning of the nature of the global city, the postmodern urban phenomenon. The flipside of such developments, the underbelly of postmodernism, is disorder, separateness, antagonism, destructive rampages against

property, and the lethal vengeance and killing of people perceived as other, apart and different.[23]

Thus, the alleged complexity and narrative concerns of post-modern geographical spaces take the dislocation and fragmentation of modernity to a nightmarish new level.

Real Indians Dance to Different Tunes

The postmodern attack on the historic and traditional identity of the Other undermines postmodernism's alleged concern for plurality. Identity is a major weapon in the struggle of the oppressed. By disarming the marginalised of the principal source of their struggle, postmodernism reduces the Other to an object of mere play. Once the Other is deprived of history and identity, it can serve no other purpose than simply to heighten the spectacle of the 'narrative content' of postmodern products. Far from giving a voice to marginalised Others, cultural plurality in postmodern cinema, for instance, is there simply to enrich the narrative, enhance orientalist voyeurism and heighten the spectacle. Pluralism is thus simulated, while the underlying structures of dominance continue unabated.

Postmodernism simulates plurality by a sleight of hand. Different worlds, cultures and ontologies are juxtaposed, superimposed, fragmented, restructured and brought together in an impossible space, what Foucault has called 'heteropoia'. In this implosion of different worlds, in this unrealisable space, the historical or contemporary reality of the Other becomes meaningless, a sense of location disappears, issues of identity evaporate and the Other is presented as an empty vessel into which can be poured the desires and concerns of the west. We can see how the Other is projected as an empty vessel in a number of postmodern films which, while pretending to argue for plurality, in fact reinforce the images of the Other of the dominant civilisation.

Paul Hogan's *Crocodile Dundee*, for example, tells the story of an Australian crocodile poacher from the remote community of Walkabout Creek who, with the help of the American media, is brilliantly marketed in New York, by collapsing three different worlds and ontologies onto its narratives: the innocent and apolitical world of Dundee, the world of Australian Aborigines and the world of hype and hysteria of the American media. But the Aborigines appear only as an appendix and their voice is filtered through the character of Dundee. Dundee become the archetype of all those white children raised by the natives who are the prime device of western appropriation. As we saw earlier with Hawkeye so with Dundee, the ultimate appropriation is the psychic/spiritual world of the Aborigines, which, once possessed, makes the Aboriginal people an unnecessary piece of exotica, whose inability to come to terms with modernity is parodied and misrepresented on a massive scale by the film. The inner and outer reality of the film come together in a truly postmodernist style: the American success of Dundee in the film is reflected in the American success of Hogan. During the course of the narrative, notes Meaghan Morris, 'Dundee does real or feigned battle with phantasmal Others of an equally phantasmal "white, male, working class" – beasts, blacks, deviants, uppity women, snobs.'[24] To counter any criticism of its treatment of the Australian Others – the Aborigines – the film places itself 'post': 'it historicizes radicalism as obsolete opinion'. This is the neatest trick of all, decontextualising the specifics of Australian conquest and settlement, as we have already seen. Moreover, its very form of 'questioning', in the form of a dialogue between Dundee's muscular innocence of politics and the enfeebled liberal conscience of Sue, the American reporter who comes to the outback to interview him, 'is a mode of American ignorance'. Postmodernism triumphs only where ignorance rules; there is no excuse for such ignorance in a society which elsewhere claims to encapsulate and disseminate all knowledge. With postmodernism as anything else, a half-truth, a partial ignorance is a constructive lie; a lie whereby the process of pre-modern mercantile expansion, modernism and now postmodernism become the self same enterprise in relation to all Others. The dialogues take place at night. Sue asks two questions:

> Each raises a problem of appropriation, framed in two different ways: bad (white land-taking, black taking back the land) and good (reciprocal borrowing between cultures). On the first night, Sue begins by posing the ultimate global question: the arms race. Dundee refutes

the need for general political statements ('gotta have a voice') by specific cultural context: 'Who's going to hear it out here?' Foiled by outback eccentricity, she tries something 'closer to home': Aboriginal land rights. He still doesn't state 'his' opinion. Instead, he paraphrases Aboriginal belief – Aborigines don't own the land, they belong to it.

This is, in one sense, true. But it is significantly partial truth ... While implying that a land-rights politics of reappropriation is un-Aborignal, he discursively appropriates the right to Aboriginal speech ... Aboriginal land claims, however, are not made for 'the land' in general, but for particular sites. Dundee effaces this distinction in a discourse on (European) romantic nature – and confirms its supremacy by casually throttling a snake.[25]

This is not to say, as Morris is quick to point out, that those who watch *Crocodile Dundee* 'emerge as anti-land-rights fanatics'; the point is that opinions are shaped not just by contents, but as much by mood – cinema is a principal source of global capital, it is a mega-industry in the global western culture, it establishes a mood across the globe.[26] When this mood is reflected and reinforced in television programmes and literature, it crystallises into something permanent. Dundee does not state his opinion because postmodernism has no opinion. But by a single sleight of hand, Dundee dismisses the Aborigines' 200-year battle to win recognition by the High Court and the Australian parliament of native title to their traditional land. Moreover, given the respect he is supposed to have for them, Dundee is totally unconcerned about the contemporary reality of the Aborigines – their marginalisation from Australian society, the absence of basic amenities such as water and electricity in Aborigine communities, the squalor of their lives, the epidemic of diseases such as diabetes and tuberculosis in their communities. The Aborigines of *Crocodile Dundee* are Uncle Tom figures, content in their misery. The crucial point in any representation of Aborigines is that they have never recovered from their historic land dispossession and the disastrous diet of western junk food and alcohol that followed. *Crocodile Dundee* leaves a constructive ignorance firmly in control, so that the more information we possess the less we actually can know about the Other.

Mira Nair's *The Perez Family* (1995), based on the novel by Christine Bell,[27] tackles the issue of what it really means to be American in a multicultural United States head on. On the surface, the narrative looks like the perfect vision of promised plurality. On screen it sounds exactly like the betrayal that postmodern plurality really is. The storyline is familiar: Cubanos making for America – and one has to hear the word as the four-note flourish Bernstein's music scored for *West Side Story*. The film is about the dispossessed and downtrodden on their migratory route to postmodern plurality, taking the rickety boat to the great melting pot of dreams. They are a rag-tag lot: Juan Raul, a political prisoner of 20 years obsessed that the loss of his teeth will make it impossible for him to kiss his wife, Carmella, who fled to America when he was imprisoned; Dorita, the quintessential plucky little *paisana*, as smart and nubile as the *Girl from Ipanema*, desperate to get away from the choice between cutting sugar cane or becoming a whore. Dorita's vision of America derives from movies – all she has ever seen of America: she dreams of a land where she will 'fuck John Wayne'. When this quaint innocent from a bygone era arrives in America, she is distraught to learn that John Wayne is dead. This ill-starred pair guide us through the world of the migrant and its recreation by the immigration process. In the migrant camp in the Orange Bowl they meet the Cubana negra Mama of decided voodoo overtones, a worldly-wise street urchin, and a lunatic mute old man who spends his time climbing trees stark naked, looking for Cuba.

To prove that this is the postmodern world of real plurality the immigration officer is an Indian, 'Not your kind of Indian, a real Indian'. This perfect Asian bureaucrat, as only Asians schooled by the Raj know how to be, is the cutting edge of American reformulation of the migrants' lives. To have any chance of getting benefits the migrants should not be lone individuals, families are better. So Dorita, who shares the same surname as Juan Raul, ensures they are marked down as a married couple. This overheard bureaucratic slip outrages brother-in-law Angel, who fumes on behalf of the besmirched honour of his chaste wife-in-suspended-animation sister and vows to deny the existence – let alone arrival – in America of Juan Raul. Cut off from the family which would have given him a foundation in a new land, Juan Raul is at the mercy of and indebted to the wits of Dorita, who learns that families of three are higher up the queue for benefits than mere couples. So the mad old man becomes their Papy, just as the street urchin becomes their lost son. In this scenario the clever little *paisana* is conniving with the knowing Asian immigration officer, making reformulation an insider's joke they share.

The new migrants are contrasted with the old migrants. There is the serene and swarthy, the refined 'Spanish' senora, Carmella, the wife of Juan Raul, who lives in a plush American house with all the trimmings provided by her overbearing, over-protective younger brother called – what else? – Angel, who spends his life worrying about her safety and installing ever more sophisticated security devices in her home. Angel himself is the most gross of all gross stereotypes, the successful immigrant who is so naïve he kept sending bribes to Cuba to free his brother-in-law, money that ensured Juan Raul spent 20 years in prison and provided his captors with a regular income. But then Angel is the perfect metaphor for what is wrong with this vision of plurality. Angel can succeed in the American dream precisely because he is too naïve to understand anything about where he came from or where he came to; he possesses the reformulations decreed for him by the stereotypes of dominant description as self-identity.

These migrants have no real history; they have only one future, to be subsumed in the dominant order; they have no cultural specificity that is not a stereotype; and nothing in the film invites any questioning of the exuberant parade that passes by. None of the central characters are played by Latinos, let alone Cubanos. Yet every one of them tries to outdo Desi Arnez on a bad day. The postmodern pluralism of *The Perez Family* is so plural that identity is rendered completely irrelevant.

To get the measure of what postmodern plurality does to real migrant experience it is as well to compare *The Perez Family* with the film version of Oscar Hujelos' *Mamba Kings*, where the wanna-be migrants from Cuba meet the real Desi Arnez (played by Desi Arnez, Jr). *Mamba Kings* deals with the trauma of broken lives, the fragmentation of identity and history, the displacement of relocation and all its attendant pain, confusion and frustration.

Hujelos' characters come from a corrupt Cuba to a New York that is the harsh world of an underclass, exploited by the same dominant order that had ruined their homeland. They dream in America as in Cuba of release, and the passport to that release is to sell their authentic cultural heritage for the amusement of white America. The brothers form a band and make one glorious song, the haunting refrain that runs throughout the film that is a poignant symbol of their inability to capture or recapture any golden moment of peace in the predestined failure that is their lot as migrants. The brothers face corruption that perverts their cultural ethos as much in America as it did in Cuba, for the problem and the predicament remain the same and the characters suffer, and they suffer in character as rounded human beings.

There are tears in *The Perez Family*, but no pain. These are happy hopefuls out on junkets, making the best of their lot. The man confined to prison for 20 years because he burnt his sugar cane to keep it from Fidel ends up with the sugar cane cutter who yearned for another choice. Both end up accepting the formulated family created for them in the migrant process, selling flowers to passing cars on the freeways of Miami, part of the underclass and its black economy. Carmella, the wife-in-waiting, is freed to restart her life as the wish fulfilment of the white welfare officer, released from cultural and historic bondage. All the characters are so busy throwing off the shackles that they need never question the meaning their history may hold, certainly not consider it might have enduring value to them. Surely it is right that Carmella should be liberated from the intolerable reimposition of family and find her first freedom outside the Cubano dispensation. She may have waited patiently for her husband, but she has lived pampered and secure in her American life – so she gets her happy ending. And Juan Raul and Dorita too get a romantic happy ending: he can kiss Dorita without his teeth, and for her it's a lot better than chasing after blond American beefcake who regard her as just a whore. There is no pain or struggle in making a living selling flowers for this exuberant, gutsy duo. The film's sales pitch is the sexual innuendo of the nubile Latin seductress and the *cojones* of the Latin lover.

The postmodernism of *The Perez Family* pales in comparison to a straight film such as *Fires Within*, based on almost exactly the same premise. In *Fires Within*, a released Cubano political prisoner has to come to terms with migration to America and rebuild his relations with the wife, who escaped under desperate circumstances as one of the boat people, and the child he hardly knew. The difference is considerable. *Fires Within* explores a political context in which being a Cubano exile in America is to be a pawn in a superpower game. *The Perez Family*, like *Crocodile Dundee*, is unaware that politics even exists. *Fires Within* explores the trauma of broken lives where lone women must struggle to make a living in sweatshops to raise their children, where there is heartbreak in longing for reunited families and searching for news of those who disappeared into the chaos of revolution and ideological power ploys. The film ends as a paeon to the struggle of women. The dislocated political crusader comes to realise the cost that has been paid by the political martyr, his wife. It is the wife who nearly died in the attempt to get to America, who fought oppression and survived with her dignity and identity intact, and thus becomes his route back to meaningful identity in a new land caught in the old dispensation of dominance and marginalisation.

Dorita, the heroine of *The Perez Family*, says of herself, 'I am Cuba, used by many, conquered by none.' It is a perverse little epithet. Cuba is the quintessential creation of conquest, product of the subjugation of many: the original Amerindian population, the Negro slaves and the mixed blood *mestizo*. Out of this cauldron of conquest was forged a distinctive Other culture with its own history, it own experience, its own struggle to be free and equal, a struggle that still has far to go. Cuba is too destabilised by economic terrorism from the United States to substantiate the arguments between left and right whether its social experiments are the ideal model of autonomous cultural and social revival or merely the meaning of Stalinist pauperisation. Postmodern parody deracinates, dislocates and degrades all that. In putting forward its argument for the arrival of plurality on every doorstep as part of the dominant order, *The Perez Family* shows us two aged Cubanos raising their tiny glasses of Cuban brew with the toast 'Next year in Havana' – the diaspora's dream, Jews and Jerusalem, Cubans and Havana. Juan Raul looks on and comments: 'I've just come from Havana. Look around you Cuba is here.' It is, like almost everything else in this film, perversely true and an intelligently fabricated lie. Cuba can only have arrived, become a real part of American life, when Cubans can describe themselves and possess both their homeland and migrant existence with autonomous choice, their identity and integrity intact.

The Perez Family is a true visualisation of postmodern pluralism. We are expected to take the deeply fused plurality so much for granted that its rainbow convention can now be played for laughs. But the pathos is what makes the film at once pathetic and excruciating. Every character is a stereotype relishing and flaunting his or her role as stereotype; we skate along the surface of experience, history and emotion without ever being challenged to question the pernicious ideology that fuels this parade of grotesques. For every puckish trick in the stereotype handbook merely confirms the ethos of dominance. When postmodern plurality enters the contemporary equation, the status quo remains strictly in control. An Asian immigration officer does not change the system, he merely operates it with a brown skin and is totally consumed by the system that has coopted him. As he correctly blares through the megaphone: 'Obey the rules of the United States Immigration Service. Welcome to Freedom.' The only trouble is these migrants find their identity in the parody created for them by the very service whose rules they are supposed to obey; and their freedom is the freedom of the infant – but truth is nothing like that. 'The truth is so easily lost, Dorita. If we lie to ourselves it opens the doors to a world of madness.' The trouble is neither Juan Raul nor postmodernists can hear what they say. As with *Crocodile Dundee*, the inner and outer reality of *The Perez Family* fuse together to produce a grotesque irony. Mira Nair, a 'real [Asian] Indian', directs white actors playing Cubanos. Earlier, Nair made *Salam Bombay*, which made her reputation and had real prostitutes and street urchins playing prostitutes and street urchins in Bombay. But like the Indian immigration official in her film, Nair has been consumed by the system that has coopted her. She has been transformed into a memsahib and gives us a vision of plurality not far removed from that of that other brown sahib, Salman Rushdie: *The Perez Family* presents us with Rushdie's thesis of migration, as it appears in *The Satanic Verses*, with all the postmodern flourishes of the master.

Postmodernism thus plays a double con-trick on non-western cultures. On the one hand, it invites plurality, attempts to liberate Other cultures from marginality and seeks their representation under conditions that are not tailored on the exclusivist and dominating cultural rationality of modernity; on the other, its visions of plurality leave all the structures of power and inequality intact. In the straight, 'modern' portraits of plurality and marginalisation in *Mambo Kings* and *Fires Within*, the existence and imposition of dominance is fully acknowledged. In postmodern cinema – in *Crocodile Dundee*, *The Perez Family* as well as numerous other postmodern films – plurality and marginalisation serve as an end in themselves: it is not the contents of Other cultures that concerns postmodernism, but simply the fact that they are different. The emphasis on difference generates a meaning in and of itself, but it is meaning without content. Postmodernism does not pose the questions, 'how do we relate to Other cultures?', 'how do we fight our own ethnocentricity?' 'How do we understand the Other in terms of its own categories and description?' It is interested *only* in registering the difference. It is a strategy both of negating the difference (by elevating it into a hyperreality) and of draining it of content. The postmodern invitation to plurality is an exercise in domination through representation, discourse and subjectivity; and it provides us with a clear indication that the imagination of the west is truly exhausted. It can no longer imagine anything different.

The Neem *Tree in Sioux City*

The different, non-western cultures of the world experience postmodernism as a lie, a lie that is sold in the guise of truth, a lie with pretensions to be taken seriously. It is a deceit that is spread far and wide by the transmitters of cultural images: fashion, pop music and advertising, cinema and television, art and architecture – by all who process and influence the reception of postmodern cultural products. When Other cultures are trapped by this deceit, they become poor replicas of their western counterparts, rather like the replicants in Ridley Scott's *Blade Runner*: authentic reproductions, with a short lifespan and enslaved to the weavers of the master narrative. But, after the experience of modernity, non-western cultures are acquiring a new, more subtle aptitude for cultural resistance.

Non-western cultures are increasingly being transformed into cultures of resistance. That is, the flight from tradition generated by and during modernity is being reversed by postmodernism; it is now becoming a flight from postmodernism to tradition. One of the most potent examples of this is the impact of the Rushdie affair on Muslim communities throughout the world: the reaction of liberal, westernised Muslims was in sharp contrast to the fundamentalists who were ready to kill and be killed. The 'modern' Muslims, in contrast, sought refuge from Rushdie's postmodern onslaught by returning to the womb of their tradition and used tradition as a critique of the new instrument of hegemony. Suddenly, almost overnight, the Muslim world had a whole new generation championing traditional culture. Similarly, the newfound confidence and pride in traditional medicine in China, the Middle East, the Indian subcontinent and southeast Asia are not simply about age-old healing and treatment systems that have proved themselves against modern scepticism; they are about moving to the future with a belief in one's own metaphysics and lifestyles without handing one's destiny to postmodernism. Indeed, there has been a mass revival in the appreciation of indigenous knowledge: from the recently discovered concern with *chi* in China to the revival of traditional irrigation systems in the Middle East to the campaign to stop the multinationals from appropriating the *neem* tree, which has numerous healing properties, in India to the global movement for the preservation and enhancement of indigenous knowledge.[28] Indeed, in the decade ahead, it will not be so easy for western consumer industries simply to take indigenous knowledge from passive and compliant natives.

While postmodernism has been embraced by some segments in the non-western world, it has also been taken to task and, in some cases, actually subverted. The declaration by the Mexican poet and Noble Laureate, Octavio Paz, that postmodernism is yet another project imported from the west with no relevance to Latin America, suggests that postmodernism's imperial ambitions have not totally escaped the non-west.[29] Indeed, throughout Latin America, where postmodernism is aggressively contested, liberation theology marks a conscious effort to displace Eurocentric conceptions of modernity and postmodernism with an indigenous historical and cultural consciousness. The discourse of 'Islamisation of knowledge' promotes the same goals in the Muslim world.[30] The decision by Kenyan novelist Ngugi wa Thiongo to abandon the novel and write mainly in Kikuyu, and Rigoberta Menchu's striking testimonial narrative of Indian resistance in Guatemala, *I, Rigoberta Menchu*, have transformed postmodernism into a culture of resistance. The re-emergence of *feng shui* (geomancy), which makes allowances for the future movement of benevolent spirits through doors and windows, in the new locally designed architecture in southeast Asia is not a nod towards eclectic postmodernism, but an effort to go forward with vernacular architecture. The *shalwar-kurta* fashion industry that has mushroomed both in Pakistan and India, which has now made serious inroads amongst the modernised middle classes, is a living testimony that traditional products too can be fashionable in traditional societies.

All this presents hope against a murderous creed that offers Other cultures only appropriation, parody and images of hyperreality: images that are always and only distortions, that have already been deconstructed and remodelled, that are merely that which can be modelled only according to the worldview of postmodernism, and that propel this worldview onto an endless trajectory. The Malaysian artist, musician and actor, M. Nasir, offers alternative images. A devout Muslim, a pop idol, a southeast Asian heart-throb, Nasir insists that modernism cannot be equated with the west: 'when people stop being so short-sighted and realise that we hinge our imagery or our music on our own cultures and our own personal experiences, then the Asian arts will truly be progressive and not simply possessive'.[31] One of Nasir's paintings, 'Ocean of Unity', underscores the point that the future of Other cultures is tied to an acceptance of their past and an appreciation of the underlying forces of modernity and postmodernism so that they can be harnessed to 'fight fire with fire'. Painted largely in blazing colours, 'Ocean of Unity' collapses past, present and the future in a dream sequence that appears to be of truly postmodern proportions. At first glance, it seems a bit naïve but the naiveté slowly disappears to reveal a traditional philosophy. The young man at the foreground, moving forward with his index finger pointing upwards, displays the traditional symbol for unity: for he cannot go forward without the old man sitting under the tree in the background dressed in the costumes of history, nor can he move to the future without addressing the demands of a fractured present: the swirling storm, the looming clouds, *Mahabharta*'s Rama and Ravana in one corner in hues of sienna – the traditional symbols of human conflict. The 'unity' expressed in the painting is not just the unity of the past and the present, it is also the unity of non-western cultures in the face of postmodernism: the illusive ogre-like figure threatening the young man in the foreground. Non-western cultures do have alternative visions of their own cultural futures. But it does not involve buying recycled shampoo from *The Body Shop*.

5. Convenient Fictions

In the summer of 1990, at the height of the Rushdie affair, a strange billboard appeared at prominent sites in London and other major cities in Britain. It consisted of a large printed image of an Islamic carpet containing three lines of Urdu at its centre. At the bottom on the internal border of the carpet one could clearly read the words: 'The Golden Verses'. Close and careful examination of the external decorative border of the carpet reveals, cleverly woven and camouflaged, the English translation of the Urdu lines:

> White people are very good people. They have very white and soft skin. Their hair is golden and their eyes are blue. Their civilisation is the best civilisation. In their countries they live life with love and affection. And there is no such thing as racial discrimination. White people are very good people.[1]

'The Golden Verses', by the British Pakistani artist Rasheed Araeen, plays on a number of signs and images that are intrinsic to western perceptions of the Self and the Other. The Islamic carpet, with its calligraphy, immediately places the billboard, and its message, in the Orient: yet here it is far from genuine. The Urdu script, incomprehensible to those to whom it is addressed, is a sign of the incomprehensible and irrational Other. Then there is that message: echoing and parodying the message of the Other 'verses' – *The Satanic Verses* by Salman Rushdie. What does such an 'alien' billboard say to the passing public? Is it totally meaningless because it does not 'speak' to them? Does it say anything beyond its mere presence?

'The Golden Verses' evokes and erases the Orientalist stereotype at the same time. It uses the conventional images of the

Other to draw its audience in; then it slaps them with total silence and incomprehensibility. It speaks to its western audience by reflecting their prejudices of the Other back to them and then it makes them feel like the Others always feel: dumbfounded. It declares its pride in the continuation of Islamic tradition – both calligraphy and carpet weaving are dynamic, thriving traditions – yet, it has more to say about the West than about the Other. Its inaccessibility masks a silenced voice and advertises the absence of space for the Other. With its deliberate play on Orientalism, its ironic comment on western civilisation, and its conscious use of postmodern conventions (a billboard on a commercial site that sells nothing, an authentic carpet that is a clear copy, seeking to represent the Other while making the Other incomprehensible), 'The Golden Verses' attempts to reveal the truly epic nature of the postmodern enterprise.

The west has always been fascinated by Oriental carpets: the intricately woven carpets from Persia, Afghanistan, Pakistan or Turkey represent a sense of wholeness, a picture of authenticity. But the authenticity that the carpet represents has been rendered meaningless by postmodernism: the west has a tendency to destroy what it seeks, decapitate what it yearns for. Postmodernism persuades, cudgels and finally forces the Other to abandon its quest for cultural authenticity and adopt the tastes, habits and cultural traits of western civilisation. But, while for the west authenticity is an individual goal, for the Others it is a largely a cultural process – a process in which the stakes are not for personal identity but the identity and therefore the survival of the community and society as a whole.[2] Afro-American literature, for example, highly values cultural authenticity as a means of ensuring communal and individual self-assertion in the black Diaspora. Similarly, some native American and Canadian writers resist what they see as the appropriation and pollution of the true essence of their culture by white writers and demand that their ownership of their stories be recognised. The postmodernist onslaught on cultural authenticity thus undermines a major mode of non-western resistance, revealing genocidal tendencies. The 'fiction' of 'The Golden Verses' – 'white people are very good people ...' – represents the instrument for this genocide of the

Other: Araeen has simply paraphrased the essence of the postmodern message, where 'white people' are equated and represented
directly with 'bourgeois liberalism'. But that nursery rhyme
parody says something else: it declares that fiction, both as lies
and as literature – the title of the work reflects the title of a *real*
novel – is an instrument of colonisation, that postmodern fiction,
with its universalising and assimilative impulses, is but another
name for the ancient colonial politics of domination and control.

The message of 'The Golden Verses' contrasts sharply with the
common wisdom on postmodern literature. Conventionally, the
representation of the Other in postmodern fiction is presented as a
new and liberating endeavour. It is argued, for example, that
'magical realism', the main school of postmodern fiction, deliberately subverts the dominant mode of narrative realism by intro-
ducing surrealistic events. This subversion of narrative forms, as
developed in Gabriel Garcia Marquez's *One Hundred Years of
Solitude*, Manuel Puig's *Kiss of the Spider Women*, Mario Vergas
Llosa's *The War of the End of the World* and Carlos Fuente's *The
Old Gringo* in Latin America, has a political dimension: 'it
involves a deliberate, self-conscious attempt to break with the
cultural imperialism of European form',[3] and as such, it is a new
and innovative mode of literature with unimaginable benefits for
the folks in the Third World. With their manipulative use of
narrative and perspectives, mixing real history and historic
characters with imaginary creations and deliberate emphasis on
plurality, these novels question the dominant notions of history
and challenge the illusion of congruous, integrated identity. But
in the final analysis, whose history, and which identity, do they
privilege – despite their stated political ambivalence? These
'Third World cosmopolitans', notes Timothy Brennan, have
'supplied sceptical readings of national liberation struggles from
the comfort of the observation tower, making that scepticism
authoritative'.[4] Indeed, Borges, Garcia, Llosa, Fuentes et al. are
more European than South American: as they themselves emphasise and as is clear in their attitudes towards the indigenous people
of Latin America. An issue in Mario Vargas Llosa's campaign for
the presidency of Peru in 1990 was the condescending attitude
towards the Peruvian Indians in his fiction. Peru, like all of South

America is a rigidly stratified society, in which the caste mark is skin colour: the paler the skin, the higher up the hierarchy one belongs. To get on the upward ladder of national inclusion in Peru requires disassociation and distance from Indianness, learning Spanish, the language of the dominant order, and radically hispanising oneself. Moreover, there is nothing really new about magical realism – it is there in Kafka and Beckett. And classical Japanese literature has always exhibited the trait, including a hostility towards logocentric systems, which are considered to be the hallmark of postmodern fiction.[5] Furthermore, the postmodern variety is not the only fiction that is concerned with history or seeks a different form and perspective on history. In Latin America itself, we can identify, as Santiago Colas notes, two new modes of fiction that seek the same goal:

> Isabel Allende's *House of Sprits* (1992), Antonio Skarmeta's *I Dreamt the Snow was Burning* (1984) and *The Insurrection* (1982), Carlos Martinez Moreno's *Inferno* (1983), Luisa Valenzuela's *Lizard's Tail* (1983) and *Other Weapons* (1992) and Marta Traba's *Conversacion al sur* (1981) and *En cualquier lugar* (1984) ... combine stylistic complexity with a concern for representing and intervening in recent history. During the same period, *testimonios* (testimonial narratives) have emerged from all over Latin America, such as Alicia Partonoy's *Little School* (1986); Hernan Valdes's *Tejas Verdes* (1974); Rigoberta Menchu's *I, Rigoberta Menchu* (1982); Domitila Chungara's *Let me Speak* (1978) and Elena Poniatowska's *Until We Meet Again* (1969), *Massacre in Mexico* (1971) and *Nada, Nadie* (1988). These *testimonios* certainly question the processes by which historical facts are constructed, passed off as given, and pressed into the service of a particular class, race, gender, or institution.[6]

So why single out postmodern fiction as the most innovative and most beneficial for the Other? The reason – as is often the case – is brute power. Postmodern fiction has acquired the power of the dominant civilisation, which has propelled it on a global trajectory while marginalising other modes and forms of fiction that question history but do it in a specifically non-western way, from the perspective of non-western hopes and aspirations. Magical realism gives the appearance of speaking from the perspective that incorporates the Other but in so doing it merely utilises that conception of the Other that fits within the established conventions of the west. The grotesqueries in Salman Rushdie's *Midnight's Children* could have sat happily in Kipling; Carlos Fuentes' murderous Mexican revolutionary in *The Old Gringo* would have no problem in finding a place in any conventional, anti-Mexican novel. With its language-games and word-play, in the mixing of the recognisably real, with dreams, fairytales, mythology and the unexpected, magical realism accomplishes what modernity is losing the power to accomplish: reinforce and further entrench the classical western ideas and stereotypes of the Other while writing the Other out of history.

It has been argued that the fragmented structure of postmodern narratives enables *western* readers to appreciate non-western works, thus opening hitherto closed texts of Other cultures to new audiences. Yoshio Iwamoto, for example, suggests that 'the emergence of postmodernist literary modes in the West should help close the gap that Western readers have apparently sensed in approaching Japanese works with their episodic, non-linear structures – say those of Yasunari Kawabata – thus rendering them less "exotic"'.[7] The well-meaning Norman Brown makes an even greater claim. Western scholars who have been unable to comprehend and appreciate the Qur'an for over a thousand years, he argues, should now be able to read it as it should be read thanks to postmodern literary modes in general and *Finnegans Wake* in particular. Brown declares:

> we are the first generation in the West able to read the Koran, if we are able to read *Finnegans Wake* ... The affinity between this most recalcitrant of sacred texts and this most avant-garde of literary experiments is a sign of our times. Joyce was fully aware of the connection, as Atherton shows in the most exciting chapter of *The Books at the Wake*; I particularly like his discovery in the *Wake* of the titles of 111 of the 114 suras. In both the Koran and *Finnegans Wake* this effect of simultaneous totality involves systematic violation of the classic rules of unity, propriety and harmony; bewildering changes of subject; abrupt juxtaposition of incongruities. Sura 18 is a good example. In addition to the melange of pseudonarratives, there are two

intrusive parables ('similitudes', vs. 33 and 46) to remind us of the Day of Judgement; intrusive allusions to the current circumstances of the Prophet (his grief, v. 6; his lack of children, v. 40); and one intrusive pointer on pious decorum or etiquette in speech (vs. 24–45). Like *Finnegans Wake* the Koran rudely insists on indecent conjunctions. The Sura on Light (14), in the words of Hodgson, contains the most ethereal passage of visionary mysticism juxtaposed with what might seem the most sordid, dealing with matters of etiquette, with sexual decency, and in particular with an accusation of infidelity levied against a wife of the Prophet. The whole texture is one of interruption (Joyce's 'interruption'); collision (Joyce's 'collideorscape'); abrupt collage, or bricolage, of disconnected ejaculations, *disjecta membra*, miscellaneous fragments. The widely accepted tradition is that the Koran was collected, after the death of the Prophet, not only from the 'hearts of men' but also from pieces of parchment or papyrus, flat stones, palm leaves, shoulder blades and ribs of animals, pieces of leather and wooden boards. In the words of *Finnegans Wake*, 'A bone, a pebble, a ramskin; chip them, chap them, cut them up always; leave them to terracook in the muttering pot' (FW, 20).

Hence, it does not matter in what order you read the Koran: it is all there all the time; and it is supposed to be all there all the time in your mind or at the back of your mind, memorised and available for appropriate quotation and collage into your conversation or your writing, or your action. Hence the beautiful inconsequentiality of the arrangement of the suras: from the longest to the shortest. In this respect the Koran is more avant-garde than *Finnegans Wake*, in which the overall organisation is entangled in both the linear and the cyclical patterns the novel is trying to transcend.

Every sura is an epiphany and a portent; and therefore not beautiful but sublime. Against He speaks in thunder and in fire! What the thunder said. Dumbfounding. Wonderstruck us at a thunder, yunder. Well, all be dumbed! (FW, 47, 262). In the Koran as in *Finnegans Wake* there is a destruction of human language.[8]

Well, as the proverb has it: better late than never. Whatever helps the helpless western scholars and readers to understand non-western texts ought to be welcomed. Unfortunately, several decades of postmodern literary practices have done nothing either to increase the understanding of non-western texts or even to increase interest in what is lovingly called 'foreign fiction'. But the murderous inclinations of postmodern fiction have been increasingly apparent.

The Cosmopolitan Head Hunters

The genocidal tendency of postmodernist fiction can be judged from the project propagated in the philosophy of Richard Rorty, the American anti-foundational apologist of postmodernism, and the translation of this philosophy into literature in the novels of, for example, Umberto Eco and Salman Rushdie. Rorty's basic thesis, outlined over a decade ago in *Philosophy, the Mirror of Nature*,[9] is that thought cannot represent the world, mind is not the mirror of nature and that western philosophy has been totally misconceived in its central project. Indeed, Rorty argues, Philosophy with a capital P is no longer a possible and credible enterprise. As nothing – mind or matter, self or world – has an intrinsic nature which may be 'expressed' or 'represented', the ultimate context within which knowledge requires meaning is conversation. There may or may not be a world out there; but for Rorty there is definitely no 'truth out there' waiting to be discovered; the quest for 'the nature of truth' is as meaningless as the discussion on 'the nature of God' and 'the nature of man'. In *Contingency, Irony and Solidarity*,[10] Rorty spells out the true dimensions of the postmodernist enterprise: 'to drop the idea of language as representation and to de-divinize the world', to get to the point where 'we no longer worship anything, where we treat nothing – as quasi-divinity, where we treat everything – our language, our conscience, our community – as a product of time and chance'.[11] How are we to proceed to this de-divinisation of the world? Since philosophy, and by extension, theory, no longer function to ground politics and social criticism, the very shape and character of criticism changes: it must become more pragmatic, ad hoc, contextual and local. Thus, Rorty's 'goal' is sought 'not by inquiry but by imagination'.[12] It is fiction rather than philosophy, narrative rather than theory, that provide a better perspective on human behaviour. Fiction, like that of Nabokov and Orwell (both of whom receive serious attention from Rorty), explains the cruelty we are capable of and awakens us to the humiliation of particular social practices. But if fiction explains our capacity for cruelty, then it explains the nature of human beings; and if it explains the nature of human beings then it is the only legitimate criterion for deciding what is and what is not cruel: it can thus, despite Rorty's clarion call that we should worship nothing, become an object of worship! The goal of postmodern fiction, then, is to uncouple the thinking self, its language and community from its telic moorings; to demonstrate the total meaninglessness of the metanarratives. Yet the vehicle for this demonstration itself acquires a meta-authority: the novel becomes god!

Umberto Eco's *Foucault's Pendulum*[13] provides an excellent mirror of Rorty's philosophy of contingency culture. According to Anthony Burgess, 'it exemplifies what postmodern fiction is about, with its learning – real and bogus – its concern with books talking to books, its elements of self-mockery, its semiological obsession. This is the way the European novel is going.' So where exactly is it going? A long, erudite novel, sprawling across close to a millennium, from the first crusade to the present day, and wandering across three continents, it plunders almost every religious and mystical tradition of thought one can think of (each chapter begins with a quotation from some worthy mystical, religious, occultist, philosophical, scientific or literary text or manuscript – from the Talmud and the Shai Imam Jafar as-Sadiq to Karl Popper, Madame Blavatsky, Henry Corbin, Francis Bacon, Borges, Hermiticus, Dante, Freemason rites), and uses them to play typographical, numerological and linguistic games. The obvious point is that there is hardly any difference between, say, Freemasonry and the thought of Imam Jafar as-Sadiq, there is nothing to choose between Karl Popper and Madame Blavatsky. Each tradition of thought, each thinker, is as meaningless and futile as the next. The narrative concerns three editors of a Milan publishing house – Belbo the disillusioned romantic, Diotallevi the dyspeptic amateur and Casaubon our hero-narrator – who by contingency get involved in an occultist mystery. The 'small but serious' publishing house of Garamond receives a visit from a mysterious Colonel Ardenti, clutching a photocopy of a manuscript excavated from a Templar stronghold in Provence. The eleventh-century parchments reveal a coded message to untap a source of extraterrestrial radioactive material 'greater than atomic energy'. Using the parchment, the three publishers decide to stage a hoax by fabricating an elaborate masterplan, a metanarrative, which explains the whole of world history. Everything from the bogus Templar plan to all the manuscript pages of hermetic thought submitted to Garamond, as well as excavated material from archives and references in printed texts are fed into a computer to build a structure of correspondences and coincidences. But the joke backfires as the twentieth-century followers of the old Templars, their dreams of ancient power still very much alive, believe in the reality of the plan. Indeed, it seems that all absurdities, however far-fetched, fit with the previously established structure of the plan. As the three publishers are pursued by the 'Diabolicals' in an attempt to discover the fictionalised plan, Eco hammers home the central point of his thesis: the world is a whirling network of kinships, a 'saraband of anagrams'; there is no truth, all is relative and man can attach his moorings, the fixed point of the world, anywhere he wishes. When all is said and done, everything is meaningless; in fact, the infinite universe is nothing more than an infinite onion which, after countless peelings, comes down to – nothing.

Like most postmodernist artefacts, *Foucault's Pendulum* offers only the suggestive power of swift juxtaposition: there is not a hint of a perspective. 'Why write novels? Rewrite history', Belbo says; especially when history and fiction are interchangeable. At the end of the novel, Belbo finds himself strung up under Foucault's contraption in the Conservatoire des Arts et Metiers in the old Paris church of Saint Martin des Champs. With Diotallevi already out of the way, Casaubon waits alone for the imminent arrival of the assassins wondering, 'Maybe I imagined the whole thing.' The lack of perspective within the novel is reflected in the lack of perspective in the new urban ensemble around Paris where Casaubon wanders aimlessly.

While the culture of postmodernism is without perspective, it is certainly not without its crusading spirit. *Foucault's Pendulum* is a sermon, albeit a learned one. It asks us, indeed rams down our throats, the theology of contingency. And Rorty himself, despite reducing everything to contingency, cherishes cultural hopes that are not so contingent. No sooner does he denounce all metanarratives as meaningless, than he erects one of his own to take over all other metanarratives: 'postmodern bourgeois liberalism', to use the title of his well-known essay.[14] It is a narrative that explains everything and marks the culmination of all human endeavour:

> For in its ideal form, the culture of liberalism would be one which was enlightened, secular, through and through. It would be one in which no trace of divinity remained, either in the form of a divinised world or a divinised self. Such a culture would have no room for the notion that there are nonhuman forces to which human beings should be responsible. It would drop, or drastically reinterpret, not only the idea of holiness but those of 'devotion to truth' and 'fulfilment of the deepest needs of the spirit'. The process of de-divination ... would, ideally, culminate in our no longer being able to see any use for the notion that finite, mortal, contingently existing human beings might derive the meaning of their lives, from anything except other finite, mortal, contingently existing human beings.[15]

The culture of liberalism, it is also argued, is also the only culture in which plurality can function. The argument goes as follows: since we cannot justify any particular culture on the basis of rationality, we are forced to tolerate a whole variety of cultural forms. Thus, the rejection of the Enlightenment faith in the power of reason, leads to pluralism. This argument, which was originally advanced by Isaiah Berlin,[16] has a well-known logical flaw. It involves an appeal to the indefensibility of all forms of cultural life in order to defend a single one. The error lies in the belief that since liberal democracy contains a plurality of beliefs, it is the only political system which reflects the fact that no one set of values is more worthwhile than any other. But to preserve that diversity one has to defend the values of liberalism and this cannot be done by declaring the indefensibility of all values. Undeterred by the serious flaw in his argument, Rorty triumphantly proclaims the metanarrative of 'anything goes', that absolutely nothing is Bad, that no action or attitude can be perceived as naturally and inherently 'inhuman', and that there is no tribunal – even in times like that of Auschwitz – higher than that of 'finite, mortal, contingently existing human beings', and that liberalism is all that really matters. Rorty's notion of 'liberalism' incorporates two ideologies: capitalism and democracy. He thus seeks to defend his contingency culture with both the power of capitalism and the institutions and practices of the rich industrialised democracies. The postmodernist onion now reveals a worm-infested hard core.

How does the original sin of contingency cope with the *real* Evil out there? The evil inherent, for example, in Serbian ethnic cleansing, in the string of serial killers stalking western cities, in the pathological concern with stockpiles of weapons of mass destruction, of autocrats and dictators who know no humanity? In a human world configured by the contingent forces of language, self and community, how are we to cope with real cruelty and the suffering it generates? Rorty provides us with a strategy to come to grips with the postmodernist onion. 'Irony', he suggests, is the only thing that can overcome public suffering and reconcile the demands of self-creation and human solidarity. Ironists are the Grand Saviours of postmodernism because they realise 'that anything can be made good or bad by being redescribed', and because they deny that 'any criteria of choice between final vocabularies exist', and because they are 'never quite able to take themselves (as well as the world and truth) seriously'.[17] So a victim of a serial killer should take comfort in irony; a displaced individual should rejoice in irony; real victims of real evil should seek solace in irony and the belief that their bad experiences can be redescribed as good. *The Perez Family* syndrome.

Once again it is Umberto Eco who provides us with a fictional demonstration of Rorty's philosophy. *The Name of the Rose* (reduced to a linear narrative in the 1986 movie)[18] is an erudite reworking of Conan Doyle (it too comes with an endorsement from Anthony Burgess) and has William of Baskerville, with an adolescent sidekick, solving a murder mystery in a medieval monastery. The novel's main protagonist is Jorge, an elderly monk who takes himself too seriously and does not laugh; a tragic figure, he is the incarnation of dogmatic belief: outdated, a kind of living dead, a remnant of the past. The main message of *The Name of the*

Rose is that lack of irony and laughter is the source of totalitarianism. This thesis, as Slavoj Žižek argues, has two basic flaws:

> First, this idea of an obsession with (a fanatical devotion to) Good turning into Evil masks the inverse experience, which is much more disquieting: how an obsessive, fanatical attachment to Evil may in itself acquire the status of an ethical position, of a position which is not guided by our egotistical interests. [Second], what is really disturbing about *The Name of the Rose*, however, is the underlying belief in the liberating, anti-totalitarian force of laughter, of ironic distance. Our thesis here is almost the exact opposite of this underlying premise of Eco's novel: in contemporary societies, democratic or totalitarian, that cynical distance, laughter, irony, are, so to speak, part of the game. The ruling ideology is not meant to be taken seriously or literally. Perhaps the greatest danger for totalitarianism is people who take its ideology literally.[19]

Irony thus can serve to maintain the status quo. What Rorty seems to be saying, and Eco trying to demonstrate in his novel, is 'laugh at bourgeois liberalism, it will ease the pain of finally accepting it'. But 'bourgeois liberalism' is no laughing matter for its victims: the non-west, the majority of mankind. Irony, ridicule and cynicism is what secularism used to undermine Christianity during the Enlightenment; now they have become weapons targeted at the non-west. Taken to its extremes irony and cynicism, as Peter Sloterdijk's classic work, *Critique of Cynical Reason*,[20] demonstrates, produce nothing but paralysis, a sensibility which is 'well off and miserable at the same time', unable to function in the real world. Other cultures, therefore, have to take postmodern liberalism, with its deep moorings in the grand narrative of secularism, *literally*. In its eagerness to subsume Other worlds and push Other cultures towards a de-divinised world, postmodernism acquires a totalitarian character: with or without irony, postmodern bourgeois liberalism spells the death of the Other.

There is also a more specific reason why postmodernism is so infatuated with 'imagination' and 'fiction', 'language games' and 'word-play'. Imagination is the one human frontier that has not been totally colonised; and fiction is the tool that can accomplish this goal. The novel is one of most powerful instruments for the colonisation of imagination. All fiction, in the final analysis, leads to the manufacture of cultural meanings which are always political meanings. Novels are thus instruments for promoting certain ideologies; and postmodern fiction is all about how the Other dreams itself to be irrelevant, obscurantist and an appendage to western liberal humanism. Moreover, while other conceptual and intellectual instruments for the projection of western desires and containing the Other – for example, 'history', 'philosophy', 'reason', 'modernity' – can be, and are, constantly challenged, argued against, and exposed, fiction is not so amenable to debate. Why take it so seriously? It is only fiction: a fictional dream of a fictional character in a fictional novel. But, as we know by now, postmodernism fiction has a nasty and persistent habit of striking back as reality: a fictional book in a fictional advertisement becomes real and ends up at the top of the bestseller list – *Fly Fishing* by J. R. Hartley from the advertisement for *Yellow Pages*. Fictional representation is thus everything; it is the stand-in for actual, real Others, with real history, real lives, real lived experiences. Postmodernism's obsession with representation of the Other in fiction is designed to project this representation back as reality and hence shape and reshape the Other according to its own desires.

A New Game of Old Images

The western desires on and of the Other play an important part in postmodern fiction. Postmodern narratives preserve both the modes of representation and the seductive gaze that was central to imperial discourse. Thus in a typical postmodern novel, like John Barth's *The Last Voyage of Somebody the Sailor*,[21] all the images of Orientalism reappear intact but now with added potency and urgency. A long, complex novel, *The Last Voyage of Somebody the Sailor* mixes the real and imaginary to knit every known fantasy in the Orientalist lore of the Other into an elaborate canvas. The narrative concerns the adventures of Simon Behlor, an ageing New Journalist 'from East Dorset, Maryland, in the fiftieth-or-so year of his life', and author of popular novels with *Arabian Nights* themes, who, while on holiday in Morocco, becomes incensed with 'the exotic otherness of Islam'. But what does this 'Otherness' consist of? The most potent of all symbols: 'market-women in veils and djellabas, men in caftans over their business suits, currency in dirhams, a predawn muezzin crying something that sounded like Wombat! Wombat! from a loudspeaker minaret near the Villa de France ...' But these symbols do not lead to an appreciation, or even an understanding of difference, of the Otherness of Islam. On the contrary, they fulfil the worst desires of our hero: 'the taste of mint tea or couscous, the smells of cumin and oleander (even of the notorious Marrakesh tanyard), the sight of camels and caftans and hammered copper, the feel of soft tooled leather, the sounds of goat-bleat, pipe and tambour, of spoken Arabic itself – most particularly the five-times-daily prayer call from the minarets of Islam – were charged for keeps with the illicit voltage of hashish and adultery'. Thus, Islam for Behlor, and Barth, only signifies hashish and adultery; which is in keeping with what Islam meant to countless other western writers who went in search of these goodies to that 'interzone' of William Burrough's *The Naked Lunch,* Tangier, where our hero falls in with the crowd of expatriate writers led by the guru, Paul Bowles.

Bowles' own fiction, dark and sinister, is directed almost exclusively by a sense of the Otherness of Islam. Bowles was followed by a host of writers – Burroughs, Cecil Beaton, Joe Orton, Tennesee Williams, Truman Capote, Stephen Tennant, to mention a just a few – for whom the dark shroud of Islam as experienced in Tangiers exerted a morbid fascination. Apart from the exotic Otherness of Islam, they came largely in search of sex – particularly homosexuality – and hashish. No wonder then that Behlor associated Islam only with promiscuous sex. When Behlor comes across an 'Islamic' image – an Arab restaurant, 'an Ingres harem scene in the Louvre', or 'an edition of *The Thousand Nights and a Night* in a London bookshop' – he thinks only of 'muskmarine vulva', 'copper-fleeced armpits' and 'unprecedentedly sustained erections'. He gets so excited while buying a watch from a woman with 'Berber and Levantine' features that he has a mystical ejaculation and ends up in 'Jmaa el Fna' (the accumulation of annihilation). The Other is there only to fulfil the sexual desires of the west.

The novel is structured like a postmodern art gallery, an inside-out mirror facade, where everything is connected to every-thing else and the predominant images on display are those of the Otherness of Muslim women. Hashish mysticism and a Seiko watch collaborate to transfer Behlor to the Baghdad of Caliph Harun al-Rashid. There in the house of Sinbad the Sailor he lives through every Oriental sexual fantasy ever penned, while Barth makes connections between medieval Islam and modern America. Language-games, word-play and semantic symmetries abound. Behlor's native Maryland is littered with condoms dubbed 'Sheikhs' and cigarettes called 'Camels'. On Sinbad's tablecloth, Behlor becomes Bey el-Loor and Sinbad the Still Stranded; he competes with Sinbad to relate the stories of his seven voyages. His wife Julia Moore is changed into 'Jew Moor'. When innocent and virtuous, Sinbad's adopted son is called Umar al-Yomm ('The Cultured Day'), when he is corrupted and becomes a pirate, he is dubbed 'Sahim al-Layl' ('Horror of the Night'). But it is the Arabic term *zahir* which provides the novel with its main connection. In normal use, *zahir* means that which can be observed. But Barth gives it a special meaning: 'it's an Arabic term for an Arabic legend ... imagine some unobtruse object ... that has the power once your eye falls innocently upon it to gradually take possession of your mind ... it might be a paper clip or the ashtray on your desk, one particular pine tree in a pine forest, or one brick no different from all the other bricks in a building, or an incidental face in crowd shot. But if it happens to be the *zahir*, then bingo'. In other words, *zahir* represents 'any unexpectedly obsessive image' – the kind of images he fills his novel with – an image that is observed as reality. Both Sinbad's ship and Behlor's yacht are called *Zahir*. Behlor shadows Tim Severin's retracing of Sinbad's voyage from Basra across the Arabian Sea to India and 'Serendib' (Sri Lanka) across the Bay of Bengal to Sumatra and Malaysia, and across the South China Sea all the way to mainland China, the fabled 'Al Sin' of Sinbad's time. But off the coast of Serendib his *Zahir* collides with the *Zahir* of Sinbad in some time-warp to produce an explosion of Orientalist obsessions.

We thus find Sinbad to be an amalgam of all the worst clichés of Arab slave-traders. His abode (like all households in medieval Islam?) is the best little whorehouse in Baghdad, complete with dancing girls, a bisexual page and a slave-girl concubine, Jayda, of such sexual prowess as to be an essential ingredient in any worthwhile orientalist wet dream. Jayda can 'fuck either human sex in four principal languages and two dialects', and, 'at certain private exhibitions' has been mounted 'by a very large guard dog, a small but ardent donkey, and a particularly lascivious chimpanzee'. She can tell the future with her ability to 'read men's *zabbs*' (penises; it should be *zibb*) as 'other folk read the Koran'. Not surprisingly she has 'the most prescient *wfhft* (colloquial term for vagina) in Islam'. But it is the vagina of Yasmin, Sinbad's daughter, that provides us with the central mystery of the novel. Like all good Muslim fathers, Sinbad is engaged in the business of selling his daughter to the highest bidder. But before the price can be determined, the quality of the merchandise has to be established. What is the status of Yasmin's vagina? Is she a virgin or 'irreparably soiled merchandise'? Was she assaulted by her pirate captives? Or by Sinbad's adopted son? A mystery of such grand proportions can only be solved by Caliph Harun al-Rashid himself. And sure enough he arrives, accompanied by his Grand Vazir Jafar al-Barmaki, like a Muslim Sherlock Holmes. But before resolving the enigma of 'the hymenal state of Sinbad's daughter', he invites wagers on this 'delicate matter'. Wagers taken, Yasmin publicly invites him to 'open and inspect'.

Barthes' Orientalist obsessions even overlook the period in which the narrative is supposed to be set. Kuzia Fukan, Sinbad's chief striptease, who performs her revealing dance with her caftans and harem-pants, beckons Behlor by 'opening her muscled, clean-shaven thighs, with two impudent fingers: Yours to enter. Yasmin is a modern feminist, an expert on the commodities market, who likes old white men (like Barthes himself?) and longs for their world where 'at least some women have the freedom that none has in ours'. Moreover, she has no problem in swallowing the postmodern definition of art as human salvation: 'raised as she had been in a culture in which autobiography was all but unknown, she found the idea of publishing one's rather ordinary adventures and misadventures (even of the more intimate sort), as if they were exemplary, for the entertainment of strangers, not self-evidently admirable; with only a little prompting, however, Yasmin came to see in it the possibility of experiencing imaginative redemption (into art, I presumed to say), and thereby, perhaps, of its vindication.' Here two vaginas are being conquered with one *zubb*: not just that we are told a historic lie – autobiography was common in classical Islam – but also we find that true salvation lies not in some 'dark superconservative' religion but in western fiction – perhaps like Barthes' own novel. Characters refer to each other simply as 'ibn' ('son of') and 'Abu' ('father of') – they obviously had a problem with basic grammar in Sinbad's Baghdad – and speak in postmodern jargon. Ibn al-Hamra, a businessman, denounces the banality of Behlor's childhood narrative by declaring: 'the high ground of traditional realism, brothers, is where I stand!' The businessman goes on to advise Behlor not to 'attempt to distract us from these grand varieties with such profitless side-shows as human copulation, which are no more agreeable to hear about in detail than are our visitor's other narrative concerns: urination, masturbation, and – your pardon, Sayyid Sinbad – regurgitation'.

What does a postmodernist novel like *The Last Voyage of Somebody the Sailor* actually accomplish? First of all, it feeds on its audience's thirst: in this case for exotic images of Otherness and the desire for sexual domination and subjugation of women of Other cultures. It is, thus, a pure exercise in, to use Ibn al-Hamara's words, 'masturbation' and 'regurgitation'. By mixing real Islamic history (incidentally, the twelfth-century period of Abbasid Caliph Harun ar-Rashid was one of the most civilised periods of any history, and is commonly referred to as 'the Golden Age of Islam') with imaginary narrative, by combining real features of contemporary Muslim societies with fictionalised versions, and knitting the whole narrative with stereotyped images, Barth presents Islam as it has always been presented in western literature: as licentious, violent, oppressive and dark. Islamic law, the reader is told, is not a law with established procedures and elaborate checks and balances concerned with justice and equity, but a kangaroo canon which demands that people should be 'halved with a scimitar' at a slightest excuse. Muslim women are merchandise to be bought and sold at the behest of men. The religion revolves around rape and dishonour. And in the time-honoured tradition of the west, what white men need to do to Islam, its men and its women is 'what men to do men who do to men as men do to women': bugger them all. Postmodern fiction thus constructs a new form of entertainment from the well established western portraits of Otherness, a new ocean of old images.

The Little Room of Torture Toys

The projection and the enveloping of the Other in grotesque and false images is only part of the agenda of postmodern fiction. To de-divinise the world totally, as Rorty would have it, postmodern fiction must go much further. That journey requires the complete removal of the insulating space of the Other, its notions of the holy and the sacred, skinning it alive as it were, so that it is totally exposed to the mercies of the postmodern wind. To accomplish this goal, postmodern fiction has to take a quantum leap directly on to the sacred territory – the holy texts, the revered personalities – of the Other. Salman Rushdie's *The Satanic Verses* makes just such a leap. Above all the recycled images of Orientalism, and beneath the offence of blasphemy and ridicule of the Prophet Mohammed which the novel has been accused of by Muslims, lurks a deeper significance which has been meticulously worked out over five years. By mimicking the life of Prophet Mohammed to its minutest detail – it is as though it was written from a standard text – the novel aims to strip Islam of its sacred space and nature, appropriate the very personality that defines Muslims as Muslims, and secularise the history that is the sole source of their identity. In a reductionist sense, *The Satanic Verses* is a fictional form of Baudrillard's simulacrum (the word actually appears in the novel a couple of times): the meticulously documented history of Islam it posits is nothing more than a mirage. The undeclared hope, the real mission, is that the novel's image of the life of Prophet Mohammed will come to shape the actual historical reality and hence the perceptions of non-Muslims and

Muslims alike. A classical postmodern exercise. In attempting to illuminate the central paradigm of Islam's mode of behaviour, *The Satanic Verses* seeks to consign the Grand Narrative of Islam to the rubbish heap of history; it attempts to cast the foundations of Islam as a secularist enterprise and therefore part of the Grand History of secularism; it erases the deep and intrinsic connection between Muslim cultural and religious identity and the Prophetic paradigm, therefore making Islamic culture and Muslim identity an appendage to western culture; and finally, as a result of all these, it succeeds in writing Islamic history and Muslim identity – at least in the minds of western readers at whom the book is largely aimed – out of existence. Thus, *The Satanic Verses* is a both a highly religious and an overtly political text: it skins one religion, Islam, to replace it with an even more homicidal, hunter theology, secularism; and it seeks to undermine the independent identity of Muslim civilisation by presenting it as a mere illegitimate child of western, secularist civilisation.

As Timothy Brennan notes in *Salman Rushdie and the Third World*, 'anyone reading the table of contents alone, with chapter headings such as "Ayesha" and "Mahound" could see that the novel was a 500-page parody of Mohammed's life'.[22] But more: *The Satanic Verses*, Brennan states, 'projects itself as a rival Qur'an with Rushdie as its prophet and the devil as its supernatural voice; it is in the postmodern culture of total doubt and panic', 'in this fertile indecision, this apotheosis of self-questioning, [that] the counter-Qur'an of the novel finds its theology'.[23] Rushdie knows, argues Brennan, that this is what his audience want to hear and 'operates in the conviction of writing for an audience that will eagerly accept this kind of joke'.[24] And he takes his assumed burden of being a postmodernist prophet quite seriously. In the novel, he provides us with systematic clues to show that he considers himself to be on par with Prophet Mohammed. Writes Brennan:

> as history records, Muhammad was about forty years old when his revelations began; so now is Rushdie, and so is his character Gibreel Farishta. Like Rushdie, Prophet Muhammad was not only a seer, but a social agitator, substituting religious brotherhood for the tribal identities of the Arab peoples; and his attack on pagan worship was a direct threat to commercial enterprise set up around the pilgrimage to

the pagan Kaaba, just as Rushdie in the novel continues the critique developed in *Midnight's Children* where religion is portrayed as 'a good business arrangement'.[25]

Such monumental arrogance could only be worked out in a work of fiction. Muslims, of all people, as their history demonstrates so vividly, are aware of the power of ideas. Faith may or may not move mountains; but ideas certainly do, particularly when they are transformed into literature or technology. For then they can be turned into ideologies, bulldozers, tools of suppression, physical and psychological torture and used to justify the eradication of entire cultures and histories. There is no vehicle more powerful for a direct onslaught on the sacred territory of Other cultures than a work of fiction. When backed by a powerful publisher, it commands an international audience, it can saturate the global marketplace. Moreover, being merely fiction, it gives no recourse to the victims to shoot it down. *The Satanic Verses*, with all its pathological symptoms of the fear and hatred of the Other, is not 'literature' as a tool for moral and poetic uplifting of people or a vehicle for illuminating the inner recesses of humanity, it is literature as a naked political and ideological weapon.

That there is nothing sacred except the sacred goal of banishing the Other is the new orthodoxy of postmodernism. The ideological and totalitarian nature of postmodern fiction is ably revealed by Salman Rushdie himself in his two highly publicised and praised essays in defence of *The Satanic Verses*: 'Is Nothing Sacred?' and 'In Good Faith'. But before we analyse the nature of postmodern narratives by examining Rushdie's essays, let me make two general points.

The first is almost a truism: literature is not the exclusive purview of Europe and North America. One can be forgiven for assuming this when almost every airport in the world is stocked only with western novels. Non-western cultures too have literary traditions and non-western people do read fiction. The Others, as Malise Ruthven put it in his book on the Rushdie affair, are not 'people unequipped by culture, education or inclination to read the work of fiction'.[26] Such statements betray an arrogance that cannot be described, or contained, in words. Even the so-called 'primitive' cultures have powerful and long-established traditions of fiction. Moreover, the literary traditions of non-western traditions are living traditions as the queues outside book kiosks in Karachi and Lahore, Delhi and Bombay, Kuala Lumpur and Jakarta, Cairo and Casablanca testify. A typical poetry recital in Pakistan does not attract scores or hundreds of people: it attracts hundred of thousands and is usually held in the kind of stadium reserved in Europe for soccer 'Cup Finals' and in America for 'World Series' baseball. Moreover, everything that *The Satanic Verses* claims to do – its questioning of God, revelation, Prophethood, its portrayal of migration, uprooting and metamorphosis – may be new to western readers but it is old and familiar to people living in even the remotest villages in Muslim countries: it has all been done before, and done far better, in Arabic, Persian and Urdu amongst other languages. In the *Children of Geblawi*, Naquib Mafouz rewrote the prophetic history; in her monumental novel *Chassma*, A. R. Khatun explored the pains and tribulations of migration, uprooting and metamorphosis (with her heroine forced to move from India to Pakistan during partition); and in his classic poem, *Complaint*, the poet-philosopher Muhammad Iqbal attacked God for being complacent about the plight of the oppressed in general, and Muslims in particular. The fact that the language of these works is not an imperial language, that they have not been published by western publishing giants, that the western *literati* are blissfully unaware of them, does not mean they do not exist – or are not read and loved by non-western people.

There is also a broader point to be made here. Non-western cultures are considered to lack literature, and hence to be inferior, because many of them are oral cultures. In the hierarchical litany of the west, the Roman alphabet, the original colonial tool *par excellence*, is the fittest not merely to survive but to triumph over the rest with their lingering associations with that most primitive stage of all, the fully oral culture. Thus, Muslims of the Subcontinent, for example, are considered to be lacking in literary appreciation since the Qur'an is incomprehensible to them as literary text. Further evidence of their orality, and hence inferiority, is provided by Islam itself. Malise Ruthven presents the following 'evidence': 'the deep connection with orality is maintained in Islamic law, where oral testimony still predominates and written affidavits are not usually taken in evidence'.[27] But writing things down has been the Muslim custom since the inception of Islam. The Qur'an says: 'When you contract a debt for fixed term, record it in writing' (2:282). The Prophet recorded all his contracts and treaties in writing. In an Islamic court, oral testimony is preferred to written affidavits for a simple reason: affidavits can be obtained under duress; oral testimony allows the person concerned to speak freely in the presence of a judge. The clearly false evidence from Islamic law is presented by Ruthven to show that postmodernist linguistic play is beyond the comprehension of the poor folk trapped in an oral culture. Thus, Ruthven asserts that while literates would regard blasphemies, expletives and insults as 'innocuous badinage or word-play, mimicking the crudities of street language', orals would take them to 'have magical potency' and be 'power-driven'.[28] But oral cultures do not just lack literary appreciation, they are also, because of their orality, incapable of democracy. Ruthven tells us that it was the 'technological revolution' of writing which created 'a democratisation of culture'. (Unfortunately, all the archaeological evidence available demonstrates that written language, a Middle Eastern invention, was used to service those states that are the primordial model for Oriental despotism, as well as to facilitate international trade and the extraction of surplus from the subject peasantry.) To substantiate his argument that a pre-modern tendency to 'go berserk' is at the root of Islam's orality,[29] Ruthven brings in Malinowski (via Walter Ong), father of modern anthropology, to support the argument that history, like so much else, is the creation of writing. But as Gellner has shown, Malinowski used the 'reserved laboratory' of oral cultures to prove conclusions about history that he had formed in the cauldron of European written history.[30] A disillusioned Pole, Malinowski preconceived the argument that the re-writing of history perennially undertaken by European political movements, most noticeably Romantic nationalists, the forefathers of fascism, was merely an exercise in creating an historical charter for present political objectives. He proved his preconceptions through his ethnographic fieldwork. It is ideology that predominates in the argument between premodern myth and modern written history: no oral culture is without history and indeed the prevalence of orality is the ultimate in democracy of culture, if democracy means the participation of all in the creation of literary forms which all understand and through which all can communicate. There is no oral culture that is without art in any of its forms. Until a century ago there were cultures with written literature whose art excluded the bulk of the population who could neither read nor write – amongst which must be ranked every European nation.

These fallacious and supremacist arguments have been around a long time; and they form the springboard of Salman Rushdie's defence of his novel. In 'Is Nothing Sacred?',[31] he relies on his audience's prejudices against oral cultures and Islam to show that the Muslim readers of his novel are incapable of appreciating literature, culturally incapable of taking part in the democratic process, and that Islam itself is beyond the redemption of history. Rushdie calls on the great names of postmodernism – Foucault, Rorty, Fuentes – to make his case. The essay is a messianic plea for 'the unimportant-looking little room' of literary fiction 'where we can hear voices talking about everything in every possible way'.[32] But is this space open to all, including oral cultures, or is it a more exclusive domain for a select few? It seems, Rushdie tells us, that 'for many millions of human beings, these (literary) books are entirely without attraction or value'.[33] So the 'unimportant-looking room' is only for those select few who aspire to the condition of imperial literature and its élitist readers. Anyhow, Rushdie informs his readers that Islam is certainly against such an enterprise. Why? Because Islam 'has set its face so resolutely against the idea that it, like all ideas, is an event inside history'.[34] Surely, there's some mistake here. The Prophet of Islam was a real person who existed inside history; he himself, as well as Islam, insist that he is merely a human being; and in so far as the idea of Islam is based on what he taught, Islam is an event in history. And the Qur'an, as it was revealed over a period of 23 years, is both a revelatory event and a permanent text inside history; indeed, even its interpretation must take history into account as many of its verses are a commentary on actual, historical events. Islam without history is Islam no longer; it could not, and cannot, work as a civilisation. This is what the Qur'an says and this is what the life of the Prophet Mohammed is all about. Moreover, to emphasise that Islam is an event in history, its basic sources provide its followers with the cardinal concept of *ijtihad*, a process that describes the continuous, perpetual and reasoned 'questioning' and 'deconstruction' to use Rushdie's own words – of its history and fundamental sources. Furthermore, anyone with a rudimentary knowledge of Islamic history and the history of literature in Muslim civilisation would know that the role that Rushdie's 'unimportant-looking room' is supposed to perform has been performed by Muslim writers and thinkers not in isolated enclaves but in the mainstream of culture.[35] However, Islam, like other religions, suggests that history does not exhaust the full meaning of human existence, nor can it provide the ultimate norms of human conduct. So why does Rushdie make this infantile and blatantly false assertion? The purpose of the exercise is not just to paint a particularly negative picture of Islam (in *The Satanic Verses* this notion occurs as the 'Untime of the Imam'), but to demonise. Placing a culture outside history is tantamount to placing it behind the times; and it has a profound impact on its present. As Randolph Pope argues,

> to live after, to be left behind – this is the colonial condition. By a prodigious tinkering with the chronological order, some cultures are labelled as behind the times, as not fully contemporary. The Spaniards declared the Aztecs and the Incas not simply different but backward, closer to humanity's starting point. Once this form of argumentation is let loose, it allows the powerful to monopolise not only territory but also Time, to claim that the present belongs only to them.[36]

The claim that Islam is outside history and hence backwards makes the opening assertion of Rushdie's essay comprehensible to his audience: 'We have been witnessing an attack upon a particular work of fiction', he writes, 'that is also an attack upon the very idea of the novel form.'[37] Backward folk from oral cultures cannot be expected to understand the significance of literature. This inductive leap in the dark – from one work of fiction to all instances of 'the novel form' – is, like all inductive leaps, logically invalid; Muslims have protested only against *The Satanic Verses*, not at any other novel, not even Rushdie's other works. The trick here is to produce a positive emotion by combining two irrationally negative ideas. If one accepts the false premise that Muslims regard their worldview to be an idea outside history, then it is a small step to believe that an attack on Rushdie is an attack on all literature.

But let us not be too harsh on logical and factual grounds. Rushdie, as he tells us, is writing a love-letter, answering an attack of the fanatical and fundamentalist Others, 'not by an attack but a declaration of love'. But this love has special qualities when compared with faith. 'Love need not be blind', he tells his readers, but 'faith must, ultimately, be a leap in the dark'.[38] So the believers, all those who have some kind of faith, are by definition irrational. They 'revere the sacred unquestioningly' and are thus 'paralysed by it'. Moreover, 'the idea of the sacred is quite simply one of the most conservative notions in any culture, because it seeks to turn other ideas – Uncertainty, Progress, Change – into crime'.[39] By this logic, where else can cultures with sacred notions go, except towards oblivion? It is indeed surprising that Islam, despite its sacred notions, made so much progress that it became a world civilisation. It is also surprising that traditional cultures, 'paralysed' by the sacred, still seem so much better at making peace with nature and conserving the environment – a constant message of all ecological writers. But the assertion is false on another ground: it assumes that all uncertainty, all progress, all change is Good. Postmodernism has deified relentless progress and change. Societies based on sacred notions make value judgements to ensure that change is progress and that progress is not at the expense of one's physical, social and psychological well being. Cultures with a sense of the sacred have a built-in mechanism that checks the price to be paid for every step of progress. This seems to be a much wiser course to follow.

But need faith be a leap in the dark? Faith can be reasoned, and many conscientious believers base their beliefs on rational grounds. Indeed, faith can be as reasoned as theoretical physics or modern cosmology much of which, after all the calculations and observations, is based on faith, on certain metaphysical assumptions about nature, space, time and so on. This much can be ascertained not just by reading Kuhn and Feyerabend, but Foucault and Rorty, both of whom Rushdie quotes with much awe and reverence. The Cosmological and Design arguments for the existence of a Creator may not convince some; but they are still reasoned arguments based on observations, just as string theory and the big bang theory of the universe are based on certain arguments derived from particular observation. There is no way reason or logic can arbitrate between the axiomatic claims of religion or of science. Indeed, every student of the modern history of ideas knows this. Only a postmodern writer like Rushdie can peddle this obsolete, nineteenth-century view and be hailed as a great thinker. Just over a hundred years ago, Pascal demonstrated in his famous wager that it is more reasonable to believe than not to believe.

However, Rushdie is not for the total abandonment of the sacred. He simply wants to transform its allegiance from traditional areas, such as God, revelation, holy text and blessed history, to another domain. 'Can art be the third principle that mediates between the material and spiritual worlds'?, he asks. 'Might it, by "swallowing" both worlds, offer us something new – something that might even be called a secular definition of the transcendence? I believe it can. I believe it must. And I believe that, at its best, it does.'[40] So the answer to the question, 'Is nothing sacred?', is 'Yes, only art is sacred'. But whatever happened to the assertion that the notion of the sacred is the 'most conservative notion in any culture, because it seeks to turn other ideas – Uncertainty, Progress, Change – into crime' and leads to 'paralysis'. It seems that this assertion is rather partial: it is true only when applied to non-western notions of the sacred; when applied to western ideas of 'art' it is magically transformed into a liberating proposition.

This belief statement in 'secular transcendence' performs a double function. It breaks free from religious tradition and historical heritage while at the same time opening up the possibility of divine creativity for postmodern man. Thus while sacred notions of Other cultures are killed, a new secular notion of art as the sacred is created. Rushdie's assertion that art – by which is meant western art – is a sacred religion with redemptive powers and its own priesthood has been echoed by many others. In his introduction to the catalogue of the *Rites of Passage* exhibition, for example, Stuart Morgan suggests that art now performs the religious role of redemption; and artists, having 'experienced their own processes of separation, transition and incorporation – in other words having themselves been delivered', should now be 'considered as *passeurs*, priests (perhaps) of that secular religion that art has become'.[41] Thus, faith in God is transformed into faith in self-creativity, unlimited perfection through art, and art as the moral conscience and guiding principle of humanity. This is one of the most potent and pathological prescriptions for the will to power. With art as the sacred territory of postmodern landscape, what is there to stop the total subjugation of the Other? Where are the moral brakes on the will to total domination? If art is all there is, what checks the impulse to greed, the demands of ever-increasing wants? Perpetuation of violence? The degradation of the earth? And, in the end, the destruction of western culture and civilisation itself? Is art supposed to answer our fundamental questions: Who am I? Where did I come from? Where do I fit in the scheme of things? Why am I responsible for my actions? What does my life mean? What is the significance of death; and how will I face it? Now that we know we cannot live by reason alone, are we now supposed to live by art alone? The abandonment of the notion of the sacred gives rise to one of the most dangerous illusions of western civilisation: the illusion that society is incessantly flexible and subject to the arbitrary whims of the White man's creative capacities. Far from providing total freedom, far from opening the panorama of self-creation on a divine plane, the illusion generates an insatiable desire for more and more power while suspending the western person in a darkness where all things are regarded with equal indifference. To dismiss the sacred, therefore, is to dismiss our own natural limits. Without a consciousness of limits, which can only come from history and religion, any attempt to limit the will to power could have catastrophic consequences.

The suggestion that art should replace traditional notions of the sacred is about as sensible as giving the commission for the design of a museum of photography to a blind architect. Rushdie, however, is unconcerned about the banality of his statements. He proceeds to state that 'religion seeks to privilege one language above all others' whereas 'the novel has always been about the way in which different languages, values and narratives quarrel'.[42] All ideologies, indeed all discursive thought, seek to privilege one language over another. In so far as the postmodern novel is a child of militant secularism, it seeks to privilege the language of secularism. It does that by pouring scorn on the notion of the sacred, by writing traditional people and worldviews out of history, by dramatising non-secular alternatives as cul-de-sacs, and by demonstrating, with all the array of literary devices at its disposal, that secularism is the only real experience we have. Indeed, Rushdie, beginning with Shakespeare then paraphrasing Marx but without showing comprehension for either, tells us that fiction begins with the acceptance that 'all that is solid has melted into air, that reality and morality are not givens but imperfect human constructs'[43] – thus by definition Rushdie's postmodern fiction starts from a metaphysical stance that dismisses all believers and everything they hold sacred, leaving relativism (cognitive as well as moral) as the only truth. This is why in his novel one cannot find a single character with reasoned faith who is a decent human being; even though in real life this is not a difficult task to accomplish. Such fiction not only privileges one language over all others, but does so while hoodwinking its readers into believing its alleged pluralism. At least religion, in so far as it declares itself to be in possession of Truth, is a more honest enterprise. As Declan Kiberd notes,

> to most Western intellectuals, Rushdie remains a hero because of his certainty that doubt is now the proper human condition, especially for an artist. His dialogic account of the novel as the form of conflicting voices, none of them privileged, seemed heroically at variance with religion, which is monologic in its devotion to a single text. The novel, he contends in a clear paraphrase of Bakhtin, 'takes the privileged arena of conflicting discourses right inside our head'. The problem with such an analysis is that it fetishises an eternal scepticism, ignoring or discounting those strong minds which, having heard many voices and arguments, come to a conclusion of definite belief. Rushdie

has no answer for them and so, in a sense, he fails his own test for a post-colonial intellectual, because he does privilege one voice, that of secular scepticism, and he does redraw the boundary between east and west as a border between belief and doubt.[44]

But Rushdie is doing more than simply privileging one voice, his voice, the voice of secularism, over others. Starting from the point that nothing matters, everything is meaningless, Rushdie's fiction proceeds to claim a rather large territory for itself. It is in 'its origins the schismatic Other of the sacred (and authorless) text, so it is also the art most likely to fill our god-shaped holes'.[45] Since god-shaped holes can only be filled by some kind of god, literature then is god. Thus the novelist has divine sanction for freely expressed contempt for all that the Other holds as sacred. Postmodern literature now becomes both *the* sacred enterprise as well as a divine authority unto itself. While Rushdie's position has given a postmodern twist to the nature of art, he is in fact echoing the classical western notion of art. In Renaissance English literature this idea is perhaps most exquisitely realised in Prospero's double fantasy: art as absolute illusion ('the baseless fabric of this vision') and art as absolute power ('graves at my command/ Have wak'd their sleepers, op'd and let 'em forth /By my so potent Art').[46] Rushdie produces both fantasies, revealing himself to be, in the words of Declan Kiberd, 'as fundamentalist as the Ayatollah': this classical western position 'arrogates to its artists the right to freely-expressed contempt for traditional beliefs and believers, in extremist language and images'. But this is an incredibly simplistic position:

> It is not even an answer hospitable to multiculturalism, since it connives in a fundamentally western reification of art as a separate category of human expression, divorced from other experiences. In the east, however, many would concur with the Balinese who told the anthropologist Margaret Mead 'we have no art: we do everything as well as we can'.[47]

'In Good Faith' takes the defence of postmodern literary theology a step forward. The essay begins with a reminder that *The Satanic Verses* is a work of fiction. But, notes Rushdie, it has been described 'as a work of bad history, as an anti-religious pamphlet'.[48] He then proceeds to announce that a 'category mistake' has been made. But who made that mistake? To read fiction as though it were fact is a category mistake, Rushdie tells us. But if the novel is totally fiction, why was it necessary to mimic the life of the Prophet Mohammed in so much detail? Why was it necessary to ensure that every major event in his biography was meticulously reproduced? And why was it necessary to paraphrase a standard text such as Martin Ling's *Life of Muhammad Based on Early Sources* page after page after page? Why is the character called 'Mahound' – a derogatory term for the Prophet Mohammed in the Orientalist lore – described in words which exactly match the description and the physical appearance of the Prophet given in classical texts? How is it possible for a deranged character, suffering from delusions, to remember the names (even a seasoned scholar of Islam would have to look them up) and physical descriptions of every one of the Prophet's wives in a dream sequence? Are the verses of the Qur'an, even though they may appear in a dream, fact or fiction? Why does the *author* take great care, even with the minutest of points, to tell his (initiated) readers that he is talking about the real Mohammed and his life – to the extent of being too clever by half? What are we to make of a text that selectively paraphrases only where it suits the ideological purpose of the author from an extensive historical corpus? And what are we to say when fiction claims the right to overturn 1,400 years of devoted striving to make clear the distinction between fact and fable?[49] A category mistake has been made. For Rushdie to tell Muslims that facts are only tangentially necessary for his fiction adds insult to that category injury.

'I am being enveloped in and described by a language that does not fit me,'[50] Rushdie complains. That is exactly what every believing Muslim said after reading his novel. Indeed, while this experience may be new for Rushdie, it is nothing new for Muslims; or indeed for Other cultures who are constantly described and enveloped in categories that paint them as demonic. The persuasiveness of these images of ignorance based upon a distorted imagination are the attitudes that constructed and are confirmed by the whole of *The Satanic Verses*.

And now to abuse and ridicule. First Rushdie offers his own crude parody of what Muslims find offensive in the novel. Then he suggests that his critics are unfamiliar with the conventions of literary fiction and quite incapable of distinguishing between the novelist and his characters. It ought to be stated categorically: it is not the bits of the novel, as Rushdie suggests, that Muslims find offensive: they find the rewriting of the life of the Prophet Muhammad as an insulting parody offensive; they find the attempt at the creation of an anti-Qur'an ridiculously arrogant and offensive; they find the attempt at writing Muslim culture out of history offensive; they find being given the point-blank choice (even in fiction) of oblivion or total acceptance of triumphant postmodern secularism offensive; they find the argument that the only future they have in Britain is without their cultural identity offensive; they find the portrayal of believers, blacks and women offensive; and they find it offensive that religion can only be discussed in the terms and conditions of secularism. In short: Muslims find the whole damn novel offensive, 'not the piece of blubber, but the whole wretched whale', to use Rushdie's own words. By isolating the alleged Muslim offensive into a few sentences, Rushdie, as Richard Webster points out, is 'doing precisely what he alleges his Muslim critics of doing. He discusses a book which simply does not exist.'[51]

The purpose of 'offensive language', argues Rushdie, is 'to create a literary language and literary forms in which the experience of formerly-colonised, still-disadvantaged people might find full expression'; further explanation is provided from the novel itself: 'to turn insults into strengths, whigs, tories, Blacks all chose to wear with pride the names they were given in scorn'.[52] First, who is Rushdie to undertake such an exercise on behalf of Muslims? Especially, when he tells us: 'I believe in no god, and have not done so since I was a young adolescent.' Thus, to argue, in Webster's words, 'that he is reclaiming language on behalf of all Muslims is an act of quite extraordinary presumption'.[53] Second, do we really want to reclaim these images? Are all nasty historical images, products of ignorant and distorted perceptions as they are, worth reclaiming? Should blacks wear the epithet 'nigger' with pride? Should Muslims reclaim the western legacy that describes them as fanatic, licentious, barbaric and bloodthirsty? Should American Indians accept Columbus's descriptions of them? Webster again: 'it is difficult to avoid the conclusion that ... Salman Rushdie is offering to Muslim readers not a renewed sense of pride and dignity but an oblique and unintended invitation to internalise centuries of Christian contempt.'[54]

And so to the central message of the novel. 'What does the novel dissent from?' asks Rushdie. 'Certainly not from people's right to faith, though I have none. It dissents most clearly from imposed orthodoxies of all types, from the view that the world is quite clearly This and not That.'[55] Wrong. By presenting faith as a cheap con-trick, the novel destroys the option of faith for the reader. Moreover, by presenting his Brown Sahib worldview as the ideology of sweetness and light, worthy of any and all respect, Rushdie's fiction thrusts the acidic dogma of postmodernism down the throats of his unsuspecting readers. It offers not dissent but the orthodoxy of doubt, the dogma of moral relativism and the creed of triumphant secularism. It is as liberating as the torture gadgetry of the Spanish Inquisition. When blasphemy is used in this fashion, as Webster points out, 'there can be nothing liberating about it. For this is exactly the way in which blasphemy tends to be used by orthodox religious thinkers in order to sustain their own repressive ideologies of purity against the challenges posed by other cultures.'[56]

Rushdie's arguments, if they can be described as such, in 'In Good Faith', are either bewilderingly naive and ignorant or are aimed at soft targets. For example, Rushdie finds it hard to believe that people 'have been willing to judge The Satanic Verses and its author, without reading it, without finding out what manner of man this fellow might be ...'[57] But since the novel is written for western audiences, and since for the vast majority of Muslims, as Rushdie tells us, fiction is quite meaningless, this is hardly surprising. Either Rushdie must concede that Muslims are intelligent and can and do read fiction as fiction, or he must concede that, being fools, they will judge him without reading his unreadable book. And what logic says that one has to read a book to judge its author? How many Marxists dipped into Das Kapital let alone read it from cover to cover before standing up for the

'revolution of the proletariat'? How many of those who fought
Hitler for the manner of man he was actually read *Mein Kamf*? But
there is another more important point to be made here. Did it
occur to the author of *The Satanic Verses* that his western readers
would accept his picture of the Prophet Muhammad without ever
trying to find out what manner of man *he* was? Did he not know
that in his novel history and fable are so merged that the potential
for truth is obscured, the ability to make reasoned evaluations
fundamentally eroded, the possibility of dialogue made a nonsense? Does he really believe that after his long and convoluted
sermon, his readers will find out for themselves what manner of
worldview is Islam?

Of course, the murderous *fatwa* of Ayatollah Khomeini against
Rushdie further eroded any possibility that readers of *The Satanic
Verses* might discover for themselves the genuine message of
Islam. But the *fatwa* itself gave the Rushdie narrative a postmodern twist where the fictional representation takes on a living,
breathing form and comes back to haunt the author. The essence
of this particular variety of postmodern irony is best captured by
Robert Coover in his short story 'Aesop's Forest' in which the
artist/Aesop sins against Apollo and is dismembered by the angry
Delphians: 'one eye is gone, the other clouded, an ear is clogged
with bees, his hide's in tatters'.[58] Aesop's heresy is that he has
denounced Apollo's Truth as fable: 'I told them the truth, they
called it sacrilege.' But while Aesop has deconstructed an absolute
truth like a true postmodernist, he has also replaced it with his
own construction of a new truth: 'men live by fictions, they have
to. But some fictions, like Aesop's deconstruction of Apollonian
Truth, start throwing their weight around. When this happens,
fictions can turn against their creator, and Aesop's moralised
animals join the Delphians in the lynching of the author.'[59]

Absolutist fiction, based on absolute freedom, becomes an arch
ideology; a power structure, a god in its own right, more powerful
than the Church it seeks to replace. It is more pernicious and repressive, for while one can fight theistic ideologies, fiction as ideology
does not present such clear-cut targets. The Others are oppressed by
a fictional reality. Far from being 'unimportant', Rushdie's 'unimportant-looking room' represents an oppressive global ideology; it is

an authoritarian postmodern enclave, which aims to desacralise the whole house of humanity. For him, and for postmodernism as a whole, fiction is sacrosanct, novelists are divine and western civilisation has the divine right, in the words of Richard Webster, 'to dominate, to subjugate, and to claim as its own imperial property even the most unwilling of brides'.[60] The kind of fiction that postmodernism produces is judge, jury and the executioner all in one. And the nonbelievers in this faith, the traditional and sacred cultures, have no alternative but to line up in the court of his kind of fiction to be written out of history. Just in case we are stupid enough not to get the point, Rushdie tells us in 'Is Nothing Sacred?' that we are 'heading towards a world in which there will be no real alternatives to the liberal-capitalist social model (except, perhaps, theocratic, foundational model of Islam)'.[61] So: submit or die! The black-and-white options of 'liberal-capitalism' or theocratic authoritarianism are given a violent undertone in 'In Good Faith'. Ride the great wave of change that is sweeping the world and bringing in the good tidings of secularism, Rushdie advises Muslims, 'renounce blood', and accept '*The Satanic Verses* as a serious work, written from a non-believer's point of view'.[62] Thus those who do not accept *The Satanic Verses* as 'a serious work' are drenched in blood; and if they do not accept secularism, they will be swept into oblivion. It is 'extremely difficult', writes Webster, 'not to read his words as an oblique and ominous threat – a secularist, apocalyptic threat made in the name of freedom against those who, because they seek to defend their religious faith against what they experience as intolerable insults, are now implicitly defined as the enemies of freedom.'[63]

Cancer Sticks in Purdah

Salman Rushdie is an articulate exponent of postmodern fiction; and as his defence of his own novel shows, postmodern fiction, despite all the claims of its champions, aims at nothing less than the total annihilation of the Other. As Diana Brydon argues, 'when directed against the Western Canon, postmodernist techniques of intertextuality, parody, and literary borrowing may appear radical and even potentially revolutionary'; but 'when directed against native myths and stories, these same techniques would seem to repeat the imperialist history of plunder and theft'.[64] Postmodern fiction has thus become a partner in the dissemination of an ideological code that has enslaved and barbarised the rest of the world. It operates, Stephen Slemon argues, as

> Euro-American western hegemony, whose global appropriation of time-and-place inevitably proscribe certain cultures as backward and marginal while co-opting to itself certain of their cultural 'raw' materials. Postmodernism is then projected onto these margins as normative, as neo-universalism to which 'marginal' cultures may aspire, and from which certain of their more forward-looking products might be appropriated and 'authorised' ... postmodernism thus acts ... as a way of depriving the formerly colonised of 'voice', of, specifically, any theoretical authority, and locking post-colonial texts which it does appropriate firmly within the European episteme. Post-modernism as a mode is thus exported from Europe to the formerly colonised, and the local 'character' it acquires there frequently replicates and reflects contemporary cultural hegemonies.[65]

As such, postmodern fiction has become a most powerful lacuna of racism and bigotry.

We have to see postmodern fiction as a power structure of the most ruthless kind. This is in sharp contrast to postcolonial fiction which is playing an important role in the rediscovery of national heritages of non-western countries, in the unfolding of native idioms, in the recovery of local histories and geographies, and in shaping a sense of community. Postcolonial writers such as Amitab Gosh, Amin Maalouf, Altaf Fatima, Pramoedya Ananta Toer, Zulfikar Ghose, Rachid Mimouni, Nuruddin Farah, Chinua Achebe and Assia Djebar are attempting to write Other cultures back into history by rearticulating the colonial and postcolonial history of non-western cultures. In postmodern narrative, however, there is a complete absence of the postcolonial subject. The power structure that is postmodern fiction eclipses these works while silencing and marginalising the literature of the non-western world which is as much ignored, passed over and unknown as it ever was.

In 'In Good Faith', Rushdie asks: 'how is freedom gained?' And answers: 'It is taken: never given.'[66] In a world where postmodern magicians wield the power of description and render invisible and inaudible any information or reasoned argument that challenges their talisma, Other cultures must rebel against the pathology of postmodernism and break out of its authoritarian spell. The basic issue, Djelal Kadir has argued, is 'survivalism'. But survival of non-western cultures cannot be ensured simply, as Kadir suggests, by 'endurance': 'at the century's end and at a millennial threshold, resilience may well be what we are after most. And our only hope might well lie in the civility of graceful endurance.'[67] While it may be 'graceful' for the west, there is nothing civil about postmodern fiction. In as much as postmodern fiction is central to the making of our contemporary structures of power and influence, essential to the setting of the agenda of what it is to be acceptable, human, worthwhile and sane, it has to be contested. In as much as postmodern fiction is determined to write Other cultures out of history, it has to be resisted. Other cultures thus have to fight to ensure that they have access and freedom to describe themselves in their own languages and categories. Postmodernism demands that Other cultures answer only as questioned, according to the agenda of relevant issues determined by the secular imagination – whether or not these are relevant to the cultural inquiry of non-western cultures. The very act of responding is an act of subjugation and willing cultural annihilation. As Webster reminds us so eloquently, in this 'secularised and agnostic culture the greatest threat to humane values seems increasingly likely to come not from murderous faith, as it has done for many centuries, but from murderous art'.

What postmodern fiction is all about is neatly summed up by Rasheed Araeen's *Jouissance* (1993–94), one of a series two-dimensional 'grid-pattern' works. In *Jouissance*, five photographs arranged in the form of a cross are combined with four 'minimal-ist' green panels. The cross and the colour green, which has strong association with Islam, represent the relationship between Islam and the west, the 'civilising mission' and the Other. Four photographs, taken from television footage, show a city being bombarded and destroyed. The centre photograph has a Muslim woman in complete *purdah*, but as her eye movement shows, quite modern for all that, being offered a cigarette by a glamorous white woman. The cancer stick of postmodern fiction is being presented with a generous smile, with all the allure of participation in something exciting, something white, something wonderful. Inhale, enjoy. Externally, as the images from television screens across the globe show, the Other is being eradicated. Internally, the Other is being induced to commit suicide. The brand name of the cigarette with which the woman in *purdah* is being seduced stands out clearly: 'West'.

6. Fairytales of Science

On a visit to Cairo, the hero of Amin Maalouf's,[1] *The First Century After Beatrice*, a world-renowned entomologist, discovers an unusual use for scarab beetles. When taken as a powder, they enhance virility and guarantee the birth of a son. Even though the powder has existed for centuries, its use hasn't done much harm to the Egyptians: the population seems to be equally balanced between males and females. But then the 'scarab powder' begins to appear in other parts of the world. The entomologist and his high-flying journalist wife discover that it is being sold in India, all over Africa and much of the third world. Worse: an examination of demographic trends reveals a sharp decline in the birth of girls throughout the South.

The First Century After Beatrice is a perceptive novel, which explores the myths and realities of modern science. We start with an ancient eastern myth which turns out to be a western invention and re-emerges as western science. We discover that the power of the 'scarab powder' to immunise women against the birth of girls derives not so much from an ancient formula but from modern molecular biology. The product is packaged in the formula of an ancient myth as a market ploy. While the narrative follows the quests of the protagonists to discover the truth about the 'scarab powder', the reader discovers how science is corrupted, statistics are manipulated and risks from new discoveries are masked by doublespeak, which make them 'negligible', 'insignificant', 'extremely limited', 'residual' and 'under control'. Far from freeing us from ancient prejudices, Maalouf asserts, science is often used to perpetuate them and, not infrequently, to confirm them.

Indeed, modern science has been instrumental in shaping some of the most potent myths – of race, of the inferiority of the non-European people, of the origins of Europe, of the 'problems' of the third world, of the inseparable distance between 'knowledge' and 'values' and the inevitability of certain futures. Science has been the dominant instrument in the subjugation of the Other – the non-west – by western civilisation, and the prime mechanism for the globalisation of the western worldview.[2] It is the bastion of Eurocentrism *par excellence*. The survival of the non-west depends on dethroning western science, on taming the instrumental rationality of the scientific enterprise with an injection of multiculturalism, redirecting it towards shaping a more humane future for humankind.

All the Rivers Run into the Sea

Science, contrary to widespread belief, is not a European creation. Almost every civilisation and culture, whether 'great' like Islam, China or India, 'complex' or 'simple' like those of Africa, the pre-Colombian Americas and the Pacific Islands, have produced its own science. Modern, western science is the heir to the sciences of all non-European civilisations. But Europe appropriated these other sciences, framing and defining them in a specific reductive and secular framework; it followed that other sciences which operated in different frameworks were not science, and thus could be written out of history. The history of the evolution and development of modern science as well as the origins of Europe were rewritten to make both the enterprise of modern science as well as Europe per se self-generating and autonomous of all Other cultures.

Paul Davies provides us with the standard Eurocentric picture of scientific advance:

> In primitive cultures, understanding of the world was limited to everyday affairs, such as the passage of seasons, or the motion of a slingshot or an arrow. It was entirely pragmatic, and had no theoretical basis, except in magical terms. Today, in the age of science, our understanding has vastly expanded, so that we need to divide knowledge up into distinct subjects – astronomy, physics, chemistry, geology, psychology and so on. This dramatic progress has come about almost entirely as a result of the 'scientific method': experiment,

observation, deduction, hypothesis, falsification ... science demands rigorous standards of procedure and discussion that set reason over irrational belief.[3]

We now know that even those cultures which were described by Europe as 'primitive' had developed highly sophisticated sciences. The pre-Columbian cultures had developed experimental agriculture into a finely tuned science: they had over 3,000 varieties of potato alone. The people of the Pacific Islands had developed highly polished principles of navigation and techniques of vessel construction that are unknown even today. Carbon steel was first produced in what is today called Tanzania over 1,500 years ago by methods so sophisticated that Europe could not match them until the beginning of the nineteenth century. Clearly such monumental feats cannot be achieved simply on the basis of 'irrational beliefs' or without some 'standards of procedure'. The conventional wisdom is to attribute 'irrationality' to non-western cultures and dismiss their achievements. However, as research into the history of science and technology of the so-called 'primitive' cultures proceeds, such arrogance will become increasingly difficult to justify.

Our knowledge of the sciences of the civilisation of Islam, China and India has taken great strides over the last two decades. The monumental work of Joseph Needham and others has shown the sophistication and empirical base of Chinese science, which was 'much more efficient than the occidental in applying human natural knowledge to practical human needs'.[4] Without China's discoveries of the magnetic needle, the rudder and gunpowder, Europe would have been confined to its geographic boundaries. The extensive research on Islamic science by numerous scholars, including Faut Sazgin, A. I. Sabra, E. S. Kennedy and Donald Hill, has established beyond doubt not just the quality and quantity of science in Islam, but also how much Europe really 'borrowed' from the Muslim scientists. There would have been no Copernicus, Kepler, Newton or Harvey without the work of al-Tusi, ibn al-Shatir, al-Haytham or ibn Nafis. Indeed, the 'scientific revolution' would not have taken place had it not been for the mathematical models of the fourteenth-century Muslim scientist, ibn Shatir, and the work of astronomers at the famous observatory in Maragha, Adharbayjan, built in the thirteenth century by Nasir al-Din al-Tusi. The Maragha astronomers developed the Tusi couple and a theorem for the transformation of eccentric models into epicyclical ones. Muslim scientists knew that Ptolemy's arrangements for planetary motion were, to use the word of al-Haytham, 'false'. Thus, the Muslim scientists were on the verge of a major breakthrough. Copernicus not only used the Tusi couple and the theorems of ibn Shatir, but used them at exactly the same points in the model. In other words, the lunar models of Copernicus and the Maragha school are identical. All that Copernicus did was to remove the earth from the centre of the model and replace it with the sun – and the 'scientific revolution' erupted.[5] If science is a universal building, then its foundations lie not in Europe but in non-western scientific traditions.

But it is not just the foundations of modern science that are deeply rooted in non-western cultures. The growth of western science is a function of the exploitation, colonisation and de-development of non-western societies. Just as colonialism and the industrial revolution went hand in hand, so the development of western science was linked intrinsically to European empires. In *Science and Empires*, Patrick Petitjean[6] and his colleagues have shown how each development in science was connected to European expansion. Indian historians of science, particularly Radhika Ramasubhan in her study, *Public Health and Medical Research in India*[7] and R. K. Kochhar in his papers on 'Science in British India',[8] have provided detailed accounts of how British colonialism in India advanced European science. Western science progressed primarily because of the military, economic and political power of Europe, focusing on describing and explaining those aspects of nature that promoted the power of the upper classes in Europe. At the same time, the colonial administrators banned the theory and practice of indigenous sciences. For example, Islamic medicine, which was the dominant medicine of the European world up to the eighteenth century, was outlawed in the Middle East and those caught practising or researching it were imprisoned. Thus, the empire played a double role: it fuelled the development of modern science – it is hardly surprising that the first thing the British did in India was to build observatories and the first European sciences to be established in India were geography and botany – and first curtailed, and then killed, the development of non-European sciences. The supposed innate rationality or the alleged commitment of European scientists to the pursuit of disinterested truths had little to do with the development of modern science. As Sandra Harding tells us, 'the professed universality of Western science was established as an empirical consequence of European expansion, not as an epistemological cause of valid claims'.[9]

Even though western science was fuelled by the scientific traditions of non-western civilisations and systemically evolved and developed, it had to be shown to be separate from all other sciences and traditions – unique to Europe and a law unto itself. A major innovation, as Wallis Harman notes,[10] was the 'ontological' assumption of separateness: separability of observer from the observed; parts from whole; organism from environment; man from nature; mind from matter; science from religion – separateness from one another of the 'fundamental particles' which are presumed to compromise ultimate reality. Once nature could be isolated and separated it could be studied in a way that was unique to western civilisation. A second innovation was the notion that only that which can be measured is real. While experimentation and measurement were crucial parts of the sciences of many non-western cultures – Islamic science in particular pioneered exact measurements and detailed experimentation – in Europe they defined what was real and what was unscientific or literally unintelligible. Ideas, notions, categories, phenomena for which no experimental or observational evidence could be discovered had to be abandoned. What was isolated, rigorously studied and measured, was the ultimate truth which, in its formulation as law, could be appropriated.

Non-western traditions of science thus became so many rivers, all of which ran into the sea of western science, which not only, as Bacon said, 'tortured' its secrets from nature but was also the rightful owner of this Truth. Unlike other civilisations, Europe transformed reason in science into an instrumentalist rationality – scientific reason now defined the world and all that it contained. Other notions of reality, however rational, were meaningless at best and dangerous at worst. They could thus be written out of history and the 'scientific revolution' connected to a more appropriate European source: Greece. The history of science thus becomes a linear story of the progress of Europe from its origins in Greece to the development of modern science during the Renaissance. A standard history of science, for example, J. D. Bernal's *Science in History*,[11] starts with ancient Greece and then (devoting only ten pages to Islamic science) jumps to Europe as though nothing happened in between or that other sciences existed. But the identification of Greek culture as European has serious problems. For one thing, Harding points out, 'the idea of Europe and the social relations such an idea made possible, came centuries later – some would date it to Charlemagne's achievement others to fifteenth century. Another point is that due to the spread of Islam, the diverse cultures of Africa and Asia can also claim Greek culture as their legacy.'[12] Islamic medicine, for example, traces its roots to Galen and Greek medicine; indeed, its technical name in Muslim civilisation is *yunani*, literally Greek – medicine. Recent studies, like the monumental works of Martin Bernal[13] and Cheikh Anta Diop,[14] have shown that Greeks were hardly 'European'. The world of Plato and Aristotle was more Egyptian and African then it was European: Bernal shows that 'the Aryan model' of the origins of Greek civilisation, which claims that the Africans and the Semites had nothing to do with the creation of classical Greek civilisation, was a fabrication of the eighteenth- and nineteenth-century Romantics and racists. Prominent amongst the fabricators were noted scientists like Boyle, Kelvin and Newton.

Having connected the 'scientific revolution' back to a manufactured Greece, and argued that modern science is totally European in origin, the west has now to demonstrate that other civilisations are unable to produce anything that could be worthy of the description of 'science'. It is normally in the analysis of the 'enigma' of the decline of Islamic and Chinese sciences that this task is performed. The diagnosis offered by Toby Huff in his *The Rise of Early Modern Science*[15] is typical. The decline of Islamic science, Huff contends, was due to the cultural factors: Islamic law, which does not recognise 'personal negligence' and corporate institutions; the 'extremely personalised nature of human relations', which has generated the ex-

tended family system; and the Islamic belief system, which denies
that nature is governed by a rational order. These three factors con-
spired to bring down Islamic science (we are not told how it manage
to reach the zenith of civilisation in the first place) and prevented
modern science from taking root in Muslim societies today. Given
the fact that one-third of the Qur'an is devoted to extolling the virtues of reason and that Islamic law has a much broader notion of
social responsibility and accountability than 'personal negligence',
one could hardly consider Islamic culture much of a hindrance to
scientific development. When it comes to Chinese science, Huff
declares that the Chinese language is not conducive to 'clear and
unambiguous communication' and is thus not suitable for scientific
inquiry. That may come as a surprise to modern China, which had no
problem in acquiring nuclear technology, and to the Japanese, who
use a parallel system and lead the world in many fields of scientific
research. Chinese notions of the organic world of primary forces
(yang and yin), Huff argues further, are hardly a metaphysics worthy
of the name. Although Chinese science does assume that 'there is a
pattern to existence in all things and that there is a unique way (tao)
for all things ... the explanation of the patterns of existence is not to
be sought in a set of law or mechanical processes, but in the structure
of the organic unit of the whole'.[16] The whole notion is little more
than 'a primitive but natural instinct'; at best, it yields meaningless
binary oppositions such as light and darkness. There is a total
absence in Chinese thought of 'a genuine dialectic of disputation and
a faith in reason'.[17] Strange, then, how the Chinese managed to build
a civilisation on this 'primitive', 'natural' notion and evolved a science without any idea of reason in their metaphysics which, according to Needham, 'was much more congruent with modern science
than was the world outlook of Christendom'.[18] While the banality of
Huff's contentions are a wonder to behold, they are standard arguments advanced both for the decline of non-western sciences and for
the claim that modern science could not have been produced by any
culture other than that of Europe. Not for nothing does the Europe of
the Middle Ages that emerges from Huff's analysis appear as a haven
of rationality where religion had willingly taken a back seat, reason
and conscience had been discovered for the first time and science
advanced unhindered by dogma, persecution or other social and

cultural impediments. In the twelfth century, we are told, Christianity in Europe had turned into a 'corporation', a legal entity that did not interfere with the work of the scientists – though critics may ask why it did not stop the emergence of the Inquisition a few centuries later. The 'cultural outlook, social organization, and economic performance' as well as 'institutionalised disinterestedness and skepticism' of Europe prepared the ground for the emergence of modern science. The universities, far from being a reluctant partner in scientific endeavour as is normally accepted, Huff contends, became the founding institution of modern science. By the fifteenth century, the search for truth had become 'part of the credo, the ethos, the cultural outlook of Europe'.[19] Of course, it was the same credo that launched Europe on its imperial adventure and colonisation of the Other. The origins of modern science lie in 'the fusion of Greek philosophy, Roman law' and that most rational of all metaphysical systems, 'Christian theology'.[20] QED: the purity of Europe and of western science is preserved from contamination by any Other culture.

Given its metaphysical assumptions as well as the nature of its development, it comes as no surprise that western science is intrinsically Eurocentric – in terms of what is selected for research – which itself depends on where the funding is coming from – what is seen as a problem, what questions are asked and how they are answered. If, for example, the problem of cancer is defined as finding a cure, then the benefits accrue to certain groups, particularly the pharmaceutical companies. But if the function of scientific research is seen as eliminating the problems of cancer from society, then another group benefits from the efforts of research. Similarly, if the problems of the developing countries are seen in terms of population, then research is focused on the reproductive systems of third world women, sterilisation techniques and new methods of contraceptives. However, if poverty is identified as the main cause, then research would take a totally different direction. But it is not just the institutional framework that is biased against the Other. The cornerstone of the ideology of science, the Scientific Method, is itself value-laden. The method of science is supposed to ensure neutrality and objectivity by following a strict logic: observation, experimentation, deduction and value-free conclusion. However, studies of how scientists work have shown this to be a myth. Historians of science (including Kuhn,[21] Feyerabend[22] and Ravetz[23]) and sociologists of knowledge (Rose,[24] Mitroff,[25] Latour and Woolgan,[26] Knorr-Cetina,[27] and many others) have shown that scientists do not 'discover' the laws of nature – rather, they manufacture them. Laws of nature are not written in indelible ink on the heavens; they are manufactured in the laboratory. Observations are not made in isolation but within a theoretical framework. The theory itself is embedded in a paradigm – a set of beliefs and dogmas. Thus, all observations are theory-laden; theories are based on paradigms, which in turn are burdened with cultural baggage. Hence, there are no such things as value-neutral, 'objective facts'. Value judgements are also at the very heart of one of the most common elements of scientific technique: statistical inference. When statisticians test a scientific hypothesis they cannot possibly decide its truth or falsity. They go for a level of 'confidence'. Different problems are conventionally investigated to different confidence limits. As Ravetz notes, 'Whether the limit is 95 or 99 per cent depends on the values defining the investigations, the costs and importance placed to social, environmental or cultural consequences.'[28] However, despite the value-laden and culturally biased nature of scientific methodology, science continues to insist on its neutrality. This emphasis in itself is a western cultural trait. 'Maximizing cultural neutrality', writes Harding, 'not to mention claiming it, is itself a culturally specific value. Both the reality and the claim are at issue here. Most cultures do not value neutrality for its own sake, so one that does is easily identifiable.'[29] The illusion of neutrality is produced by stripping a scientific fact of its unique historical features. The 'essential nature' of a scientific fact, argues Claude Alvares, 'is abstracted, in order that the new information can fit other similarly anaesthetised historical events. The fact that an experiment distorts reality is no longer doubted. Strikingly, such distorted information or "objective knowledge" is passed off as the only true picture of reality. The method thus arrogates to itself the right to function as the sole absolute criterion of truth. What science creates are artificial facts. Violence results when the "artificial" fact is imposed on "natural" nature in its ascientific state.'[30] While western cultural values are deeply ingrained in the methodology of science, compassion is totally excluded. 'Both the method and its metaphysics', notes Alvares, 'demand the constant mutilation of the Other. Vivisection, for instance, is an essential component of the strategy of achieving "scientific truth".'[31]

The cultural baggage of science is not limited to its institutions and method. Certain laws of science, based on 'both Judeo-Christian religious beliefs and increasing familiarity in early modern Europe with centralized royal authority and royal absolutism',[32] are also formulated in a Eurocentric manner. For example, a detailed examination of the second law of thermodynamics – which states that heat cannot be transferred from a colder to a hotter body without some other effect, e.g. work, being done – led the Indian physicist C. V. Seshadri to conclude that it is 'ethnocentric'.[33] Seshadri charges that due to its industrial origins the second law presents a definition of energy that favours the allocation of resources to big industry; and a notion of efficiency that values high temperatures, and resources like petroleum and nuclear power that can generate such high temperatures, over ambient temperatures. Together, the notion of energy and the concept of efficiency were thus 'fused with one kind of resource-utilization'. As work done at ordinary temperature is by definition inefficient, both nature and the non-western world are losers. For example, Seshadri points out, the monsoon, transporting millions of tons of water across a subcontinent must be 'inefficient' since it does its work at ordinary temperatures. Similarly, traditional crafts and technologies are designated as inefficient and marginalised. Capitalism and big industry win by the force of 'natural law'.

Finally, the costs and benefits of science are also distributed along racial lines. Harding observes:

> the way Westerners both distribute and account for the consequences of modern science appear distinctively Western. The benefits are distributed disproportionally to already over-advantaged groups in the West and their allies elsewhere, and the costs disproportionally to everyone else. Whether it is sciences intended to improve the military, agriculture, manufacturing, health or even the environment, the expanded opportunities science makes possible have been distributed

predominantly to already privileged people of European descent, and the cost to the already poorest, racial and ethnic minorities, women, and people located at the periphery of global economic and political networks.[34]

Thus, for Other cultures, science's Eurocentrism manifests itself in its violence, in the de-development of the Third World, in the racial portrayals of their culture and worldviews, in the suppression of their modes of knowledge, and in the degradation of the very environments that sustain their physical existence. Science perpetually seeks to dominate and control the Other: 'the character of science', writes Alvares, 'compels it to colonize areas previously outside its domain of control. In this regard, it resembles the great proselytizing religions which attempt to compel people to their point of view because of their unshakeable belief that they alone possess the ultimate truth concerning God and nature.'[35]

No Particular Place to Go

As modern science marches on its self-proclaimed quest for truth, God appears to be entering the scientific equation more and more. Both theoretical physics and molecular biology, it appears, have brought us to the brink of the final curtain: a Theory of Everything and a 'Code of Codes', which lay bare every gene in our bodies, are within our grasp. As the blurb on the jacket of Leon Lederman's *The God Particle*[36] announces: 'we may be close to discovering the ultimate atom – the God particle – which orchestrates the cosmic symphony, and that its discovery may reduce the laws of physics to an equation so simple that it can fit on a T-shirt'. The famous closing paragraphs of Stephen Hawkins' *A Brief History of Time*, reflect the same sentiments:

> If we do discover a complete theory, it should in time be understand-able in broad principle by everyone, not just a few scientists. Then, we shall all, philosophers, scientists, and just ordinary people, be able to take part in the discussion of the question of why it is that we and the

universe exists. If we find the answer to that, it would be the ultimate triumph of human reason – for then we will know the mind of God.[37]

But would the ultimate triumph of western instrumental rationality really tell us something about ourselves? Would the end of reductive science really make us happy and induce us to be nice to each other? Would the reduction of the entire universe to a single equation that can be printed on an outsize T-shirt really answer the burning questions that confront humankind? Would a theory of everything enable us successfully to manipulate the world to all our advantage?

The history of science teaches us that the 'correct' understanding of how the world works is not necessary for a successful manipulation of the world. After all, even the most chauvinist historians are forced to acknowledge that the Chinese were very good at manipulating the world to their advantage; but, given the fact that they did not subscribe to the notions of western science, they could hardly have had a 'correct' understanding of the world. Most 'primitive' cultures could manipulate the world without possessing a scientific theory in the western genre. But a theoretical, rational explanation of how the universe works serves an important purpose in western thought: that of possession and legitimisation. The western notion of science and rationality is deeply rooted in mathematical realism. Only that which can be described by mathematics is real and can be believed. The conviction that the true meaning of nature is to be found only in mathematical formulae goes back to Pythagoras, who believed that both reason and intuition can be encapsulated in the harmonies that numbers display, and to Plato, for whom mathematics is a pointer to the ultimate reality of the world of forms that overshadows the visible world of sense data. Whatever western scientists actually believe, they work – indeed, the dominant paradigm of science forces them to work – as though pi is really in the sky. This approach, as John Borrow notes, 'elevates mathematics pretty close to God in traditional theology. Mathematics is part of the world, but transcends it. It must exist before and after the Universe.'[38] Thus translating a natural phenomenon into an equation is tantamount in western thought to possessing it.

Most non-western cultures believe that the world is potentially and actually intelligible because at some level it is algorithmically compressible and can be described by mathematics. Witness the mathematical achievements of the civilisations of India (where the zero, the decimal, the ability to deal with very large numbers – e.g. 10 to the power 53, irrational and negative numbers were discovered), China (where mathematics was first integrated with aesthetics) and Islam (where algebra, trigonometry and spherical geometry were formulated).[39] However, while the western perception equates mathematics with truth and reality, the non-western cultures and civilisations have always held reality and truth to be infinitely more complicated and certainly not totally amenable to a single (mathematical) approach. When al-Biruni, the eleventh-century Muslim mathematician and scholar who first measured the specific gravity of numerous base metals, encountered Yoga in India, he immediately declared his mathematical knowledge to be useless in the study of the new science he had encountered. The relevant questions one can ask of Yoga, he declared, are not amenable to mathematical answers; a different reality was at work here and one needed a different method and approach to study it. For him there was no question of superiority or inferiority: the two subjects, Yoga and the determination of the coordinates of Indian cities, required two different approaches, each as valid as the other. But a western mind would immediately relegate Yoga to the status of an inferior science because it is not amenable to the western deity: mathematical formulation.

The different approach to mathematics in the west and the non-west also generates different notions of truth. In most non-western cultures truth is *a priori*, given; in Islam, for example, its source is revelation. In western perception, truth is arrived at by some act of observation and mathematical formulation; it is known only *a posteriori*. Thus, while non-western cultures start with a set of basic axioms, western civilisation is forever searching for truth, something to believe in. The Grand Desire of western science to encapsulate in a unitary code, thus reducing the entire universe to a single equation, is a manifestation of its inner emptiness.

That this is a purely western enterprise is well illustrated by

Lederman. The quest for the ultimate particle, he tells us in a chart labelled 'The Standard Model', started with Thales in 60 BC, moved on to Empedocles (460 BC) and Democritus (430 BC) from where we take a quantum leap to 1687 and Newton.[40] The black hole in between and the atomic theories of Indian, Chinese and Muslim scientists do not concern him. For Steven Weinberg, the main travellers on the quest for the string theory are known to 'everyone': 'Copernicus, who proposed that the earth is not the center of the universe, Galileo, who made it plausible that Copernicus was right, Bruno who guessed that the sun is only one of a vast number of stars, and Newton who showed that the same laws of motion and gravitation apply to the solar system and to bodies on the earth.'[41] Lederman describes the Higgs Boson, the so-called God particle which is crucial to the understanding of the structure of matter, in brutish metaphors:

> We are building a tunnel fifty-four miles in circumference that will contain the twin beam tubes of the Superconducting Super Collider, in which we hope to trap our villain. And what a villain. The biggest of all time. There is, we believe, a wraithlike presence throughout the universe that is keeping us from understanding the true nature of matter. It is as if something, or someone, wants to prevent us from attaining the ultimate knowledge.[42]

Weinberg places his faith in mathematical realism: the difference between the earlier theories of physics and the string theories is that 'the space-time and internal symmetries are not put in by hand; they are mathematical consequences of the particular way that rules of quantum mechanics are satisfied in each particular string theory'.[43] Thus string theories offer a 'rational explanation of nature'. So, how long *is* a piece of string? What would the effects of a final theory be? What would we discover when we 'trap' the ultimate 'villain'? We may discover things about the working of the universe that would be as surprising to us as say Newtonian mechanics would have been to Thales. But with the discovery of Higgs Boson and the construction of the final theory of everything, says Lederman, 'the road to reduction will come to end; we will essentially know it all'.[44] Quoting Einstein, Weinberg tells us that we will learn that 'God Himself could not have arranged these connections in any other way than that which factually exists',[45] and warns that we will 'regret that nature has become more ordinary, less full of wonder and mystery'. But the discovery 'would give us some special insight into the handiwork of God'. However, this will not provide us with a 'standard of value or morality. And so we will find no hint of God who cares about any such things.'[46] The end of reductive physics, like the end of history, would spell the triumph of western rationality and liberal capitalist democracy, but it will leave a rather boring universe behind. The ultimate discovery of the theory of everything will be that there is no point to the universe: it's just a physical system. 'There are ways that we ourselves could invent a point to our lives, including trying to understand the universe.'[47] So in this pointless universe we will continue in our meaningless quest to make sense of it. We cannot sit around and 'have nothing else to do', says Lederman: 'we need to think beyond the SSC (Superconducting Super Collider) energy of 40 trillion volts to more powerful machines which will make this barrier seem docile'.[48] Even when possessed, the final frontier brings no satisfaction. The journey may be meaningless but it must be perpetual.

The inconsequential external universe of modern science is but an echo of the inner being of western man. The truth is, E. O. Wilson has declared in his classic defence of sociobiology, *On Human Nature*, 'we have no particular place to go. The species lacks any goal external to its own biological nature.'[49] In the next hundred years or so we could solve the few remaining problems of energy and material resources, control reproduction, stabilise our ecosystems, and so on – 'but then what?' We need something more: 'in order to search for a new morality based upon a more truthful definition of man, it is necessary to look inwards, to dissect the machinery of the mind and to retrace its evolutionary history.'[50] When we look 'inwards' we will find 'innate censors and motivators' that 'exist in the brain that deeply and unconsciously affect our ethical premises; from these roots, morality evolved as instinct'.[51] Apart from being on the verge of conquering the universe and wrapping it in an equation, science will also 'soon be in a position to investigate the very origin and meaning of human values, from which all ethical pronouncements and much of political practice flow'.[52] Natural selection over thousands of generations, Wilson informs us, has programmed all 'human emotional responses and the more general ethical practices based on them' in our genes. Soon, in the not-too-distant future, it will have the 'power to identify many genes that influence behavior'.[53] We will thus possess not just the universe, but the very morals and ethics that shape our behaviour. Back in 1978 when Wilson published *On Human Nature*, and the earlier *Sociobiology*,[54] biological determinism was frowned upon and sociobiology was attacked as a new variant of eugenics. Now it has become respectable and is the dominant theme of biology.

The thesis is simple. All living beings are made of elementary life-particles called genes, which are themselves made of DNA molecules; we will understand what we are and who we are when we know what our genes are made of. The genes are really our driving force: they are propagating themselves through us, using us as temporary means of transportation, as a medium through which these replicators spread through the world. As Richard Dawkins has it:

> they swarm in huge colonies, safe inside gigantic lumbering robots, sealed off from the outside world, communicating with it by tortuous indirect routes, manipulating it by remote control. They are in you and me; they created us, body and mind; and their preservation is the ultimate rationale for our existence. They have come a long way, these replicators. Now they go by the name of genes, and we are their survival machines.[55]

As machines, human beings do not have much free will, let alone any responsibility, for all our behaviour is genetically determined. We do what our genes tell us to do. We behave as our genes wish us to behave. Chauvinism, xenophobia, sexual dominance are *a priori*, given. There are genes for free market entrepreneurs, for male aggression and dominance, for homosexuality. It is the genes that make different societies different. Whether a particular race is aggressive or docile, creative or banal, musical or tone deaf, is all coded in its genes. The corollary is that the hierarchical structure of the modern world, with the professorial-type white man at the top of the ladder and the indigenous cultures of the third world at the bottom, is actually a function of our human nature. If we differ in our cultural traits and fundamental abilities because of innate differences, and if these innate differences are written in our genes and are biologically inherited, then hierarchy is coded in human nature. The world is the way it is because that is exactly how it should be. A proposed scientific explanation thus becomes the instrument for legitimising the status quo. But in essence it is something even more remarkable: it is western science returning to precisely the formulation it supposedly fractured to struggle free. The conception of gene dominance and the necessity of all hierarchical arrangements derived from there is merely a contemporary restatement of the very old notion, most cherished of the medieval Christian worldview, articulated repeatedly in Shakespeare and pervasive in the formation of modernist attitudes to life, the universe and everything – the Great Chain of Being. The chain is one of order and degree, with all of life from the lowest microbe upwards ordered in a hierarchical system of not merely physical attributes but natural endowments, both mundane and moral. At the top, of course, the final link in the chain is man who at his best shades into the orders of angels. But not all men. It was the conception of the Chain of Being that stirred the deep debates of expanded early modern Europe over whether the newly discovered peoples were indeed human or *similitudines homines*, a conditional category of beast men. Native Americans and Africans were included in this category and thus affected the way all Others came to be seen. The idea was old, vouchsafed by no less an authority than St Augustine in the fourth century, included in Linaeus and Buffon and the basis of the nineteenth-century foundational debate between mono- and poly-genesists, amongst whom the whole notion of evolution came to be debated. Sociobiology is but the latest paraphrase of the whole history of western thought, and highly representative of the aspect of that thought that had supposedly died a proper death: innate racism. Human nature dictates that Other cultures should always be conquered, suppressed, exploited, marginalised, consumed, and eradicated – and in the final analysis we can only blame our genes. Hence the Holy Grail of modern biology: the Human Genome Project.

The declared objectives of the Human Genome Project are pretty straightforward: to map out and analyse the complete genetic blueprint for a human being. A gene is a long sequence of four kinds of nucleotide identified by the letters A, T, C and G. Writing down the nucleotide sequence of the A's, T's, C's and G's of all human genes is a complex project which, given current technology, states R. C. Lewontin, 'will take about 30 years and use tens or even hundreds of billions of dollars'.[56] The knowledge will be useful in treating and curing some genetically caused diseases, like cystic fibrosis, thalassaemia and sickle-cell anaemia. But what else will the Human Genome Project achieve?

It is not just a question of learning 'the genetic spelling of cystic fibrosis', says Tom Wilke: the Human Genome Project is an 'attempt to find out how to spell "human"'.[57] Wilke cites Walter Gilbert, a Nobel Prize-winning geneticist, boasting that 'when we know the complete human genome we will know what it is to be human'.[58] Thus, the very concept of human nature will be transformed as a result of the Human Genome Project, which, Wilke argues, will usher in the most important scientific revolution since Darwin; indeed, it will be a culmination of the scientific revolution begun by Darwin. At the very least, the Human Genome Project will have direct consequences 'for patients seeking medical care, would-be parents planning a family, prudent investors seeking to save for a pension in their old age, for insurance companies trying to assess the actuarial risk of giving someone life assurance, and for prospective employers assessing the health and capabilities of their workers'.[59]

The reduction of the human being to no more than the biological expression of the programme of instructions encoded in his or her DNA will also have moral consequences for how we look at our bodies. If an individual believes that he or she is no more than a DNA code, that his or her biographical life is valueless, then there is no bar to suicide or euthanasia. And 'humans who possess only the capacity for biological life (such as those born with gross mental retardation) may be of less moral value in this scheme of things than a normal chimpanzee or orangutan'.[60] Moreover, it would be no less morally permissible to carry out 'scientific experiments involving vivisection on a grossly handicapped human baby than on a standard laboratory animal such as a rhesus monkey'.[61] Certainly, the end-product of the Project will encourage cultural, social, racial and sexual discrimination on the grounds of biological determinism. Biology has always been used to justify the status quo; and the Human Genome Project will further institutionalise the existing array of prejudice against the Other. Difference, more specifically genetic difference, will become the criterion for judging all Others. Wilke asks: given that 'the democracies of the Western industrialised nations have on occasion displayed a surprisingly illiberal streak and have discriminated against those whose genetic constitution (actual or presumed) made them different, how is society to ensure that, with the much more powerful tools available from the Human Genome Project, such actions are not repeated?'[62] The frank answer: science has always used new tools for the oppression of the Other and no matter what legislation is introduced, whatever safety mechanisms we may produce, the new tools will become instruments in the subjugation and oppression of the Other.

Would we, in knowing the molecular configuration of our genes, know everything that is biologically worth knowing about ourselves? Only if all human beings are exactly alike; but we are not. Lewontin explains:

> there is an immense amount of variation from normal individual to normal individual in the amino acid sequence of their protein because a given protein may have a variety of amino acid compositions without impairing its function. Each of us carries two genes for each protein, one that we get from our mother and one from our father. On the average, the amino acid sequence specified by our maternally inherited and paternally inherited genes differ in about one every 12 genes. In addition, because of the nature of the genetic code, many changes occur at the level of DNA that are not reflected in proteins themselves. That is, there are many different DNA sequences that correspond to the same protein. We do not have good estimates for humans at the moment, but if humans are anything like experimental animals, about

one in every 500 nucleotides will differ in DNA taken from any two individuals chosen at random. Since there are roughly 3 billion nucleotides in human genes, any two human beings will differ on the average in about 600,000 nucleotides. And an average gene that is, say, 3,000 nucleotides long will differ between any two normal individuals by about 20 nucleotides. Who's genome, then, is going to provide the sequence for the catalog for the normal person?[63]

Moreover, Lewontin asserts, there is a serious problem with identifying genes as the 'cause' of this or that disorder, let alone determining the individual. An alteration in a cancer gene cannot be assumed to be *the* cause of cancer, for the alteration could in turn have been caused by a pollutant, which was a product of an industrial process, which was the consequence of investing money at 6 per cent. The cancer is an accumulative product of all these factors and not a result of the alteration of a single gene. Cancer treatment involves removing the growing tumour or destroying it with radiation therapy; progress in cancer therapy has hardly received a boost from progress in our understanding of cell growth and development despite the fact that nearly all cancer research is focused on cell biology. Indeed, as Lewontin notes, progress in genetics has had very little input in discovering therapies for most of our common diseases. Cardiovascular diseases are treated by surgery whose anatomical bases go back to the nineteenth century; antibiotics were originally developed without the slightest notion of how they do their work; and diabetics continue to take insulin as they have done for over 60 years. The medical track-record of genetic research leaves a great deal to be desired.

Given the medically limp record of genetic research, the serious shortcomings in the methodology and the morally dubious nature of the enterprise, why are scientists so keen on the Human Genome Project? Scientific enterprise is totally committed to the ideology of perpetual research – stop the research and the whole venture threatens to collapse on itself. There is also a 'rather crass' reason:

The participation in and control of a multibillion-dollar, 30- or 50-year project that will involve the everyday work of thousands of technicians and lower-level scientists is an extraordinarily appealing prospect for an ambitious biologist. Great careers will be made. Nobel Prizes will be given. Honorary degrees will be offered. Important professorships and huge laboratory facilities will be put at the disposal of those who control this project and who succeed in producing thousands of computer discs of the human genome sequence.[64]

But apart from personal aggrandisement, there is also the social and economic amplification of the power of western civilisation. Normally, patent laws prohibit patenting anything that is natural. But genes are not natural; they are isolated in the laboratory, and they can be patented. Lewontin notes that 'if human DNA sequences are to be the basis of future therapy, then exclusive ownership of such DNA sequences would be money in the bank'.[65] But more: their ownership could mean the ownership of 'human nature', clandestine experiments on third world populations, and their military and political use in subjugating the Other. This is why the Human Genome Project is being pursued with such zeal and determination. It confirms biological determinism as an explanation of all social and individual variation: it is the biological Theory of Everything. Possessing the 'Code of Codes' is tantamount to possessing the human being itself and, once possessed, the 'lumbering robots' could be controlled and manipulated at will.

There Are More Things in Heaven and Earth, Horatio!

Both the moral dimension, as well as its perpetual descent into reductionism, is changing the nature of science. We are moving from science based on modernity – the self-declared pursuit of the 'Grand Design' of seeking the Truth, total control, absolute certainty, ontological assumption of separateness to a western science of postmodern dimensions. The 'Grand Design of improving Natural Knowledge, and perfecting all Philosophical Arts and Sciences',[66] as the editor of the first volume of *Philosophical Transactions of the Royal Society* put it, stands discredited: most self-respecting scientists now accept that far from being the pursuit of some romantic truth, science is one gigantic 'puzzle-solving' industry. Governments, increasingly unwilling to fund the unlimited growth of 'pure' research, now demand that science produces 'practical results' with direct impacts on the GNP. The public is increasingly suspicious of science and associates it with most of our environmental and global problems. The continued 'unplanned' progress of science is threatened by a dilemma of control: at the point when research can still be controlled, its harmful social consequences cannot be predicted with enough certainty to justify that control; by the time that the undesirable consequences of research have become apparent, the research is too far advanced to be easily controlled. 'Increasingly', write Crook et al., 'science and technology are required to turn their attention to another kind of control: the "damage control" of the unforeseen consequences of the project for the control of nature.'[67] The certainty of scientific results is evaporating. As Funtowics and Ravetz point out, 'issues of risk and the environment present the most urgent problems for science, uncertainty and quality are moving in from the periphery, one might say the shadows of scientific methodology, to become the central, integrating concepts'.[68] The boundaries between what is natural and what is artificially produced are breaking down. Genetic engineering is blurring the distinction between natural, social and technical processes. 'Is a fly engineered to transmit sterility to its descendants and released into the wild to be considered as a part of "nature" or as a pest-control "technology"?' Science policy in most western countries, as Crook et al. put it, now has an air of 'panic production': it produces 'a simulation of organization in a rapidly disorganizing world'.[69]

   In physics, it is the movement towards a general theory of strings that is ushering in postmodern science. Because string theories incorporate gravitons and hosts of other particles and seem to have solved the problems of infinities, they mark, says Steven Weinberg, 'the beginning of a new, postmodern, era in physics'.[70] But the sciences that really display all the characteristics of postmodernism – an emphasis on diversity, the abolition of the ontology of separateness, an accent on the interconnectedness of everything and an accommodation of different notions of truth

– and so deserve the label 'postmodern' are the new sciences of chaos and complexity.

Chaos theory is the new science of non-linear systems. Chaos itself has been defined in a number of different ways: 'a kind of order without periodicity'; 'apparently random recurrent behavior in a simple deterministic (clockwork-like) system'; and 'dynamics freed at last from the shackles of order and predictability ... systems liberated to randomly explore their every dynamical possibility ... exciting variety, richness of choice, a cornucopia of opportunity'.[71] Complexity is somewhat more difficult to define. Its concern is with spontaneous, disorderly 'complex systems' in which a host of interdependent agents act with each other to produce, by an 'adoptive strategy', 'spontaneous self-organisation'. Complex systems have the ability to balance order and chaos, the balancing point being 'the edge of chaos'. Complexity grapples with big questions: what is life, why is there something rather than nothing, why do stock markets crash, why did the Soviet empire collapse within a few months, why do ancient species remain stable in fossil records after millions of years? and so on. Both chaos and complexity undermine reductionism and paint a more pluralistic picture of reality than modern science. The complexity produced from simplicity by non-linearity and feedback makes chaotic all the assumptions and assurances on which science has been operating for the last four hundred years of its dominance of modernity, and the two millennia of the exclusively western history that it traces all the way back to Euclid and his geometry. Chaos and complexity demonstrate that the universe cannot be approximated in straight lines, as a ball rolling down a table through time; equally they show that predictability is a rare phenomenon, one operating only within the constraints that science has filtered out from the rich diversity of our complex world. Quite simply, chaos theory and the new science of complexity show that 'there are more things in heaven and earth, Horatio,/ Than are dreamt of in your philosophy' (*Hamlet*, I.v.166). The most significant question we have to ask is whether the deeply entrenched enterprise of scientism, all that has been built on the foundations of the scientific method, will react to this jolt like that other Horatio, Horatio Nelson, who, when sent a signal he did not wish to receive, placed his telescope to his blind eye.

Chaos and complexity promise a postmodern revolution in science based on the notions of holism, interconnection, order out of chaos and self-governing, autonomous nature. But where do the new ideas of complexity come from? Why, they are the very same non-western notions that modern science rejected in the fifteenth century as irrational and Huff described as 'a primitive but natural instinct of mankind'. In his *Complexity: The Emerging Science at the Edge of Order and Chaos*, Mitchell Waldrop reports the following conversation with Brian Arthur, a stalwart of the Santa Fe Institute, which pioneered the work on complexity:

> You can look at the complexity revolution in almost theological terms, he says. The Newtonian clockwork model is akin to standard Protestantism. Basically there's order in the universe. It's not that we rely on God for order. That's a little too Catholic. It's that God has arranged the world so that the order is naturally there if we behave ourselves ...
>
> The alternative – the complex approach – is total Taoist. In Taoism there is no inherent order. 'The world starts with one, and the one become two, and the two become many, and the many led to myriad things.' The universe in Taoism is perceived as vast, amorphous, and ever changing. You can never nail it down. The elements always stay the same, yet they are always arranging themselves. So it's like a kaleidoscope: the world is a matter of patterns that change, that partly repeat, but never quite repeat, that are always new and different ...
>
> In complexity there is no duality between man and nature, says Arthur. We are part of nature ourselves. We're in the middle of it. There is no division between the doer and the done-to because we are all part of this interlocking network ...
>
> Basically what I am saying is not at all new to Eastern philosophy. It's never seen the world as anything else but a complex system. But it's a world view that, decade by decade, is becoming more important in the West – both in science and in the culture at large. ... what is happening is that we are beginning to loose our innocence, our naiveté.[72]

Precisely: eastern philosophy has never seen the world in any other but complex terms. While modern science saw that as a problem, postmodern science sees it as an opportunity – when western thought reaches a dead end, it unreservedly turns towards the Other to appropriate and devour its thought and continue on its irrational and grotesquely skewed goal.

Despite its obvious challenge to the linear outlook of modern science, however, complexity is not a rupture from modern science but an attempt at a quantum leap to a new level of multidimensional reduction and pluralistic control. 'My own aim', writes Stuart Kauffman, one of the key founders of complexity, 'is not so much to challenge as to broaden the neo-Darwinian tradition. For, despite its resilience, that tradition has surely grown without seriously attempting to integrate the ways in which simple and complex systems may spontaneously exhibit order.'[73] The goal of complexity is to expand evolutionary theory 'to combine the themes of self-organisation *and* selection' and thus produce a new edifice. The object of the exercise is thus to transcend scientific control beyond Darwinian determinism to multidimensional, pluralistic, self-organising systems.

Both chaos and complexity, like modern science itself, postulate the universe as a computer. Kauffman's hope that 'we may, in the not distant future, create new life'[74] begins with the creation of cellular automata in the computer. In merely blurring the boundary and extending the confusion between natural life and genetically manufactured 'life' to 'life' generated inside a computer, complexity presents itself as a new self-glorifying phase of western science. But what is really 'new' about the 'new science' of complexity and chaos is the mathematics. The insights revealed by chaos theory and complexity are hardly new for non-western cultures. The aesthetics of the Mandelbrot set, for example, have astounded scientists and non-scientists alike; but for someone whose visual sense has been formed by Islamic art and design, what is the revelation? Go into any historic mosque and look at the ceiling. There you will find simple patterns generating complexity as a mental tool to focus the intellect on the contemplation of the Infinite. But cherished non-western notions have become real for western science because they have been proved mathematically. The mathematical codifications of the notions of nature, holism, interconnectedness and complexity lead the west to the illusion that they can be 'possessed'. Postmodern science extends the absolutist Grand Desire of western civilisation into hitherto 'irrational' domains of non-western notions of nature and reality. It is hardly surprising that Roger Lewin describes complexity as 'a theory of everything'.[75]

The philosophy and methodology of western science did not develop in a vacuum. The social context of both chaos and complexity, as well as much of modern science, is that most notorious of all non-linear dynamic systems: western civilisation. The semantic field of the terms 'chaos' and 'complexity' are deeply embedded in the western psyche. Chaos has an ancestry as a term for the primordial condition, or anti-condition out of which the world as we know it, the natural world, the world of human existence and thought was created. It is the term for all that is not ordered, what lies beyond the boundaries of the ethos, ideology and philosophy that established the means of knowing, being and doing of the world in the right way. Chaos is antithesis, or perhaps more properly anti-matter, to all that makes life sustainable and knowable. It has played a part in every speculation about social or material order, it has taken the role of the alternative, the Other, the unacceptable backdrop operating as imperative and necessity urging on the human constructs that seek to promote order. Chaos is something more than disorder: it is the absence of any possibility of rule or rationality. Disorder is something that can emerge within or as a consequence of order itself. Disorder marches to the same drummer, but mischievously or maliciously, it recognises that which it flouts or defies. The new propositions being demonstrated with postmodern science are that order can come out of chaos, simple rules can give rise to complex behaviour and complexity answers to simple rules. Chaos is not chaos per se; it is the failure to confirm the reductionist vision of predictable operations according to the laws elucidated by science. Complexity is an effort to subdue complex systems by way of mathematical description. If the misnomers of chaos and complexity have anything to teach us in the social and cultural realm, then it would seem to be that this is the most natural way for the world to proceed. But once again it is the west that must bear the burden of change.

Travelling in Thought

Before the emergence of the postmodern sciences of chaos and complexity, the non-west had its own conventional chaos and complexity to deal with. And in each of the traditional civilisations of the non-west, in India, the Muslim world and China as well as in other civilisational pockets, a conservational and prudential resistance was already in motion – movements of cultural resistance in search of authenticity that spawned a new interest in their own discrete sciences and technologies. It is not too much to say that these traditional non-western sciences are better fitted to integrate the 'new' vision of complexity for they have conserved a more complex, non-reductionist vision at their core and have always considered the holistic view as essential to the pursuit of science as an intellectual and cultural undertaking.

Given the Eurocentrism and the racial economy of modern science, and the insights of postmodern science of chaos and complexity, non-western cultures have a new imperative to revive their own unique sciences based on their own perceptions of nature and reality. If the Islamic, Chinese and Indian traditions could scale such heights of scientific endeavour in history, there is nothing that says they cannot be 'rediscovered' and prove equally valuable for our time. Indigenous knowledge systems, which are sometimes described as 'traditional' or 'local' knowledge systems, are based on genuine complexity where systematic inquiry is integrated with cultures, values and lifestyles as well as the religious outlook of a community. Often the notion of 'rationality' in non-western cultures appears quite bewildering from a western perspective; but this does not mean that non-western knowledge systems are not based on objectivity, systematic inquiry or experimentation. There is nothing that dictates that reason can only be defined in a single, western way. Consider, for example, how sophisticated and complex is the shamanistic concept of environmental accounting amongst the Tanimuka and Yukuna tribes of the Colombian Amazon:

> These societies have a strong cultural tradition of indigenous sustainable development based on a model of resource management which

allows for long term maintenance of human and environmental well-being without depleting the resource base. The shamans and some ritual specialists assess the trends in land use patterns and guide the community's production level as well as their conservation strategies. They practice 'traveling in thought' to map areas, re-establish ecosystem boundaries, and survey land, water and air to determine the size of population of various species. This environmental audit considers the impact of human activities on the universe and the cosmos and demonstrates the state of debt, credit or balance with nature as a whole. The shaman then prescribe or prohibit certain activities, prescribe forms of resource utilisation, and commit the community as a whole to sustainable development.[76]

Tanimuka and Yukuna's 'traveling in thought' appears similar to the 'songlines' of the Australian Aborigines or the theoretical basis of Chinese medicine responsible for acupuncture: even though they are beyond the scope of western perception and rationality, they 'work' within their own system and 'work' just as well as western science. Indeed, sometimes traditional systems of rationality work better than western science. Paddy farmers in Sri Lanka, for example, had developed a system of pest control which was intrinsically linked to their ritual behaviour. Certain practices, like the offering of food, flowers, and lighted oil lamps, were designed to reduce pests. Birds were attracted to the food while insect pests were attracted to the light. Birds thus preyed on the destructive insects. When these time-tested, environmentally safe and economically viable systems were replaced by the application of science – pesticides – the results were devastating for the farmers.[77] Even on a simple technological level, indigenous knowledge often foxes western science and technology. For example: upland rice farmers in Batangas, Philippines, developed an animal-drawn five-tined furrow opener and inter-row cultivator called *lithao*. After primary land preparation the *lithao* is used to open parallel furrows. Rice seed is broadcast and then harrowed into the furrows: the seed germinates in rows. The system requires less labour than the traditional system of furrowing by plough and seed drilling. Since the wooden *lithao* cannot break the sandy Batangas soil easily, agricultural engineers were asked to improve the system. After a decade of development, the *lithao* was declared 'unstable' and the work abandoned. Meanwhile, farmers in Tupi, South Cotabato, managed to change the Batangas wooden *lithao* to a steel *panudling* and happily adopted it for heavier soils and developed a highly productive upland rice system based on use of the implement and associated practices.[78] In his brilliant *Science, Development and Violence*, Claude Alvares shows how indigenous Indian knowledge systematically proved to be more environmentally sound, economically viable, empowering and highly complex. The knowledge system that produced *gur* (traditional Indian sweetener), *rotis* (Indian bread) and *idli* are far more complex – and therefore humane and sustainable – than that which produces white sugar, white bread and biotechnology. Such complex systems are not 'emergent' – they are already there and have been there for centuries. Their existence not only demands recognition and acknowledgement, but space for growth and development.

But non-western cultures have to create this 'knowledge space' for themselves. Neither modern science, nor its postmodern equivalent, would willingly give up its hegemonic tendencies. It is only by developing contemporary civilisational sciences, with a sound theoretical as well as empirical base, that western science can be humbled. Indian work on a science based on Indian metaphysics, which can achieve a precise and unambiguous formulation of universal statements without quantification, is a beginning. The work on medicine and agriculture shows considerable promise. Equally promising is the attempt, particularly in Pakistan, India and Malaysia, to formulate the theory and practice of a contemporary Islamic science – a science based on Islamic metaphysics and its notion of nature as a trust, which incorporates the ideals of justice and public interest in its processes and methods and is geared to the needs and requirements of Muslim societies.[79] Rudimentary models of what this enterprise may look like have already appeared in the *Journal of Islamic Science*. Similarly lines of inquiry could be pursued in Chinese science and the sciences of the Pacific Islands, various African cultures and indigenous people of America.

It is worth emphasising that champions of contemporary models of indigenous knowledge and non-western sciences are not arguing for a magical or mystical notion of science. The debate is about *science* – that is, systematic inquiry, albeit grounded in different notions of rationality, different perceptions and approaches to nature, based on empirical observations and work, whose results are universally applicable. The argument is not that the laws of nature 'discovered' by western science do not or will not work in other cultural locations, but, as Sandra Harding puts it, 'they are not the only possible such universal laws of nature – there could be many universally valid and culturally distinctive sciences'.[80]

From the perspective of the Other, the key question is, however, what it always was. How ready is the dominant establishment of western science to enter into a multiplex polylogue of diverse sciences and technologies, how ready is it to share a complex world with diverse explorations of nature and reality? What is at issue is our ability effectively to incorporate a complex future of plurality as an integrated diverse world order of the future. Other cultures have always treated their myths as myths; western civilisation systematically translates its myths into science. Would postmodern science create new myths about the Other – ironically using non-western notions of nature and reality – and then institutionalise them in mathematical codes? For a genuinely new departure, complexity must demonstrate that it has the capability of transforming western science, like the narrator's caterpillar in Amin Maalouf's *The First Century After Beatrice*, into a butterfly, a higher level of knowledge that recognises different ways of knowing and promotes symbiosis with non-western sciences.

7. The Rivers of Belief

Martin Scorsese's *The Last Temptation of Christ* begins with a quotation that is immediately followed by a declaration. The quotation, taken from Nikos Kazantazakis' novel on which the film is based, reads:

> The dual substance of Christ – the yearning, so human, so superhuman, of man to attain God – has always been a deep inscrutable mystery to me. My principal anguish and source of all my joys and sorrows from my youth onwards has been the incessant merciless battle between the spirit and the flesh! And my soul is the arena where these two armies have clashed and met.

The declaration announces that 'this film is not based upon the Gospels but upon this fictional exploration of the eternal spiritual conflict'.

Despite the declaration, the film follows the Gospels fairly faithfully: all the basic landmarks of the accepted narrative of Jesus of Nazareth are there – Jesus, son of Mary and Joseph, is a carpenter; he acquires a small band of disciples, including Judas, Peter and the rest; he preaches his message of love and the coming Kingdom of God in Galilee using stories and parables; he is concerned about the oppressed, the poor and the meek of the earth; he meets and is baptised by John the Baptist; at the Last Supper in Jerusalem he is betrayed by Judas and is crucified by the Romans. Up to the crucifixion, the story is presented with only a couple of twists. Mary Magdalene becomes more than a repentant prostitute, more than a woman reformed by Jesus: she seems to be sexually infatuated with Christ, who in his turn appears to have wronged her by his neglect of her desires. And Judas Iscariot, the putative original Other of Christianity, is shown, contrary to the conventional narrative, as a loyal disciple whose 'betrayal' was only apparent and not real: he did what he did only at the request, indeed insistence, of Jesus. So the fictionalisation, up to the crucifixion of Jesus, amounts to nothing more than massaging the accepted 'facts' of the Christian narrative with postmodern political correctness.

But towards the end of the film, when Jesus is dying on the Cross, the film adds a long dream sequence which violates the conventional Christian narrative. Just like the dream sequences in the 'Mahound' chapter of *The Satanic Verses*, the dream sequence in *The Last Temptation of Christ* constructs an alternative life history of Christ; and just as *The Satanic Verses* suggests that the Prophet Mohammed was duped by Satan, *The Last Temptation of Christ* implies that Jesus was led astray by the Devil.

While hanging on the cross a hallucinating Jesus sees a little girl appear at his side. 'I am the angel who guards you,' she says. 'Your father is the God of Mercy, not punishment. He saw you and said, "Aren't you his guardian angel? Well, go down and save him. He has suffered enough." Remember when he said to Abraham to sacrifice his son. Abraham was just about to kill the boy with his knife and God stopped him. So if he saved Abraham's son, don't you think He wants to save his own son? He has tested you and He is happy with you. He doesn't want your blood. He said: "Let him die in a dream; but let him live his life".' The girl angel then helps Jesus from the Cross and leads him away from the shouting and cursing crowd. 'I don't ask to be sacrificed,' says Jesus. 'No you don't,' says the angel. 'I am not the Messiah?' asks Jesus. 'No you are not,' answers the angel. The harsh landscape of the earlier film now transforms into a lush green. 'Is this the world of God?', asks Jesus. 'No this is earth.' 'Why is it changed so much?' 'It hasn't changed. You have. Now you can see its real beauty. Harmony between earth and the heart. That's the world of God.' The angel leads Jesus straight into a wedding ceremony where he is married to Mary Magdalene. He makes love to her, she becomes pregnant, but dies before giving birth. The angel consoles a grieving Jesus: 'There is only one woman in the world.

One woman with many faces. This one falls, the next one rises. Mary Magdalene died; but Mary, Lazarus' sister, she lives. She would like to live with a different face. She is carrying your greatest joy inside her: your son.' So Jesus moves in with Mary of Bethany, sister of Lazarus. He also accepts the invitation of Martha, Lazarus' second sister, to come into her room. He acquires a large family; and he becomes happy and contented.

The dream sequence continues. Jesus meets Paul who is preaching to a crowd. He doesn't like what he hears. The following dialogue takes place:

Jesus: 'I was never crucified. I never came back from the dead. I am a man like everybody else. Why are you telling these lies?'

Paul: 'What are you talking about?'

Jesus: 'I am the son of Mary and Joseph. I am the one who preached in Galilee. I had followers; we marched on Jerusalem; Pilot condemned me and God saved me.'

Paul: 'No He didn't!'

Jesus: 'Who are you talking about? Don't try and tell me what happened to me because I know. I live like a man now: I work, eat, have children – I enjoy my life. For the first time I am enjoying it. Do you understand what I am saying? So don't go around telling lies about me ...'

Paul: 'What's the matter with you? Look around you! Look at all these people! Look at their faces! You see how unhappy they are? You see how much they are suffering? Their only hope is the resurrected Jesus. I don't care whether you are Jesus or not. The resurrected Jesus will save the world and that's what matters.'

Jesus: 'These are lies. You can't save the world by lying.'

Paul: 'I created the truth out of what people needed and what they believed. If I have to crucify you to save the world then I will crucify you. And if I have to resurrect you then I will do that whether you like it or not.'

Jesus: 'I won't let you. I will tell everyone the truth.'

Paul: 'Go ahead! Go on! Tell them now. Who is going to believe you ...? You see: you don't know how much people need God. You don't know how happy He can make them. He can make them happy to do anything. He can make them happy to die – and they will die. All for the sake of Christ! Jesus Christ! Jesus of Nazareth! Son of God! The Messiah! Not you. You know I am glad I met you. So now I can forget about you. My Jesus is much more important and much more powerful...'

Unlike *The Satanic Verses*, which tries to establish doubt as the permanent human condition, *The Last Temptation of Christ* tries to reconfirm faith in the manner of postmodernism. Jesus becomes old; and the disciples come to see him for the last time. An angry Judas arrives to denounce Jesus and exposes the girl angel as the Devil in disguise. Jesus sees his folly; asks his Father for forgiveness, and returns to the Cross. End of the dream sequence: Jesus dies!

The Last Temptation of Christ thus presents us with a duality: the suffering, life-denying aspects of Christian tradition are contrasted with the happiness of married (polygamous?) life – the dry harsh scenery, the renunciation necessary to pass through the portals of belief as compared to the rollicking jolly life of a green and pleasant land with compliant women. But this duality, simulated for the argument of the film is that, as far as belief is concerned, it really doesn't matter what happened in history. Both narratives are equally believable, both are equally valid truth claims, there is nothing to choose between God and the Devil. Both the way the problem of religion is formulated, as 'the incessant merciless battle between the spirit and the flesh', and the way it is resolved, the triumph of the humanness of human beings, are intrinsically western in their conception. Indeed, the very notion of God, as a flawed but ultimately humane white man, that permeates the narrative of *The Last Temptation of Christ* and much of western history, is Eurocentric. This is a God of European perceptions, emerging out of European experience and ultimately at the mercy of western desires. He can be killed at will; resurrected if needed; moulded and remoulded, formulated and reformulated, conjured up and vanished. In postmodern times, when truth is a function of contingency and relativism, and where, in the words of Don Cupitt, it is *a priori* that 'everything, but everything, burns and burns out and passes away',[1] it doesn't really matter what we make of God: take him as *you* want to take him. In other words, God is not only a product of our perceptions and needs, he is our servant.

But the postmodern thesis about God is not all that new. As we learn from *The Last Temptation of Christ*, St Paul reformulated Christianity as a cult of Jesus. His Jesus was not a prophet, like so many before and after him, but something 'much more important and much more powerful': 'The Son of God'. The attribution of divinity to Jesus has had serious consequences for non-western cultures. The logic of this position has become a two-edged sword. If Jesus is God, then God allows himself to be edged out of the world and on to the cross. Thus God is weak and totally powerless in the world. He helps us not through his omnipotence but through his weakness and suffering. This has led Christians to impose a submissive love on the members of non-western cultures they converted, thus paving the way for their colonisation or sustaining the unjust status quo. And if Jesus is God and it is not possible to attain salvation, or indeed become fully human, except through acknowledging his Lordship, then any and all means are justified to attain that salvation for the less fortunate occupants of the globe. Moreover, if you have attempted salvation by being 'in Christ', then you are naturally a member of a privileged class – you have already carved out a piece of paradise for yourself. Thus the claim about the absolute uniqueness of Jesus, and the absolute necessity of the encounter with the person of Jesus for human salvation, brought God into the service of Europe. Unlike Islam, which gives due recognition to all religions in general, and Christianity and Judaism in particular; or Judaism which limits its purview to a particular group of people; or other religions of the world all of which accept that the notion of Divine Truth is not an exclusive right of any single reverent outlook; Christianity's universal mission amounted to little more than the total subjugation of all Others in the name of God and salvation through Jesus.

During the medieval period, the barbarism of Christianity's subjection of non-western cultures worked itself out in the form of the crusades. While Islam had no problem with Christianity, it presented Europe with three distinct problems. First: what was the purpose of a new revelation to an Arabian prophet over six hundred years after the crucifixion and resurrection of God's own son? Second: as a world civilisation, Islam was perceived as a political threat to Europe. And third: the scholarly and scientific achievements of the Muslim civilisation made Islam an intellectual problem. Europe tried to solve these problems by representing Islam as the darker side of Christianity, the evil Other. When Others are classified as pure evil their existence becomes a problem for the classifier: the only true solution for evil is to eliminate it. Hence the crusades; the subjugation of Islamic Spain; and the process of colonisation in the wake of Columbus. Europe's representation of Islam and Muslims, and in particular its representation of Moorish Spain, was utilised in the framing of all those non-western cultures Europe encountered in the so-called 'voyages of discovery'. Just as Moors and Ottomans were enemies of God, and wars conducted against them were necessarily just, so the violence inflicted on the people of the 'New World' was just and necessary. However, the sanction to conquer and enslave all Others came not only from Christianity; it was also a fundamental tenet of humanism and rationalism. Whereas the unrestrained Christian imperialist has a god, the unrestrained humanist imperialist, in the words of the Florentine humanist Marsilio Ficino, 'strives to be God everywhere'.[2] European humanists were not only concerned with establishing the superiority of the white man, they were insistent about demonstrating that superiority by means of instrumental rationality.

The non-western cultures played an important part in shaping the intellectual and scholarly tradition that crystallised modernity and humbled Christianity. The *philosophes* – the intellectuals who conceived and perfected the Enlightenment – looked at exploration not just for new knowledge but also new attitudes towards knowledge. From science they acquired the sceptical attitude of systematic doubt, and from exploration a new relativistic attitude towards belief and used them as ammunition against traditional Christian norms and values. Voltaire's sage Chinese, Diderot's virtuous Tahitians, Montesquieu's Persians, coming after Fountenelle's plurality of worlds, all served as weapons to knock down European society and suggest a better one. Yet, the effect of such scepticism and relativism was to glorify and magnify man in general and European man in particular.

The Enlightenment generated the modernist discourse of secularism. This discourse was constructed, as John Milbank has argued in *Theology and Social Theory*,[3] in direct opposition to (perverted) Christian theology. In other words, modernist secularism replaced Christianity as a total theory of salvation, complete with its own theology and ideas of redemption and grace. If Christianity was the enemy of modernist secularism in Europe, then all religions everywhere were adversaries of secularism; and any society that identified strongly with a religious worldview – and that actually meant *all* Other societies – had to be beaten and dragged into 'modern, secular civilisation'. Since religion and tradition go hand in hand in most third world societies, tradition too was identified as 'backward', 'dogmatic' and 'against progress': traditional societies had to be swept aside to make way for their modern counterparts. The creation of highly unstable and insecure secular 'nation states' in the non-western world owes much to these assumptions.

How Christian thought and experience were universalised as the global, generic religious outlook is well illustrated by Aldous Huxley. Arguing from the authority of Blessed Cecilia, a thirteenth-century Roman Catholic nun, that the nobility of man in Christianity has been construed as a mandate for treating nature as evil, Huxley relates the following story in her own words:

One evening, St Dominic came to preach, from behind the grille, to the Sisters of his convent. His theme was devils; and hardly had he begun his sermon, when 'the enemy of mankind' came on the scene in the shape of a sparrow and began to fly through the air, hopping even on the sisters' heads, so that they could have handled him had they so minded, and all this to hinder the preaching. St Dominic observing this, called Sister Maximilla and said: 'Go up and catch him and bring him here to me'. She got up and putting out her hand, had no difficulty in seizing hold of him, and handed him out through the window to St Dominic. St Dominic held him fast in one hand, and commenced plucking off his feathers with the other, saying the while: 'You wretch, you rogue!' When he had plucked him clean of all his feathers, amidst much laughter from the Brothers and Sisters, and awful shrieks of the sparrow, he pitched him out saying: 'Fly now if you can, enemy of mankind! You can cry out and trouble us, but you cannot hurt us!'[4]

Now the Otherisation of nature as evil is a specifically Christian position. Secularism adopted the same position for it permitted nature, without the pains of conscience, to be dominated, 'tortured' in the words of Bacon, and subjugated so that her secrets could be wrested from her. This tale, and its moral, however, do not represent the characteristically monotheistic attitude towards nature. But Huxley generalises the anecdote and universalises the Christian position by presenting it as an example of the perversion of 'monotheistic' ethics. Contrast St Dominic's attitude towards birds with the teachings of the Prophet of Islam who declared unequivocally that 'no bad omen comes from birds' and that the people who enter paradise will have hearts as pure as those of birds; he also advised Muslims to plant trees for 'never a Muslim plants a tree, but he has the reward of charity for him, for what is eaten out of that is charity; what is stolen out of that, what the beast eat out of that, what the birds eat out of that is charity for him'.[5] There is no comparison between the Christian stand on nature and the Islamic ethics of nature. Huxley's generalisation is not only absurd but betrays a colossal western ignorance of the non-Christian monotheistic traditions.

Just as in medieval Europe there was only one religion, modernist secularism too acknowledges the existence of only one religion: subsuming all Other religions, particularly the monotheistic ones, into the ambit of Christianity. Even the monotheism of the two recognised 'monotheistic' faiths, Islam and Judaism, is not the same as Christian monotheism. Islam, for example, differs in radical ways from Christianity. Consider, for example, the Christian and Islamic approach to nature. The Hebrew story of creation is transformed in Christianity into the doctrine of the fall. Creation thus appears to the Christian mind as 'fallen' and nature is viewed as opposed to grace. St Augustine, to take but a prominent example, believed that nature was 'unredeemed', just as many Christian theologians maintain even today that nature cannot teach man anything about God and is therefore of no theological and spiritual interest. Salvation, in the Christian scheme of things, is the humbling of nature by the miraculous; the intrusion of the supernatural in history. Moreover, the nearest thing in the physical universe that reflects the miraculous is man. Holiness then exists only in the man-made environment: 'In the Christian view, it was not emanation from the earth but ritual that consecrated the site; man not nature bore the image of God and man's work, the hallowed edifice, symbolised the cosmos.' Nature, so devoid of God's presence and grace, may then be 'tortured'; it may justifiably be subjected to scientific experimentation. In short, Christianity achieves a genuine desacralisation and disenchantment of the world.

The Islamic view is very different. Though it agrees with Christianity on the necessity of de-divinising the world (indeed, such a stance is incumbent upon both Judaism and Islam), it does not accept its devalorisation. For creation (nature) in the Qur'anic view, always bears the 'signs of God' and is necessary for man's 'salvation'. It is in accordance with this that Islam holds that 'there is no such thing as a profane world. All the immensity of matter constitutes a scope for the self-realisation of the spirit. All is holy ground. The Prophet has expressed the same truth as "the whole of this earth is a mosque".'[6] Earth, creation and nature thus have a sacramental efficacy in Islam which can be ill-accommodated with the perverse applications of the 'dominion ethics'. The claim for nature's 'salvational worth', however, may never be construed as a token of its autonomy. In fact, Muslim theologians have always claimed that nature has no meaning without reference to God; without Divine purpose it simply does not exist. (Hence, nature, in Islam, is simply known as the created order.) But it is not just book-based monotheist religions that are painted with the same brush as Christianity, other non-western religions have been consistently projected as the pagan Other of Christianity. For example, all African religions are projected as superstitious cults rather than legitimate belief systems. The varying labels that are appended to them – 'animists', 'magical' and voodoo-based – relegates them to the twilight zone beyond civilisation. Ella Shohat and Robert Stam list the ways in which Eurocentric Christian and secular thinking has denigrated African religions:

1. Oral rather than written, they are seen as lacking the cultural imprimatur of the religion 'of the Book' (when in fact the text simply takes distinct, oral semiotic form, as in Yoruba praise songs);

2. they are regarded as polytheistic rather than monotheistic (a debatable hierarchy and in any case a misrepresentation of most African religions);

3. they are viewed as superstitious rather than scientific (an inheritance from the positivist view of religion as evolving from myth to theology to science), when in fact all religions involve a leap of faith;

4. they are considered disturbingly corporeal and ludic (danced) rather than abstractly and austerely theological;

5. they are thought insufficiently sublimated (for example, involving actual animal sacrifice rather than symbolic or historically commemorative sacrifice);

6. they are seen as wildly gregarious, drowning the personality in the collective transpersonal consciousness, rather than respecting the unitary, bounded individual consciousness. The Christian ideal of the *visio intellectualis*, which Christian theology inherited from the neo-Platonists, flees in horror from the plural trance and visions of the 'trance' religions of Africa and many indigenous people.[7]

Non-western religions were not supposed to survive the impact of colonial Christianity, let alone the instrumental rationality of the Enlightenment. The Enlightenment expounded the belief that progress and the influence of religion were mutually exclusive and predicted that religion would disappear with the advancement of knowledge. This expectation was enhanced as secularisation progressed in the west during the eighteenth, nineteenth and twentieth centuries. But in the colonies, religion not only proved to be astonishingly persistent but turned out to be a major focus of resistance to colonialism. The fight against colonialism and European imperialism was led largely by religious figures. Jamaluddin Afghani and Mohammad Abuh in Egypt, the Mahdi in the Sudan, Uthman dan Fadio in Nigeria, scores of ulama or religious scholars in Iran and Algeria – all led movement after movement against the colonial powers. In India, religious leaders led several uprisings against the British and played a prominent part in the famous 1857 'mutiny'; and the independence movement too was led by religious leaders: Mahatma Gandhi, Mualana Abu Kalam Azad, the Muslim poet Muhammad Iqbal (known as 'the philosopher of the east'); while religious figures also fought for the establishment of Pakistan as the first 'Islamic state'. Both the persistence of religions in the colonial territories and the resistance they mobilised against the colonial power led to further demonisation of Other religions.

Under modernity, the Enlightenment belief in secularisation was enhanced further – despite the evidence of colonial experience in Other cultures. Modernisation, it was thought, would do for non-western societies what the Protestant Reformation and the Catholic Counter-Reformation did for Europe. In most Other cultures, however, religion and politics are considered to be two sides of the same coin and religion often serves as a vehicle for social and political change. Furthermore, religion shapes both individual and communal identities. For example, in the Middle East identity is reflected by one's religious affiliation: one is either a Sunni Muslim or a Shi'a Muslim, an Alawite or a Druze, or Christian of Roman Catholic, Maronite, Copt or Eastern Orthodox persuasion or Jewish. In other non-western countries, religion defines communal identities: the Sudan, India and Malaysia are good examples. The *raison d'être* for the very existence of Pakistan is Islam. To abandon religion totally in favour of an imported and imposed secularism in such circumstances amounts to a denial of one's own identity and existence.

Thus, it is not surprising that even after Third World countries obtained their independence, the role and influence of religion in non-western societies continued. While in certain countries religion manifested itself largely as a reactionary force, in others it played an important part in developing popular opposition to military and authoritarian rule. In Latin America, the Catholic Church's opposition to military dictatorships and grinding poverty led to the mobilisation of the poor and a strong sense of communal solidarity. In the Philippines, the clergy led the opposition and spearheaded the downfall of the Marcos dictatorship. In Iran, a revolution based on religion led to the ousting of the Shah. In the Lebanon, religion has been the key to resisting foreign domination and oppressive rule, and led to the demand for equitable redistribution of available resources. In Poland, the Church led the movement for democracy. Across Eastern Europe religion was one of the factors contributing to the collapse of communism and overthrow of the Soviet hegemony.

Thus modernity, rather then weakening the influence of religion in Other societies, or indeed as anticipated by the west, making it disappear altogether, has in fact had the totally opposite impact: religion has made its public role stronger, it has emerged as a revolutionary force, it has become an essential part of the process of state-formation, and it is increasingly providing inspiration for resisting instrumental modernity and the west. The failure of modernisation programmes to provide any solutions to the economic, social and political problems of non-western countries, as well as the failure of secular ideologies to provide an alternative to subjugation by the west, has now made religion an inescapable part of the non-western political agenda. Not only has the revitalisation of traditional religions increased political participation and made politics relevant for many traditional societies, but increasingly religion is being seen as a major form of resistance against the encroachment of modernity. Social institutions in most non-western societies tend to be religious institutions, which also provide a support base for the ruler or the backbone for the opposition. As Emile Sahliyeh notes, religion provides 'its adherents with strong ideological justifications to undertake political risks that otherwise may not be contemplated. The exaltation of personal sacrifice and martyrdom by the Sikh and Shiite cultural and religious traditions have in part been responsible for the emergence of a militant religious movement in both communities. The recent history of Lebanon, Iran, and India provide numerous examples of men and women who sacrificed their lives in the name of achieving higher religious and communal goals.'[8]

Principles of Lust are Burnt in Your Mind

The resurgence of religion in the non-western world should not be all that surprising. Contrary to widespread belief, secularism does not lead to a decline in religiosity: its rejection leads to religious entrenchment and its acceptance simply transfers, as Griffin notes, 'religious devotion from one kind of religious object to another – from one that transcends the world, at least in part, to one that is fully worldly, that is, secular'.[9] In modernity, this religiosity has been expressed in such ideologies as Fascism, Communism, Nationalism, Scientism, Aestheticism, Nuclearism and Ecologism – to mention only the most notable ones. There is also an accompanying shift in the way power is justified. In conventional religions, the use of cogent power is justified by invoking God or higher principles. In modernity, however, 'the "death of God" is taken to mean that no norms exist to restrain our will-to-power', 'no reason exists, beyond the power of others, to restrain one's own use of power in striving to realise one's interests: "Might makes right".'[10] As a critique of modernity, one would expect postmodernism either to provide a superior justification for coercive power or condemn and reject it. In fact, the dominant mode of postmodern thought does neither. Indeed, it adds a new form of power to the modernist list: the power of ridicule summed up by Rorty's declaration that 'the best way to cause people long-lasting pain is to humiliate them by making the things that seem most important to them look futile, obsolete and powerless'.[11] This new form of amorphous, postmodern power is a continuation of the old Orientalist tradition; indeed, it is simply a reinstatement of the predominant mores of what T. H. White called the *Age of Scandal* – the era that bred the *philosophes* and Enlightenment and shaped the general temper of the eighteenth century.[12] Irony and ridicule were used during the Enlightenment to dethrone Christianity; postmodernism gives the techniques a new justification and hence a new lease of life in fiction, movies, plays and the media. Both *The Last Temptation of Christ* and *The Satanic Verses* are examples of the use of postmodern power to cause 'long-lasting pain' to believers and Other cultures and to highlight their total powerlessness.

The rampant use of Orientalising postmodern abuse, irony and ridicule has had two consequences for non-western cultures. They have either accepted their absolute powerlessness and shrunk into insecurity and nihilism, or entrenched themselves in western-hating fundamentalism. Religious fundamentalism in general, and Islamic fundamentalism in particular, are panic reactions to postmodern nihilism. Thus postmodernism retains Christianity's will to power. The divinity of Jesus, replaced in modernity with the divinity of European man, is preserved. Salvation is now sought not just through secularism, and its offshoots like bourgeois liberal democracy, art and literature: the symbolic Judas is replaced with irony and ridicule which work their magic by rendering all religious symbols meaningless and showing the absolute powerlessness of all traditional, religious societies.

Given postmodernism's categorical determination to de-divinise the world, one would expect its discourse to be free of all theological trappings. On the contrary: most postmodern texts come elegantly wrapped in theological jargon and liturgy. As examples we could consider Derrida's *Of Spirit*, Baudrillard's *The Transparency of Evil* and *America* – which, as Andrew Wernick points out, appears to be a quest not just to fill the classical 'God shaped hole' but also a Marx-shaped one[13] – Lyotard's fascination with the 'Sublime' and the obsession of many postmodernists with Buddhist thought, mysticism and spirituality. Why is postmodernism so concerned with quasi-religious sanctimony? To understand postmodernism's concern with the religious, John Milbank writes,

> one must pay attention to a difference in the 'modes of suspicion' exercised by modern and postmodern thought respectively. Characteristically, modern thought seeks to reduce the burden of what it identified as 'irrational' phenomena by showing that they are traceable to an error, a failure of reason, or else that they secretly subvert rational purposes: for example, Freud traced pathological mental phenomena to failures of self-recognition, but also showed how irrational manifestations help us to cope with the subjectively intolerable. Yet Nietzsche and his contemporary French followers do not, on the whole, seek to show that apparently strange and arbitrary is not purely arbitrary. On the contrary, they seek to demonstrate almost the

reverse: that apparently rational, common-sense assumptions about self-identity, motivation and moral values themselves disguise historically instituted mythological constructs. So, for example, the whole complex of attitudes to do with free will and guilt is but a rationalisation of a low degree of power, and plebeian *resentment*. Where modernity lifted the burden of power and obscurity in favour of a light-travelling reason, postmodern hyper-reason makes arbitrary power into the hydra-headed but repetitious monster whose toils we can never escape, yet whom we should joyfully embrace.

What happens, though, to 'obscurity', by which I mean the religious? To be sure, obscurity is here regarded as itself a ruse of power, but since power will always operate through ruses and self-disguising, and half-concealed inventions of mysterious new creeds, one can no longer will the end of religion. For every socially instituted creed and code of practice must lack foundations beyond the essence that it creates through its own self-elaboration. Religion will not depart, because all social phenomena are arbitrary and therefore 'religious'. Quite clearly, these conclusions will tend to suggest affinities between postmodernism and those kinds of sacricity which lay stress of the wilfulness of God, the positivity of revelation, the total and absolute inaccessibility of the divine unity beyond the always divisive manifestations of this unity in time.[14]

If one cannot will the end of religion, one can at least share in its power. Hence the manufacture of postmodern religion. Postmodern religion, like postmodernism itself, is a fragmented discourse. There are as many postmodern theologies as there are self-proclaiming postmodernist preachers. For some, like Richard Rorty, postmodernism suggests the death of God (yet again) and the disappearance of religion from the planet; for others, like David Griffin and John Milbank, the return to premodern, traditional but somewhat reformulated faith; and for still others, like the Revd Don Cupitt, the possibility of recasting religious ideas to cleanse them of realism, all transcendence, and expressing the religious ideal by something as simple as 'love'.

Don Cupitt regards modernity as the sole product of western civilisation. 'Our modern industrial civilisation which now rules the whole world', he writes 'was forged in just one particular place and period, and influenced by just one religious tradition.'[14] The formation of this 'civilisation' involved 'the slow process of secularisation, the impact of science and then biblical and historical criticism, the shift to an ever more man-centred outlook, the encounter with other faiths, and then finally the awesome and still incomplete transition to modernity – all this makes up a story which for Christians has extended over some three or four centuries'.[15] But this is not just 'a' story; it is *the* story of civilisation. For Cupitt, secularism is a universal worldview:

> There are people in other traditions, and most notably in Islam, who say that the story is a purely Christian one that reflects only Christianity's weakness in controlling developments in its own culture and its failure to resist the corrosive effects of scepticism. They flatter themselves that they will be able to escape the fate that has overtaken Christianity, some Muslims even adding that they will be able to create an Islamic science free from the undercurrent of scepticism that has marked Western science. They are, I fear, mistaken. The story we have to tell may be local, but its moral is universal. Christianity has had the great advantage of a long period in which to understand and in some measure to adjust itself to what has happened, whereas in other cultures the process of modernisation is all the more abrupt, confusing and traumatic for being telescoped to within the span of a single lifetime.[16]

Notice how Christianity is still projected as a superior system. At an earlier stage of history it was superior because of its religious creed; now it is superior due to its 'great advantage': its experience as a handmaiden to secularism for over three centuries. But this superiority is set up in contrast to Islam which lacks 'scepticism' and its followers are little more than self-deluding flat-earthers. 'Islamic science', by *definition*, must shun 'undercurrents of scepticism', presumably because Islam itself cannot tolerate uncertainty or nurture the scientific spirit. The good reverend is quite ignorant of the fact that his ancestors learned their scepticism, their rationality, their science, indeed even their much flaunted humanism, from the Muslims.[17] Cupitt reveals his ignorance not just of Islam, but also of science, which he describes as 'value-neutral and independent of local political or religious beliefs': just as the entire history of Islam is dismissed in a single sentence, so all modern research in the history and philosophy of science and the sociology of knowledge, which has revealed science to be anything but value-neutral and free from ideological, political and social, as well as religious, influences, is brushed aside. For Christian postmodernists like Cupitt, belief in Christianity has given way to belief in science and secularism, but the original structures in which these beliefs were situated remain intact. White man still reigns supreme.

Cupitt wishes to cleanse 'religion' of the doctrine of original sin, spirit–body duality and other oppressive aspects. He accuses the clergy in western Christianity of arrogating all sacredness to themselves. And above all, he maintains, the myth of an 'extra-terrestrial' and 'supernatural' redeemer 'who died for our sins' cannot be maintained. But the criticism leads to a troubling question: 'Can it be that the faith on which a great civilisation was built has deteriorated within a few generations into a popular superstition, treated with indulgent tolerance?'[18] Cupitt, who considers himself to be 'a deep existential thinker', performs the task with a neat but all too familiar trick. The incoherent and untenable nature of Christian doctrine is universalised so that the Christian encounter with secularism is presented as universal history. Christianity's fate therefore must necessarily be the fate of all other religions: if the superior creed degenerated so rapidly, what hope could there be for the inferior? But the Other has to be softened up to allow the 'great civilisation' to continue on its historic mission. Cupitt thus aims straight at the heart of Other cultures: 'instead of seeing the world in terms of poetry, myth and symbol – always seeing one thing in terms of another, and almost everything in terms of stories and human imagery – we have come to see the world in terms of mathematical frameworks and structural regularities'.[19] Science is posited against the element of sacredness: and you cannot choose both; you cannot explain things 'from above', only 'from below'. We should, Cupitt tells us, 'dispense with signs and wonders' and tie ourselves firmly to science, 'a jealous wife who rightly demands complete fidelity'.

The sacred is thus replaced by an idealised but highly instrumental perception of science.

While Cupitt has no problem in recognising the omnipotence of science and secularism, he has trouble with the omnipotence of God, which he describes as an 'infantile fantasy'. Soon, he tells us, science will solve all problems and give meaning and direction to our lives: 'as the body of available scientific knowledge and technology grows ever larger and more powerful, science progressively takes over from religion, in one area of life after another, the task of explaining what is happening and prescribing what is to be done'; 'within the next generation or two the theoretical physicists will succeed in producing their ToE (theory of everything)' and everything will become totally transparent.[20] All of this means that 'religious belief and practice' will become little more than 'a hobby, a minority world-view and an optional but basically unimportant leisure-time pursuit on the part of those who have a psychological need for "roots" in an ethnic past or a cultural tradition'.

What is the postmodern, secular man (sic) to do in such a world? Being a totally autonomous individual, he makes his morality as he goes along:

He has no hesitation in simply appropriating many Christian virtues, such as concern for prisoners, the sick, the hungry and the oppressed. At the same time he sharply criticises many traditional Christian doctrines and teachings such as those to do with original sin and the disciplining of children, the subjection of women, and the prohibitions against nakedness, homosexuality and contraception. In other areas, such as fasting and abstinence, he has cheerfully abandoned and forgotten the traditional religious disciplines and has independently invented new and secular equivalents such as sponsored mortifications for charity. So modern secular man invents his own autonomous ethic and is no longer accustomed to allowing religious authority to prescribe his morality to him.[21]

Belief, then, becomes a matter of 'pick and mix'; 'our most fundamental beliefs have simply to be chosen. Their "truth" is not descriptive or factual truth, but the truth about the way they work out in our lives.'[22] Religious beliefs, then, are actually falsehoods which are constantly reinvented, according to the dictates of society and needs and desires of individuals. There is, however, an object of worship in the non-realist variety of religions that postmodernists like Don Cupitt propagate: love. You can worship love, he tells us, and you will say nothing untrue. In a world of contingency, there is nothing to hold on to: 'in the end everything must be given up, in such a way as to turn loss into oblation. That's non-realism: love unto death.'[23] So the religious wisdom of several thousand years amount to little more than a 'Beatles' song – 'All you need is love; love, love is all you need.' Or to put it in the more theological formulation of 'Enigma':

Principles of lust are burnt in your mind
Do what you want – do it until you find: *love*.[24]

Cupitt's postmodern religion amounts to little more than a feeble attempt to legitimate white man's lust. It also replaces Christian domination with market imperialism. His alleged pluralism hides the merciless authoritarianism of the market; which amounts to a celebration of the power of the west. Despite all his apparent openness, Cupitt displays all the hatred of the Other that we find in perverted Christianity. He wants all Other religions to go the way of Christianity and abandon their fundamental beliefs for some vague notion of charitable love (which is exactly what Christendom claimed it wanted to spread to Other cultures under colonialism) and bury themselves in the meaninglessness of his nihilistic theology, thus erasing the final traces of all Other identities. Here, then, we have a logical postmodern conclusion of modernity's goal to transform every white man into a god and to prove his superiority by reason: hence Cupitt's emphasis on science as an essential arbiter of what is good and desirable, his insistence on the total autonomy of (white) man, his reduction of all morality to the contingent ethics of the 'modern secular man'. Finally, Cupitt's unshakeable belief that secularism is the future, indeed the only future, is as misguided as Enlightenment predictions of the decline and disappearance of religion. It is the last hurrah of a desperate but empty-headed Christian bigot, who looks at the sky and howls.

The Returning Silence

There is no place for God, or indeed notions of the divine or the sacred, in deconstructive postmodernism. When Cupitt brings God into the picture, even in such a naive form as 'love', he is simply putting a saintly gloss on secularism's nihilistic picture of reality. Cupitt is in the business of formulating a secular religion which gives a modicum of comfort in the totally meaningless universe of the west. In contrast, there is a variety of constructive postmodernism, pioneered by David Griffin, Richard Falk, David Bohm, Rupert Sheldrake, Charlene Spretnak and others, which aims not only to preserve the idea of God and the sacred, but also to build on the best that modernity has to offer by combining it with the best of premodern thought. Constructive postmodernism is about giving positive meaning to the human self, recognising that history is ever present in us and everything we do, that it is possible to recover truth from premodern ideas of divine reality, cosmic man and enchanted nature. The constructive nature of this postmodernism is emphasised by the creative synthesis it seeks of modern and premodern ideas and values.

Whereas Cupitt's postmodern theology relies on a modernist view of science – which is rapidly becoming dangerously obsolete – Griffin offers an alternative postmodern theology based on a view of science and 'radical empiricism' that does not require either 'supernatural intervention' or a leap of faith. Here we are presented with 'naturalistic theism' which is said to be 'distinct from the supernaturalistic theism of premodern and early modern theology and the nontheistic naturalism of the late modern worldview'.[25] Its main epistemological basis is the affirmation of non-sensory perception, which allows for 'a dimension or element of perceptual experience that is not a product of culturally conditioned frameworks and is therefore common to us all'.[26] A key term for this postmodern theology is 'panexperientialism', which involves the attribution of feelings and innate values to all that constitutes nature:

Our ineradicable realism is thereby honored, in that dogs, cells, and molecules are said to be real in the same sense in which we are real, while both dualism and materialism are avoided. This panexperientialism is the ontological basis for naturalistic theism, which seems so strange to the modern mind, given this mind's assumption that experience is not natural. If modernity has had trouble thinking of the human soul as natural, all the more could it not think of a cosmic soul as a natural reality and its interaction with the world as part of the natural process. Postmodern theology, by contrast, with its assumption that experience is fully natural, finds it natural to speak of a divine, all-inclusive experience.[27]

All experience in this framework is considered to be creative experience and creativity itself is 'considered the ultimate reality, which is embodied by all individuals, from God to electrons'. Thus creative power is not the sole prerogative of God; indeed, He does not have the power to intervene or unilaterally control or change the world. The embodiment of creativity in the divine individual, writes Griffin, means that 'postmodern theology, while agreeing with modernity that the problem of evil undermines supernaturalistic theism, argues that theism itself, if naturalistically conceived, is fully compatible with the reality of genuine evil'.[28] Finally, the new formulation allows for the affirmation of life after death without compromising any of its basic principles. Thus, in the postmodern naturalistic theology, we have a 'robust doctrine of God, providence, and even life after death'; 'people no longer have to choose between having a meaningful faith and being fully empirical and reasonable'.[29] We are certainly entering the realm of the best of all possible worlds.

Where does the Other come in this, perhaps more conciliatory, take on postmodern religion? The specific aim here, Griffin asserts, is to 'make explicit the ways in which theological truth is *liberating* truth'. So is constructive postmodern theology liberating for non-western cultures? Does it, as a natural theology, provide a perspective in which Jewish, Muslim, Buddhist and Hindu can share and contribute? Constructive postmodern theology is Christian, Griffin asserts, in two ways. First, Jesus is accorded a central position in this vision. However, while divine character and purpose have been manifested through Jesus of Nazareth, he is not accorded any divinity himself nor are any claims made about God's unique presence – thus he is not the sole mode of salvation. Such an interpretation of Jesus is ruled out by naturalistic theism which defines itself by the metaphysical position that God does not intervene directly in the world – a conception borrowed from the otiose – high – god of many Other traditions. Jesus then becomes another prophet along with so many others. While postmodern Christians may hold him in special awe, and refer to him in a specially normative way, he is in effect deposed from the throne of God. This view of Jesus will find resonance not just with Muslims, who have always held Jesus to be a great prophet, but also with Hinduism and Buddhism which see great individuals as embodying universal aspirations and divine guidance. This aspect of constructive postmodern theology is liberating for the Other: it grants them the basic ecumenical decency of acknowledging that Christianity is not the sole repository of theological Truth and that there are Other ways to traditional religious salvation; a basic courtesy that Christianity has denied to all Others for some two thousand years.

Second, constructive postmodern theology is Christian in that it 'necessarily reflects a Western Christian perspective on the nature of reality'. Its philosophical outlook has been shaped primarily by Alfred North Whitehead and Charles Hartshorne, both of whom were sons of Anglican priests and products of western Christian civilisation. In as much as the philosophical dimension of postmodern theology is meant to provide criteria (rationality, self-consistency, adequacy of relevant facts including facts of experience and illuminating power) for assessing its truth-claims, no one would really argue against it. But should constructive postmodern theology's perspective on the nature of reality 'necessarily' be that of western Christianity? And, in fact, is it? From a non-western perspective, both the presumed necessity and claim are problematic.

The concept of God constructed by Griffin and other constructive postmodernists, like Richard Falk, Catherine Keller and Charlene Spretnak, owes little to Christianity and a great deal to Buddhism and Taoism. The constructive postmodern vision sees the world as the creation of a personal deity; but this deity is not the all-powerful monotheistic God of the Abrahamic tradition, which incorporates Judaism, Christianity and Islam. Theistic postmodernity challenges the idea of divine power traditionally associated with the generic idea of God. What we are presented with then is a notion remarkably similar to Tao with bits of Christianity grafted on. Here is Griffin's description of the deity:

> The postmodern God created our present world not by calling it into existence out of absolute nothingness, but by bringing order out of a chaotic realm of energetic events. This God neither controls all things nor interrupts the natural processes here and there. God does not coerce, but persuades. God does not create unilaterally, but inspires the creatures to create themselves by instilling new feelings of importance in them. This constant inspiration is a necessary part of the natural process, not an intervention into it. In this world, the vast amount of evil does not count against the reality and goodness of a divine creator, because all the creatures have some degree of power to act contrary to the purposes of the creator. The idea of an all-pervasive providential spirit is not contradicted by the evidence for extensive 'chance and necessity' throughout the evolutionary process.[30]

When this notion of God is combined with the idea that creative power resides in every momentary event, we get the complete picture. Everything from quarks to quasars, from cells to the human mind, is realising its creative potential at every instance and is influencing God. God exists; but He exists only in a dynamic equilibrium with the creation. He may be the supreme power but His power to influence events in creation is limited: 'God does not have and could not have a monopoly on power and therefore cannot unilaterally determine the events in the world.'[31] The limitation of the power of God also has consequences for the creation of the world. If God created the world by creatively 'persuading' it, then He could not have created it out of absolute nothingness – there must have been something there to persuade. Thus constructive postmodern theology argues that the universe was created out of previous creative state and creation moves things along from simpler towards more complex forms of order.

The idea of God as energy, the creative potential of every entity and every being and the associated notion of creation has a valuable payoff: because everything has creative potential and experience, everything has value and importance in and for itself. Nothing can be treated as a mere object – a mere end to our ends. And everything deserves respect. Thus respect for Other cultures is generated, not just because traditional societies have endured for over two thousand years, survived five hundred years of subjugation from savage colonialism and barbarous modernity, but also because of their intrinsic value and worth. However, respect for tradition does not mean acceptance of obscurant traditionalism: constructive postmodernism argues for transformative traditionalism that does not altogether shun innovation. Constructive postmodernism also marks a radical departure from conventional, deconstructive postmodernism in making its position on the cardinal issue of our time emphatic: our total alienation from nature (for which both liberal humanism and that Judeo-Christian heresy, Marxism, are equally responsible) and the consequent need to recover our sense of oneness with nature. Moreover, it also offers us a new relationship with time – with the past as well as the future. It sets out to recover a healthy respect for all our pasts, arguing that knowledge of the past is essential to self-knowledge and that 'the present moment of experience is seen to enfold within itself, in some respect and to some degree, the entire past'. Indeed, in the highly original ideas of Bohm on science and Sheldrake on life and evolution, we can see how the undercurrents of the past come to influence the present. In Bohm's theory of implicate order, every natural unit as an act of enfoldment in some sense enfolds the activity of the universe as a whole within it. Bohm's attempt to construct a postmodern science based on 'implicate order' implicitly incorporates a reference to divine activity. He is thus reversing the de-divinisation or secularisation of nature.[32] Sheldrake's hypothesis of morphic resonance, which attributes a cumulative power to the repetition of similar forms, depends on an influence at a distance, over both temporal and spatial gaps.[33] The past therefore has a serious role to play in the present. The common-sense conclusion from all this is categorically stated by Griffin:

The idea that the human psyche embodies not only influences from its body but also the repeated experiences of past psyches ... leads us to be wary of assuming that we can adopt radically new forms of being human without suffering severe, perhaps terminal, psychic distress. Good reason therefore exists to suspect that the modern attempt to live without religious convictions and practices, and without the support of intimate communities, will not produce a sustainable society.[34]

So who needs 'constructive nihilism' to survive the future? Constructive postmodernism offers a 'rational' and genuine reason to protect the planet and be optimistic about the future without resorting to mental gymnastics or restating established values in new, allegedly postmodern forms: 'we care about the future of the world because we care about the everlasting divine reality'.

Whereas deconstructive, Cupitt-type postmodern theology seeks to banish the Other and subsume everything in the grand designs of western civilisation, constructive postmodern religion leans on the Other in an attempt to save western civilisation. Noble sentiments notwithstanding, there is hardly anything new in the 'constructive postmodern thought' project. We are told by Griffin that the roots of his postmodern organicism are to be found in Aristotelian, Galilean and Hermetic paradigms. Catherine Keller glorifies neo-Platonism, Greek gnosis and the alchemists.[35] Richard Falk ascribes the lineage of his thought to 'Socrates, Jesus, the Buddha, even St Francis'.[36] In short, constructive postmodernism is an eclectic mix of the authoritarianism of Greek rationalist and Gnostic thought combined with Buddhism and nature worship, which produces, as have most philosophers in western history who have appealed to nature for ethics, a totally totalitarian system of thought.

It is worth noting that whenever the western mind turns to learn from the Other it almost always look towards Buddhism. Why? Because Buddhism is the easiest system to appropriate: it affirms the individuality of experiential and transcendental understanding, without any social and textually confirmed orthodoxy. The trick is in the means of appropriation. The interpretational gloss put upon Buddhism retains all the authoritarianism intrinsic in western thought while liberating it of all its guilt. Hence the popularity of Buddhism, and associated varieties of karma cola mysticism, like transcendental meditation, from the east. So what is presented as a constructive postmodern religion is little more than standard American empirical theology with a perverse Buddha integrated to justify the pluralistic validity of the entire edifice: the God of perverted Christianity reduced to an amorphous universal energy with lashings of neo-Platonic gnosis: the 1960s Jesus freaks and flower children meet the Greek perennialists. Constructive postmodern theology, therefore, holds little attraction for the Other, who would prefer to be understood in their own terms and categories before being swallowed whole and reformulated for postmodern delicatessence.

The Voice and the Snake

Just because modern and postmodern secularism have killed God, and postmodern religion (both the deconstructive and constructive variety) has cut Him into a badly fitting designer jacket, does not mean that western societies do not need God. If there is one message that we constantly get from postmodern culture, it is this: western folks feel that they have lost something but do not know, or remember, what they have lost. This quest has become an end in itself: what is crucial for postmodern culture is that the search must be constant, meaningless and perpetual; without any idea of the destination. The exponential increase in cults in the west during the last two decades is but a postmodern manifestation of the secular soul's ever-present need for spiritual search, 'an abiding hunger for extreme belief in an unbelieving world'.[37]

When Jesus, in *The Last Temptation of Christ*, finds it difficult to resolve the paradox that 'everything has two meanings', he resolves to find the path that God wants him to take. He walks into the wilderness, draws a circle and sits inside declaring, 'I am not going to leave here unless you speak to me ... speak to me in human words, whatever path you want I will take ...' He is tempted by Satan who appears first in the form of a snake and then as a voice from behind a fire. But Jesus sees through the temptation of evil. In contrast, postmodern seekers have no moral discernment simply because there are no criteria for judging good from evil. In postmodern times, belief in everything from aliens, witches, dead and alive pop stars, charismatic leaders to the ideology of the *X Files* is mushrooming. Many of the new Christian cults are nothing more than bizarre reworkings of the cult of Jesus that official Christianity has been trying to distance itself from. If you can believe that Jesus was 'son of God' what is there to stop you from believing that Reverend Jim Jones or David Korash or Yehweh bin Yehweh is a 'son of God'?

It is worth noting that the highest claim of those who pervert Islam is that they are a prophet – and the only noteworthy contemporary Muslim cult that comes to mind is that propagated by Rashid Khalifa, who 'discovered' that the Qur'an is encoded with a mathematical structure based on the number 19, and who styled himself 'Rashid Khalifa, PhD, Messenger of Allah'. In contrast, Christian cult leaders almost always attribute divinity to themselves, a claim that can be justified not just on the basis of perverted Christianity but also on the basis of modernity – if 'man strives to be god everywhere' it is not surprising that few of them actually claim to have made it. The accent on Christian religious revival in the west seems firmly to be on megalomania and madness: discoveries of the statues of crying Madonnas are becoming as common as sightings of UFOs (which never seem to land on non-western countries); people in various churches are falling to the floor or laughing uncontrollably and ascribing these activities to the 'Holy Spirit' working through the so-called 'Toronto Blessing'; armies of 'Christian patriots' are marching everywhere to save souls by hook or crook. Indeed, the indigenous cultures of South America can be forgiven for thinking that God is actually an American and a capitalist to boot.[38]

Being in tune with both modernity and postmodernity, many fundamentalist Christian cults, like the Jesus Fellowship Bugbrooke (Jesus Army), the Unification Church of Reverend Sun Myung Moon and numerous tele-evangelists have turned perverted Christianity into a business – big business, in some cases. This is an extension of medieval Christianity when colonising the Other involved both the mission to civilise and to extend the profits of the empire; today, the mission to save souls fits neatly with the need to make a fast buck. Many of the apocalyptic cults have roots in medieval

Christianity and incorporate all the fear and loathing of the Other that gave this period its particular flavour, though paradoxically virtually all of them operate out of a Protestant theological perspective. Muslim and Arab racism is a particular hallmark of Christian apocalyptic and millenarian writings. Saddam Hussein, Ayatollah Khomeini, Colonel Qaddafi have all been identified as 'anti-Christ' by modern apocalyptic writers, just as their medieval counterparts branded Salahuddin Ayyubi ('Saladin') and other Muslim leaders with similar labels. For many modern apocalyptic writers 'the Arab world is an Anti-Christ world'.[39] A flavour of the kind of hatred apocalyptic Christians have for the Other can be obtained from the writing of the sixteenth-century seer, Nostradamus. A vast industry has grown over the last decade around Nostradamus, including over 200 best-selling books, a movie, an American spin-off TV show, monopoly-style board games, virtual reality games and special Nostradamus watches.

When it comes to Islam or Muslims, Nostradamus's predictions are particularly revealing. Some samples:

V.55 A mighty Muslim chief shall come to birth
      In country fortunate of Araby.
      He'll take Granada, trouble Spanish earth
      And conquer the Italian from the sea.

III.27 A Libyan leader in the West ascendant
        Shall make the French against Islam irate.
        To literary scholars condescendent,
        The Arabs into French he shall translate.

VII.7 After the combat 'twixt the horse light
       Great Islam they shall claim at bay to keep.
       Death, shepherd-dressed, shall stalk the hill at night:
       The clefts flow red in all the chasms deep.

IX.67 Upon the mountain all about Isere
       They gather at Valence's rocky gate
       From Chateauneuf, Pierrelatte and Donzere:
       There shall Rome's flock the Muslim force await.[40]

And on and on ... Whatever one makes of this nonsense, its deep
fear of the Other, the darker side of Christianity, Islam, is evident.
When the Other is not being projected as the 'anti-Christ', its
spiritual traditions are being turned into so many consumer
products, there simply to be used, abused and thrown away. Just as
in Georgian Britain, when young black slaves were considered to
be essential fashion accessories, so in postmodern times, appropriating non-western spiritualities has come to be regarded as a
quintessential symbol of being chic. At least two generations have
grown up in the west desperate for meaning and happy to follow
actors, pop stars, fashion designers and other celebrity personalities in acquiring various non-western spiritualities as essential
designer accessories. A bit of quick-fix Indian mysticism, a touch
of Chinese acupuncture, a little native American spirituality, yogic
exercises or Buddhist meditation.

Theologians like Cupitt are completely at home on the Internet,
the world wide network of all computer networks. Here countless
individuals, with names like 'Doctress Neutopia', 'snake oil'
(which gives guidance on 'Kooky Kontemporary Kristian Kul-
ture') and 'Anders Magick', are busy creating their on-line
religion, mixing neo-paganism (nature worship) with Zen, teachings of *The Bhagavad Gita*, poetry of Sufi mystics and Satanism,
fundamentalist Christianity with xenophobic nationalism, and
western soothsayer literature with eastern religious classics. Postmodernism has elevated such pathetic 'spirituality', a kind of
motorway cafeteria religion, to the level of high theology. Often an
individual's search for spirituality ends up with those classics of
Orientalist lore: sex and justification of western authoritarianism.
Notice how many spiritual imports from the east have simply
turned out to be poor excuses for free sex in congregation:
Baghwan ('master of the vagina') Rajneesh's devotees are eager to
believe that meditation involves nudity, sex and making sound
barrier-breaking grunts; the LSD-induced sex sessions that became the trademark of the Hare Krishna movement in the 1970s;
the increasing fascination with tantra (the Hindu cult of sex)
amongst middle-class, yoga practising and meditating Europeans
and Americans – to give just three examples. Many imported
eastern mystical philosophies are put to good use for justifying the

status quo and the inhumanity of postmodern times. Nichiren Shoshu, a militant, thirteenth-century Japanese form of Buddhism that emphasises material progress, for example, has become very popular amongst professionals in the west. The karma-based secular spirituality of Nichiren Shoshu serves as an excellent balm for middle-class guilt:

> The most famous British follower of Nichiren Shoshu is (BBC's) Clothes Show presenter Jeff Banks. In a notorious interview in 1994, Banks explained his belief that people always get the fate their karma deserves: he was asked whether this would extend to starving Somalian child or the Holocaust. Banks claimed that Somalia 'has a bad national karma' and 'the Jews have had bad money karma'. Asked how he would explain a girl who was murdered, Banks replied: 'It would be something in her karma which made her a victim of the attack.'[41]

It's a genuine miracle that, given the western history of oppression and domination, the white man's karma always puts him on top.

The spirituality of Other cultures and societies thus serves two main purposes in postmodernism. Taken out of their historical and traditional context, they can be consumed to alleviate spiritual boredom. Many non-western spiritual traditions, like Yoga and Tantra, are reduced to techniques that one acquires. Or they can be used to glorify the meanest, basest and most brutal elements in western society and actually used against the Other. For example, the abuse of native American spirituality has become so common that the American Indian people were forced to set up an organisation to protect their spiritual inheritance: SPIRIT – Support and Protection of Indian Religious and Indigenous Traditions. SPIRIT claims that native Indian spirituality has been 'commercialised and bastardised' by New Age seekers who use them to promote their own 'harmful fantasies and stereotypes' of native Indians. SPIRIT sees this development as a new form of 'colonisation and oppression', which would lead to the 'spiritual genocide' of native American people.[42] An enlightened film-maker is now reduced to issuing health warnings in his films. Lou Diamond Phillips' *Sioux City* ends with the following warning: 'the Lakota ceremonies, rituals and religious items depicted in this film have been altered to protect the sacredness of the Lakota religion'. The spirituality of non-western cultures, like their realities, are not there simply to be used, abused and appropriated by the west. None of the Truth that is out there in the world of the Other is about bestiality, authoritarianism and shameful consumerism. It is about sanctity, about sacredness that unifies and unites us in purposeful meaning with the whole of creation. One can only pity postmodern spiritual bankruptcy because such madness cannot sustain the humane instinct or the caring operation of any society. Spirituality makes sense, as the non-western cultures have always known, only in the guise of full-blown historic religions.

Knocking on Forbidden Doors

Postmodernism has made traditional, historic religion a forbidden territory – a grand narrative that, like Enlightenment Reason, is absolutist, oppressive, isolationist and totalising. This interpretation of religion, as I have argued, is based almost exclusively on Christian dogma and history and does serious violence to non-western religious worldviews. The crux of the case against 'religion', as formulated, for example, by William Connolly's letter to St Augustine, is the price paid for insistence upon a religion in which faith *must* be made to accord with the possibility of eternal salvation for human beings.[43] That price is certainly too high as non-western cultures have discovered, over several centuries. Connolly's main concern, however, is the cost to European paganism. Christianity crumbles, Connolly argues, when presented with the problem of evil: if God is good and omnipotent, why is there so much evil in the world? Connolly contends that paganism, particularly Manicheanism, offered a more viable solution to the problem of evil by positing a dualistic god: a good and an evil god battling it out in the heavens and on earth. That not only solves the problem of evil but makes paganism a worthwhile enterprise. However, it generates another problem that Connolly omits to discuss: how do we know that the good god is more powerful than the bad one; and if the bad god has an equal chance of being more powerful than the good god, than how can we be sure that good will triumph? Indeed, why should we be good? But by solving the problem of evil, Manicheanism 'appears not as an external affront to a faith that has attained internal coherence and unity but as an alternative possibility of faith that must be constituted as heresy to protect the integrity of the self-identity it threatens through its existence'.[44] Thus the need for protecting one notion of God and good and evil is established by circumscribing counter-possibilities as deviations and heresy: 'humans drawn to paganism or Manicheanism must be made to suffer in order to vindicate the self-identity of those who find their deepest hopes disturbed, destabilised, or threatened by these alternative possibilities of interpretation. In a more general sense, Augustine's solution to the first problem of evil both delimits the sites at which responsibility can be located and intensifies the demand to identify agencies of responsibility.'[45] But there is no logical connection between a theistic solution to the problem of evil and defining otherness as a deviation from that solution: that is a uniquely Christian formulation. There is, for example, no notion of theological Otherness in Islam; Islam does not see Christianity or Judaism as 'counter-possibilities' that have to be eliminated to preserve the self-identity of Islam. On the contrary, it recognises Christianity and Judaism as *viable* and *legitimate* counter-possibilities, although it contains its own critique of both of them. Indeed, it is a basic contention of Islam that every nation on earth has its own prophet and as such every religious idea contains some notion of eternal truth. Similarly, Hinduism, which despite popular beliefs is a variety of monotheism, does not see deviation from the Hindu norm as a problem to its self-identity. The problem arises from the Europeanisation of Christianity; in formulating the Other, deviations and counter-possibilities, as a negation and hence a threat to one's own worldview. Connolly calls the Christian/European process of othering the second problem of evil:

> The second problem of evil is the evil that flows from the attempt to establish security of identity for any individual or group by defining the other that exposes sore spots in one's identity as evil or irrational.

The second problem of evil is *structural* in that it flows from the defining characteristic of a doctrine as it unravels the import of its own conceptions of divinity, identity, evil, and responsibility; but it is a temptation rather than a necessity because it is juxtaposed to other interior elements – such as, in Augustine, the orientation to mystery, a certain presumption in favor of leaving judgment to his god – that could be drawn upon to disrupt or curtail it. It is a temptation rather than an implication, and a structural temptation rather than simply a psychological disposition.[46]

The second problem of evil is not just structural, Connolly argues, but universal: 'the definition of difference is a requirement built into the logic of identity' and identity, particularly religious identity, can only be shaped by demonising the Other. This logic generates a paradox: 'without a set of standards of identity and responsibility there is no possibility of ethical discrimination, but the applications of any such set of historical constructions also does violence to those to whom it is applied'.[47] So, if you have identity your ethical stance does violence to others; and if you are a nice non-violent person you shouldn't be too concerned with self-identity.

But self-identity can be secure within itself – without reference to difference and Others. Muslims and Hindus, Australian Aborigines and the Bedouin of the Negev, the Malays and the Mongols, do not define themselves by pointing to differences they have with others – their identities are defined internally by their worldviews. Moreover, religious identities based on claims of absolute truths do not have to invoke difference either. Individuals in different religions experience absoluteness in their particular ways. Difference enters the equation, and identity becomes a problem, when a scale of measurement is brought into the identity equation: our religion not only defines our identity but it is the *only* way to salvation for everyone; *we* are civilised, *they* are the savages; *our* history is *universal* history; *we* are developed, *they* are underdeveloped. And who has been making such claims? And for whom are the questions of identity paradoxical?

Beyond Connolly's structural 'second problem of evil', there is the more earthly question of the postmodern embrace of evil. Postmodernism has replaced the classical western equation between

seeing and knowing with a genuinely dark mode of seeing and thinking. The relativisation of truth-claims makes postmodernism totally
blind: it is incapable of distinguishing between religions with
millennia of living history and instant, transient cults, between religious and traditional thought aimed at producing goodness and
justice and cultist theology based on evil. The special issue of
Colors[48] published by the Italian clothing multinational, Benetton,
provides an insight into the postmodern perception of religion.
Photographs of followers of historic religion, mainly non-western,
are juxtaposed with photographs of followers and leaders of cults
(mostly western) – the comparison is not only designed to demonstrate that there is nothing to choose between the two but also to
ridicule the Other. Almost all the points are made at the *expense* of
the Other. The centrefold that spreads out to four pages equates
Muhammad, Jesus, Krishna and Buddha with Haile Selasse, David
Koresh, Rev Sun Myung Moon, Yahweh ben Yahweh (leader of the
American black Hebrew cult). Another spread compares a weeping
American evangelist preacher, Jimmy Swaggart, with the feats of an
Indian Sahdu standing on wooden shoes of nails while an ecstatic
face of an African looks down from the opposite page. A two-page
spread juxtaposes Christ with David Koresh. Over an illustration of
Christ, under the banner question 'God?', we read: 'some say he was
the son of God. A carpenter and handyman who gave followers wine,
he was killed at 33. Nearly 200,000,000 people believe he's God.'
Over a photograph of Koresh, scanned from television, and under
the question 'God?', we read: 'He said he was the son of God. A
former gardener and gas station attendant who gave followers beer,
he was killed at 33. More than 200 people believed he was God.' The
message is clear: there is nothing to distinguish between Christ and
Koresh, between western cults and eastern mysticism, between historic religion and instant theology – buy Benetton and live happily
ever after! Evil may be 'transparent' in the word of Baudrillard, but it
does not stand out clearly enough for postmodernism to distinguish
it from good.

The real problem of modernity was the problem of belief. The
efforts to find meaning and exaltation in literature and art as a substitute for religion have left the problem untouched. Postmodernism
compounds the problem of modernity by an ahistorical representa-

tion of religion and its consequent embrace of evil. Whereas all historic religions seek to control individual desire and ego, postmodernism glorifies the uncontrolled expression of individual desires and inflated egos. But religion is not about ego-massage or the quest for a feel-good factor or appropriation of other visions of Other cultures or spiritual voyeurism that demeans non-western beliefs and spirituality or indoctrination. Religious faith is about metaphysical and moral commitment; and it need not be irrational. Faith without reason is as blind as a science without faith. Just as the practice of science demands that certain assumptions about nature, time, space and universe be taken for granted, so do the great world religions demand that certain propositions about the origins and purpose of life be accepted as true. No one is under any compulsion to accept these propositions; but every one has a moral and intellectual obligation not to misrepresent historic religion.

The Way to Eternity

The central concern of religion is the discernment of good and evil and eliciting from people a commitment to good in all aspects of human existence, thought and reverence. However, the question of good and evil is not merely a postmodern confusion, conflation and chaotic hodgepodge. Western civilisation has been exercised on the subject of 'why evil, and what is good?' for centuries: it was the central problematic of medieval society, part of the drive that authored modernity as well as being the defining perplexity of postmodernity. It is a very good question, certainly not a question exclusive to western civilisation. But there is a major distinction: the means of formulating the question in western thought has produced a tradition of inquiry and set of answers that can only lead to the cul de sac of postmodern neutrality, the indistinguishability of good and evil. What the tradition of western answers seems to ignore is human responsibility. Evil is not a problem of God, as for example 'the problem' has been framed by Connolly, but a human problem. It is not a question of why God does not intervene to prevent evil but why humans do not, and perhaps cannot, organise themselves to abolish evil. It is not a question of whether God Himself (Herself? Itself?) is Good or Evil but whether we can distinguish which principle we will commit ourselves to – good or evil. Good men in the name of good do evil works. Example: the postmodern temperament looks at the Conquistadors, those robust uncompromising Christians who settled the New World and laid the foundation of western dominance over the whole world, and sees only the will to power, the lack of any distinction between brutality and the profit motive and any good intent. Postmodernism accepts the profits, the world order cast in the mould of western dominance, and shakes its head in disbelief at how its forebears could so cravenly delude themselves on the justifications for their actions. The one thing postmodernism cannot accept is that the Conquistadors believed most passionately in the concept of heaven and the necessity of earning eternal life. So passionately did they believe that this was the one and only good thing in existence that redeeming grace could be enforced at the point of the sword or in the fiery heart of the *auto de fe*. The brutality of enforced conversion to Christianity or the purgation of heresy by the Inquisition defied the Devil and evil while it opened the way to Heaven. The justifications for such acts provided by conscientious faith were widely accepted. The means employed to achieve the only good end were known to be brutal, yet the brutality was commensurate with the unthinkability of leaving people as they were – outside the dispensation of heavenly life. No fire or pain on earth would be as hot or horrid as the eternal pains of hell. Where in all this, the postmodernist asks, is the difference between good and evil? The answer is elementary: it lies not in the abstract essences of good and evil but in the operative vessels, the rules and regulations, the whys and wherefores, of how good is to be done and evil obviated. In other words, the problem of evil, like the search for good, is a process of human operation, understanding and comprehension. Human interpretation creates the institutional forms of religion: religious laws have to be comprehended and employed by people. Since all the rules are acts of human interpretation, it is not God who is fashioning the sword or lighting the match. It is people who have the distorted imagination, the vivid, lurid capacity to conjure up demonic behaviour to save themselves from devils. And people are just as capable of interpreting and understanding conscientious faith otherwise. To the faithful the message of transcendence is such that human imagination can never get to the end of its meaning, hence no human interpretation is ever the final, absolute and inherently necessary operative embodiment of religious law. Distinguishing between good and evil does not transcend the rules and regulations but operates through the limitations of the rules and regulations to struggle towards the abstract essence of good – and most often fails. Failure, limitation, wrongheadedness, human perversity – none of these obviates the possibility of good or the value of perpetual search for the good, indeed they are the rationale for continuity, for perpetual struggle.

The key difference between the west and the rest is that non-western cultures comprehend humanity primarily in terms of its limitations, its finiteness. To be human is to be interrelated, integrated as part of a created order, which is not in and of itself transcendent. Non-western perspectives are as full of rules and regulations, operative processes and whys and wherefores – and just as prone to human error. But acceptance of human limitations and finiteness is the cardinal principle that bolsters the religious impulse. In contrast, the incorporation of religion in the west created an institutional form of putative human transcendence – the Church which in its Magisterium partakes of the power of God. The corruption of this institutional form, the impediments it created in its idealised conception and earthly operation promoted the movement to transfer more and more spheres of existence from the body of Christ, the perpetual and mystical authority of the Church, to the mores and control of the seculum, the 'present world'. Indeed the corruption and venal operation of the rules and regulations of the Church came to be seen by many as the main limitation which was preventing mankind from being good. Secularisation attained its own hagiography: organised religion bad, secular humanism good; priests and priestcraft the worst, the lone seeker after truth the best. The principles of secularism working through philosophy and all the disciplines of thought became a war upon the institutional interpretations of religion and as such a movement which saw itself as freeing human potential, without the mediation of clergy, to attain

this destiny. Such a movement could be engaged in as wholeheart-
edly by the religiously minded as the secular minded. But only with
the given starting point of institutionalised Christianity could one
end with the theological illiteracy that pervades western thought
today, for the process of secularisation is grounded on a profound
confusion. The Church's self-identification with the identity of God
led the rebellion against priestly institutionalism and all the rules
and system of authority based on it, a human creation, to result in a
rebellion against God. So successful was the institution of the
Church in making itself a logical necessity inherent in the interpretation of scripture that the logic of purging the errors of human
interpretation and action in the name of religion acquire the necessity of defining mankind as the only god, the individual taking the
place of the Church in the structure of argument. Instead of curing
the problem the disease has become the central tenet of postmodernism: the deification of man and consequent insignificance of God.
Postmodernism's inability to distinguish between good and evil is
the inevitable result of its failure to retain any sense of the nature of
God when it so misidentifies and overstates its claims for the nature
of man. The other salient detail is that for the west religion is, and
has always only been, Christianity, whose problems are the universal
problems of all religions. From the perspective of the non-west, this
is simply absurd.

Islam, as one non-western tradition, can say with postmodernism that interpretation is all we have. But Islam like other
non-western traditions cannot say that as a result of this inevitable, unavoidable circumstance we, personkind, therefore make up
the rules. The cardinal principle of human limitation and
finiteness comes in association with a set of enduring values,
concepts, categories that endure, are enduringly relevant and
which retain their meaning despite human frailty, failings, errors
or perverse bloody mindedness. In short, the rules and regulations
are never relative, the interpretations always are, it is always
necessary for people to go back and relearn the meaning and
import of the rules and regulations, accept the possibility of
change of form that is not change of meaning but a nearer
approach to the meaning. The misidentification of the source of
the problem, placing responsibility on God for the failures of

humankind, is the problem of postmodernism, its historic inheritance from western tradition of which it is a logical culmination,
not a brave new post-enlightenment. The acceptance that interpretation is all we have, and therefore any rule is a moveable feast, a
contingent and contextual possibility, has not helped in resolving
the problem of good or evil, it has made them even more identical
with each other than was ever the case for the Conquistadors. The
consequence has been moral inertia. In this vortex more and more
people in the west are scurrying off to find some new answer to the
religious void. A large number of them seek out cults allegedly
based on non-western religion, and the headline attraction they
offer is authoritarian control. Irony and paradox abound, for this
merely serves to strengthen the misidentification of the first part,
the identification of the essence and totality of organised religion
as a parody of the actuality of organised religion.

Whether they wanted or not, all non-western societies have been
secularised, à la Occident. They have been secularised because the
force of modern dominance has been imposed upon them to create
their present world, in all its inefficacy, contradiction, corruption
and incompatibility. Non-western believers live in a world not of
their making. Yet religion, the plurality of religious traditions, ideas
and imperatives have not ceased to have meaning for the non-west.
Indeed it is in the non-west that the failure of the secular dispensation has reconfirmed the good name of religion. This is not an un-
qualified benefit. Often what has been reconfirmed is a truncated,
distorted religious heritage: the fundamentalist route. The challenge of religion remains alive in the non-west, as does the ability to
take sacredness, reverence and spirituality in ordered forms, as
systems of rules and regulations, conceived as purposeful dispensa-
tions that stretch human understanding within its limitations and
finiteness. It is the non-west that husbands and retains the language,
reflexes and repertoire of ideas to articulate a dialogue on the distinction between good and evil, though this is not a covert way of saying
the non-west has all the answers or any special purchase on the
question of good and evil.

The dialogue, however, cannot solely be a discourse within each
tradition of the non-west or among traditions of the non-west. The
dialogue must include and engage the west. Today the challenge

of good and evil necessitates plurality, not religious pluralism in the sense of denying and diminishing the differences between distinctive religions and merging all traditions into identikits. It must be a plural debate through the defining differences of diverse religious traditions, like, for example, efforts being made in Malaysia to create a dialogue between Islam and Confucianism that makes clearer the potential for the two systems of thought to cooperate, and constructively cohabit while mutually supporting agreed moral and ethical programmes that promote a common understanding of good in a specific social context. But here is the rub. Christianity and its derivative postmodern secularism have profound difficulties with plurality that disable their humility, make it difficult for them to participate as equals within a plural debate. The problem of good and evil in our time is all about willingness to submit to the subversion of worldly dominance; only then can religion offer us new avenues for the exploration of our human and social condition. It is natural for a Muslim to suggest that submission is the basic religious impulse, but it is a notion that is endorsed by any religious imagination. Submission, however, is not a passive, quiescent activity: to the religious its meaning is diametrically contrary to the secular interpretation. Submission is the portal through which the religious imagination becomes alert to its limitations and finiteness, its frailties and failings and therefore sensitive to the fact that no human system of ideas or forms of interpretation can be allowed absolute dominance; all systems of worldly dominance must be subject to amelioration and curtailment because of the existence of a transcendent order. So long as one system of ideas remains the dominant order there can only be one model of modernity and no plurality. The chairman's veto exists and all other parties to the dialogue are required to formulate themselves according to the chairman's agenda. The historic formulation of Christian understanding is taken as the definition of the universal nature of all religious problems, and through that distorting lens all religions are asked to address issues that are irrelevant to them and express their own understanding according to a language that is meaningless to their necessary concerns. The dominance of western perspectives makes plural debate a resounding silence. To engage with religion one has to be able to submit to its categories. Only then can submission become the active principle for the subversion of a dominant perspective that is delivering us all into the hands of evil. Despite its self-declared good intentions, postmodernism, like *The Last Temptation of Christ*, has nothing new to say. Postmodernism takes western imperialism into a new phase where uncontrolled and self-glorified lust and all-encompassing consumption, including the consumption of the Other, become the norm. *The Last Temptation of Christ* manipulates the sensibilities of the faithful for no discernible reason. The dream sequence of the film is dream-like in its illogic and yet totally redundant – since all it argues is not so much that Jesus could or was seduced by the Devil, but that everything points to the necessity of the redemptive sacrifice as an intervention in human affairs. Rather than arguing against the Christian message, the dream sequence substantiates that message. In a sense it suggests that preposterous inquiry has a superior right – but since preposterous inquiry comes back to the orthodox view it is self-evidently purposeless; inquiry for its own sake. Self-indulgence needs no sense of reverence, even when it can provide no real alternative. We are left only with a worldview that cannot differentiate between good and evil and hence cannot cultivate virtue. It can thus have no long term future. One will be surprised if, in the history of ideas, postmodernism registered more than a pathological glitch.

8. Surviving Postmodernism

The minaret is clearly there. It looks as if serried ranks of people are huddled around, even on top of the minaret, in a representation in which the rules of realist perspective have been abandoned. The painting is, however, subtly Other. The Chinese painters Lin Yong and Su Hua have become famous in Pakistan for a series of works that draws on the tradition of Persian and Turkish miniatures to depict contemporary life in modern Pakistan.[1] 'Friday prayers', like the classic miniatures which illustrated the sixteenth-century masterpiece *Shahnama* ('Book of Kings'), uses a single plane to represent a number of dimensions. The congregation, the minaret of the mosque, and the *neem* tree in late autumn, all appear to exist in a single plane. Closer examination shows that we are actually outside looking in, taking an aerial view that encompasses what is outside the walls of the mosque and what is within its precincts. While the scene is clearly rural Pakistan, the painting is distinctively Chinese: with its characteristic brush-strokes, the *neem* tree rendered in the style of bamboo, the line of Chinese calligraphy at the left-hand corner, and the unmistakable signature. Other paintings by Lin Yong and Su Hua in the 'Pakistan' series can also be mistaken for representations of classic Islamic miniatures or Chinese paintings. 'Park', for example, seems like an illustration from an old Muslim text of fairytales or the work of an old Chinese master. In fact, it shows families and friends enjoying a day out in the Shalimar Gardens, Lahore in the mid-1980s. But while true to both Islamic and Chinese traditions, 'Friday prayers', 'Park' and the other paintings in the series are not products of an ossified and historically frozen past. There is here a technique that is entirely the work of tradition, it is a wholly identifiable 'gaze', which can embrace the conventions of other civilisations, whether they be the conventions of Persian miniatures or western realist portraiture, to produce a new kind of art, one that is intercommunicative, that engages many observers from many different backgrounds, without violating its unique point of origin. Here tradition is presented as a dynamic force: alive, innovative, life-enhancing. What we witness in these paintings is a thriving, dynamic culture ready to confront the problems of modernity and the nihilism of postmodernism: these parameters, as the paintings illustrate so breathtakingly, are common to both Islamic and Chinese traditions, and by corollary to all non-western traditions.

From the perspective of non-western societies, surviving post-modernism is all about moving forward to tradition. Cultural resistance to postmodernism begins with tradition, as did opposition to modernity. Non-western cultural resistance *to* postmodernism – which, as I have consistently argued, does not represent a disconti-nuity with history, a sharp break from modernity, but an extension of the grand western narrative of secularism and its associated ideol-ogy of capitalism and bourgeois liberalism – can come only from non-western traditions. More: tradition can actually transform non-western societies into cultures *of* resistance.

But tradition is a double-edged sword. Traditions of resistance have maintained non-western enclaves of cultural autonomy as heavily defended redoubts. But fortified earthworks cannot be moved. There is a cultural resistance that does not go forward and is coming perilously, indeed fatally, close to being a dead weight, sub-merging Other cultures in illusory pasts instead of anchoring them to the continuing flow of history. Non-western cultures must distin-guish between tradition and traditionalism. Tradition is the summa-tion of the absolute frame of reference provided by the values and axioms of a civilisation that remain enduringly relevant and the conventions that have been developed in history into its own dis-tinctive 'gaze': patterns of organisation, ideas, lifeways, techniques and products. Tradition can be periodised, it can be studied as a work of human history wherein there has been change. *Most* signifi-cantly tradition *is*, and in its being is proactive, whether or not the bearers of a particular tradition have lived up to this challenge or not.

Traditionalism, on the other hand, is a reflex-action, a response to external pressure. In retention it is passive; its only activity is to retain. It reifies formalist aspects of tradition as it operated in a defined past to be the guarantor of the survival of a community, while holding tenaciously to those practices and ideas of autonomous tradition that have continued in an embattled present. It can, and indeed has, become ossified, oppressive and backward-looking in many societies and cultures. This happens when tradition is romanticised and fixed in specific space–time coordinates. It is traditionalism that dominates fundamentalist activity throughout the non-west. By offering the past as the ultimate answer to contemporary problems it falsifies both tradition and the past and fails to generate or inculcate the acquisitive knowledge impulse that is the essence of any living tradition. Tradition is a way of knowing; traditionalism deals only with the imperishable content of what is known. Traditionalism has done a fine job in maintaining some aspects of the non-western heritage, in retaining something for Other cultures to fight for. It has developed ramparts and barricades that make today's citizens of the non-west conscious that there are lines that cannot be crossed or compromised. But in its preservational task, traditionalism, as personified by fundamentalist movements, has become a pathological factor of postmodern times: it can fight only to destroy and reinstall; it cannot build anew.

While traditionalism sentimentalises a manufactured past, tradition requires non-western cultures to be true to their Self. But this Self is not the 'I' of western individualism, what is known in Islamic parlance as *nafs*: subservience to *nafs* leads to selfishness, greed, perpetual desire and cynicism. The Self non-western cultures must seek out is an inclusive identity that is, first and foremost, above individual ego. Postmodernism celebrates egoism – and it is the ego that ultimately leads, as Mohammad Iqbal suggests, to the demonisation of the Other and the ensuing conflict:

> It makes from itself to be Other than itself,
> It makes itself from the form of Other,
> In order to multiply the pleasure of strife.[2]

Iqbal is hailed in the Indian subcontinent as 'the poet-philosopher of the east' and much of his poetry, like the work of so many eastern poets and philosophers before him, is devoted to the exploration of how the Self can be liberated from the ego. Two of his great epic poems, *Asrar-I Khudi* ('The Secrets of the Self') and *Rumuz-I-Bekhudi* ('The Mysteries of Selflessness') are devoted to the subject. In 'The Mysteries of Selflessness' Iqbal argues that the community and the individual are not discrete categories, but inseparable elements that become fused through a living consciousness of tradition. The semantic field of the term Self employed in the poems makes clear the parameters in which the poet is operating. *Khud* means self while the suffix 'i' signifies coming. The terms are related to *khuda*, which means the self existing God. The Self that Iqbal is discussing implicitly and explicitly refers to a concept of unitary creation. It reminds readers that within the Islamic framework *nafs*, the individual ego, is not the only concept that defines the individual human being. The more familiar and extensive concept is *fitrah*, which translates as innate human nature. The *fitrah* of all human beings gives us the qualitative measure of what it is to be human: to begin with knowledge, a propensity to make, to do and to learn, as well as to speak; a capacity to discern right from wrong; a capacity to recognise one's origin and purpose. It is the *fitrah* which makes human beings capable of experiencing a sense of belonging and necessitates community. Indeed, within the Islamic framework it is inconceivable for an individual to exist except in community, hence the full development and realisation of their humanity requires building mutual compatibility with the community. As the suffix in the term *khudi* indicates, neither the Self nor the community within which it must exist are static givens. The moral and ethical framework of values, origin and purpose endures; Self and, by implication, community must be created, striven for, reforged in each generation. Islam has never been interested in that quintessentially western concept of 'the good citizen'; the whole focus of Islamic discourse on politics, society and the individual concerns how to foster the holistic conception of the 'moral human being': only a good society can generate good people, while good people cannot be fulfilled without exerting themselves to achieve a good community. The notion of *fitrah* is the antithesis of western individualism, not because it denies individual

personality, identity and responsibility – all these are basic ideas
fundamental to an Islamic outlook – but because in the Islamic purview the individual is only conceivable within a web of essential
relationships wherein their individuality is neither the dominant
nor the only significant consideration if the person is to realise and
be true to his or her innate nature.

A community, argues Iqbal, is like a child. A child acquires a
sense of its worth when it learns to remember and link tomorrow
with its yesterday, and hence 'createth its own history'. It is the
personal history of the child that opens its 'Being's eye': 'so his
memory maketh him aware of his own Self'. Similarly, it is its
memory, its living history, its tradition, that makes a community
'self-aware'; and only through self-awareness can a collection of
individuals actually become a community:

> Know, then, 'tis the connecting thread of days
> That stitches up thy life's loose manuscript;
> This selfsame thread sews us a shirt to wear,
> Its needle the remembrance of old yarns.
> What thing is history, O self-unaware?
> A fable? Or a legendary tale?
> Nay, 'tis the thing that maketh thee aware
> Of thy true self, alert to the task,
> A seasoned traveller; this is the source
> Of the soul's ardour, this is the nerve that knits
> The body of the whole community.[3]

Historical tradition is not static, it must be reinvented by each
new generation as it takes over its cultural inheritance from those
preceding it. Only through the interweaving of past and present
can change attain meaningful form:

> The skilful vision that beholds the past
> Can recreate before thy wondering gaze
> The past anew; wine of a hundred years
> That bowl contains, an ancient drunkenness
> Flames in its juice; a cunning fowler it
> To snare the bird that from our garden flew.[4]

The constructive capacity of human nature, its innate ability to
become skilled, refined – hence the word civilised – is all about
making interconnections, maintaining continuity of meaning.
This is the antithesis of rupture, fragmentation and discontinuity.
It leads us to gaze anew upon the past, not as the pattern that must
slavishly be repeated in the present and for the future but in its
spiritual essence. In the conventions of Persian and Urdu poetry
wine and all references to drinking and drunkenness refer to
spiritual essence in the sense of perception and experience of the
divine. What each generation must lay hold of is the passionate,
intoxicated, creative essence of human skilfulness, the need to be
doing and being which changes things in its environment, adapts
and refines the material world and the human organisation of this
world; to maintain the meaning of values, morality and ethics
despite apparent differences. Living memory, reinterpreted history, dynamic tradition not only enable a community to survive
and thrive, they are prerequisites for life:

> If thou desirest everlasting life,
> Break not the thread between the past and now
> And the far future. What is life? A wave
> Of consciousness of continuity,
> A gurgling wine that flames the revellers.[5]

The recovery of their Self is thus the strongest hurdle that Other
societies can place before postmodernism. Although Iqbal's ideas are
rooted in Islamic thought, its concepts and categories, they have a
resonance and relevance for all non-western societies. It is not
merely that Iqbal's poetry has been eagerly embraced by Indians and
Chinese. It is the more general point that non-western cultures share
a holistic instinct, which is derived from their diverse but intercommunicative individual traditions as illustrated by the paintings of
Lin Yong and Su Hua. What all Others share today is what separates
them from and impels their resistance to postmodernism. Each non-
western tradition has to recover the Self that enables it to begin
making its present and future anew within the continuity of its own
history. This is not an isolated or lonely struggle: culturally alive
non-western writers, academics and activists share many premises in

their struggle for cultural renewal, though the cultural premises they draw from are different for each, according to the tradition from which they come. It is not a homogenisation of all Others that one is talking about, but a kind of solidarity through difference, a compatibility through plurality, which can strengthen them in their contest with the massed forces of postmodernism. The cultures of resistance that the non-west must seek to create are not about eradicating the individual in the search to re-establish the community as a viable thriving entity. It is rather the rejection of the notion that human beings can find and are fulfilled through the existential loneliness and angst of postmodern existence. The quest is to find a new dispensation, their own multiple and diverse cultural means beyond the straitjacket of western modernity and postmodernism where individual and community form a symbiotic whole.

The proliferation of cultures of resistance in the non-west will multiply the 'gazes' that are turned upon the west. It has been characteristic of the 'gaze' of Orientalism, for example, that the object of its interest has been seen to be passive. Indeed, the Other has always been a passive object for the west, a negative awaiting its overwriting in order to become human, predictable, able to be included in its processes of political, social and economic control. The outward vision of cultures of resistance, however, must be true to the Self of the non-west. Their 'gaze' must become not a languorous stare of incomprehension, but a sharpened vision, which can engage and hold a plurality of objects, styles and ideas in a critical, simultaneous moment; it is an outward look that takes things in their whole and divergent being and is prepared to deal with them as they are. Perhaps this was the reason why the non-west facilitated its own domination. It took the scions of the conquering west, as it took all things, on their own limited and finite terms expecting them to be flawed, and in so doing misconceived the nature of the danger posed. Now, having resisted and endured through that long onslaught of the category mistake, the non-west can make an active virtue from what was an immobilising error. To look on the west and see limitations, frailty and flaws is not to take the west on its own idealised terms but in the round, in its reality and in distinctly non-western terms.

As I have tried to show, while actively seeking plurality and representation for 'Other voices', postmodernism in fact dismembers Other cultures by attacking their immune system: eradicating identity, erasing history and tradition, reducing everything that makes sense of life for non-secular cultures into meaninglessness. It places the inhuman and degrading on a par with the humane and ethical. From the standpoint of the concept of *fitrah* by removing the innate capacity to distinguish between good and evil postmodernism can be classified as anti-human. It is thus the most pathological of all creeds of domination, the final solution of the cultural logic of secularism: the acquired inhuman domination syndrome (AIDS) of our time. The movement forward to the Self provides Other cultures with a much needed antidote to the virulent and ever-changing virus of postmodernism.

But the revival of Other traditions is necessary not only for resisting postmodernism. It is also essential for the creation of a genuinely pluralistic world. Postmodernism, with its globalising and secularising tendencies, turning all cultures into ahistorical, liberal, free markets, is set to eliminate any possibility of dialogue with cultures that are truly Other: who will be there to dialogue with once the earth and humanity are completely westernised? This is the subtext of the postmodern appropriation of multiculturalism, as I have tried to demonstrate. It is the appropriation of those facets which are conducive to the thrust of dominance, appropriation of elements that account for the losses suffered by the modern self. The corollary is that what postmodernism leaves behind, soundless and unmentioned, what they do not want of the totality of the Other or actively traduce, parody, ridicule and deride, is then useless. In the process the Other as a going concern is as comprehensively destroyed as ever it was under modernism and its colonial endeavour, it is as successfully fragmented and destabilised. What postmodernist multiculturalism wants of the Other has one further subversive twist of the knife. Postmodernism seeks to appropriate its own romanticised and unbalanced conception of the 'soul' of the Other, the psychic/spiritual power which is one way of describing aspects of non-western worldviews. Not only does the New Age agenda, which makes multiculturalism a respectable and marketable commodity, deform the reality of non-western worldviews, it also plays havoc within the non-west. It disproportionately empowers those who hold firmest to ossified traditionalism and pietistic outlooks, thus making it easier for the totalitarian power of the project of postmodernism to consume them entirely. It makes unholy allies of the old traditionalists and the new onslaught from the west, leaving no space for the new discourses of the non-west to occupy and develop. Tradition is either what the traditionalists say or what the west deems it to be through its scholarship or co-option. The traditionalists and the postmodernists justify each other's existence neatly by the virulence of their adversarial rhetoric. They fight, therefore they are. Recovery of the Self in non-western cultures needs more than sabre-rattling, and does not finds its *raison d'être* in the mere existence of the postmodernist threat. Cultures of resistance must be nurtured because they are the only humane answer to the pressing need for liveable options, sustainable choices for the people of the non-west. It is only in their Self that the Other can find hope, sanity and fulfilment. The survival and the flowering of non-western traditions make viable alternatives to the west conceivable, and genuine pluralism, with thriving cultures that are truly Other, a possibility.

All non-western cultures will change and are changing. The issue for them is to change within meaningful boundaries, reformulate traditions into contemporary configurations, rediscover their history and heritage in forms that empower and resist the onslaught of modernity and postmodernism and, on the basis of tradition, to author new answers to contemporary questions. This rethinking of the concept of tradition is a process of recovery of indigenous meaning and a development of inherent, autonomous potential to initiate stable but dynamic change. It requires serious attention to the way in which the corpus of traditional worldviews becomes fossilised and tradition confined and made into a preserve of private, domestic and exotic peasant 'culture'. More specifically, it requires releasing internal forces of dynamism and change that are intrinsic to all non-western cultures. For example, within Islam the dynamic principle of *ijtihad* – sustained and reasoned struggle for innovation and adjusting to change – has been neglected for centuries. A strategy for desirable futures for Islamic cultures would articulate methods for the rediscovery of this principle – a rediscovery which would lead to reformulation of Islamic tradition into contemporary configurations.[6] The highly complex and multidimensional concept of *han* in Korean thought represents similar notions of opening up new horizons for future life. As Tae-Chang Kim argues so forcefully, the fossilisation of the past in Korean tradition can be overcome by discovering new ways of practising traditional notions: *'han* is, *par excellence*, a horizon – opening force. *Han* has been underlying the Korean people's endless passion to try to go through the dark times of trials and tribulations and find a new alternative world.'[7] Other cultures have similar principles hidden from view. In other words, desirable futures can be conceived of and planned for only where plural processes of autonomous cultural adaptation are the accepted norm.

The Incredible Lightness of Authenticity

Rethinking tradition also requires an appreciation of cultural authenticity and cultural autonomy. Cultural authenticity means that traditional physical, intellectual and spiritual environments and values should be respected and accorded their proper place in society. It is not a question of re-instituting Puritanism in all its stark determinism. What is most needed is the unabashed embrace of self-confidence, the pride that dares to walk its talk. The figure that really terrifies the west most is the unapologetic Other with the competence and the confidence to accommodate the contemporary world and amend it in ways undreamed of and unconsidered by the hosts of modernity and postmodernism. How could this be done? First, by seeing traditional systems as a source of strength and a reservoir of solutions for people's problems. Clearly this does not mean that all the urgent questions that beset non-western cultures can find ready answers in the past – that is the cloud cuckoo land of fundamentalists who substitute evangelical euphoria for thought. What the past offers is more complex. What makes the Other different from the west is a civilisational corpus of ways of knowing, being and doing defined by value parameters. These active principles have been in suspended animation often for centuries, under the onslaught of modernity and colonialism. They need the animation of thought, critically undertaken in the sincere belief that the value parameters matter and must be maintained. This is as much a leap of knowledge as it is a leap of faith. When the 'gaze' of tradition is turned upon the modern world as a knowledge enterprise, working through the value-defined categories and concepts of tradition, its geography looks radically different. This geo-morphing raises new questions, and renders old ideas fruitful repositories of new ways to think about what have so far been considered intractable problems. The stark truth is that no one in the non-west and certainly not the west itself has any idea of what potency this enterprise will release. It is not the form of the past that such an undertaking requires or seeks, but its conceptual power, the power that can integrate, synthesise and innovate within the parameters of enduring values to author meaningful change, change that delivers us into a future our forebears could not have imagined but where they would eventually recognise themselves as at home.

Meaningful change is the currency of cultural authenticity. It will include authentic mistakes, for which the non-west must accept responsibility, as well as food for thought that can stimulate the barren landscape of ideas of the west. The drive for cultural authenticity will be far easier if there is cultural autonomy. This is the crux of the problem. Postmodernism simply does not tolerate cultural autonomy, nor do the totalitarian reflexes of free market capitalism and liberal democracy. Creating the space, resources and empowerment needed to nurture the cultural autonomy that will permit cultural authenticity to mature will be hard. It is the only battlefield, and it most definitely cannot be won with landmines, small arms or artillery, let alone long-range bombers and high octane explosives. It is a work of imaginative reconstruction.

The second requirement, the detail of engineering cultural autonomy, is emphasising indigenous development stemming from traditions and encouraging the norms, language, beliefs, arts and crafts of a people – the very factors that provide meaning, identity and richness to people's lives. The corollary of all this is a sensible check on postmodern consumer goods that represent the omnipotence of technology – which induce dependency, thwart self-reliance and expose non-western societies to physical and mental domination. As A. K. N. Reddy has so elegantly pointed out, appropriate technology is more sophisticated intellectually and just as technological as the dominant consumer variant. The difference is that appropriate technology submits itself to more demanding criteria, ones that respect and integrate the values of indigenous cultures and humane social and economic considerations.[8] What is important is not the abandonment of technological advance but the refashioning of what criteria determine whether an advance has been made, and the devising of new criteria to generate new forms of local production processes and products to satisfy local needs. The very expression of cultural authenticity, leading to a degree of self-reliance, self-respect and pride, transforms a culture into a force of resistance. Desirable futures require articulation and implementation of strategies for cultural authenticity and hence transformation of traditions into cultures of resistance.

Postmodernism is at pains to discredit and destabilise the very concept of authenticity. It is either rendered as a romanticised notion that is unknowable to members of Other cultures themselves because they have been adulterated by colonialism, or ridiculed and derided as inferior. The battle to reassert cultural authenticity is the most precarious balancing act for non-western people. It must embrace the culturally authentic proposition that none of our civilisations is monolithic. This is not the meaning of tradition, certainly not the definition of tradition on which I have been operating. The balance comes in recognising that non-western authenticities will be, as they once were, multiple, that there will and indeed must be multiple ways of doing and being that can be elicited within the commonly held consensus of publicly agreed parameters.

Surviving postmodernism also demands strategies for cultural autonomy. Cultural autonomy does not mean isolating a culture from the outside world or shunning the benefits of modern society. It means the ability and the power to make one's own choices based on one's own culture and tradition. Contrary to popular belief, cultural autonomy does not compromise 'national sovereignty', it is not an invariant threat to unstable nation states. There are two dimensions of cultural autonomy. The external dimension requires non-western societies to seek their economic and political development with the accent firmly on local traditions and cultures. The internal dimension requires nation states to provide space and freedom for ethnic minorities within their boundaries to realise their full cultural potential, make their own choices and articulate their own cultural alternatives. Cultural autonomy has to be seen as a dialectical concept. It embraces both the macro level of cultural, religious or ethnic groups and the micro level of the human mind. It begins with the simple idea that cultures, and individuals within cultures, have a right to self-expression and leads to the burgeoning of pluralism and multiculturalism.

It is mere historic accident that the European definition of nationalism and hence the nation state should emphasise one unique and dominating cultural identity. In part, this is derived from the cultural homogeneity of European communities. Its other prop was the historic legacy of a system of thought that defined the only rightful citizen as the orthodox – that is, one who subscribed to the orthodox beliefs of the Church which underpinned the whole concept of governance in medieval Europe. When religious orthodoxy broke down in Reformation Europe, new political entities were formed. Where this did not happen, populations changed their religious affiliation to match that of the sovereign. The quest for liberty of conscience is the origin of both the movement for political enfranchisement and citizens' rights and the secularisation of thought and society in Europe. Even then it was a quest that did not imply an accepted place for multiculturalism and heterogeneity since dissenting citizens shared the same cultural ancestry and, in many respects, culture as the rest of the nation state.

The non-western experience has been quite different. Genuine heterogeneity of culture, within communities and systems of governance, has been an integral part, for example, of Islamic, Indian and southeast Asian history and experience. Recovery of tradition should focus on the rediscovery of the means of stable plurality within communities and states. Today, Asia is virtually the only place where this desperately needed human resource can be championed. Ironically, given contemporary events, it is the only logical place to search for working, historical models of pluralism and multiculturalism that are not based on secularism.

It should also lead to the preservation of what is good and life-enhancing in traditional thought; legal, economic and political arrangements for the equal participation of all cultures in wealth and social opportunity; the elimination of distrust between cultural groups; the encouragement of meaningful communication between peoples and cultures; and the elimination of extremist positions and actions. Thus, strategies for cultural autonomy are the *sine qua non* for surviving postmodernism.

Just as we can document the transition in western discourse of the singular form of the terms culture and civilisation to the plural, so we need to effect a change in the usage and meaningful content of the term 'modernity'. At present, the term means, and implies, only one thing: the slavish replication of the process of social, cultural, political and economic transformation, which occurred in Europe and in western civilisation. Non-western societies need to redefine modernity in their own terms and cultural frameworks. This requires using traditional concepts and ideas as analytical tools, incorporating the knowledge of the past into the thought processes and products of today. As Susantha Goonatilake points out, 'Asians have tried to use the past, but in the nineteenth and twentieth centuries, they have largely emphasised the presumed "spiritual" aspects. It is in the more mundane, material aspects, however, that Asian cultural elements could be fruitfully used.'9 Cultural elements from non-western history, traditions and lineages need to be identified in such areas as science, medicine, technologies, materials and agriculture, and reprocessed and incorporated into modern systems of distribution and dissemination.

In the contemporary information age the battle for norms and values is won not so much in the political arena as by the control of the tools of perception. For postmodernism the image is all and the imagist industries, film and the media, are genuine centres of power and influence. One cannot shut out the satellite feed, or close down or stand aside from the information superhighway, though the greatest part of the non-west will remain an unconnected branch line for a very long time. Countermanding the global information and image industry with alternative imagery and information is the essence of empowering cultural autonomy with cultural authenticity. For a brief moment it appeared as if Japan might be opening this enclosed conundrum through the power of the almighty yen by buying into the US entertainment industries: films, music, games, software. The strategy has been a resounding failure. Not only did Hollywood successfully use the Japanese as a convenient punchbag for its own excess, but the Japanese clearly had no concerted 'cultural' imprint ready to infiltrate into the axioms of Hollywood. Ownership and control are the failed headlines of the old left analysis of the media. They are only one facet to explain the supremacy of the western media industry. Its most insidious achievement is co-option of all points on the social and political scale within the west through cultural identity: the fact that there is such a thing as western civilisation and a western worldview which unifies owners and controllers with the operatives of the media, those who actually do the manufacturing of the cultural products.

Owners, controllers and operatives share a common conception that they 'understand' their audience, the arrogant notion that it is they, jointly and severally, who 'know' what should be produced, when in fact they are all merely serving the most basic and brutal of free market notions – you get only what is most profitable. But now the non-west is beginning to have a marked effect on the film industry. The audiences of Asia now affect the market value of Hollywood stars. The ability to make profits from films that flopped in America from non-western audiences is generating a genre of films driven by marquee value star names that are long on action, short on dialogue – a kind of all-purpose comic book, special effects-driven epic of global communication. Out of this morass of meaninglessness, opportunities that empower cultural authenticity and autonomy have to be effected. But such opportunities cannot be created from cringing apologetics and lack of self-confidence in one's own cultural identity which are the kiss of death for the non-west. Mouth-to-mouth resuscitation of indigenous cultural traditions demands concerted strategic thought and the investment of financial resources: serious efforts have to be made for the production of indigenous cultural products, local film production has to be encouraged, investment has to be made in making local television programmes. In short, wherever possible, meaningless western culture has to be replaced with products that impart indigenous cultural meaning. Cultural autonomy cannot be gained without human and financial commitment; it requires a *volte face* from the passive acceptance of the notion that 'things change' to actively changing things.[10]

Beyond the pursuit of cultural authenticity and cultural autonomy, resistance to postmodernism requires non-western cultures to come to terms with their own darker side. The point is not to indulge in the postmodern embrace that glories in evil, but to combat it and constrain the deformity it imposes on society. In as far as all cultures are human products, they have an unsavoury darker side. Many non-western cultures have an undeniably authoritarian streak that needs to be checked. For example, the argument that the 'individual' does not exist in the communal milieu of Asia as an absolute individual has become an excuse for the violation of the human integrity and the dignity of individuals. There is a place for political dissent in the Asian purview that needs both to be acknowledged and enhanced. Communal values embellish participatory governance; they should not be used as a licence for the ruthless suppression of dissenting voices. It is precisely because of the stability produced by strong extended family commitments, community structures and social concerns that non-western societies need to be open societies, with accountable political structures, actively promoting and encouraging all that is good and healthy in human endeavour. To achieve this, non-western societies have consciously to come to terms with the unsavoury side of their history. The Japanese, for example, have to do more than say 'no' to the west, abandon their old policy of 'Leave Asia, turn to the West' (*'Datsu-Ah, Nyuu-Oh'*) in favour of the new clarion call, 'Leave the West, turn to Asia' (*'Datsu-Oh, Nyuu-Ah'*), as the novelist and film director, Shintaro Ishihara, argues so well in *The Japan That Can Say No*;[11] they must also address the painful facts of their history if Japan is to play a prominent role in Asia and, through it, in non-western politics. Similarly, the corruption and abuse of power that has a certain history in non-western societies needs to be directly addressed. What Anwar Ibrahim has said about Asia applies equally to all Other cultures:

We must have the courage to address the stark contradictions within our society. Although we take pride in religiosity continuing to be a major element in our lives, yet at the same time, and most paradoxically, our society seems to be indifferent to the moral decadence and the erosion of social fabric through widespread permissiveness and corruption. Of course, some would say that many of the vices rampant are but the inevitable consequences of abject poverty. No doubt there is a grain of truth in that. Yet, we cannot help feeling that if the practice of religion had been entrenched together with its moral and ethical dimensions, then this degeneration could have been kept in check.

Our self-induced euphoria in respect of our remarkable economic growth must not blind us to the parallel rise in corruption, bribery, nepotism and the abuse of power. While some seem content to regard this as a necessary evil, we firmly hold that this is a fundamental issue at the core of our moral and ethical foundations. There can be no compromise on this.

The experience of Southeast Asia in economics, social and political development is indeed rich and varied. Because we wanted our development to be indigenous, ASEAN remained neutral during the Cold War. Each member embarked on its own particular mode of democracy. However, some may have entertained the idea that authoritarianism is the most efficacious means for economic success. To them, democracy is, maybe, too cumbersome for orderly development. It may even be seen as inimical to political stability, which is a precondition for rapid economic growth and social well being. Even Asian, especially Confucian, values have now come to be invoked in support of that proposition. This notion has been effectively debunked by the experience of Malaysia and Thailand. Political liberality is *not* incompatible with strong economic performance. Both these countries have sustained economic growth for more than three decades while practicing open and vibrant forms of democracy. As for Asian values, they produced great civilisations in the past. However, if these values are to contribute towards a renaissance of Asia, they must serve as a source of liberation. Asian cultural renewal must mean the cultivation of all that is true, just and caring from our heritage, not perpetuating the narrow and oppressive order of the feudal past ...[12]

Pre-eminently one is not saying that Other cultures are inherently virtuous, just as resolutely as I oppose the notion that they are inherently evil. Nor will a recovery of public consensus and concern for shared values as the glue of traditional cultures end for them the worry of wrestling with the problem of evil in our times – that is, their own evil in times they shape and determine for themselves. Consciously and deliberately one is looking to avoid utopian vision; utopias have always betrayed their adherents. It is the unglamorous realm of the real, with all its complexity, confusion and constraints, that one is seeking to influence with remedies of its own kind: complexity, a measure of confusion and constraints. The first lesson for the reconstructors of Other civilisations is they have no ready answers and an urgent need to confront and deal with their own limitations through the categories and concepts of their own knowledge systems. Only the people of the non-west can realise how far this is from being an instant panacea. It is a project that requires a willingness to accept complexity of argument, confusion of voices – a proof of diversity as well as concerned creativity and vibrancy of debate – and an acknowledgement of the limits within which such debate must range. However, in advance even what is an unbreachable barrier may not be instantly obvious. It is not a case of asking people to die on the barricades but making it possible for them to live within the boundaries. Cultural resistance, as for example in Iran and other places, has come to mean asking people to die for the utopian rhetoric of cultural authenticity rather than asking them to live according to what one believes as part of a complex rethinking of inherited tradition. Living one's resistance is far harder, not self-evident in the world we now inhabit, and likely to look and act quite contrary to the modes of inherited traditionalism still extant and powerfully authoritative within our societies.

The one characteristic of traditional lifeways that most urgently needs to be recaptured by culturally resistant Others is tolerance. Anecdotal evidence generates the argument that traditional societies used tolerance as the connective tissue of their existence. The importance of personal networks in the structuring of society, for example, makes for a measure of latitude, a tolerance of individual eccentricity or divergence from the norm precisely because the individual is known in a very real sense and maintains relations with all those who would otherwise abstractly condemn such behaviour in a stranger. In traditional worldviews individuals are never abstractions by dint of the conception of the structure and organisation of society. Analyses of Other cultures which have concentrated on building up ideal-types of how things are or were seldom chronicled the spaces such societies offered for the individual. Western scholarship provides documentation of what ideal marriage rules are preferred, how kinship networks and ascribed social positions are ideally operated, but only belatedly did it consider that at any one time there may be more unpreferred marriages than those that fulfil the 'rule' and that there may be multiple ways of operating and being innovative within or around the confines of ascription. Tolerance also develops from the inherent fact that no one person, group or institution within traditional civilisations possesses the absolute. The absolute values and qualities that generate and animate Other outlooks are transcendent. As has been argued within contemporary Muslim scholarship, it makes interpreters of us all. The absolute frame of reference is always there: all that successive generations of Muslims can do is stand in an interpretative relationship to that reference frame, and only learning, cogency and contextual importance can distinguish an individual opinion. Any individual opinion is always open to re-examination. Whether the challenge is accepted or not it is the responsibility of each new generation to strive to ensure they maintain the best possible interpretative relationship with Islam, or put another way, that they utilise the basic values and axioms of Islam as the adaptive instruments to determine change in society. The classical Muslim scholar would say: this is what I think, the best I can do under the circumstances, but God alone knows all. Today, as yesterday, cultural reformers must be content to agree that so long as one holds to the supreme importance of the formulation that God alone knows all there is, humility and tolerance of multiple discourses become an imperative. The necessity of a conscientious, interpretative search for truth that is common to all leads to the acknowledgement and acceptance of the fact that the truth that can be made knowable by human efforts is limited.

By declaring that there is no truth and no morality, that all is meaningless and that life itself is a meaningless problem; by announcing that religion and philosophy, history and tradition are symptoms of will to power and symbols of decadence; by raising doubt, cynicism and ambivalence to an arch value; by its acceptance of barbarism and embrace of evil and hence legitimisation of every act of cruelty, neglect and intolerance; by appropriating the knowledge, history and cultural products of the Others; by embarking on a crusade to transform Other cultures into ahistorical, identity-less masses and perpetual consumers of its cultural products; by isolating and further marginalising Other cultures by irony and ridicule; by attempting to subsume Other cultures into the Grand Narrative of bourgeois liberalism, free market capitalism and secularism; by giving a new life to the old tools of colonial domination and subjugation – by all these means, postmodernism has declared a war on non-western cultures and societies. Yet, while postmodernism may displace, fragment and even momentarily occupy Other cultures, the innate and powerful desire for historic meaning and identity in non-western societies cannot be eradicated. It is the urge of every culture to be true to its Self, to be self-confirming and self-propagating. It is this unfathomable urge – which has 'presence' as its prime value and forms the matrix of every idealism – that will lead to the return of dynamic tradition and give the twenty-first century its defining character. The invincible, life-denying forces of postmodernism are about to encounter the immovable object of life-enhancing tradition.

Notes

Introduction

1. Charles Jencks, *What is Postmodernism?*, Academy Edition, London, 1989, p. 14.
2. Bryan S. Turner, ed., *Theories of Modernity and Postmodernity*, Sage, London, 1990, pp. 3–4.
3. Jean-François Lyotard, *The Postmodern Condition*, Manchester University Press, Manchester, 1979, p. xxiv.
4. Steven Best and Douglas Kellner, *Postmodern Theory: Critical Interrogations*, Macmillan, London, 1991, p. 11.
5. Richard Rorty, *Contingency, Irony and Solidarity*, Cambridge University Press, Cambridge, 1989.
6. Umberto Eco, *Foucault's Pendulum*, Secker and Warburg, London, 1989.
7. John R Gibbons, ed., *Contemporary Political Culture: Politics in a Postmodern Age*, Sage, London, 1989, p. 14.
8. Terry Eagleton, 'Awakening from Modernity', *Times Literary Supplement*, 20 February 1987.
9. George Yudice, 'Morality and the Ethics of Survival', in Andrew Ross, ed., *Universal Abandon? The Politics of Postmodernism*, Edinburgh University Press, Edinburgh, 1988, p. 214.
10. Ross, *Universal Abandon?*, p.vii.

Chapter 1

1. Charles Jencks, *What is Post-Modernism?*, Academy Edition, London, 1986, p. 7.

2. Ibid.
3. Walter Truett Anderson, *Reality Isn't What it Used to Be*, Harper, San Francisico, 1990, p. 7.
4. Jencks, *What is Post-Modernism?*, p. 7
5. Anderson, *Reality Isn't What it Used to Be*, p. 114.
6. Idriss Jazairy, Mohiuddin Alamgir and Theresa Panuccio, *The State of World Rural Poverty: An Inquiry into its Causes and Consequences*, IT Publications for International Fund for Agricultural Development, London, 1992. The figure of one billion living below the poverty line comes from this report.
7. This was first realised in the early 1970s, see, for example, J. A. Kautsky, *The Political Consequences of Modernization*, Wiley, New York, 1972, and the reference cited therein. For more recent analysis see Claude Alvares, *Science, Development and Violence: The Revolt against Modernity*, Oxford University Press, Delhi, 1992; and UN agency reports, e.g.: Economic and Social Commission for Asia and the Pacific (ESCAP), *Fourth Asian and Pacific Ministerial Conference on Social Welfare and Social Development*, United Nations, New York, 1992, as well as earlier conference proceedings. Tariq Benuri's literature review, 'Development and the Politics of Knowledge: A Critical Interpretation of the Social Role of Modernization', in F.A. Marglin and S.A. Marglin, eds, *Dominating Knowledge: Development, Culture and Resistance*, Clarendon Press, Oxford, 1990, provides an up-to-date outline of how development systematically strips traditional societies of their choices.
8. See Ziauddin Sardar, *Islamic Futures: The Shape of Ideas to Come*, Mansell, London, 1985, particularly chapter 2, 'The Dialectics of Islamic Resurgence'; see also Yusul Ali al-Qaradawi, *Islamic Awakening between Rejection and Extremism*, International Institute of Islamic Thought, Herndon, VA, 1991.
9. See the evidence in Catholic Institute for International Relief (CIIR), *Proceedings of the 1990 International Conference on Right Wing Religion*, CIIR, London, 1992. For a general background of how, instead of collapsing, faith is actually strengthening, see Richard T. Antoun and Mary E. Hegland, eds, *Religious Resurgence: Contemporary Cases in Islam, Christianity and Judaism*, Syracuse University Press, New York, 1987.
10. Anderson, *Reality Isn't What it Used to Be*, p. 23.

11. The impact of westernisation on the third world has been assessed from every conceivable point; the literature on the subject is vast and ranges from Pierre Jalee, *The Pillage of the Third World*, Monthly Review Press, New York, 1968 to my own *Science, Technology and Development in the Muslim World*, Croom Helm, London, 1977, to Jalal Ali Ahmad, *Occidentosis: A Plague from the West*, Mizan Press, Berkeley, 1984, to Jorge E. Hardoy et al., *Environmental Problems in Third World Cities*, Earthscan, London, 1992. The diversity of evidence and the plurality of arguments against westernisation are truly of postmodern proportions!

12. Anderson, *Reality Isn't What it Used to Be*, p. 68.

13. Jean Baudrillard, 'Simulacra and Simulations', in *Selected Writings*, ed. Mark Poster, Polity Press, Oxford, 1988, p. 170.

14. Jean Baudrillard, 'The Reality Gulf', *Guardian*, 11 January 1991.

15. Jean Baudrillard, 'La guerre du Golfe n'a pas eu lieu', *Libération*, 29 March 1991.

16. Christopher Norris, *Uncritical Theory: Postmodernism, Intellectuals and the Gulf War*, Lawrence and Wishart, London, 1992, p. 26.

17. Ibid., pp. 110–11.

18. Baudrillard, 'Simulacra and Simulations', p. 171.

19. Fredric Jameson, *Postmodernism or the Cultural Logic of Late Capitalism*, Verso, London, 1991.

20. Quoted by Timothy Mitchell, *Colonising Egypt*, University of California Press, Berkeley, 1991, p. 32.

21. Ibid., pp. 32–3.

22. Ibid., p. 12.

23. The term is normally associated with the Edward Said's book of the same name: *Orientalism*, Routledge and Kegan Paul, London, 1978. In fact, it has been around for much longer and other authors analysed it in some detail before Said. See, for example, A. L. Tibawi, *English Speaking Orientalists*, Islamic Centre, Geneva, 1965. For a more contemporary examination of Orientalism, see Ziauddin Sardar and Merryl Wyn Davies, *Distorted Imagination: Lessons from the Rushdie Affair*, Grey Seal, London, 1990.

24. Adam Ferguson, *An Essay on the History of Civil Society*, Edinburgh University Press, Edinburgh. 1966 (first published 1767).

25. See Ashis Nandy, *Traditions, Tyrannies and Utopias: Essays in Politics of Awareness*, Oxford University Press, Delhi, 1987.

26. Tariq Benuri, 'Modernization and its Discontent: A Cultural Perspective on the Theories of Development', in Marglin and Marglin, *Dominating Knowledge*, p. 84.

27. Ibid., p. 88.

28. Ibid., p. 87.

29. Daniel Lerner, *Passing of the Traditional Society: Modernizing the Middle East*, The Free Press, New York, 1958.

30. Benuri, 'Modernization and its Discontent', p. 80.

31. Jencks, *What is Post-Modernism?*, p. 9.

32. Warren Montag, 'What is at Stake in the Debate about Postmodernism?', in E. A. Kaplan, ed., *Postmodernism and its Discontents*, Verso, London, 1988, p. 88.

33. Ibid.

34. Anderson, *Reality Isn't What it Used to Be*, p. 212.

35. See Bruce Lawrence, *Defenders of God: The Fundamentalist Revolt against the Modern Age*, I.B. Tauris, London, 1990. For broader perspectives on how Islamic fundamentalism developed as a critique of modernisation, see John Esposito, *Islamic Revivalism*, American Institute for Islamic Affairs, Washington DC, 1986; Nikki Keddie and Eric Hooglund, eds, *The Iranian Revolution and the Islamic Republic*, Syracuse University Press, New York, 1986; and James P. Piscatori, *Islam in a World of Nation-States*, Cambridge University Press, Cambridge, 1986.

36. For a systematic account of the emergence of Sufism as a critique of dominant modes of thought in Muslim society, see M. M. Sharif, ed., *A History of Muslim Philosophy*, 2 vols, Otto Harrassowitz, Wiesbaden, 1963.

37. Jean Baudrillard, 'Symbolic Exchange and Death', in Baudrillard, *Selected Writings*, p. 143.

38. See Ziauddin Sardar, 'Editor's Introduction: Islam and the Future', *Futures* 23 (3) (April 1991), 223–30.

39. Quoted by Anderson, *Reality Isn't What it Used to Be*, p. 258.

40. Ibid.

41. Ibid., p. 13.

42. Ibid., p. 153.

43. Ibid., p. 155.

44. A quote from the seventeenth-century Indian/Malay Muslim mystic, Nur al-Din al-Raniri.

45. The Muslim exposition of realities is based on the monumental works of Professor Syed Muhammad Naquib al-Attas. See his *Islam, Secularism and the Philosophy of the Future*, Mansell, London 1985; *The Mysticism of Hamzah Fansuri*, University of Malaya Press, Kuala Lumpur, 1970; *A Commentary on the Hujjat al-Siddiq of Nur al-Din al-Raniri*, Ministry of Culture, Kuala Lumpur, 1986); and numerous other works.

46. For a more detailed exposition of Indian logic, see M. D. Siriniva, 'Logical and Methodological Foundations of Indian Science', in Ziauddin Sardar, ed., *The Revenge of Athena: Science, Exploitation and the Third World*, Mansell, London, 1988; Susantha Goonthalake, 'The Voyages of Discovery and the Loss and Re-discovery of "Others" Knowledge', *Impact of Science on Society* 167 (1992) 241–64, and numerous references cited therein.

47. Nandy, *Traditions Tyrannies and Utopias*, in particular the essay 'Towards A Third World Utopia'.

Chapter 2

1. *Independent*, 24 July 1995.

2. Stjepan Mestrovic, *The Barbarian Temperament*, Routledge, London, 1993.

3. Zygmunt Bauman, *Modernity and the Holocaust*, Polity Press, Oxford, 1989.

4. Eric Hobsbawm, 'Barbarism: A User's Guide', *New Left Review* 206 (July/August 1994) 44–54.

5. Ibid.

6. Diana Brydon, 'The White Inuit Speaks: Contamination as Literary Strategy', in Ian Adam and Helen Tiffin, eds, *Past the Last Post*, Harvester Wheatsheaf, London, p. 192.

7. John Kenneth Galbraith, *The Culture of Contentment*, Sinclair-Stevenson, London, 1992, p. 10.

8. Christopher Bellamy, '20,000 Still Missing in "Zone of Death"', *Independent*, 17 July 1995.

9. Zoran Radosaljevic, 'Muslims' Flight Brings No Escape from Despair', *Independent*, 15 July 1995.

10. Paul Hockenos, 'Behind Serb Lines', *New Statement and Society*, 2 June 1995.

11. *Independent*, 30 October 1995.
12. After announcing that 'normality has been restored to "Free Sre-brenica"' Bosnian Serb radio played the following song: *'Die you scum, the Serbs are the champions. Come out onto your balconies and hail the white Serb race.'*
13. Robert Block, 'They Were Led Away and They Were Killed', *Independent*, Section Two, 21 September 1995.
14. John Sweeney, 'UN Cover-up of Srebrenica Massacre', *Observer*, 10 September 1995.
15. Mary Dejevsky, 'France Throws Down Gauntlet', *Independent*, 15 July 1995.
16. Charlotte Eager, 'From Haven into Hell', *Observer*, 16 July 1995.
17. Martin Bell, *In Harm's Way: Reflections of a War Zone Thug*, Hamish Hamilton, London, 1995.
18. Jean Baudrillard, *The Transparency of Evil*, Verso, London, 1993.
19. Harold Elletson, 'A War the West Can No Longer Ignore', *Independent*, 27 December 1995.
20. Victoria Clark, 'Chechnya's Silent Scream to the West', *Observer*, 26 February 1995.
21. Sam Kiley, *The Times*, 15 November 1995.
22. Richard Barnet and John Cavanagh, 'The World the Transnationals Have Built', *Third World Resurgence* 40 (December 1993) 21–2; see also Richard Barnet and John Cavanagh, *Global Dreams: Imperial Corporations and the New World Order*, Simon and Schuster, New York, 1994.
23. Jeremy Seabrook, 'Soft-soaping India', *New Statesman and Society*, 13 January 1995.
24. Geoffery Lean, 'One Western Life is Worth 15 in the Third World, says UN Report', *Independent on Sunday*, 23 July 1995.
25. Agnes Heller and Ferenc Feher, *The Post-Modern Political Condition*, Polity Press, Cambridge, 1988, p. 10.
26. On how deeply 'sleaze' is embedded in British politics, see the special supplement on 'Sleaze' in *Independent*, 23 July 1995.
27. John Laughland, 'Mitterrand's Deadly Legacy', *Independent*, 11 January 1996.
28. Andrew Adonis and Geoff Mulgan, 'Back to Greece: The Scope for Direct Democracy', *Demos* 3 (1994) 3–9.
29. Jeremy Corbyn, 'Political Dimensions of Northern Global Domina-

tion and its Consequences for the Rights of Five-sixths of Humanity',
in Chandra Muzaffar, *Human Wrongs*, Just World Trust, Penang,
1996.
30. George Makdisi, *The Rise of Humanism in Classical Islam and the
Christian West*, Edinburgh University Press, Edinburgh, 1990.
31. See Richard J. Smith, *China's Cultural Heritage*, Westview Press,
Boulder, Colorado, 1994.
32. See Merryl Wyn Davies, *Knowing One Another: Shaping an Islamic
Anthropology*, Mansell, London, 1988.
33. See Clifford Geertz, *The Interpretations of Cultures*, Basic Books, New
York, 1973.
34. See, for example, John Kenneth Galbraith, *The Culture of Contentment*, Sinclair-Stevenson, London, 1992; Robert Hughes, *The Culture
of Complaint*, Oxford University Press, Oxford, 1993; and Richard
Stivers, *The Culture of Cynicism*, Blackwell, Oxford, 1994.
35. Miklos N. Szilagyi, *How To Save Our Country: A Nonpartisan Vision
for Change*, Pallas Press, Tucson, 1994.
36. See Michael R. Ogden, 'Politics in a Parallel Universe: Is There a
Future for Cyberdemocracy?', *Futures* 26 (7) (September 1994)
713–29; see also Ziauddin Sardar, 'alt.civilizations. faq: Cyberspace as
the Darker Side of the West', *Futures* 26 (7) (September 1994) 777–95.
37. Bhikhu Parekh, 'The Cultural Particularity of Liberal Democracy',
in David Held, ed., *Prospects for Democracy*, Polity Press, Cambridge,
1993.
38. See Ali Mazrui, *Cultural Forces in World Politics*, James Currey,
London, 1990.
39. For example, V. G. Simiya, 'The Democratic Myth in the African
Traditional Societies', in W. O. Oyugi and A. Gitonga, eds, *Democratic Theory and Practice in Africa*, Heinemann, Nairobi, 1987.
40. Godwin Sogolo, 'The Futures of Democracy and Participation in
Everyday Life: The African Experience', in Bart van Steenbergen, R.
Nakarada, F. Marti and J. Dator, eds, *Advancing Democracy and
Participation: Challenges for the Future*, Centre Catala de Prospectova,
Barcelona, 1991.
41. N. Sithole, *African Nationalism*, Oxford University Press, Cape Town,
1959.
42. See William Pfaff, 'New Colonialism', *Foreign Affairs* 74 (1)
(January–February 1995) 2–6.

43. Meddi Muguenyi, 'Development First, Democracy Second: A Comment on Minimalist Democracy', in W. O. Oyugi and A. Gitonga, eds, Democratic *Theory and Practice in Africa*, Heinemann, Nairobi, 1987.
44. Richard Falk, *Explorations at the Edge of Time*, Temple University Press, Philadelphia, 1992, p. 21.
45. Walter Truett Anderson, *Reality Isn't What It Used to Be*, Harper, San Francisco, 1990.
46. Donald Kuspit, 'The Contradictory Character of Postmodernism', in Hugh J. Silverman, ed., *Postmodernism: Philosophy and the Arts*, Routledge, London, 1990, p. 54.
47. On this point, see David Little, John Kelsay and Abdualaziz A. Sachedina, *Human Rights and the Conflict of Cultures: Western and Islamic Perspectives on Religious Liberty*, University of South Carolina Press, Columbia, 1988; Max L. Stackhouse, *Creeds, Society, and Human Rights: A Study in Three Cultures*, W.B. Eerdmans, Grand Rapids, 1984; Arlene Swidler, ed., *Human Rights in Religious Traditions*, Pilgrim Press, New York, 1982; Leroy S. Rouner, ed., *Human Rights and the World's Religions*, University of Notre Dame Press, Notre Dame, 1988; Irene Bloome, Paul Martin and Wayne Proudfoot, eds, *Religion and Human Rights*, Columbia University Press, New York, 1994.
48. Vinay Lal, 'The Imperialism of Human Rights', *Focus on Law Studies* 8 (1) (Fall 1992) 5–11.
49. S. Parvez Manzoor, 'Human Rights: Secular Transcendence or Cultural Imperialism?', *Muslim World Book Review* 15 (1) (1994) 3–10.
50. See Robert Traer, *Faith in Human Rights: Support in Religious Traditions for a Global Struggle*, Georgetown University Press, Washington DC, 1991.
51. See Muhammad Ayub, 'Asian Spiritual and Moral Values and Human Rights', in Chandra Muzaffar, *Human Wrongs*, Just World Trust, Penang, 1995.
52. See Aliran, *The Human Being: Perspectives from Different Spiritual Traditions*, Aliran, Penang, 1991.
53. Raimundo Panikkar, 'A Hindu/Jain/Buddhist Reflection', *Breakthrough* 10 (2–3) Winter/Spring 1989.
54. Abdul Aziz Said, 'The Islamic Context for Human Rights', *Breakthrough* 10 (2–3) Winter/Spring 1989.

55. Mohammad Kamali, 'Fundamental Rights of the Individual', *The American Journal of Islamic Social Sciences*, X:3 (Fall 1993) 340–66.
56. M. Umar Chapra, *Islam and the Economic Challenge*, Islamic Foundation, Leicester, 1992.
57. Mohammad Hashim Kamali, *Freedom of Expression in Islam*, Barita, Kuala Lumpur, 1994.
58. Islamic Council of Europe, *Universal Islamic Declaration of Human Rights*, Islamic Council of Europe, London, 1981; see also Islamic Council of Europe, *Universal Islamic Declaration*, Islamic Council of Europe, London, 1980.
59. Upendra Baxi, 'Law, Democracy and Human Rights', in Smitu Kothari and Harsh Sethi, eds, *Rethinking Human Rights*, New Horizon Press, New York, 1989; and Upendra Baxi, 'From Human Rights to the Right to be Human: Some Heresies', in Smitu Kothari and Harsh Sethi, eds, *Rethinking Human Rights*, New Horizon Press, New York, 1989.
60. John Stuart Mill, *On Liberty*, 1859.
61. John Rawls, *A Theory of Justice*, Harvard University Press, Cambridge, Mass., 1971.
62. See Noam Chomsky, *World Orders, Old and New*, Pluto Press, London, 1994, 1997; and *Deterring Democracy*, Verso, London, 1991; and Edward S. Herman and Noam Chomsky, *Manufacturing Consent*, Pantheon, New York, 1988.
63. Chandra Muzaffar, *Human Rights and the New World Order*, Just World Trust, Penang, 1993, p. 13.
64. Ibid., p. 15.
65. For an interesting analysis of how the IMF underdevelops the non-west, see the articles in the special issues of *Third World Resurgence*: 'Reconquest of the South', *Third World Resurgence* (monthly) Penang, December 1992 and the *New Internationalist*, 'Squeezing the South', Oxford, July 1994.
66. See Jeremy Seabrook, *Victims of Development: Resistance and Alternatives*, Verso, London, 1993.
67. United Nations, *Human Development Report 1994*, Oxford University Press, Oxford, 1994.
68. D. L. Sheth, 'An Emerging Perspective on Human Rights in India', in Smitu Kothari and Harsh Sethi, eds, *Rethinking Human Rights*, New Horizon Press, New York, 1989.

69. K. Balagopal, 'Ruling Class Politics and People's Rights', in Smitu Kothari and Harsh Sethi, eds, *Rethinking Human Rights*, New Horizon Press, New York, 1989.

70. Alex de Waal, 'Compassion Fatigue', *New Statesman and Society*, 17 March 1995.

71. The NGO Bureau, *Report of Inquiry into NGOs*, Government of Bangladesh, Dekkah, 1992.

72. de Waal, 'Compassion Fatigue'.

73. Lindsey Hilsum, 'Save us from our Saviours', *Observer*, 31 December 1995.

74. de Waal, 'Compassion Fatigue'.

75. Samuel P. Huntington, 'The Clash of Civilizations?', *Foreign Affairs* 72 (3) (July/August 1993) 22–49.

76. Ibid., p. 22.

77. Ibid., p. 3.

78. Fouad Ajami, 'The Summoning', *Foreign Affairs* 72 (4) (September/October 1993) 2–10.

Chapter 3

1. Felipe Fernandez-Armesto, *Millenium*, Bantam, London, 1995.

2. 'From the very beginning of this project the filmmakers were determined to make a movie that would be both entertaining and true to history,' says Donald Ogden Stiers in the commentary of the documentary, *Pocahontas: Two Different Worlds, One True Love*, produced by the Wrightwood Company for the Walt Disney Company, 1995.

3. Francis Jennings, *The Invasion of America*, University of North Carolina Press, Chapel Hill, 1975, p. 46.

4. From the documentary, *Pocahontas: Two Different Worlds, One True Love*.

5. Quote from *Map of Virginia with a Description of the Country the commodities people government and religion Written by Captain John Smith sometimes Governor of the Country*, published Oxford, 1612.

6. This was too much even for Samuel Purchas, who wrote that reports of child sacrifice must have been confused. However, it is Smith's interpretation of the ceremonial customs of the Powhatan that

survived and spawned a lively tradition, for it was Smith's interpretation that confirmed the expectations of the European scholarship. As
William Strachey noted when he included similar material on child
sacrifice in his account of Virginia, the practice was encountered
'over all the Indies'. The original source is the experiences of William
White, a young labourer who was sent to live with the Indians to
learn their language. White's account of the ceremonial concluded by
stating he did not know what happened to the young boys who
participated in what is most likely to have been an initiation
ceremony.

7. Quoted in H. C. Porter, *The Inconstant Savage: England and the North
   American Indian*, Duckworth, London, 1979, p. 324. John Smith first
   used the epithet 'inconstant' of the native inhabitants in a letter
   written in 1608.

8. William Strachey, *The History of Travel into Virginia Britania*, ed. L. B.
   Wright and V. Freund, Hakluyt Society, London, 1953; originally
   published in 1612.

9. Ibid., p. 72.

10. *Instruction of the London Council of the Virginia Company from Records of
    the Virginia Company of London*, 4 vols, ed. Susan Myra Kingsbury,
    Washington DC, 1906.

11. From a letter by Sir Thomas Dale in Ralph Homor's *A True Discourse
    of the Present Estate of Virginia and the success of the affaires there till the
    18 of June 1614*, facsimile edition, Richmond, Virginia, 1957,
    pp. 53–5.

12. Ibid., pp. 53–5.

13. From the Ashmole MS, reprinted in Philip L Barbour, *Pocahontas
    and Her World*, London, 1971. Appendix III, pp. 247–52.

14. Ibid., all subsequent quotes from Rolfe's letter are from the same
    source.

15. Porter, *Inconstant Savage*, p. 112.

16. Quoted in *Court and Times of James I*, 2 vols, ed. R. F. Wilkins,
    London, 1849, p. 415.

17. Samuel Purchas, *Hakluytus Posthumus or Purchas His Pilgrims*,
    London, 1625. pp. 118–19.

18. John Rolf, *True Relation of the State of Virginia*, H. C. Taylor, New
    Haven, 1951; written in 1616; quoted in Porter, *Inconstant Savage*,
    p. 407.

19. See the excellent Peter Mason, *Deconstructing America: Representations of the Other*, Routledge, London, 1990.
20. From the documentary, *Pocahontas: Two Different Worlds, One True Love*.
21. John White's drawings are in the collection of the British Museum and were first reproduced to illustrate Thomas Hariot's *A Briefe and True Report of the New Found Land of Virginia*, Frankfurt, 1590; facsimile edition, New York, 1972.
22. See Malik Alloula, *The Colonial Harem*, Manchester University Press, Manchester, 1986.
23. For an extended discussion of these points, see Ziauddin Sardar, Merryl Wyn Davies and Ashis Nandy, *Barbaric Others: A Manifesto on Western Racism*, Pluto Press, London, 1993.
24. Janet Siskind, 'The Invention of Thanksgiving: A Ritual of American Nationality', *Critique of Anthroplogy* 12 (2) (1992) 167–91.
25. John Rolfe, Letter to Sir Edwin Sandys in Kingsbury, vol. III, p. 243.
26. John Smith, *A Description of New England*, London 1616, p. 191. Smith states that while negroes are 'the most idle and devilish people in the world', they make 'the best servants', ibid., p. 995.
27. 'loh the poor Indian' is taken from the a poem by John Donne and became a standard means of referring to native inhabitants of North America. John Donne, poet, preacher, Dean of St Paul's Cathedral, London, had very nearly been appointed an official of the Virginia Company.
28. For a more detailed discussion of this point, see Ziauddin Sardar, 'alt.civilisation.faq: Cyberspace as the Darker Side of the West', in Ziauddin Sardar and Jerome R. Ravetz, eds, *Cyberfutures: Politics and Culture on the Information Superhighway*, Pluto Press, London, 1996.
29. Mary Fuller and Henry Jenkins, 'Nintendo and New World Travel Writing: A Dialogue', in Steven G. Jones, ed., *Cybersociety: Computer-mediated Communication and Community*, Sage, London, 1995, p. 59.
30. Sid Meier, 'Civilization', *Micro Prose*, Hunt Valley, MD, 1991.
31. *Microsoft Bookshelf*, Microsoft Corporation, 1993 edition.
32. Dorling Kindersley, *History of the World*, London and New York, 1995. All quotes from the CD-ROM.
33. John Smith, *General History of Virginia, New England and the Summer Isles*, London, 1624, p. 688.

Chapter 4

1. The Body Shop Team, *The Body Shop Book*, Macdonald, London, 1985, p. 7.
2. Ibid., pp. 9–10.
3. Polly Ghazi and Roger Tredre, 'Green Queen of All She Purveys?', *Observer*, 28 August 1994.
4. The Body Shop Team, *Mamatoto: A Celebration of Birth*, Virago, London, 1991, p. 94.
5. Label attached to *East India Company* apparel bought in Kuala Lumpur early 1995.
6. Paul Smith, 'Visiting the Banana Republic', in Andrew Ross, ed., *Universal Abandon? The Politics of Postmodernism*, Edinburgh University Press, Edinburgh, 1988, p. 142.
7. Ibid., p. 143.
8. Ibid., p. 141.
9. Ashis Nandy, *The Intimate Enemy: Loss and Recovery of Self under Colonialism*, Oxford University Press, Delhi, 1983, p. 57.
10. Les Back and Vibeke Quaade, 'Dream Utopias, Nightmare Realities: Imaging Race and Culture within the World of Benetton Advertising', *Third Text* 22 (Spring 1993) 65–80.
11. Phil Davidson, '"Peasants"' Golf War puts Mexico in a Spin', *Independent*, 15 September 1995.
12. Hakim Bey, Lamia Naji and Hassan Massoudy, *Voyage International: Overcoming Tourism*, Lilim, Paris, 1995, pp. 6–7, 8.
13. Regional magazines like the *Far Eastern Economic Review* and *Asiaweek* (both of which carry the Hong Kong Bank advertisement) regularly carry features about the increasing number and decreasing age of Asian consumers. See also the quarterly special reports of the *International Herald Tribune*; the second quarterly report of 1995 is entitled 'Asia/Pacific: The New Consumers'.
14. Arthur Kroker and David Cook, *The Postmodern Scene*, Macmillan, London, 1988, p. 270.
15. 'Youth: The Wilder Ones', *Asiaweek*, 25 May 25 1994, pp. 24–33.
16. Heinrich Klotz, 'Postmodern Architecture', in Charles Jencks, ed., *The Post-Modern Reader*, Academy Editions, London, 1992, p. 238.
17. Charles Jencks, *The Architecture of the Jumping Universe*, Academy Edition, London, 1995.

18. Scott Meek, *Independent*, 14 July 1988; quote by David Harvey, *The Condition of Postmodernity*, Blackwell, Oxford, 1989.
19. Ibid., p. 292.
20. William Gibson, 'Disneyland with the Death Penalty', *Observer*, 'Life' Section, 14 August 1994.
21. Jim Masselos, 'Postmodern Bombay: Fractures Discourses', in Sophie Watson and Katherine Gibson, eds, *Postmodern Cities and Spaces*, Blackwell, Oxford, 1995. p. 212. For a more detailed analysis of the political, social and economic consequences of the urban development of Bombay, see the essays in Sujata Patel and Alice Thorner, eds, *Bombay: Metaphor for Modern India*, Oxford University Press, Delhi, 1995.
22. Ibid., p. 212.
23. Ibid., pp. 213–14. For a more detailed analysis of the causes – both modern and postmodern – of the Bombay riots, see Ashis Nandy, Shikha Trivedy, Shail Mayaram and Achyut Yagnik, *Creating a Nationality: The Ramjanmabhumi Movement and Fear of the Self*, Oxford University Press, Delhi, 1995.
24. Meaghan Morris, 'Tooth and Claw: Tales of Survival and Crocodile Dundee', in Ross, *Universal Abandon?*, p. 114.
25. Ibid., p. 116.
26. On the notion of cinema as global capital, see Jonathan L. Beller, 'Cinema, Capital of the Twentieth Century', *Postmodern Culture* 4, 3 (May 1994).
27. Christine Bell, *The Perez Family*, Virago, London, 1990.
28. While the indigenous knowledge movement is global, it is strongest in India. For the true breadth and scope of indigenous knowledge in India, see *Congress on Traditional Sciences and Technologies of India*, 28 November–3 December 1993, Indian Institute of Technology, Bombay. For developments in the indigenous knowledge movement in general, see the *Indigenous Knowledge and Development Monitor*, published by the Centre for International Research and Advisory Networks (CIRAN), The Hague, Netherlands.
29. Octavio Paz, 'El romanticismo y la poesia contemporanea', *Veulta* 11, 127 (1987) 26–7; see also Neil Larsen's polemic, 'Postmodernism and Imperialism: Theory and Politics in Latin America', *Postmodern Culture* 1, 1 (1990). On the whole question of how postmodernism is now beginning to be questioned in Latin America, see *Boundary* 2 (Fall

41111113111111333333311

1993), Special Issue: 'The Postmodern Debate in Latin America', ed. John Beverley and Jose Oviedo, Duke University Press, NC.

30. 'Islamisation of Knowledge' is a complex debate involving Islamic notions of knowledge, science, economics, culture and the future; the literature on it is truly vast. For an overview, see Merryl Wyn Davies, 'Rethinking Knowledge: Islamization and the Future', *Futures* 23, 3 (April 1991) 231–47; for the science debate, see Ziauddin Sardar, ed., *The Touch of Midas: Science, Values and Environment in Islam and the West*, Manchester, Manchester University Press, 1984, and *Explorations in Islamic Science*, London, Mansell, 1989; and Nasim Butt, *Science and Muslim Societies*, London, Grey Seal, 1991; for the economic aspects, see M. Umar Chapra, *Islam and the Economic Challenge*, Leicester, Islamic Foundation, 1992.

31. J. Anu, 'Portraying the Pulse of our Time', *Sunday Star*, 30 April 1995.

Chapter 5

1. Rasheed Araeen's 'The Golden Verses' was produced as part of a project sponsored by the Artangel Trust in 1990; apart from in Britain, the billboard also appeared in selected European and American cities.

2. Pennina Barnett, 'Rugs R Us (And Them): The Oriental Carpet as Sign and Text', *Third Text* 30 (Spring 1995) 13–28.

3. Malise Ruthven, *A Satanic Affair: Salman Rushdie and the Wrath of Islam*, The Hogarth Press, London, 1990, p. 132.

4. Timoth Brennan, *Salman Rushdie and the Third World*, Macmillan, London, 1989, p. ix.

5. See Kojin Karatani, *Criticism and the Postmodern*, Fukutake Shoten, Tokyo, 1985.

6. Santiago Colas, *Postmodernity in Latin America: The Argentine Paradigm*, Duke University Press, Durham, NC, 1994.

7. Yoshio Iwamoto, 'A Voice from Postmodern Japan: Haruki Murakami', *World Literature Today* 67 (2) (Spring 1993) 295–300.

8. Norman Brown, *Apocalypse and/or Metamorphosis*, University of California Press, Berkeley, 1991, pp. 89–90.

9. Richard Rorty, *Philosophy, the Mirror of Nature*, Princeton University Press, Princeton, NJ, 1979.

10. Richard Rorty, *Contingency, Irony and Solidarity*, Cambridge University Press, Cambridge, 1989.
11. Ibid., pp. 21 and 22.
12. Ibid., p. xvi.
13. Umberto Eco, *Foucault's Pendulum*, Secker and Warburg, London, 1989. All quotes from the novel are from this edition.
14. Richard Rorty, 'Postmodern Bourgeois Liberalism', *Journal of Philosophy* 80 (October 1983) 585.
15. Rorty, *Contingency, Irony and Solidarity*, p. 45.
16. See Isaiah Berlin, *The Crooked Timber of Humanity: Chapters in the History of Ideas*, John Murray, London, 1990.
17. See the chapter on 'Private Irony and Liberal Hope', in Rorty's *Contingency, Irony and Solidarity*.
18. Umberto Eco, *The Name of the Rose*, G. K. Hall, Boston: Mass., 1984.
19. Slavoj Zizek, *The Sublime Object of Desire*, Verso, London, 1989, pp. 27–8.
20. Peter Sloterdijk, *Critique of Cynical Reason*, University of Minnesota Press, Minneapolis, 1987.
21. John Barth, *The Last Voyage of Somebody the Sailor*, Hodder and Stoughton, London, 1992. All quotations from the novel are from this edition.
22. Brennan, *Salman Rushdie and the Third World*, p. 144.
23. Ibid., p.152.
24. Ibid., p. 126.
25. Ibid., p. 147.
26. Ruthven, *A Satanic Affair*.
27. Ibid., p. 147.
28. Ibid., p. 148.
29. Ibid., p. 148.
30. Ernest Gellner, 'Malinowski Go Home', *Anthropology Today* 1 (5) (October 1985).
31. Salman Rushdie, 'Is Nothing Sacred?' in *Imaginary Homelands: Essays and Criticism 1981–1991*, Granta Books, London, 1991, pp. 415–29.
32. Ibid., p. 429.
33. Ibid., p. 415.
34. Ibid., p. 424.
35. For a brief history of Muslim achievments in literature, see Ziauddin Sardar and Merryl Wyn Davies, *Distorted Imagination: Lessons from the*

Rushdie Affair, Grey Seal, London, 1991, Chapter 4, 'The Legacy of Muslim History'.

36. Randolph Pope, 'Letters in the Post, or How Juan Goytisolo Got to La Chanca', *World Literature Today* 69 (1) (Winter 1995) 17–21.
37. Rushdie, 'Is Nothing Sacred?', p. 415.
38. Ibid., p. 416.
39. Ibid., p. 416.
40. Ibid p. 420.
41. Stuart Morgan, 'Introduction', *Rites of Passage: Art for the End of the Century*, by Stuart Morgan and Frances Morris, Tate Gallery Publications, London, 1995, p. 12.
42. Rushdie, 'Is Nothing Sacred?', p. 420.
43. Ibid., p. 417.
44. Declan Kiberd, 'Multiculturalism and Artistic Freedom: Rushdie, Ireland and India', Occasional Paper Series No. 12., Department of Sociology, University College, Cork, 1992, p. 10.
45. Rushdie, 'Is Nothing Sacred?', p. 424.
46. William Shakespeare, *The Tempest*, IV.1 and V.1.
47. Kiberd, 'Multiculturalism and Artistic Freedom', p. 11.
48. Salman Rushdie, 'In Good Faith', in *Imaginary Homelands: Essays and Criticism 1981–1991*, Granta Books, London, 1991, pp. 393–414.
49. For a detailed analysis of *The Satanic Verses* and other novels by Salman Rushdie, see Sardar and Davies, *Distorted Imagination*.
50. Rushdie, 'In Good Faith', p. 405.
51. Richard Webster, *A Brief History of Blasphemy: Liberalism, Censorship and the Satanic Verses*, The Orwell Press, Southwold, Suffolk, 1990, p. 91.
52. Rushdie, 'In Good Faith', p. 402.
53. Webster, *A Brief History of Blasphemy*, p. 94.
54. Ibid., p. 94.
55. Rushdie, 'In Good Faith', p. 396.
56. Webster, *A Brief History of Blasphemy*, p. 88.
57. Rushdie, 'In Good Faith', p. 397.
58. Robert Coover, 'Aesop's Forest', in Heide Ziegler, *Facing Texts: Encounters between Contemporary Writers and Critics*, Duke University Press, Durham, NC, 1988.
59. Roberto Maria Dainotto, 'The Excremental Sublime: The Postmod-

ern Literature of Blockage and Release', *Postmodern Culture* 3 (3) (May 1993).

60. Webster, *A Brief History of Blasphemy*, p. 96.
61. Rushdie, 'In Good Faith', p. 426.
62. Ibid., p. 413.
63. Webster, *A Brief History of Blasphemy*, p. 102.
64. Diana Brydon, 'The White Inuit Speaks: Contamination as Literary Strategy', in Ian Adam and Helen Tiffin, eds, *Past the Last Post*, Harvester Wheatsheaf, London, 1991, pp. 195–6.
65. Stephen Slemon, 'Introduction', in Adam and Tiffin, *Past the Last Post*, p. viii.
66. Rushdie, 'In Good Faith', p. 396.
67. Djelal Kadir, 'What Are We After?', *World Literature Today* 69 (1) (Winter 1995) 17–21.

Chapter 6

1. Amin Maalouf, *The First Century After Beatrice*, Quartet, London, 1993.
2. For analysis of how science dominates the non-West, see Ziauddin Sardar, ed., *The Revenge of Athena: Science, Exploitation and the Third World*, Mansell, London, 1988; Ashis Nandy, ed., *Science, Hegemony and Violence*, Oxford University Press, Delhi, 1988; and Sandra Harding, ed., *The Racial Economy of Science*, Indiana University Press, Bloomington, 1993.
3. Paul Davies, *The Mind of God*, Penguin Books, Harmondsworth, 1992, pp. 22–3.
4. Joseph Needham, *The Grand Titration: Science and Society in East and West*, University of Toronto Press, Toronto, 1969, p. 56; quoted in Sandra Harding, 'Is Science Multicultural?', *Configurations: A Journal of Literature, Science and Technology* 2 (2) (1994).
5. For a general introduction to Islamic science, see Donald Hill, *Islamic Science and Engineering*, Edinburgh University Press, Edinburgh, 1994; see also: Faut Sazgin, *Geschichte des Arabischen Schrifttum*, 8 vols, Brill, Leiden, 1974–82; E. S. Kennedy, *Studies in the Islamic Exact Sciences*, American Univerity of Beirut, Beirut, 1983; A. I. Sabra, *The Optics of ibn al-Haytham*, 2 vols, The Warburg Institute,

University of London, 1989; and numerous entries in the *Dictionary of Scientific Biography*, Scribners, New York, 1970–80.

6. Patrick Petitjean, *Science and Empires*, Kluwer, Dordrecht, 1992.

7. Radhika Ramasubhan, *Public Health and Medical Research in India*, SAREC, Stockholm, 1982.

8. R. K. Kochhar, 'Science in British India', *Current Science*, Parts I & II 63 (11) & 64 (1) (1992–93).

9. Harding, 'Is Science Multicultural?', and David Theo Goldberg, ed., *Multiculturalism: A Reader*, Blackwell, Oxford, 1994.

10. Willis W. Harman, 'Rethinking the Central Institutions of Modern Society: Science and Business', *Futures* 25 (10) (1993) 1063–9.

11. J. D. Bernal, *Science in History*, 4 vols, MIT Press, Cambridge, Mass., 1979.

12. Harding, 'Is Science Multicultural?'.

13. Martin Bernal, *Black Athena*, 2 vols, Free Association Books, London, 1987.

14. Cheikh Anta Diop, *Civilization or Barbarism: An Authentic Anthropology*, Lawrence Hill Books, New York, 1991.

15. Toby Huff, *The Rise of Early Modern Science*, Cambridge University Press, London, 1993.

16. Ibid., p. 215.

17. Ibid., p. 299.

18. Needham, *The Grand Titration*, p. 56.

19. For how Huff rewrites the history of Europe and science, see chapters 3, 6 and 9. But for a more enlightened account, see Colin A. Ronan, *Science: Its History and Development among the World's Cultures*, Facts on File, New York, 1982; and the magnificant George Sarton, *Introduction to the History of Science*, 4 vols, Robert E. Krieger, New York, 1975, and historic papers, particularly on scientific revolution in J. R. Ravetz, *Merger of Knowledge with Power*, Mansell, London, 1990.

20. Huff, *The Rise of Early Modern Science*, p. 314.

21. T. S. Khun, *The Structure of Scientific Revolutions*, University of Chicago Press, Chicago, 1962.

22. Paul Feyerabend, *Against Method*, NLB, London 1975; *Science in a Free Society*, Verso, London, 1978; and *Farewell to Reason*, Verso, London, 1987.

23. J. R. Ravetz, *Scientific Knowledge and its Social Problems*, Oxford

University Press, Oxford, 1991, and *The Merger of Knowledge with Power*.

24. H. Rose and S. Rose, eds., *Ideology of/in the Natural Sciences*, 2 vols, Macmillan, London, 1976.

25. Ian Mitroff, *The Subjective Side of Science*, Elsevier, Amsderdam, 1974.

26. Bruno Latour and Steve Woolgan, *Laboratory Life: Social Constructions of Scientific Facts*, Sage, London, 1979.

27. Karin Knorr-Cetina, *The Manufacture of Knowledge*, Pergamon, Oxford, 1981.

28. J. R. Ravetz, 'Science, Ignorance and Fantasies', in Sardar, *The Revenge of Athena*. p. 35.

29. Harding, 'Is Science Multicultural?'.

30. Claude Alvares, *Science, Development and Violence*, Oxford University Press, Delhi, 1992, p. 65.

31. Ibid., p. 64.

32. Harding, 'Is Science Multicultural?'.

33. C. V. Seshadri, *Development and Thermodynamics*, MCRC, Delhi, 1982; cited by Alvares, *Science, Development and Violence*.

34. Harding, 'Is Science Multicultural?'.

35. Alvares, *Science, Development and Violence*, p. 85.

36. Leon Lederman, *The God Particle*, Bantam Press, London, 1993.

37. Stephen Hawkins, *A Brief History of Time*, Bantam Press, London, 1988, p. 175.

38. John D. Borrow, *Theories of Everything*, Vintage, London, 1991, p. 184.

39. On the mathematics of non-western civilisations, see George Gheverghese Joseph, *The Crest of the Peacock: Non-European Roots of Mathematics*, Penguin, London, 1990.

40. Lederman, *The God Particle*, p. 340.

41. Steven Weinberg, *Dreams of a Final Theory*, Vintage, London, 1993, p. 196.

42. Lederman, *The God Particle*, p. 22

43. Weinberg, *Dreams of a Final Theory*, p. 173.

44. Lederman, *The God Particle*, p. 408.

45. Weinberg, *Dreams of a Final Theory*, p. 194.

46. Ibid., p. 200.

47. Ibid., p. 204.

48. Lederman, *The God Particle*, p. 408.

49. E. O. Wilson, *On Human Nature*, Harvard University Press, Cambridge, Mass., 1978, p. 3.
50. Ibid., p. 4.
51. Ibid., p. 5.
52. Ibid.
53. Ibid., p. 46.
54. E. O. Wilson, *Sociobiology*, Harvard University Press, Cambridge, Mass., 1975.
55. Richard Dawkins, *The Selfish Gene*, Oxford University Press, Oxford, 1976, pp. 19–20.
56. R. C. Lewontin, *The Doctrine of DNA*, Penguin, London, 1991, pp. 48–9.
57. Tom Wilkie, *Perilous Knowledge*, Faber and Faber, London, 1993, p. 3.
58. Ibid., p. 182.
59. Ibid., pp. 69–170.
60. Ibid., p. 177.
61. Ibid., p. 178.
62. Ibid., p. 188.
63. Lewontin, *The Doctrine of DNA*, pp. 49–50.
64. Ibid., p. 51.
65. Ibid., p. 75.
66. Royal Society of London, *Philosophical Transactions* 1: 1665–66 (Johnson Reprint Company, New York, 1963): 2, p. 197.
67. Stephen Crook, Jan Pakulski and Malcolm Waters, *Postmodernization*, Sage, London, 1992, p. 211.
68. Silvio Funtowics and Jerome R Ravetz, 'Science for the Post-normal Age', *Futures* 25 (7) (1993) 739–56.
69. Cook et al., *Postmodernization*, p. 207.
70. Weinberg, *Dreams of a Final Theory*, p. 172.
71. James Gleick, *Chaos*, Cardinal, London, 1987, p. 306.
72. Mitchell Waldrop, *Complexity: The Emerging Science at the Edge of Order and Chaos*, Viking, London, 1993, pp. 330–3.
73. Stuart A Kauffman, *The Origins of Order*, Oxford University Press, Oxford, 1993, p. 26.
74. Ibid., p. 341. On computer-generated life, see also Steven Levy, *Artificial Life*, Penguin, London, 1993.
75. Roger Lewin, *Complexity*, J. M. Dent, London, 1993, p. 191.

76. Elizabeth Reichel, 'Shamanistic Modes for Environmental Account-
ing in the Colombian Amazon: Lessons from Indigenous Etho-
Ecology for Sustainable Development', *Indigenous Knowledge and
Development Monitor* 1 (2) (1993) 17–18.

77. Rohana Ulluwishewa, 'Indigenous Knowledge System for Sustainable Development: The Case of Pest Control by Traditional Paddy
Farmers in Sri Lanka', *Indigenous Knowledge and Development Monitor*
1 (2) (1993) 14–15.

78. S. Fujisaka, E. Jayson and A. Dapusala, '"Recommendation Domain"
and a Farmer's Upland Rice Technology', *Indigenous Knowledge and
Development Monitor* 1 (3) (1993) 4–7.

79. For a detailed examination of the contemporary issues in Islamic
science, see Ziauddin Sardar, *Explorations in Islamic Science*, Mansell,
London, 1989.

80. Harding, 'Is Science Multicultural?'.

Chapter 7

1. Don Cupitt, 'All You Need is Love', *Guardian*, 10 December 1994
('Face to Faith' column, in 'Outlook' section).

2. Marsilio Ficino, *Theologica Platonica*, 1480; quoted by Kirkpatrick
Sale, *The Conquest of Paradise: Christopher Columbus and the Columbian
Legacy*, Alfred Knopf, New York, 1990, p. 38.

3. John Milbank, *Theology and Social Theory: Beyond Secular Reason*,
Blackwell, Oxford, 1990.

4. Aldous Huxley, *On Art and Artists*, Meridian Books, New York, 1960.
p. 121.

5. All these *hadith*, or sayings of Prophet Muhammad, are from the
authentic collection of Sahih al-Bukhari: 7608, 6808 and 3764.

6. Muhammed Iqbal, *The Reconstruction of Religious Thought in Islam*,
London, 1932, p. 155.

7. Ella Shohat and Robert Stam, *Unthinking Eurocentrism*, Routledge,
London, 1994, p. 202.

8. Emile Sahliyeh, ed., *Religious Resurgence and Politics in the Contemporary
World*, State University of New York Press, Albany, NY, 1990, p. 301.

9. David Ray Griffin, ed., *Spirituality and Society: Postmodern Visions*,
State University of New York Press, Albany, NY, 1988, p. 5.

10. Ibid., p. 7.
11. Quoted by Graham McCann, 'Rortysomething', *The Modern Review*, February–March 1993, p. 30.
12. T. H. White, *Age of Scandal*, Jonathon Cape, London, 1950.
13. John Milbank, 'Problematising the Secular: the postmodern agenda', in Philippa Berry and Andrew Wernick, *Shadows of Spirit: Postmodernism and Religion*, Routledge, London, 1992, p. 31.
14. Don Cupitt, *The Sea of Faith*, BBC, London, 1984, p. 7.
15. Ibid.
16. Ibid., pp. 7–8.
17. In this regard, see the brilliant works of George Makdisi, *The Rise of Colleges*, Edinburgh University Press, Edinburgh, 1981, and *The Rise of Humanism*, Edinburgh University Press, Edinburgh, 1990, which settle the debate as to where Europe acquired its 'scepticism' and 'humanism'.
18. Cupitt, *The Sea of Faith*, p. 10.
19. Ibid. p. 30.
20. Don Cupitt, 'The Pure Bliss of Like in an Eternal Flux', *Guardian*, 4 September 1993 ('Face to Faith' column, in 'Outlook' section).
21. Cupitt, *The Sea of Faith*, p. 30.
22. Ibid., p. 19.
23. Cupitt, 'All You Need is Love'.
24. Enigma, 'Principles of Lust', from the album 'MCMXC a.D.', Virgin, CD 262 029. The heading of this chapter and all the subheadings are taken from the titles of the songs in this album!
25. David Ray Griffin, *God and Religion in the Postmodern World*, State University of New York Press, Albany, NY, 1989, p. 3.
26. Ibid., p. 4.
27. Ibid., p. 5.
28. Ibid.
29. Ibid., p. 7.
30. Ibid., p. 25.
31. Ibid., p. 65.
32. See David Bohm, 'Postmodern Science and a Postmodern World', in David Ray Griffin, *The Reenchantment of Science: Postmodern Proposals*, State University of New York Press, Albany, NY, 1989, pp. 57–68; see also his *Wholeness and the Implicate Order*, Routledge and Kegan Paul, London, 1980.

33. See Rubert Sheldrake, 'The Laws of Nature as Habits: a Postmodern Basis for Science', in David Ray Griffin, *The Reenchantment of Science: Postmodern Proposals*, State University of New York Press, Albany, NY, 1989, pp. 79–86; see also his *A New Science of Life: The Hypothesis of Formative Causation*, Blond and Briggs, London, 1981; and *Seven Experiments that Could Change the World*, Fourth Estate, London, 1994.

34. David Ray Griffin, ed. *Spirituality and Society: Postmodern Visions*, State University of New York Press, Albany, NY, 1988, p. 16.

35. Catherine Keller, 'Towards a Postpatriarchal Postmodernity', in Griffin, ed., *Spirituality and Society*, pp. 63–80.

36. Richard A. Falk, 'In Pursuit of the Postmodern', in ibid., pp. 81–98.

37. Robert Cornelius, 'A–Z of Cults', *Guardian*, 14 May 1995.

38. See Soren Hvalkof and Peter Aaby's classic study, *Is God An American?*, Survival International, London, 1981.

39. Paul Boyer, *When Time Shall Be No More: Prophecy Belief in Modern American Culture*, Harvard University Press, Cambridge, Mass., 1992.

40. Peter Lemesurier, *Nostradamus: The Next 50 Years*, Piatkus, London, 1993.

41. *Observer*, 10 May 1995. 'Life' Section, p. 10.

42. *American Indian Review*, No 10 (1995), p. 27.

43. 'A Letter to Augustine' in William E. Connolly, *Identity/Difference: Democratic Negotiation of Political Paradox*, Cornell University Press, Ithaca, NY, 1991, pp. 123–57.

44. Ibid., p. 7.

45. Ibid., p. 8.

46. Ibid.

47. Ibid., p. 12.

48. *Colors*, Issue VIII, Rome, Religion Special, 1994.

Chapter 8

1. Lin Yong and Su Hua, *Pakistan*, Beijing,1985.

2. From the poem 'Will and the Way' by Sir Muhammad Iqbal, in Chughtai, *The Poet of the East and Chughtai*, Karachi, 1968.

3. Sir Muhammad Iqbal, *The Mysteries of Selflessness*, translated by A. J. Arberry, John Murray, London, 1953, p. 61. (First published 1910.)

4. Ibid., p. 62.

5. Ibid.

6. For a discussion of *ijtihad*, see Ziauddin Sardar, *The Future of Muslim Civilisation*, 2nd editon, Mansell, London, 1987.

7. Tae-Chang Kim, 'Coherence and Chaos in Our Uncommon Futures: A *Hun* Philosophical Perspective', in Mika Mannermaa et al., eds., *Coherence and Chaos in Our Uncommon Futures: Visions, Means, Actions*, World Future Studies Federation, Turku, 1994, p. 44.

8. A.K.N. Reddy, 'Appropriate Technology: A Reassessment', in Ziauddin Sardar, ed., *The Revenge of Athena: Science, Exploitation and the Third World*, Mansell, London, 1988.

9. Susantha Goonatilake, 'The Futures of Asian Cultures: Between Localisation and Gobalisation', *The Futures of Cultures*, Unesco Publishing, Paris, 1994.

10. Anwar Ibrahim, 'From Things Change to Change Things', in Ziauddin Sardar, ed., *An Early Crescent: The Future of Knowledge and the Environment in Islam and the West*, Mansell, London, 1989.

11. Shintaro Ishihara, *The Japan That Can Say No*, Simon and Schuster, New York, 1991.

12. Anwar Ibrahim, *New Strait Times*, 21 September 1994.

Bibliography

Adair, Gilbert, *The Postmodern Always Rings Twice*, Fourth Estate, London, 1992

Adonis, Andrew, and Geoff Mulgan, 'Back to Greece: the scope for direct democracy', *Demos* issue 3 3–9 (1994)

Ahmad, Jalal Ali, *Occidentosis: A Plague from the West*, Mizan Press, Berkeley, 1984

Aliran, *The Human Being: Perspectives from Different Spiritual Traditions*, Aliran, Penang, 1991

Alvares, Claude, *Science, Development and Violence*, Oxford University Press, Delhi, 1992

Anderson, Walter Truett, *Reality Isn't What It Used To Be*, Harper, San Francisco, 1990

Antoun, Richard T., and Mary E. Hegland (eds), *Religious Resurgence: Contemporary Cases in Islam, Christianity and Judiasm*, Syracuse University Press, New York, 1987

Appignanesi, Lisa (ed.), *Postmodernism: ICA Documents*, Free Association Books, London, 1989

Araeen, Rasheed, *The Other Story: Afro-Asian Artists in Post-War Britain*, South Bank Centre, London, 1989

Arlene Swidler, Arlene (ed.), *Human Rights in Religious Traditions*, Pilgrim Press, New York, 1982

Ayub, Muhammad, 'Asian spiritual and moral values and human rights' in Chandra Muzaffar, *Human Wrongs*, Just World Trust, Penang, 1996

Back, Les, and Vibeke Quaade, 'Dream utopias, nightmare realities: imaging race and culture within the world of Benetton advertising', *Third Text* 22 65–80 (Spring 1993)

Balagopal, K., 'Ruling class politics and people's rights', in Smitu Kothari and Harsh Sethi (eds), *Rethinking Human Rights*, New Horizon Press, New York, 1989

Barber, Benjumin R., *Jihad vs McWorld*, Times Books, New York, 1995

Barnet, Richard, and John Cavanagh, 'The world the transnationals have built', *Third World Resurgence*, 40 21–22 (December 1993)

Barnet, Richard, and John Cavanagh, *Global Dreams: Imperial Corporations and the New World Order*, Simon and Schuster, New York, 1994

Barnett, Pennina, 'Rugs R Us (And Them): The Oriental Carpet as Sign and Text', *Third Text* 30 13–28 (Spring 1995)

Barth, John, *The Last Voyage of Somebody the Sailor*, Hodder and Stoughton, London, 1992

Baudrillard, Jean, *America*, Verso, London, 1988

Baudrillard, Jean, *Selected Writings*, edited by Mark Poster, Polity Press, Oxford, 1988

Baudrillard, Jean, *The Transparency of Evil*, Verso, London, 1993

Baudrillard, Jean, *The Gulf War Did Not Take Place*, Power Publications, Sydney, 1995

Bauman, Zygmunt, *Modernity and the Holocaust*, Polity Press, Oxford, 1989

Bauman, Zygmunt, *Postmodern Ethics*, Blackwell, Oxford, 1993

Bauman, Zygmunt, *Life in Fragments: Essays on Postmodern Morality*, Blackwell, Oxford, 1995

Baxi, Upendra, 'From human rights to the right to be human: some heresies' in Smitu Kothari and Harsh Sethi (eds), *Rethinking Human Rights*, New Horizon Press, New York, 1989

Baxi, Upendra, 'Law, democracy and human rights' in Smitu Kothari and Harsh Sethi (eds), *Rethinking Human Rights*, New Horizon Press, New York, 1989

Bell, Christine, *The Perez Family*, Virago, London, 1990

Bell, Martin, *In Harm's Way: Reflections of a War Zone Thug*, Hamish Hamilton, London, 1995

Beller, Jonathan L., 'Cinema, Capital of the Twentieth Century', *Postmodern Culture*, May 1994

Benuri, Tariq, 'Development and the Politics of Knowledge: A Critical Interpretation of the Social Role of Modernization' in F. A. Marglin, and S. A. Marglin (eds), *Dominating Knowledge: Development, Culture and Resistance*, Clarendon Press, Oxford, 1990

Benuri, Tariq, 'Modernization and its Discontent: A Cultural Perspective on the Theories of Development' in F. A. Marglin, and S. A. Marglin (eds), *Dominating Knowledge: Development, Culture and Resistance*, Clarendon Press, Oxford, 1990

Berlin, Isaiah, *The Crooked Timber of Humanity: Chapters in the History of Ideas*, John Murray, London, 1990

Bernal, J. D., *Science in History*, MIT Press, Cambridge MA, 1979, 4 vols

Bernal, Martin, *Black Athena*, Free Associaton Books, London, 1987, 2 vols

Berry, Philippa, and Andrew Wernick, *Shadows of Spirit: Postmodernism and Religion*, Routledge, London, 1992

Best, Steven, and Douglas Kellner, *Postmodern Theory: Critical Interrogations*, Macmillan, London, 1991

Beverley, John, and Jose Oviedo (eds), *Boundary 2*, Special Issue: 'The Postmodern Debate in Latin America', Duke University Press, Durham NC, (Fall 1993)

Bey, Hakim, Lamia Naji and Hassan Massoudy, *Voyage International: Overcoming Tourism*, Lilim, Paris, 1995

Blackburn, Robin (ed.), *After the Fall: The Failure of Communism and the Future of Socialism*, Verso, London, 1991

Bloome, Irene, Paul Martin and Wayne Proudfoot, (eds), *Religion and Human Rights*, Columbia University Press, New York, 1994

The Body Shop Team, *The Body Shop Book*, Macdonald, London, 1985

The Body Shop Team, *Mamatoto: A Celebration of Birth*, Virago, London, 1991

Bohm, David, *Wholeness and the Implicate Order*, Routledge and Kegan Paul, London, 1980

Borrow, John D., *Theories of Everything*, Vintage, London, 1991

Boyer, Paul, *When Time Shall Be No More: Prophecy Belief in Modern American Culture*, Harvard University Press, Cambridge MA, 1992

Boyne, Roy, and Ali Rattansi (eds), *Postmodernism and Society*, Macmillan, London, 1990

Brennan, Timothy, *Salman Rushdie and the Third World*, Macmillan, London, 1989

Brinker-Gabler, Gisela (ed.), *Encourtering The Other(s): Studies in Literature, History and Culture*, State University of New York Press, Albany, 1995

Brown, Norman, *Apocalypse and/or Metamorphosis*, University of California Press, Berkeley, 1991

Brown, Stephen, *Postmodern Marketing*, Routledge, London, 1995

Brydon, Diana, 'The White Inuit Speaks: Contamination as Literary Strategy' in Ian, Adam and Helen Tiffin (eds) *Past the Last Post*, Harvester Wheatsheaf, London, 1991

Callinicos, Alex, *Againt Postmodernism*, Polity Press, Cambridge, 1989

320   POSTMODERNISM AND THE OTHER

Catholic Institute for International Relief (CIIR), *Proceedings of the 1990 International Conference on Right Wing Religion*, CIIR, London, 1992

Chapra, M. Umar, *Islam and the Economic Challenge*, Islamic Foundation, Leicester, 1992

Chomsky, Noam, *Deterring Democracy*, Verso, London, 1991

Chomsky, Noam, *World Orders, Old and New*, Pluto Press, London, 1994

Churchill, Ward, *Indians Are Us: Culture and Genocide in Native North America*, Common Courage Press, Manroe ME, 1994

Colas, Santiago, *Postmodernity in Latin America: The Argentine Paradigm*, Duke University Press, Durham NC, 1994

Connolly, William E., *Identity/Difference: Democratic Negotiation of Political Paradox*, Cornell University Press, Ithaca, 1991

Cooper, B, *The End of History: An Essay on Modern Hegelianism*, Toronto, University of Toronto Press, 1984

Coover, Robert, 'Aesop's Forest' in Heide Ziegler, *Facing Texts: Encounters between Contemporary Writers and Critics*, Duke University Press, Durham NC, 1988

Corbyn, Jeremy, 'Political dimensions of northern global domination and its consequences for the rights of five-sixths of humanity', in Chandra Muzaffar, *Human Wrongs*, Just World Trust, Penang, 1996

Crook, Stephen, Jan Pakulski and Malcolm Waters, *Postmodernization*, Sage, London, 1992

Cupitt, Don, *The Sea of Faith*, BBC, London, 1984

Dainotto, Roberto Maria, 'The excremental sublime: the postmodern literature of blockage and release', *Postmodern Culture* 3 (3) (May 1993)

Davies, Merryl Wyn, *Knowing One Another: Shaping An Islamic Anthropology*, Mansell, London, 1988

Davies, Paul, *The Mind of God*, Penguin, Harmondsworth, 1992

Dawkins, Richard, *The Selfish Gene*, Oxford University Press, Oxford, 1976

Denzin, Norman, *Images of Postmodern Society*, Sage, London, 1991

Diop, Cheikh Anta, *Civilization or Barbarism: An Authentic Anthropology*, Lawrence Hill Books, New York, 1991

Docherty, Thomas, *Postmodernism: A Reader*, Harvester Wheatsheaf, London, 1993

Eco, Umberto, *The Name of the Rose*, G. K. Hall, Boston MA, 1984

Eco, Umberto, *Foucault's Pendulum*, Secker and Warburg, London, 1989

Esposito, John, *Islamic Revivalism*, American Institute for Islamic Affairs, Washington DC, 1986

Falk, Richard, *Explorations At the Edge of Time*, Temple University Press, Philadelphia, 1992

Featherstone, Mike, *Consumer Culture & Postmodernism*, Sage, London, 1991

Ferguson, Adam, *An Essay on the History of Civil Society*, Edinburgh University Press, Edinburgh, 1966 (original 1767)

Fernandez-Armesto, Felipe, *Millennium: A History of Our Last Thousand Years*, Bantam Books, New York, 1995

Feyrabend, Paul, *Against Method*, New Left Books, London, 1975

Feyrabend, Paul, *Science in a Free Society*, Verso, London, 1978

Feyrabend, Paul, *Farewell to Reason*, Verso, London, 1987

Fisher, Jean, 'Dancing with Words and Speaking with Forked Tongues', *Third Text* 14 27–40 (Spring 1991)

Friedberg, Anne, *Window Shopping: Cinema and the Postmodern*, University of California Press, Berkeley, 1993

Friedman, George, and Meredith Lebard, *The Coming War with Japan*, St Martin's Press, New York, 1991

Fujisaka, S., E. Jayson and A. Dapusala, '"Recommendation domain" and a farmers' upland rice technology', *Indigenous Knowledge and Development Monitor* 1 (3) 4–7 (1993)

Fukuyama, Francis, *The End of History and the Last Man*, Hamish Hamilton, London, 1992

Funtowics, Silvio, and Jerome R Ravetz, 'Science for the post-normal age', *Futures* 25 (7) 739-56 (1993)

Galbraith, John Kenneth, *The Culture of Contentment*, Sinclair Stevenson, London, 1992

Geertz, Clifford, *The Interpretations of Cultures*, Basic Books, New York, 1973

Gellner, Ernest, 'Malinowski go home', *Anthropology Today* 1 (5) October 1985

Gibbons, John R. (ed.), *Contemporary Political Culture: Politics in a Postmodern Age*, Sage, London, 1989

Giddens, Anthony, *The Consequences of Modernity*, Polity Press, Cambridge, 1990

Gillespie, M. A., *Hegel, Heidegger and the Ground of History*, University of Chicago Press, Chicago, 1984

Gleick, James, *Chaos*, Cardinal, London, 1987

Goonatilake, Susantha, 'The futures of Asian cultures: between localisation and globalisation', in *The Futures of Cultures*, Unesco Publishing, Paris, 1994

Goonatilake, Susantha, 'The voyages of discovery and the loss and re-discovery of "others" Knowledge', *Impact of Science on Society* 167 241–64 (1992)

Griffin, David Ray (ed.), *Spirituality and Society: Postmodern Visions*, State University of New York Press, Albany NY, 1988

Griffin, David Ray, *The Reenchantment of Science: Postmodern Proposals*, State University of New York Press, Albany NY, 1988

Griffin, David Ray, *God and Religion in the Postmodern World*, State University of New York Press, Albany NY, 1989

Haddad, Y. Y., *Contemporary Islam and the Challenge of History*, State University of New York Press, Albany NY, 1982

Harding, Sandra (ed.), *The Racial Economy of Science*, Indiana University Press, Bloomington, 1993

Harding, Sandra, 'Is Science Multicultural?', *Configurations: A Journal of Literature, Science and Technology* 2 (2) (1994) and in David Theo Goldberg (ed.), *Multiculturalism: A Reader*, Blackwell, Oxford, 1994

Harman, Willis W., 'Rethinking the central institutions of modern society: science and business', *Futures* 25 (10) 1063–9 (1993)

Harvey, David, *The Condition of Postmodernity*, Blackwell, Oxford, 1989

Hawkins, Stephen, *A Brief History of Time*, Bantam Press, London, 1988

Heller, Agnes, and Ferenc Feher, *The Post-Modern Poltical Condition*, Cambridge, Polity Press, 1988

Herman, Edward S., and Noam Chomsky, *Manufacturing Consent*, Pantheon, New York, 1988

Hill, Donald, *Islamic Science and Engineering*, Edinburgh University Press, Edinburgh, 1994

Hobsbawm, Eric, 'Barbarism: a user's guide', *New Left Review* 206 44–54 (July/August 1994)

Huff, Toby, *The Rise of Early Modern Science*, Cambridge University Press, Cambridge, 1994

Hughes, Robert, *The Culture of Complaint*, Oxford University Press, Oxford, 1993

Huntington, Samuel P., 'The clash of civilizations?', *Foreign Affairs* 72 (3) 22–49 (July/August 1993)

Huxley, Aldous, *On Art and Artists*, Meridian Books, New York, 1960

Hvalkof, Soren, and Peter Aaby, *Is God An American?*, Survival International, London, 1981

Ibrahim, Anwar, *The Asian Renaissance*, Times Books, Singapore, 1996

Ibrahim, Anwar, 'From things change to Change Things' in Ziauddin Sardar (ed.), *An Early Crescent: The Future of Knowledge and the Environment in Islam and the West*, Mansell, London, 1989

Ibrahim, Anwar, *Managing Change*, Barita Books, Kuala Lumpur, 1991

Iqbal, Muhammad, *The Reconstruction of Religious Thought in Islam*, Ashraf, Lahore, 1962 (original 1932)

Iqbal, Sir Muhammad, *The Mysteries of Selflessness*, translated by A. J. Arberry, John Murray, London, 1953 (original 1910)

Ishihara, Shintaro, *The Japan That Can Say No*, Simon and Schuster, New York, 1991

Iwamoto, Yoshio, 'A voice from postmodern Japan: Haruki Murakami', *World Literature Today* 67 (2) 295–300 (Spring 1993)

Jameson, Fedrick, *Postmodernism or The Cultural Logic of Late Capitalism*, Verso, London, 1991

Jazairy, Idriss, Mohiuddin Alamgir and Theresa Panuccio, *The State of World Rural Poverty: An Inquiry into Its Causes and Consquences*, IT Publications, London, 1993

Jencks, Charles, *The Architecture of the Jumping Universe*, Academy Editions, London, 1995

Jencks, Charles, *What is Postmodernism?* Academy Editions, London, 1989

Johnston, Douglas, and Cynthia Sampson, *Religion, the Missing Dimension of Statecraft*, Oxford University Press, Oxford, 1994

Jones, Christopher B., 'Eco-Democracy: synthesizing feminism, ecology and participatory organisations' in Bart van Steenbergen, R. Nakarada, F. Marti and J. Dator (eds), *Advancing Democracy and Participation: Challenges for the Future*, Centre Catala de Prospectova, Barcelona, 1991

Joseph, George Gheverghese, *The Crest of the Peacock: Non-European Roots of Mathematics*, Penguin, London, 1990

Kadir, Djelal, 'What are we after?' *World Literature Today* 69 (1) 17–21 (Winter 1995)

Kamali, Mohammad Hashim, 'Fundamental Rights of the Individual', in *The American Journal of Islamic Social Sciences*, X: 3, 340–66 (Fall 1993)

Kamali, Mohammad Hashim, *Freedom of Expression in Islam*, Barita, Kuala Lumpur, 1994

Kaplan, Amy, and Donald E. Pease (eds), *Cultures of United States Imperialism*, Duke University Press, Durham NC, 1993

Karatani, Kojin, *Criticism and the Postmodern*, Fukutake Shoten, Tokyo, 1985

Katzenberger, Elaine (ed.), *First World, Ha Ha Ha!: The Zapatista Challenge*, City Lights, San Francisco, 1995

Kauffman, Stuart, *The Origins of Order*, Oxford University Press, Oxford, 1993

Kennedy, E. S., *Studies in the Islamic Exact Sciences*, American Univerity of Beirut, 1983

Khun, T. S., *The Structure of Scientific Revolution*, University of Chicago Press, Chicago, 1962

Kiberd, Declan, 'Multiculturalism and Artistic Freedom: Rushdie, Ireland and India', Occasional Paper Series No. 12, Department of Sociology, University College, Cork, 1992

Kim, Tae-Chang, 'Coherence and Chaos in Our Uncommon Futures: A Hun Philosophical Perspective' in Mika Mannermaa et al. (eds), *Coherence and Chaos in Our Uncommon Futures: Visions, Means, Actions*, World Future Studies Federation, Turku, 1994

Klotz, Heinrich, 'Postmodern Architecture' in Charles Jencks (ed.), *The Post-Modern Reader*, Academy Editions, London, 1992

Knorr-Cetina, Karin, *The Manufacture of Knowledge*, Pergamon, Oxford, 1981

Kochhar, R. K., 'Science in British India', *Current Science* Parts I & II 63 (11) & 64 (1) (1992–93)

Kolakowski, Leszek, *Modernity on Endless Trial*, University of Chicago Press, Chicago, 1990

Kothari, Smitu, and Harsh Sethi (eds), *Rethinking Human Rights*, New Horizon Press, New York, 1989

Kroker, Arthur, and David Cook, *The Postmodern Scene*, Macmillan, London, 1986

Kruger, Barbara, *Remote Control*, MIT Press, Cambridge MA, 1994

Kumar, D. (ed.), *Science and Empire*, Anamika Prakashan, Delhi, 1991

Kumar, D., *Science and the Raj*, Oxford University Press, Delhi, 1995

Kuspit, Donald, 'The contradictory character of postmodernism' in Hugh J. Silverman (ed.), *Postmodernism: Philosophy and the Arts*, Routledge, London, 1990

Kymlicka, Will, *The Rights of Minority Cultures*, Oxford University Press, Oxford, 1995

Lal, Vinay, 'The imperialism of human rights', *Focus on Law Studies* 8 (1) 5–11 (Fall 1992)

Larsen, Neil, 'Postmodernism and imperialism: theory and politics in Latin America', *Postmodern Culture* 1, 1 (1990)

Latour, Bruno, and Steve Woolgan, *Laboratory Life: Social Constructions of Scientific Facts*, Sage, London, 1979

Lawrence, Bruce, *Defenders of God: The Fundamentalist Revolt Against the Modern Age*, I. B. Tauris, London, 1990

Lederman, Leon, *The God Particle*, Bantam Press, London, 1993

Levy, Steven, *Artificial Life*, Penguin, London, 1993

Lewin, Roger, *Complexity*, J. M. Dent, London, 1993

Lewontin, R. C., *The Doctrine of DNA*, Penguin, London, 1991

Lin Yong, Lin, and Su Hua, *Pakistan*, Beijing, 1985

Little, David, John Kelsay and Abdualaziz A. Sachedina, *Human Rights and the Conflict of Cultures: Western and Islamic Perspectives on Religious Liberty*, University of South Carolina Press, Columbia, 1988

Lyon, David, *Postmodernity*, Open University Press, Buckingham, 1994

Lyotard, Jean-Francois, *The Postmodern Condition*, Manchester University Press, Manchester, 1979

Maalouf, Amin, *The First Century After Beatrice*, Quartet, London, 1993

Maccoby, Hyam, *Judas Iscariot and the Myth of Jewish Evil*, Peter Halban, London, 1992

Makdisi, George, *The Rise of Humanism in Classical Islam and the Christian West*, Edinburgh University Press, Edinburgh, 1990

Manzoor, S. Parvez, 'City and salvation: confronting the secular myth', *Muslim World Book Review* 13 (3) 3–9 (1993)

Manzoor, S. Parvez, 'Human rights: secular transcendence or cultural imperialism?', *Muslim World Book Review* 15 (1) 3–10 (1994)

Manzoor, S. Parvez, 'Return of tribalism: end of empire and the quest for western identity', *Muslim World Book Review* 14 (3) 3–12 (1994)

Marglin, F. A., and S. A. Marglin (eds), *Dominating Knowledge: Development, Culture and Resistance*, Clarendon Press, Oxford, 1990

Masselos, Jim, 'Postmodern Bombay: Fractures Discourses' in Sophie Watson and Katherine Gibson (eds), *Postmodern Cities and Spaces*, Blackwell, Oxford, 1995

Mazuri, Ali, *Cultural Forces in World Politics*, James Currey, London, 1990

McHale, Brian, *Postmodernist Fiction*, Routledge, London, 1987

Mestrovic, Stjepan G., *The Balkanization of the West*, Routledge, London, 1994

Mestrovic, Stjepan, *The Barbarian Temperament*, Routledge, London, 1993

Milbank, John, *Theology and Social Theory: Beyond Secular Reason*, Blackwell, Oxford, 1990

Mill, John Stuart, *Essay on Liberty*, 1859

Mitchell, Timothy, *Colonising Egypt*, University of California Press, Berkeley, 1991

Mitroff, Ian, *The Subjective Side Science*, Elsevier, Amsterdam, 1974

Miyoshi, Masao, and H. D. Harootunian (eds), *Postmodernism and Japan*, Duke University Press, Durham NC, 1989

Mohamad, Mahathir, and Shintaro Ishihara, *The Voice of Asia*, Kodansha International, Tokyo, 1995

Montag, Warren, 'What is at Stake in the Debate about Postmodernism?' in E. A. Kaplan (ed.), *Postmodernism and Its Discontents*, Verso, London, 1988

Morgan, Stuart, and Frances Morris, *Rites of Passage: Art for the End of the Century*, Tate Gallery Publications, London, 1995

Morris, David, 'Free Trade: The Great Destroyer', *Ecologist* 20 (5) September/October 1990, 190–5

Morris, Meaghan, 'Tooth and Claw: Tales of Survival and Crocodile Dundee' in Andrew Ross (ed.), *Universal Abandon? The Politics of Postmodernism*, Edinburgh University Press, Edinburgh, 1988

Muguenyi, Meddi, 'Development first, democracy second: a comment on minimalist democracy', in W. O. Oyugi and A. Gitonga (eds), *Democratic Theory and Practice in Africa*, Heinemann, Nairobi, 1987

Muzaffar, Chandra, *Human Rights and the New World Order*, Just World Trust, Penang, 1993

Muzaffar, Chandra, *Human Wrongs: Reflections in Western Global Dominance and its Impact Upon Human Rights*, Just World Trust, Penang, 1996

Nader, Ralph, et al., *The Case Against 'Free Trade'*, Earth Island, San Francisco, 1993

Nandy, Ashis, *The Intimate Enemy: Loss and Recovery of Self Under Colonialism*, Oxford University Press, Delhi, 1983

Nandy, Ashis, *Traditions, Tyrannies and Utopias: Essays in Politics of Awareness*, Oxford University Press, Delhi, 1987

Nandy, Ashis (ed.), *Science, Hegemony and Violence*, Oxford University Press, Delhi, 1988

Nederveen, Jan, and Bhiku Parekh (eds), *The Decolonization of Imagination: Culture, Knowledge and Power*, Zed Books, London, 1995

Needham, Joseph, *The Grand Titration: Science and Society in East and West*, University of Toronto Press, Toronto, 1969

New Internationalist, 'Squeezing the South', *New Internationalist*, Oxford, July 1994

Nicholson, Linda J. (ed.), *Feminism/Postmodernism*, Routledge, London, 1990

Norris, Christopher, *Uncritical Theory: Postmodernism, Intellectuals and the Gulf War*, Lawrence and Wishart, London, 1992

Norris, Christopher, *The Truth About Postmodernism*, Blackwell, Oxford, 1993

Ogden, Michael R., 'Politics in a parallel universe: Is there a future for cyberdemocracy?', *Futures* 26 (7) 713–29 (September 1994)

O'Neill, John, *The Poverty of Postmodernism*, Routledge, London, 1995

Panikkar, Raimundo, 'A Hindu/Jain/Buddhist reflection', *Breakthrough* 10 2–3 (Winter/Spring 1989)

Parekh, Bhikku, 'The cultural particularity of liberal democracy' in David Held (ed.), *Prospects for Democracy*, Polity Press, Cambridge, 1993

Parfrey, Adam (ed.), *Apocalypse Culture*, Feral House, Los Angles, 1987

Paz, Octavio, 'El romanticismo y la poesia contemporanea' *Veulta* 11, 127 26–7 (1987)

Petitjean, Patrick, *Science and Empires*, Kluwer, Dordrecht, 1992

Pfaff, William, 'A new colonialism?', *Foreign Affairs* 74 (1) 2–6 (January–February 1995)

Piscatori, James P., *Islam in a World of Nation-States*, Cambridge University Press, Cambridge, 1986

Pope, Randolph, 'Letters in the Post, or How Juan Goytisolo Got to La Chanca' *World Literature Today* 69 (1) 17–21 (Winter 1995)

Ramasubhan, Radhika, *Public Health and Medical Research in India*, SAREC, Stockholm, 1982

Rattansi, Ali, and Sallie Westwood, *Racism, Modernity and Identity: On the Western Front*, Polity Press, Cambridge, 1994

Ravetz, J. R., *Scientific Knowledge and its Social Problems*, Oxford University Press, Oxford, 1971

Ravetz, J. R., *Merger of Knowledge With Power*, Mansell, London, 1990

Reichel, Elizabeth, 'Shamanistic Modes for Environmental Accounting in the Colombian Amazon: Lessons form Indigenous Etho-Ecology for Sustainable Development', *Indigenous Knowledge and Development Monitor* 1 (2) 17–18 (1993)

Reimer, Bo, 'Postmodern Structures of Feeling: Values and Lifestyles in the Postmodern Age' in John R. Gibbons (ed.), *Contemporary Political Culture: Politics in a Postmodern Age*, Sage, London, 1989

Rieff, David, *Slaughterhouse: Bosnia and the Failure of the West*, Vintage, London, 1995

Ritzer, George, *The McDonaldization of Society*, Pine Oak Press, Thousand Oaks, 1993

Roberts, J. M., *The Triumph of the West*, London, BBC, 1985

Ronan, Colin A., *Science: Its History and Development among the World's Cultures*, Facts on File, New York, 1982

Rorty, Richard, *Philosophy and the Mirror of Nature*, Princeton University Press, Princeton NJ, 1979

Rorty, Richard, 'Postmodern Bourgeois Liberalism', *Journal of Philosophy*, 80 585 (October 1983)

Rorty, Richard, *Contingency, Irony and Solidarity*, Cambridge University Press, Cambridge, 1989

Rorty, Richard, *Objectivity, Relativism and Truth*, Cambridge University Press, Cambridge, 1991

Rose, H., and S. Rose (eds), *Ideology of/in the Natural Sciences*, Macmillan, London, 1976, 2 vols

Ross, Andrew (ed.), *Universal Abandon? The Politics of Postmodernism*, Edinburgh University Press, Edinburgh, 1988

Rouner, Leroy S. (ed.), *Human Rights and the World's Religions*, University of Notre Dame Press, Notre Dame, 1988

Rowls, John, *A Theory of Justice*, Harvard University Press, Cambridge MA, 1971

Rushdie, Salman, *The Satanic Verses*, Viking, London, 1988

Rushdie, Salman, *Imaginary Homelands: Essays and Criticism 1981-1991*, Granta Books, London, 1991

Rutherford, Jonathan (ed.), *Identity: Community, Culture, Difference*, Lawrence and Wishart, London, 1990

Ruthven, Malise, *A Satanic Affair: Salman Rushdie and the Wrath of Islam*, The Hogarth Press, London, 1990

Sabra, A. I., *The Optics of ibn al-Haytham*, The Warburg Institute, University of London, London, 1989, 2 vols

Sahliyeh, Emile (ed.), *Religious Resurgence and Politics in the Contemporary World*, State University of New York Press, Albany NY, 1990

Said, Abdul Aziz, 'The Islamic context for human rights', *Breakthrough* 10 (2-3) Winter/Spring 1989)

Said, Edward, *Orientalism*, Routledge and Kegan Paul, London, 1978

Sangwan, Satpal, *Science, Technology and Colonisation*, Anamika Prakashan, Delhi, 1991

Sardar, Ziauddin, *Islamic Futures: The Shape of Ideas to Come*, Mansell, London, 1985

Sardar, Ziauddin, *The Future of Muslim Civilization*, Croom Helm, London, 1979; Mansell, London, 1987

Sardar, Ziauddin (ed.), *The Revenge of Athena: Science, Exploitation and the Third World*, Mansell, London, 1988

Sardar, Ziauddin, *Explorations in Islamic Science*, Mansell, London, 1989

Sardar, Ziauddin, 'Surviving the Terminator: The Postmodern Mental Condition', *Futures* 22 (2) 203–9 (March 1990)

Sardar, Ziauddin, 'Total Recall: Aliens, Others and Amnesia in Postmodernism', *Futures* 23 (2) 189–302 (March 1991)

Sardar, Ziauddin (ed.), 'Islam and the Future', *Futures*, Special Issue 23 (3) (April 1991)

Sardar, Ziauddin, 'Terminator 2: Modernity, Postmodernity and Judgement Day' *Futures* 24 (5) 493–506 (June 1992)

Sardar, Ziauddin, 'When Dracula Meets the "Other": Europe, Columbus and the Columbian legacy', *Alternatives* 17 (4) 493–517 (Fall 1992)

Sardar, Ziauddin, 'Lies, Damn Lies and Columbus: The Dynamic of Constructed Ignorance' *Third Text* 21 47–56 (Winter 1992–93)

Sardar, Ziauddin, and J. R. Ravetz (eds), *Cyberfutures: Politics and Culture on the Information Superhighway*, Pluto Press, London, 1996

Sardar, Ziauddin, and Merryl Wyn Davies, *Distorted Imagination: Lessons from the Rushdie Affair*, Grey Seal, London, 1990

Sardar, Ziauddin, Merryl Wyn Davies and Ashis Nandy, *Barbaric Others: A Manifesto on Western Racism*, Pluto Press, London, 1993

Sarton, George, *Introduction to the History of Science*, Robert E. Krieger, New York, 1975, 4 vols

Sazgin, Faut, *Geschichte des Arabischen Schrifttum*, Brill, Leiden, 1974–82, 8 vols

Schlosstein, Steven, *Asia's New Little Dragons*, Contemporary Books, Chicago, 1991

Seabrook, Jeremy, *Victims of Development: Resistance and Alternatives*, Verso, London, 1993

Seabrook, Jeremy, 'Soft-soaping India', *New Statesman and Society*, 13 January 1995

Seshadri, C. V., *Development and Thermodynamics*, MCRC, Delhi, 1982

Sheldrake, R., *A New Science of Life: The Hypothesis of Formative Causation*, Blond and Briggs, London, 1981

Sheldrake, R., *Seven Experiments That Could Change the World*, Fourth Estate, London, 1994

Sheth, D. L., 'An emerging perspective on human rights in India' in Smitu Kothari and Harsh Sethi (eds), *Rethinking Human Rights*, New Horizon Press, New York, 1989

Shintaro, Ishihara, *The Japan That Can Say No*, Simon and Schuster, New York, 1991

Shohat, Ella, and Robert Stam, *Unthinking Eurocentrism*, Routledge, London, 1994

Simiya, V. G., 'The democratic myth in the African traditional societies' in W. O. Oyugi and A. Gitonga (eds), *Democratic Theory and Practice in Africa*, Heineman, Nairobi, 1987

Simons, Herbert W., and Michael Billig, *After Postmodernism*, Sage, London, 1994

Siriniva, M. D., 'Logical and Methodological Foundations of Indian Science' in Ziauddin Sardar (ed.), *The Revenge of Athena: Science, Exploitation and the Third World*, Mansell, London, 1988

Sithole, N., *African Nationalism*, Oxford University Press, Cape Town, 1959

Slaton, Christa Caryl, 'Democracy's quantum leap', *Demos* 3 32–3 (1994)

Slemon, Stephen, 'Introduction' in Ian Adam and Helen Tiffin (eds) *Past the Last Post*, Harvester Wheatsheaf, London, 1991

Sloterdijk, Peter, *Critique of Cynical Reason*, University of Minnesota Press, Minneapolis, 1987

Smith, Paul, 'Visiting the Banana Republic' in Andrew Ross (ed.), *Universal Abandon? The Politics of Postmodernism*, Edinburgh University Press, Edinburgh, 1988

Smith, Richard J., *China's Cultural Heritage*, Westview Press, Boulder CO, 1994

Sogolo, Godwin, 'The futures of democracy and participation in everyday life: the African experience' in Bart van Steenbergen, R. Nakarada, F. Marti and J. Dator (eds), *Advancing Democracy and Participation: Challenges for the Future*, Centre Catala de Prospectova, Barcelona, 1991

Solomon-Godeau, Abigail,'Living with Contradictions: Critical Practices in the Age of Supply-Side Aesthetics' in Andrew Ross (ed.), *Universal Abandon? The Politics of Postmodernism*, Edinburgh University Press, Edinburgh, 1988

Spurr, David, *The Rhetoric of Empire*, Duke University Press, Durham NC, 1993

St Augustine, *The City of God*, Penguin Classics, Harmondsworth, 1984 (original 1467)

Stackhouse, Max L., *Creeds, Society, and Human Rights: A Study in Three Cultures*, W.B. Eerdmans, Grand Rapids, MI, 1984

Stephanson, Anders, 'Regarding Postmodernism – A Conversation with Fredric Jameson' in Andrew Ross (ed.), *Universal Abandon? The Politics of Postmodernism*, Edinburgh University Press, Edinburgh, 1988

Stivers, Richard, *The Culture of Cynicism*, Blackwell, Oxford, 1994

Syed, Muhammad Naquib al-Attas, *The Mysticism of Hamzah Fansuri*, University of Malaya Press, Kuala Lumpur, 1970

Syed, Muhammad Naquib al-Attas, *A Commentary on the Hujjat al-Siddiq of Nur al-Din al-Raniri*, Ministry of Culture, Kuala Lumpur, 1986

Szilagyi, Miklos N., *How To Save Our Country: A Nonpartisan Vision for Change*, Pallas Press, Tucson AZ, 1994

Tarnas, Richard, *The Passion of the Western Mind*, Ballantine Books, New York, 1991

Tester, Keith, *The Inhuman Condition*, Routledge, London, 1995

Third World Resurgence, 'Reconquest of the South', *Third World Resurgence*, Penang, December 1992

Tibawi, A. L., *English Speaking Orientalists*, Islamic Centre, Geneva, 1965

Torgovnick, Marianne, *Gone Primitive: Savage Intellects, Modern Lives*, University of Chicago Press, Chicago, 1990

Traer, Robert, *Faith in Human Rights: Support in Religious Traditions for a Global Struggle*, Georgetown University Press, Washington DC, 1991

Trigger, Bruce G., *Natives and Newcomers*, McGill-Queen's University Press, Kingston, 1985

Turner, Bryan S. (ed.), *Theories of Modernity and Postmodernity*, Sage, London, 1990

Ulluwishewa, Rohana, 'Indigenous Knowledge System for Sustainable Development: The Case of Pest Control by Traditional Paddy Farmers in Sri Lanka', *Indigenous Knowledge and Development Monitor* 1 (2) 14–15 (1993)

United Nations, *Human Development Report 1994*. Oxford University Press, Oxford, 1994

Waal, Alex de, 'Compassion fatigue', *New Statesman and Society*, 17 March 1995

Waldrop, Mitchell, *Complexity: The Emerging Science at the Edge of Order and Chaos*, Viking, London, 1993

Webster, Richard, *A Brief History of Blasphemy: Liberalism, Censorship and the Satanic Verses*, The Orwell Press, Southwold, 1990

Weinberg, Steven, *Dreams of a Final Theory*, Vintage, London, 1993

Welford, Richard, *Environmental Strategy and Sustainable Development: The Corporate Challenge for the 21st Century*, Routledge, London, 1995

White, Hayden, *Tropics of Discourse*, Johns Hopkins University Press, Baltimore, 1985,

Wilkie, Tom, *Perilous Knowledge*, Faber and Faber, London, 1993

Wilson, E. O., *Sociobiology*, Harvard University Press, Cambridge MA, 1975

Wilson, E. O., *On Human Nature*, Harvard University Press, Cambridge MA, 1978

Wollen, Peter, 'Cinema/Americanism/The Robot' in James Naremore and Patrick Brantlinger (eds), *Modernity and Mass Culture*, Indiana University Press, Bloomington, 1991

World Bank, *The East Asian Miracle: Economic Growth and Public Policy*, Oxford University Press, Oxford, 1993

World Bank, *Adjustment in Africa*, Oxford University Press, Oxford, 1994

Yudice, George, 'Morality and the Ethics of Survival', in Andrew Ross (ed.) *Universal Abandon: The Politics of Postmodernism*, Edinburgh University Press, Edinburgh, 1988

Zizek, Slavoj, *The Sublime Object of Desire*, Verso, London, 1989

Index

Abuh, Mohammad, 240
accountability, in Islam, 72
acupuncture, 228
advertising, 131–3
Afghani, Jamaluddin, 240
Africa, 76, 120, 132; imposition of
    nation state on, 66–7; religions
    of, 239–40; science in, 203;
    traditional participatory
    politics in, 60, 65–6
aid: conditional foreign, 57, 68;
    and NGO domination, 77–81
Ajami, Fouad, 83
Algeria, democracy in, 58
alterity, 13
Alvares, Claude, 209–10, 211, 229
Anderson, Walter, 17–19, 38, 39;
    construction of reality, 23, 26;
    duality of religion, 36; and
    human rights, 68
anthropology, 7; and oral culture,
    185–6; view of non-Europeans,
    30–1, 96
Araeen, Rasheed, 164, 166;
    Jouissance, 199–200
architecture: modern, 145, 147;
    postmodern, 2, 6, 145–9; and
    space, 149, 150–2
Argall, Samuel, 95

art, 6, 35; as sacred, 189–91, 192
Arthur, Brian, 224
Asia: cultural plurality in, 284–5;
    suppression of dissent in, 287–8;
    tourism in, 134–5; traditional
    medicine, 161; western youth
    culture in, 142–3, *see also* China;
    India; Japan; Philippines
asylum seekers, 20
Augustine, Saint, 238, 261
Austen, Jane, 105
Australia, 118–19, 153–4, 228
authenticity, 165; cultural, 281–3
Avenging Lance (film), 104
Azad, Mualana Abu Kalam, 241
Azerbaijan, 51
Aztec civilisation, 100

Banana Republic chain store,
    128–30, 131, 133
Bangkok, tourism in, 134–5
Bangladesh, 77, 78–9, 80
Banks, Jeff, 260
barbarism, 30–1, 44–6
Barth, John, *The Last Voyage of
    Somebody the Sailor*, 176–81
Baudrillard, Jean, 39, 51, 244;
    duopoly of control, 37; and Gulf
    War, 25, 26; on reality, 24

Index by Auriol Griffith-Jones